COMMONER RITUAL AND IDEOLOGY IN ANCIENT MESOAMERICA

MESOAMERICAN WORLDS
FROM THE OLMECS TO THE DANZANTES

GENERAL EDITORS: DAVÍD CARRASCO AND EDUARDO MATOS MOCTEZUMA

The Apotheosis of Janahb Pakal: Science, History, and Religion at Classic Maya Palenque, GERARDO ALDANA

Commoner Ritual and Ideology in Ancient Mesoamerica, NANCY GONLIN AND JON C. LOHSE, EDITORS

Eating Landscape: Aztec and European Occupation of Tlalocan, PHILIP P. ARNOLD

Empires of Time: Calendars, Clocks, and Cultures, Revised Edition, ANTHONY AVENI

Encounter with the Plumed Serpent: Drama and Power in the Heart of Mesoamerica, MAARTEN JANSEN AND GABINA AURORA PÉREZ JIMÉNEZ

In the Realm of Nachan Kan: Postclassic Maya Archaeology at Laguna de On, Belize, MARILYN A. MASSON

Life and Death in the Templo Mayor, EDUARDO MATOS MOCTEZUMA

The Madrid Codex: New Approaches to Understanding an Ancient Maya Manuscript, GABRIELLE VAIL AND ANTHONY AVENI, EDITORS

Mesoamerican Ritual Economy: Archaeological and Ethnological Perspectives, E. CHRISTIAN WELLS AND KARLA L. DAVIS-SALAZAR, EDITORS

Mesoamerica's Classic Heritage: Teotihuacan to the Aztecs, DAVÍD CARRASCO, LINDSAY JONES, AND SCOTT SESSIONS

Mockeries and Metamorphoses of an Aztec God: Tezcatlipoca, "Lord of the Smoking Mirror," GUILHEM OLIVIER, TRANSLATED BY MICHEL BESSON

Rabinal Achi: A Fifteenth-Century Maya Dynastic Drama, ALAIN BRETON, EDITOR; TRANSLATED BY TERESA LAVENDER FAGAN AND ROBERT SCHNEIDER

Representing Aztec Ritual: Performance, Text, and Image in the Work of Sahagún, ELOISE QUIÑONES KEBER, EDITOR

The Social Experience of Childhood in Mesoamerica, TRACI ARDREN AND SCOTT R. HUTSON, EDITORS

Stone Houses and Earth Lords: Maya Religion in the Cave Context, KEITH M. PRUFER AND JAMES E. BRADY, EDITORS

Tamoanchan, Tlalocan: Places of Mist, ALFREDO LÓPEZ AUSTIN

Thunder Doesn't Live Here Anymore: Self-Deprecation and the Theory of Otherness Among the Teenek Indians of Mexico, ANATH ARIEL DE VIDAS

Topiltzin Quetzalcoatl: The Once and Future Lord of the Toltecs, H. B. NICHOLSON

The World Below: Body and Cosmos in Otomi Indian Ritual, JACQUES GALINIER

COMMONER RITUAL AND IDEOLOGY IN ANCIENT MESOAMERICA

edited by

NANCY GONLIN *and* JON C. LOHSE

University Press of Colorado

© 2007 by the University Press of Colorado

Published by the University Press of Colorado
5589 Arapahoe Avenue, Suite 206C
Boulder, Colorado 80303

All rights reserved
First paperback edition 2016

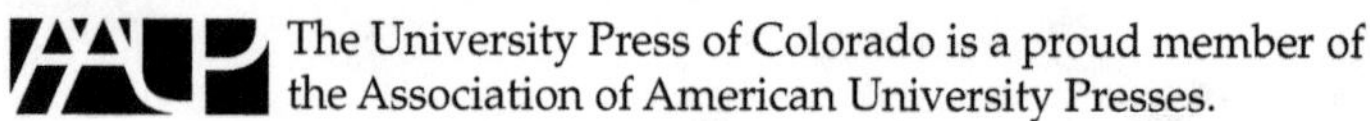

The University Press of Colorado is a cooperative publishing enterprise supported, in part, by Adams State College, Colorado State University, Fort Lewis College, Mesa State College, Metropolitan State College of Denver, University of Colorado, University of Northern Colorado, and Western State College of Colorado.

Library of Congress Cataloging-in-Publication Data

Commoner ritual and ideology in ancient Mesoamerica / [edited by] Nancy Gonlin and Jon C. Lohse.
p. cm. — (Mesoamerican worlds)
Includes bibliographical references and index.
ISBN: 978-0-87081-845-5 (hardcover)
ISBN: 978-1-60732-588-8 (pbk.)
1. Indians of Mexico—Rites and ceremonies. 2. Indians of Mexico—Religion. 3. Indians of Mexico—Social life and customs. 4. Indians of Central America—Rites and ceremonies. 5. Indians of Central America—Religion. 6. Indians of Central America—Social life and customs. I. Gonlin, Nancy. II. Lohse, Jon C., 1968–
F1219.3.R56C65 2006
299.7—dc22

2006036736

Design by Daniel Pratt

To our parents,
Sophie (Sue) and the late Henry Gonlin,
and Margie and Lloyd Elliott,
for providing a foundation of character.

CONTENTS

List of Figures *ix*

List of Tables *xv*

Preface *xvii*

1. Commoner Ritual, Commoner Ideology: (Sub-)Alternate Views of Social Complexity in Prehispanic Mesoamerica—*Jon C. Lohse* 1
2. Tradition and Transformation: Village Ritual at Tetimpa as a Template for Early Teotihuacan—*Gabriela Uruñuela and Patricia Plunket* 33
3. Commoner Ritual at Teotihuacan, Central Mexico: Methodological Considerations—*Luis Barba, Agustín Ortiz, and Linda Manzanilla* 55
4. Ritual and Ideology Among Classic Maya Rural Commoners at Copán, Honduras—*Nancy Gonlin* 83

5. Smoke, Soot, and Censers: A Perspective on Ancient Commoner Household Ritual Behavior from the Naco Valley, Honduras—*John G. Douglass* 123
6. Commoner Rituals, Resistance, and the Classic-to-Postclassic Transition in Ancient Mesoamerica—*Arthur A. Joyce and Errin T. Weller* 143
7. Shrines, Offerings, and Postclassic Continuity in Zapotec Religion—*Marcus Winter, Robert Markens, Cira Martínez López, and Alicia Herrera Muzgo T.* 185
8. Altar Egos: Domestic Ritual and Social Identity in Postclassic Cholula, Mexico—*Geoffrey G. McCafferty* 213
9. A Socioeconomic Interpretation of Figurine Assemblages from Late Postclassic Morelos, Mexico—*Jan Olson* 251
10. Steps to a Holistic Household Archaeology—*Mark W. Mehrer* 281

List of Contributors 295

Index 297

FIGURES

0.1. Map of Mesoamerica showing archaeological sites referred to in the text. *xviii*
0.2. Chronological chart of Mesoamerican archaeological phase names used by authors throughout the text. *xx*
1.1. A view of the place of religion in archaeological models of historic and prehistoric societies. 4
1.2. Thatched huts as decorative elements on public architecture. Structure 2 at Chicanná, Campeche, México, and the Arch at Labná, Yucatán, México. 17
1.3. Artist's reconstruction (looking northwest) of Operation 19 houselot, based on archaeological data recovered during excavations (garden to south and pathways are inferred), Dos Hombres, Belize. 20
1.4. Artist's reconstruction (looking northwest) of Operation 25 houselot, based on archaeological data recovered during excavations, Dos Hombres, Belize. 21

2.1. Map showing sites mentioned in Chapter 2. 34
2.2. Typical house layout at Tetimpa, Puebla, Mexico. 36
2.3. Small Tetimpa *talud-tablero* platform with vestiges of wattle-and-daub walls (a rectangular sub-floor storage pit is visible to one side of the building). 37
2.4. *Talud-tablero* platforms around the Moon Plaza at Teotihuacan, Mexico, with the Pyramid of the Sun rising in the background. 38
2.5. Anthropomorphic sculptures crowning a volcano effigy shrine with concentration of gravel-sized stones. 42
2.6. Interior *talud-tablero* altar of a central room (Unit 3, Operation 19), with an earlier burial in front (20-cm scale), Tetimpa, Puebla. 43
2.7. Two decapitated skulls placed in the fill used to cover the altar shown in Figure 2.6, Tetimpa, Puebla. 44
2.8. Courtyard altar at the Tetitla apartment compound at Teotihuacan, Mexico. 45
2.9. Papier-maché volcano effigy at the base of the Volador pole set up for the Altixcáyotl dance festival in Atlixco, Puebla, Mexico in 1996. 47
3.1. Location of the Oztoyahualco compound in the Classic city of Teotihuacan, Mexico. 57
3.2. Patron family gods related to the domestic hierarchy at Teotihuacan: Tlaloc in the upper registers, Huehueteotl and the Butterfly God in the middle, and a rabbit in the lower register. 62
3.3. Three household sectors within the Oztoyahualco compound, Teotihuacan, Mexico. 63
3.4. Ritual elements found in and around ritual courtyards C33 and C25 of the Oztoyahualco compound, Teotihuacan, Mexico. 65
3.5. Chemical residues at Xolalpan floor C41a, Oztoyahualco, Teotihuacan, Mexico. 71
3.6. Chemical residues at courtyard C41, Oztoyahualco, Teotihuacan, Mexico. 72
3.7. Chemical residues at courtyard C25, Oztoyahualco, Teotihuacan, Mexico. 74
3.8. Chemical residues at courtyard C33, Oztoyahualco, Teotihuacan, Mexico. 75

3.9. Ritual elements in and around main ritual courtyard C41 in the Oztoyahualco compound, Teotihuacan, Mexico. 77
3.10. Ritual elements in the Oztoyahualco compound, Teotihuacan, Mexico. 78
4.1. The Classic Maya center of Copán, Honduras. The monumental architecture is commonly referred to as the Main Group. Note the location of the Great Plaza, where polity-wide congregations likely assembled. 86
4.2. The location of completely excavated rural Type 1 sites in the Copán Valley, Honduras, by Webster's Rural Sites Project 1985–1986. 88
4.3. Plan map of a possible ritual structure in the Copán Valley, Honduras, at Site 11D-11-2. Structure 1 and 1-sub make up a residence, with Structure 1 the possible ritual structure. 92
4.4. Site 7D-3-1, Copán Valley, Honduras; the cist inside Structure 1, containing ceramics, an eccentric, a spear point, and a tiny piece of jade. 97
4.5. Frog/toad sculpture in green tuff recovered from Structure 1-sub, Site 11D-11-2, Copán Valley, Honduras. 101
4.6. Drawing of the miniature altar recovered in front of Structure 3, Site 34C-4-2, Copán Valley, Honduras. 104
5.1. Map of the Naco Valley, Northwest Honduras. 127
5.2. Late Classic multi-chamber *candelero* from Honduras. 131
5.3. Late Classic ladle censer from Honduras. 133
6.1. Plan of the Main Plaza at Monte Albán, Oaxaca, Mexico. 153
6.2. Plan of Xunantunich, Belize, Group A, Late Classic period. 157
6.3. Plan of Xunantunich, Belize, Group A, Terminal Classic period. 157
6.4. Plan of Altun Ha, Belize, A Plaza. 159
6.5. Plan of Río Viejo, Oaxaca, Mexico, showing mounds and locations of excavations in 2000. 164
6.6. Carved stone monuments from Río Viejo, Oaxaca, Mexico. 165
6.7. Plan of Op. RV00 A excavations Río Viejo, Oaxaca, Mexico. 167
7.1. Map of the Valley of Oaxaca, Mexico, with sites mentioned in the chapter. 187
7.2. Chronological chart. 188
7.3. Map of the center of Monte Albán, Mexico, with locales mentioned in the chapter. 191

7.4. Map of Xoo phase complex excavated at Macuilxóchitl, Oaxaca, Mexico. 194
7.5. Ceramic jaguar head found on the stairway of Mound 55, Macuilxóchitl, Oaxaca, Mexico. 195
7.6. Monte Albán: miniature vessels from the South Platform altar and Mound B offerings, Oaxaca, Mexico. 196
7.7. Macuilxóchitl Mound 35, one of the stone sculptures representing a *penate*, Oaxaca, México. 198
7.8. Comparative table of miniature vessels from Monte Albán and Macuilxóchitl, Oaxaca, Mexico. 199
7.9. Macuilxóchitl Mound 1: plan of the excavated residential patios, Oaxaca, Mexico. 201
7.10. Macuilxóchitl Mound 1: paired vessels from south patio, Oaxaca, Mexico. 203
7.11. Vessels representative of the Chila phase forms found in Mound 1 at Macuilxóchitl, Oaxaca, Mexico, including gray (G), Huitzo Polished Cream (H), brown (B), polychrome (P), and orange/yellow (O). 204
7.12. Celebration of the Santa Cruz atop Cerro Danush at Macuilxóchitl, Oaxaca, Mexico. 206
8.1. Plan of UA-1, Cholula, Mexico. 219
8.2. Platform altar in Room 3, UA-1, Cholula, Mexico. 222
8.3. Anthropomorphic braziers, or *xantiles,* found in the niche next to the altar, UA-1, Cholula, Mexico. 223
8.4. *Temazcal,* or sweatbath, with circular seating area connected to tunnel to firebox, UA-1, Cholula, Mexico. 225
8.5. Multiple burial at Cholula, Mexico. 228
8.6. Common forms of UA-1 incense burners, Cholula, Mexico: (a) long-handled *sahumadores,* (b) tripod *incensarios,* (c) pinched appliqué *braseros,* and (d) lantern censers. 230
8.7. Distribution of figurines at UA-1 Structure 1, Cholula, Mexico. 231
8.8. (a) Complete head and torso (UA-1); (b) male sacrificial victim (UA-1); (c) miniature figurine masks; (d) Tlaloc head (UA-1); (e) possible figurine of Tlazolteotl (UA-1); (f) figurine of seated female from Well 3; (g) figurine of standing female from Well 1. 233
8.9. Polychrome pottery from UA-1 Structure 1, Cholula, Mexico. 237

9.1. Map of Postclassic sites Yautepec, Cuexcomate, and Capilco in Morelos, Mexico. 253
9.2. Figurines from the Mexican Postclassic sites Yautepec, Cuexcomate, and Capilco that illustrate the figurine group classification. 256
9.3. Figurines from the Mexican Postclassic sites Yautepec, Cuexcomate, and Capilco that illustrate the figurine type classification. 257
9.4. Middle Postclassic period figurine type and group for Capilco and Yautepec, Mexico. 262
9.5. Late Postclassic–A period figurine types for Capilco commoner, Cuexcomate elite, Yautepec commoner, and Yautepec elite, Mexico. 264
9.6. Late Postclassic–A period figurine groups for Capilco commoner, Cuexcomate elite, Yautepec commoner, and Yautepec elite, Mexico. 264
9.7. Late Postclassic–B period figurine types for Capilco commoner, Cuexcomate commoner, Yautepec commoner, and Yautepec elite, Mexico. 268
9.8. Late Postclassic–B period figurine groups for Capilco commoner, Cuexcomate commoner, Yautepec commoner, and Yautepec elite, Mexico. 269
9.9. Colonial figurine types and groups from Yautepec, Mexico. 271

TABLES

0.1. Two ends of the continuum: Common assumptions about ancient Mesoamerican commoners and elites *xxv*
8.1. Burial data for Structure UA-1, Cholula, Mexico 227
9.1. Figurine group categories for Postclassic Central Mexico 255
9.2. Figurine type categories for Postclassic Central Mexico 258
9.3. Percent data for figurines ordered by chronology and socioeconomic class for Cuexcomate, Capilco, and Yautepec in Morelos, Mexico 259
9.4. Mean percentages for figurine positions by chronology and socioeconomic class at Yautepec in Morelos, Mexico 261
9.5. Mean percentages of animal species for known animal figurines by chronology and socioeconomic class at Yautepec in Morelos, Mexico 261

PREFACE

Jon C. Lohse and Nancy Gonlin

This volume begins with the premise that the ritual and ideological lives of commoners in the Mesoamerican past were rich and vibrant but remain seriously undertheorized by archaeologists and moderately underrepresented in the evidence often targeted by data recovery. Using frameworks such as household and landscape archaeologies, community studies, and finely resolved artifact and chemical analyses, the authors in this volume present a variety of approaches, themes, and theoretical viewpoints that provide answers to questions about ideational aspects of the past while remaining firmly grounded in the material record. The ritual life of commoners has not been significantly explored in the literature to the extent provided here, although certainly there has been an awareness of such activities since the times of Bishop Diego de Landa (Tozzer 1941) and Fray Diego Durán (Horcasitas and Heyden 1971), which has been occasionally addressed, at least implicitly and sometimes explicitly (e.g., Lucero 2003; Plunket 2002; Smith 1992). Much of the attention given to commoner ritual

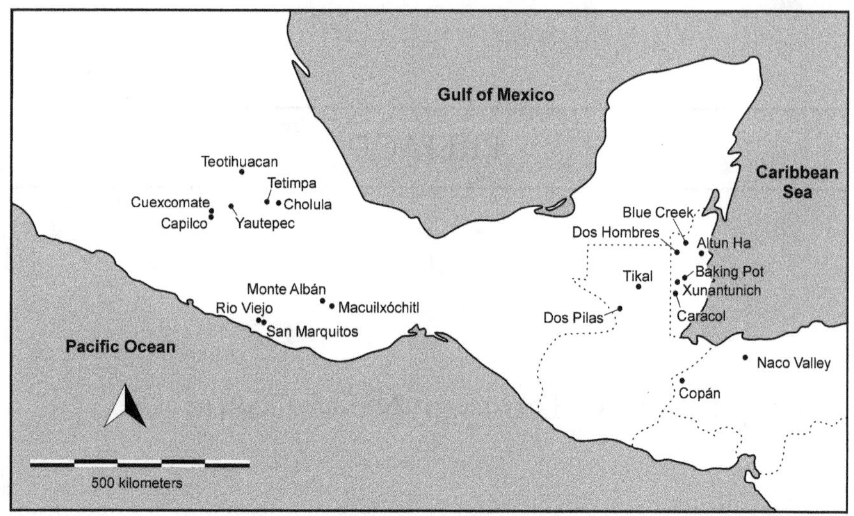

0.1. Map of Mesoamerica showing archaeological sites referred to in the text.

and ideological expression in recent years has paralleled, or in some cases has anticipated, the general shift in archaeology toward a more inclusive and multivocal understanding of the past.

The household, an important analytical unit for all members of society, was not the only location for ritual behaviors and ideological expressions, and we caution that the study of the household is not to be equated with the study of commoners, as is well illustrated by recent publications on royal households (Inomata et al. 2002; Inomata and Houston 2001). Such practices transcended domestic settings (see McAnany 1995). Evidence from sites located in different times and places throughout ancient Mesoamerica reveals patterns, both broad and diverse, in the role of ritual performances and their ideological meanings with respect to commoners. Rather than focusing on a spatial location, such as the domestic setting (a task that has been successfully completed by Patricia Plunket [2002] in her seminal work), the authors present material from the perspective of a socially defined class, segment, or group of individuals. Geographically, Plunket's volume primarily focuses on domestic ritual in Central Mexico at sites such as Teotihuacan, Tetimpa, and Cholula. Although there is some overlap between our volume and Plunket's in terms of location and even authorship, we have strived for wider geographical coverage of Mesoamerica by including sites from most core areas (Figure 0.1). As in Plunket's volume, the contributors to our volume primarily examine ritual from a domestic perspective but not exclusively so. Rituals on a community-wide basis are treated in both volumes; however, the volumes depart in their emphases. The Plunket volume sees ritual as creating and fomenting social solidarity and forging group identity (Plunket 2002:9). Contributors to this volume also see ritual acts by commoners as undercutting elite authority and as an occasional expression of autonomy rather than solidarity. In direct contrast to the Dominant Ideology Thesis (see Lohse, Chapter 1), the voice of commoners is seen as multivocal, multi-ideological. By focusing in this way on commoner ritual and ideology, this volume is able to include a perspective on the past not often portrayed—one of resistance and independence of thought by the masses.

The initial impetus for this work came from a symposium that originated from our discussion about the possibilities of and obstacles to investigating ritual and ideology in archaeological contexts that can somehow be associated with social non-elites. In 2002, we organized for the Society of American Archaeology meetings in Denver a session titled "Commoner Ritual, Commoner Ideology: Evidence from Households and Beyond Across Mesoamerica." The methodological, theoretical, chronological, and geographical coverage offered in those papers has been expanded by the inclusion of some authors who did not present their work at the original symposium. Also, Elizabeth Brumfiel originally served as one of the session discussants and provided important insights to many of the papers, although she is not represented here. Likewise, Amy Kovak contributed a noteworthy study on figurines and their role in commoner ritual at Piedras Negras, Guatemala, but declined to publish her work in the present volume. Furthermore, two figures have been included in the preface to orient readers because the following case studies are drawn from a range of regions and time periods across ancient Mesoamerica prior to the arrival of the Spaniards. Figure 0.1 is a regional map showing sites highlighted in the volume and Figure 0.2 is a chronological chart integrating all the archaeological phase names referred to in the individual chapters. Religion, ritual, and ideology, concepts often associated with power and control over commoners, are explored in Chapter 1, to eliminate the need for each chapter to discuss in depth the ways in which these terms are applied.

WHO ARE COMMONERS?

To help integrate the studies that follow and because this particular topic is so enormous, it is necessary to address at a fundamental level what

	Teotihuacan	Morelos	Tetimpa	Cholula	Monte Albán	Oaxaca	Maya Lowlands	Copán	Naco Valley
A.D. 1600		Colonial (1540–1650)			Convento (1521–1600)				
A.D. 1500		Late Postclassic B (1440–1540)	Los Ranchos	Late Chololan					
A.D. 1400		Late Postclassic A (1300/50–1440)			Chila		Late Postclassic	Ejar	Late Postclassic
A.D. 1300				Early Cholollan		Late Postclassic			
A.D. 1200		Middle Postclassic (1100–1300/50)			(V)				Early Postclassic
A.D. 1100				Late Tlachihualtepetl			Early Postclassic	Late Coner	
A.D. 1000				Middle Tlachihualtepetl	Liobaa				Terminal Classic
A.D. 900						Early Postclassic	Terminal Classic		
A.D. 800				Early Tlachihualtepetl				Early Coner	Late Classic
A.D. 700					Xoo Late (IIIB-IV)		Late Classic		
A.D. 600	Metepec		Nealtican	Late Quinametepec		Late Classic			
A.D. 500	Xolalpan				Xoo Early			Acbi	
A.D. 400					Pitao (Dxú) (IIIA)		Early Classic		Early Classic
A.D. 300	Tlamimilolpa			Early Quinametepec	Niza Late	Early Classic		Bijac	
A.D. 200	Miccaoti						Terminal Preclassic		
A.D. 100	Tzacualli				(II)				
			Late Tetimpa	Terminal Formative	Niza Early	Terminal Formative			Terminal Preclassic
100 B.C.	Patlachique							Chabij	
200 B.C.				(?)	Pe		Late Preclassic		
300 B.C.				Late Formative	(I)	Late Formative			Late Preclassic
400 B.C.			Early Tetimpa		Danibaan				
500 B.C.									
600 B.C.				Late Cabanas	Rosario	Middle Formative		Uir	
700 B.C.							Middle Preclassic		Middle Preclassic
800 B.C.					Guadalupe				
900 B.C.				Early Cabanas					
1000 B.C.					San José				
1100 B.C.						Early Formative			
1200 B.C.							Early Preclassic	Rayo	
1300 B.C.					Tierras Largas				
1400 B.C.									

0.2. Chronological chart of Mesoamerican archaeological phase names used by authors throughout the text.

is meant by the term *commoner.* Odd as it may seem, this concept is not examined exhaustively by any of the contributors to this volume. But it is one that will endure long after the dust settles over these efforts as future scholars seek to untie the complex knots of many-stranded relations that characterized many ancient and historical societies. One inherent problem with the use of the term *commoner* is that it automatically implies a dichotomy between commoner and its opposite, elite or noble. Life was certainly more complicated in the past than what the use of these two divisions of society connotes, as kinship, gender, age, and economic ties incorporated individuals into factions along multiple lines (Brumfiel 1992). For example, inhabitants of "elite" Type 4 sites at the Classic Maya site of Copán, Honduras, included those of varying status (Hendon 1991). To label something as "common" is to denote that it was something shared by all. Here, we reject outright that *all* people in hierarchical societies shared, or held in common, identical beliefs and practices. The terms *commoner* and *elite,* however, are most useful as heuristic devices and have served to frame much research (Chase and Chase 1992; Lohse and Valdez 2004a), and will continue to be used in the extant literature. As with all heuristic devices, simplification is inherent.

The intractable linkages between elites and commoners and outstanding historical bias in favor of the former provide a starting point for understanding commoners. A discussion of the term *elite* as used in cultural anthropology is provided by George Marcus (1983). Elites have often been viewed as prime movers, causal agents, and those in possession of power. By extension, then, commoners have not been viewed as prime movers, causal agents, or those with power, when viewed at all. Marcus (1983:19) supplies us with a worthy quote that we might well heed for commoner research: "Much of elite research has been based on the presupposition that we already know what elites are about, and that priority attention should be given to their social impact." Systemic, behavioral contexts of elites are essential for understanding them and their impact on society. The same is true for commoners, although at the current stage of research, it remains important to guard against presupposing that we know exactly what commoners "were about."

With cautions put aside, what do we mean by the term *commoner*? This question is complex and involves multiple approaches, many of which are related. Max Weber addressed these relationships and their complexity in his discussion of status groups, which are defined by "a claim to positive or negative privilege with respect to social prestige so far as it rests on one or more of the following bases: (a) mode of living, (b) a formal process of education which may consist in empirical or rational training and the acquisition of the corresponding modes of life, or (c) on the prestige of birth, or of an occupation" (Weber 1947:428). Any society consists of multiple status groups, or social positions, many of which are ranked in relation to one another (Fried 1967), while others are not. Weber's class statuses (distinct from social statuses) are more often stratified and depend "on the kind and extent of control or lack of it which the individual has over goods or services and existing possibilities of their exploitation for the attainment of income or receipts within a given economic order" (Weber 1947:424). Contrasted by Weber's honor- and prestige-based status groups and materially defined class statuses, some Marxist approaches to class have privileged an emphasis on the relationships between individuals as expressed through social labor (see Saitta 1994, 1997). Adherents to this perspective (Resnick and Wolff 1987) have identified fundamental classes that include producers and appropriators of labor surplus. Importantly, relationships between these two are not inherently exploitative, although the question of when and how they are remains to be systematically addressed by most Mesoamerican archaeologists. The present volume could conceivably be considered a step in this direction inasmuch as parts of it address commoner consciousness and awareness.

The ties between Weberian status groups and class statuses, or Marx-informed labor producer and appropriator classes, and the "economic orders" in which they are grounded (one might consider these economic orders comparable to modes of production, following Wolf [1982]) embed the concepts in culturally and historically specific contexts in which different kinds of classes might arise. Weber (1947) discusses property, acquisition, and social class statuses. Karl Marx and Friedrich Engels, in *Capital, Volume Three,* identify wage-laborers, capitalists, and landlords as the "three big classes" of modern society (in Tucker 1978:441). Stephen Resnick and Richard Wolff (1987) talk about fundamental classes (producers and appropriators) and subsumed classes (which include distributors and receivers of social labor). Each of these essays foregrounds a particular constellation of unevenly allocated social commodities: labor, prestige, material well-being, knowledge, productive property, and resources. To this list could be added control over ritual and religious information (see Lohse, Chapter 1). Resulting imbalances along any or all of these dimensions, which can operate quite independently of each other, are perceived as social inequality and provide the basis for recognizing commoners in the past. Clearly, "commoners" can be categorized according to a very wide array of considerations.

The specific relations that bind together these groups and the mechanisms by which they distinguish themselves are historically contingent and must be examined on a case-by-case basis. We cannot reiterate forcefully enough that given the essential linkages between the two, defining *elite* and *commoner* is best accomplished in temporally and geographically (or culturally) bounded studies, or at least where these framing principles are clearly defined. It is quite often the case that access to material, prestige, property, and labor between status groups or classes seems to overlap, and commoners and elites are identified by combinations of these factors. The historical and cultural particularism that underlie these relationships, however, also mean that the bases by which classes or status groups are defined changed through time. This model was certainly the case for prehispanic Mesoamerica, as economic, political, and ideological orders varied from region to region and from the Preclassic to the Postclassic. For example, the Terminal Classic to Early Postclassic in most of Mesoamerica appears to have been a time when commoners experienced new freedoms as the bonds of social and political obligation to elites had started to unravel by the close of the Classic period (see Joyce and Weller, Chapter 6; Winter et al., Chapter 7). Forewarned by the possibility of overlapping but not necessarily conjoining dimensions of inequality, archaeologists must avoid presumptions that unbalanced accessibility to exotic materials, for example, signifies exploitative relationships or was also accompanied by unequal access to labor. Specificities such as these will need to be worked out for each time period and cultural unit. It is also important to note that this framework to defining commoners (and elites) renders many of the definitions that have been offered for *elite* oversimplistic to the point of questionable utility.

OPERATIONALIZING COMMONER

We have abundant evidence from Mesoamerica that the social categories approximating elite and commoner were emically perceived and ascribed and remain accessible to archaeologists. In the Colonial era, Spaniards observed that membership in a class status was oftentimes fixed at birth and that social proscriptions, such as those against class exogamy, prohibited individuals born in one category from crossing into the other. Each class often had its own self-referential terms; for example, some sixteenth-century Maya commoners used *yalba winik* or *pach kah winikob* to identify themselves, respectively, as "small or short in stature" or "townspeople" (Martínez Hernández 1929; see J. Marcus 2004). These terms were different from those used for nobles, or *almehenob.* Among Nahua speakers, those born of low rank were called *macehualtin,* or *maceguales* in Spanish; nobles and rulers frequently went by such terms as *pipiltin* or *tlatoque* (Gibson 1964; Lockhart 1992). Across most of pre-Colonial Mesoamerica (as represented in the chapters of this volume), the concept of prestige at birth was probably the critical determining factor of a person's social standing, with the honor accorded to these positions also providing mechanisms for exploiting or attaining income and services. Mobility and fluidity are inherently part of each class or ranked status group, meaning that a person's position in society may actually have consisted of layers of identity and belonging (by gender, age, occupation or task group, family lineage, material and nonmaterial interests, and so forth), although hard fast lines existed between class statuses.

Identifying distinctions between these categories using material data is a difficult task (Chase and Chase 1992), particularly when dealing with well-off commoners or low-ranking elites. Typical measures of unequal distribution of resources have included access to productive agricultural lands; health (as measured by isotope studies [Reed 1998] or distribution of foodstuffs per Lentz [1991]); trade goods such as polychrome pottery or jade; building materials and styles; access to water; housing location; and access to hunting, gathering, and fishing grounds. Using these material lines of evidence, however, can be confusing, as, for example, building size, complexity, and style varied throughout the Copán Valley but access to such items as polychrome pottery and a basic domestic assemblage did not (Gonlin 1993). Sites labeled as Type 1 or "commoner" at Copán present a continuum of expressions from urban to rural areas in terms of architecture, burial patterns, and status (Gonlin 1994). These findings show that simple correlations between urban and rural with elite and commoner, respectively (a dichotomy recently examined and deconstructed by Iannone and Connell [2003]), are frequently problematic.

In *Ancient Maya Commoners,* Joyce Marcus (2004:259) writes: "One of the biggest stereotypes is that all commoners were alike; it parallels another stereotype, that all elites were alike. Each group, in fact, has been stereotyped to facilitate making contrasts." This volume, to some extent, is no exception. If we examine the criteria most often used to determine the status of ancient households, a laundry list of characteristics can be

Table 0.1. Two ends of the continuum: Common assumptions about ancient Mesoamerican commoners and elites

Characteristic	*Commoner*	*Elite*
Status	Low	High
Geographical locale	Rural/Periphery	Urban/Center
Architecture	Small Simple Low-quality materials	Large Complex High-quality materials
Occupation	Agrarian Craft production of utilitarian goods	Administrative Craft production of non-utilitarian goods
Burials	Simple No or few grave goods	Elaborate Numerous grave goods
Artifacts	Utilitarian Local Few forms	Utilitarian and non-utilitarian Local and exotic Many forms
Writing	Illiterate	Literate
Ritual	Domestic Simple	Public Complex
Ideology	Acquiescent	Dominant
Power	None	All

easily drawn up. Table 0.1 takes the material correlates most often used in archaeological contexts to infer status, and that status is usually conceived of as "high" or "low." Nonmaterial cultural characteristics, such as literacy, ritual beliefs and practices, ideology, and power, are also subject to stereotyping in studies of commoners and elites.

Another complication in defining commoners is related to location. At Copán, most Type 4 sites were situated on the best agricultural lands, near the main waterway, and within a few kilometers of the civic-ceremonial complex (Webster et al. 2000). But, as stated above, Type 4 sites housed people of varying statuses. The Copán examples support the conclusion that we cannot and should not assume that commoners' access to resources was expressed similarly throughout all of Mesoamerica. Criteria need to be operationalized on a site-by-site basis (a point also made by Lohse and Valdez 2004b:5), and we make no attempt to generalize. Not all contributors to this volume define *commoners* in the same manner and we have not expected them to do so.

Designating elite or commoner status has ramifications for other parts of culture, such as ritual, ideology, and power, the main topics of this volume. Many of the contributors use the material correlates listed in the table in much the same fashion as archaeologists have used them for decades, but the differences lie in the interpretation of the meanings of these characteristics. Were most commoners in ancient Mesoamerica poor? In a material sense, yes, probably so. Were they poor in their beliefs and culture? Certainly not, as the authors of these chapters convincingly demonstrate.

ORGANIZATION OF THE VOLUME

In contending with the commoner concept we collectively have attempted to recognize the myriad ways in which ritual and ideological expression was inherent at all levels of society. Jon Lohse provides a discussion of ritual and ideology and their anthropological uses in Chapter 1. Ensuing chapters present case studies from different chronological and geographical areas of Mesoamerica. These studies are ordered by time period—from Formative, or Preclassic, to Postclassic—to provide an overview of how many of the defining relationships between commoners and noncommoners changed through the millennia of Mesoamerican prehistory. This organization also allows readers to quickly find the information most directly related to their own areas of interest.

In all cases, the authors have used a polythetic set of identifiers to infer commoner status from the archaeological remains. Some cases are more convincing than others, drawing on extensive excavation data. Working assumptions are integral to each contribution and not always made explicit. It is taken for granted by all contributors, for example, that commoners existed in ancient Mesoamerica and that by excavating the remains of houses and other social contexts we are able to identify that segment of society. Furthermore, it is presumed that commoners did indeed participate in their own rituals and express their own ideologies, many of which were shared with other factions of society. Some chapters move immediately beyond these assumptions and explore how understanding commoners in their own right contributes to other, large-scale inquiries of Mesoamerican complexity. One of the volume's strengths is its reliance on material data to come to conclusions about nonmaterial aspects of culture. In his summary chapter, Mark Mehrer echoes his support of this empirical approach.

In Chapter 2, Gabriela Uruñuela and Patricia Plunket discuss the Late and Terminal Formative occupation of Tetimpa, Puebla, Mexico. The authors state that they are not dealing with a hierarchically organized settlement per se; however, they see the roots of complex, urban societies as emerging partly from rural domestic village life that included the practices of ancestor veneration, selective burial treatment, and emphasis on patrilineages. The material manifestation of these practices at Tetimpa includes a preponderance of male burials within the house compound and a central placement of patio shrines. These practices are maintained but reinterpreted and reformulated in state-level Classic Teotihuacan. The authors contend that the origins of such characteristics, which become broadly shared—but amplified to underscore status and class differences in state societies—emanate from earlier times and places that antecede the development of sharp social stratification (also Sugiyama 2004). This case study is important in adding a historical context to the much-examined urban phenomenon in prehispanic Mesoamerica.

The discussion of the Oztoyahualco apartment compound of Classic Teotihuacan in Chapter 3 by Luis Barba, Agustín Ortiz, and Linda Manzanilla demonstrates that commoners lived within an urban setting as parts of larger households. The apartment compound is located within 1.5 km of the center of the Pyramid of the Moon complex. Following Manzanilla (2004), this compound appears far less elaborate than others at that site, suggesting its occupants were of relatively low rank, although it exhibits internal variation indicative of different roles and positions assumed by its constituent families. The inhabitants were stucco plasterers rather than farmers, as evidenced by the remains of their trade within the compound. Researchers elsewhere also have documented the role of urban non-farming populations that provide goods and services. Within this large compound, however, status differences were discernible from the quality of building materials, the differential distribution of plaster flooring, size differences in ritual courtyards, variance in the use of religious symbols on ritual objects, and the amount of foreign materials present in each sector of the compound. The scale and size of ritual buildings, rather than being seen as pertaining to exclusively high or low status, are interpreted as incorporating increasingly larger numbers of people, from the single family to the entire compound to the community. Mapping out the locations of certain activities at Oztoyahualco, including ritual, through artifact distribution and chemical residue analyses allows researchers to suggest religious practice as one of the behavioral dimensions that corresponded to social differentiation within extended family networks.

The use of the term *commoner* in the Copán Valley of Honduras initially depended on observations of architecture. The typology presented by Willey and Leventhal (1979) has been little modified since its origination in the 1970s (but see Freter 1988). If anything, the categories have been reinforced by additional evidence coming from studies of artifacts, ecofacts, grave types, and human remains. The extensive Copán database, however, has provided an understanding of the heterogeneity of both commoners and elites at Copán (see J. Marcus [2004] for an excellent discussion on the stereotype and reality of Maya commoners). Nancy Gonlin's chapter on the Classic Maya commoners at Copán primarily focuses on the rural low-status population but also includes an important recognition of urban commoners and illustrates how some ritual practices were shared communally despite vast differences in social standing among practitioners.

John Douglass discusses the Late Classic non-Maya occupation of the Naco Valley in central Honduras. Commoners typically had small houses, lived in rural areas, farmed the landscape, and had fewer valuable goods. Douglass interprets these differences to indicate that "households . . . differed in kind from elites primarily in access to economic, social and political spheres" (Douglass, Chapter 5). Naco elites emulated certain Maya practices, whereas commoners were more likely to maintain traditional local practices, using what Douglass has called a "ritual toolkit." Douglass's study also provides an important reminder that distinctions between built domestic and experienced natural landscapes were not always impermeable and absolute; thus, archaeologists might expect to find additional evidence of commoner ritual behavior beyond constructed environments (also Brown 2004).

In Chapter 6, Arthur Joyce and Errin Weller discuss commoners in reference to the Classic period collapse that was widespread throughout Mesoamerica and the developments of the succeeding Early Postclassic period. They make clear that all people in society had some power, but differences in social standing framed how and where (in public or private) expressions of will, identity, and empowerment were formulated. They note that the "hidden transcript" of resistance is indeed challenging to identify in the archaeological record. In their chapter we once again find commoner status associated with modest architecture, modest burial offerings, and peripheral location. Some commoners chose to live in areas distant from the political centers because of the advantages of loose supervision conferred on such locations. Commoners are discussed in terms of their exclusion from ceremonial space at major centers, "where the dominant discourse is overwhelmingly represented in overt, public expressions in writing, architecture, art, and ritual performance" (Joyce and Weller, Chapter 6). In contrast to Classic period patterns, Early Postclassic habitational remains attributable to commoners are located atop the collapse of Classic period royal compounds and include defaced monuments depicting former elites, providing a provocative account of non-elite actions, in response not just to their perceived subordination but to the memory of those conditions.

The contribution by Marcus Winter, Robert Markens, Cira Martínez López, and Alicia Herrera Muzgo T. traces Zapotec religious practices from the Classic through Early Postclassic transition, a period marked by the sharp decline of local seats and institutions of authority (see Joyce and Weller, Chapter 6). Commoners in the Oaxaca Valley are associated with the remains of small households, burials distinguished by few grave goods and simple pits, and a lower amount of polychrome vessels. Deity representations are not present in commoner households, perhaps signaling the autonomy of the individual family. In the literate society of the Zapotec, there is no evidence that commoners had a command of writing. Instead, evidence for mortuary practices and life-cycle events characterizes the archaeological remains. Winter and his colleagues suggest that practices organized and carried out by commoners in different communities from the Late Classic to Early Postclassic contributed significantly to the maintenance of ideological traditions across that tumultuous time span. In this case, cultural continuity as opposed to changes, such as those noted by Joyce and Weller, can be ascribed to commoner practice.

Geoffrey McCafferty summarizes a commoner household excavation at Cholula, Puebla, Mexico. The UA-1 structure is admittedly a small sample of domestic architecture at this grand Postclassic site. However, the detailed excavations provide an excellent example of a low-status habitation. Although the size of this structure is small, it has elaborate architectural features not prevalent at other commoner sites discussed in this volume, such as a sweatbath, decorated façades, painted plaster floors and walls, and an altar (see also chapters on Tetimpa and Teotihuacan). The distinction between this site and elite sites rests on the following criteria: small house size, distance from the center (1 km east of the Great Pyramid), different burial patterns, large numbers of child burials, few exotic items, and anthropomorphic figurines. An interesting conclusion of McCafferty's work is that not all figurines may have functioned in an exclusively ritual context since many were found in areas suggesting other activities, such as children's play. Ample evidence for dedicatory and mortuary/ancestor rituals is discussed.

Rather than looking exclusively at architecture as most authors in this volume have done, Jan Olson focuses on middens, some of which were associated with structures. Her study of an extensive Late Postclassic collection of figurines from dozens of middens from three sites—Yautepec, Cuexcomate, and Capilco—in Morelos, Mexico, provides abundant data on differences through time and in socioeconomic status. For middens that are associated with structures, domestic architectural remains provide the best indicator of class. The assignment of status to the artifactual remains of those middens not associated with houses relies on analysis of an artifact sample comprising more than one million figures. Figurine consumption differed significantly by chronology and status. Commoners typically had higher percentages of figurines manufactured from local materials, the forms and symbols varied from those recovered at elite sites, and there were few imports. In some circumstances, figurine use at commoner sites exceeded that at elite sites, indicating differences in behavior. Interestingly, differences were noted among the three communities, underscoring the need for broad archaeological testing to verify conclusions regarding commoner-elite discourse in the past.

THE ARCHAEOLOGICAL LOOK AHEAD

The primary contribution of this volume does not lie in the alteration of the list of material correlates that archaeologists often use to identify commoners (see Table 0.1). In fact, these chapters reinforce it. Every author has used some of the criteria to define commoner status throughout Mesoamerica in time and space, either explicitly or implicitly. We reiterate sentiments expressed by many researchers (e.g., Gonlin 2004; Hirth 1993; Masson and Lope 2004; Smith 1987; Stark and Hall 1993) that "where precise determinations between elite and commoner are unclear, multiple lines of evidence must be used concurrently" (Lohse and Valdez 2004b:5). The purpose of such an approach is *not* to demonstrate which artifact categories—for instance, counts of jade or polychrome pottery—can be used as an indication of social rank but rather to understand how material culture reflects the expression of ideas and values conditioned to a large degree by social inequalities. Compiling site or community-based inventories derived from multiple social contexts represents perhaps the best way not only of characterizing the varying shades that existed between clear-cut social distinctions but also of understanding the roles and behaviors undertaken by various members of a community according to knowledge and skill. Taken together, the chapters in this volume accomplish just that, while also breaking down many of the assumptions around ritual and religion that have grown from the long use of the generalized elite-commoner heuristic dichotomy. The primary significance of this work, then, lies in the attention to commoner rituals and ideologies in a land of hierarchical social circumstances, where dominant ideologies have long been given primary consideration.

The interpretation of the material evidence of rituals on commoner sites has been shaped by our expectations of what types of rituals we expect that commoners would have performed. For example, Patricia McAnany and Shannon Plank (2001:table 4.2) list ritual practices that are essential to a household. They divide them into three categories: mortuary/ancestor, "house" dedication, and agricultural/calendrical. Other types of rituals that McAnany and Plank identified as not important at the household level and found in only royal courtyards fall into the categories of succession/heir designation, military/ballgame, and delimitation of territory (on a polity-wide scale, rather than at the household level). The evidence for all three categories of household rituals has been recovered at nearly all sites discussed in this volume. Life-cycle events were also surely celebrated by commoners. Although not having the political significance of the installment of a new monarch, succession/heir designation ceremonies were possibly held when one lineage or household head passed on authority to the next, when a newborn child was welcomed into the family, or when the participants in a marriage ceremony were received at home. It is currently unknown to what extent commoners may have participated in military operations or ballgames of their own or what rituals may have been associated with these activities.

Contributions by Barba, Ortiz, and Manzanilla; Gonlin; Joyce and Weller; and Winter, Markens, López, and Muzgo T. make it clear that domestic and community spheres of ritual behavior did not always overlap, and that distinctions between elite and commoner at times may be clearly understood in terms of differences in how and where ritual practice occurred as well as the message content of those rituals (see also Lohse, Chapter 1). In particular, elites appear to have been largely responsible for the public gatherings that served to integrate populations. Ballgame ceremonies, coronations, and accession events seem to dominate elite-specific ritual behavior (although see R. Joyce and Hendon [2000] for contrasting discussion of rural ballcourts in dispersed communities in the Cuyumapa Valley, Honduras). We collectively find little evidence for commoner ritual conduct beyond the domestic or extended family scale. Noteworthy exceptions include the aforementioned observation by Douglass that natural places were used as elements of ritually charged landscapes, and the documentation by Winter and his colleagues of large-scale Early Postclassic offerings at Macuilxóchitl, Oaxaca. These exceptions are important when considered together with domestic rituals and go some distance in dispelling the myth that esoteric knowledge was universally controlled and administered by elites (also Brown 2004; Mathews and Garber 2004; Zaro and Lohse 2005). Critical differences appear to be found in the message content of ritual, the status and role of individual ritual practitioners, and the scale at which it was performed (Gonlin, Chapter 4). Future studies that focus on ritual expression and ideological motivation specifically at commoner levels will provide additional balance to our understanding of how people of unequal social standing articulated with the divine and otherworldly.

It is our view that research integrating multiple scales of analysis, starting at the household and extending up to the community, is particularly promising in helping researchers recognize and understand how both rulers and the ruled managed and defined their social roles on a daily basis. Extreme differences in social rank were most often, and most directly, experienced at the community level. To be sure, elites interacted with fellow elites over long distances in a number of ways, although we lack firm evidence explaining how the lives of commoners were similarly linked across regional scales. It is unclear, for example, how or whether elites at Tikal directly affected a commoner's life elsewhere in the Maya Lowlands. Multi-scalar research allows archaeologists to fully contextualize and account for differences in access to the trade goods by which social positions were defined or to quantify social labor and one's entitlement to it. Many of the contributors to this volume employ a multi-scalar approach in understanding how their respective data reveal the religious and ideological lives of their subjects.

Additional aspects of "commoner" studies that are essential to consider are temporal and situational in nature. Certain individuals and groups in almost any social relationship are at some disadvantage in terms of the resources to which they have access or the degree of autonomy they retain in maintaining their own livelihoods without obligations to others. In the terms described above, such differences may be seen as permanent (or at least of long duration) and absolute in how they are experienced by the participants themselves. Oftentimes, however, these relationships are entirely situational. That is, social categories distinguished by prestige imbalances expire when participants move on to other encounters. In the abstract, the structure of these relationships can be understood along similar, although perhaps more theoretical, lines as those between *yalba winik* and *almehenob.* The term *structural commoners,* or *situational commoners,* may refer to individuals who are periodically or situationally characterized by unequal social standing or entitlement as defined by social norms around honor. For example, neighbors in a community might enjoy similar ranks most of the time, although they temporarily assume ranked (not necessarily stratified) positions based on membership in a church or other organization. Heads of non-elite lineages were both commoners by birth and non-commoners in that they commanded reverence and perhaps tribute from their extended families. In this way, individuals may experience both superordinate and subordinate positions in relation to others over the course of their lifetimes or even on a daily basis. Putting this framework to use allows us to begin delineating distinctions within society, such as those based on ritual specialization while also acknowledging the hard fast lines that existed between some social classes.

The periodic or situational relationships described above can also be examined on the basis of power differentials in more enduring or permanent distinctions and are fertile fields for understanding strategies of domination, alliance-building, resistance, persistence, and many other ideologies that reflect individuals' attempts to come to terms with their social experiences. Archaeologists are often prone to see the structure of such relationships as static and unchanging, although increasing influences from postmodernist subaltern schools and resistance literature are providing tools for understanding how elite-commoner dialogues can change through time. Examples from historical and contemporary societies, including the rise of feminism, grassroots movements, labor strikes, student protests and uprisings, shareholder class action suits, and even community-based movements in religious institutions such as the Catholic Church, all provide compelling reminders of how individuals and factions previously characterized by power imbalances can alter structural or institutional inequalities. Changes inspired by subordinated factions can occur episodically or over long periods, but they do occur (e.g.,

A. Joyce 2004). The chapters by Urunuela and Plunket; Joyce and Weller; and Winter, Markens, López, and Muzgo T. all deal with issues involving change or continuity through time in the social relationships that bound different ranked and stratified factions of society. Similar studies, if scaled to households and corporate groups, might yield critical information on the internal dynamics of family factions.

Returning to archaeology, the field of commoner studies stands to contribute much to our understanding of complex societies not just by cataloging and describing the material remains of the underclasses but also through recognizing the diversity of responses to situational and institutional inequality. Given the complex and interrelated relationships that undoubtedly characterized all archaeological subjects, one challenge we face is viewing elite-commoner interactions as a dialogue that involved give and take from both directions, and also from multiple directions within these categories. The probability is that there was more taking than giving done by elites, but nevertheless, theoretical frameworks pertaining to religious leadership, political action, resource management, economic production, and so forth that view this ebb and flow exclusively or even primarily from only one perspective seem out of balance. Another, related challenge is to foreground the assumptions and implications of such frameworks for the underclassed or underprivileged. This volume makes particular headway here with respect to our understanding of what it means for ideology to be materialized and "dominant."

Commoner studies will not, and should not, replace those focused on other elements of society. In broadening the dialogue around the ritual, religious, and ideological roles of different status groups as elements of complex societies, we urge that such analyses be viewed in conjunction with, and not opposed to, those that focus heavily or exclusively on the record of the elite few. Commoner studies are becoming increasingly central, however, to achieving a more integrated and comprehensive perspective of the past. Although it is recognized that Mesoamerica is a diverse area, the following statement seems applicable to the region as a whole: "It seems clear from both Colonial documents and Classic period hieroglyphic texts that the ancient Maya had much less trouble than we do in recognizing who was a noble and who was a commoner" (J. Marcus 2004:261). Had any of us been present in pre-Columbian times, we also may not have had trouble distinguishing elites from commoners. Hopefully, archaeologists of the twenty-first century will become more adept at this task. Our goal for this volume is to contribute to the growing awareness of the richness and diversity of commoner lives in all aspects of what it means to be "common" and recognize the significance of their contributions to ancient social complexity. These chapters provide a starting point for discussing the interaction of commoners, ideology, ritual, and religion. We look forward to seeing future work on these subjects.

ACKNOWLEDGMENTS

We sincerely thank the authors for contributing their original work to make this volume a success, for doing it so energetically and good-naturedly, and for respecting deadlines with a ritual solemnity. Three anonymous reviewers helped us to clarify and refine our thoughts on these complicated subjects, and their detailed input is greatly appreciated. Darrin Pratt of the University Press of Colorado embraced this project from the very beginning, and it has been a pleasure to work with him. We also thank Laura Furney of the University Press of Colorado for her copy editing of the manuscript. At Bellevue Community College, the personnel of the Social Sciences Division (in particular, Trina Ballard, Deanna Veyna, Beverly White, and Tom Pritchard) and the Academic Computing Services (read HELP! desk) were of notable assistance, especially in the final stages of completion. We thank our parents, Sophie (Sue) and the late Henry Gonlin, and Margie and Lloyd Elliott, for supplying us with continuous love, support, and encouragement, and it is to them that we dedicate this volume.

REFERENCES CITED

Brown, Linda A.

2004 Dangerous Places and Wild Spaces: Creating Meaning with Materials and Space at Contemporary Maya Shrines on El Duende Mountain. *Journal of Archaeological Method and Theory* 11:31–58.

Brumfiel, Elizabeth M.

1992 Breaking and Entering the Ecosystem: Gender, Class, and Faction Steal the Show. *American Anthropologist* 94:551–567.

Chase, Arlen F., and Diane Z. Chase

1992 Mesoamerican Elites: Assumptions, Definitions, and Models. In *Mesoamerican Elites: An Archaeological Assessment,* edited by Diane Z. Chase and Arlen F. Chase, pp. 3–17. University of Oklahoma Press, Norman.

Freter, AnnCorinne

1988 The Classic Maya Collapse at Copán, Honduras: A Regional Settlement Perspective. Ph.D. dissertation, Pennsylvania State University. University Microfilms, Ann Arbor.

Fried, Morton H.

1967 *The Evolution of Political Society: An Essay in Political Anthropology*. McGraw Hill, New York.

Gibson, Charles

1964 *The Aztecs Under the Spanish Rule: A History of the Indians of the Valley of Mexico, 1519–1810*. Stanford University Press, Stanford.

Gonlin, Nancy

1993 Rural Household Archaeology at Copán, Honduras. Ph.D. dissertation, Pennsylvania State University. University Microfilms, Ann Arbor.

1994 Rural Household Diversity in Late Classic Copán, Honduras. In *Archaeological Views from the Countryside: Village Communities in Early Complex Societies*, edited by Glenn M. Schwartz and Steven E. Falconer, pp. 177–197. Smithsonian Series in Archaeology Inquiry, Smithsonian Institution Press, Washington, D.C.

2004 Methods for Understanding Classic Maya Commoners: Structure Function, Energetics, and More. In *Ancient Maya Commoners*, edited by Jon C. Lohse and Fred Valdez Jr., pp. 225–254. University of Texas Press, Austin.

Hendon, Julia A.

1991 Status and Power in Classic Maya Society: An Archaeological Study. *American Anthropologist* 93:894–918.

Hirth, Kenneth G.

1993 Identifying Rank and Socioeconomic Status in Domestic Contexts: An Example from Central Mexico. In *Prehispanic Domestic Units in Western Mesoamerica*, edited by Robert S. Santley and Kenneth G. Hirth, pp. 121–146. CRC Press, Boca Raton.

Horcasitas, Fernando, and Doris Heyden (translators and editors)

1971 *Book of the Gods and Rites of the Ancient Calendar, by Fray Diego Durán*. University of Oklahoma Press, Norman.

Iannone, Gyles, and Samuel V. Connell (editors)

2003 *Perspectives on Ancient Maya Rural Complexity*. Monograph 49, Cotsen Institute of Archaeology. University of California, Los Angeles.

Inomata, Takeshi, and Stephen D. Houston (editors)

2001 *Royal Courts of the Ancient Maya*, Volumes 1 and 2. Westview Press, Boulder.

Inomata, Takeshi, Daniela Triadan, Erick Ponciano, Estela Pinto, Richard E. Terry, and Markus Eberl

2002 Domestic and Political Lives of Classic Maya Elites: The Excavation of Rapidly Abandoned Structures at Aguateca, Guatemala. *Latin American Antiquity* 13:305–330.

Joyce, Arthur A.

2004 Sacred Space and Social Relations in the Valley of Oaxaca. In *Mesoamerican Archaeology,* edited by Julia A. Hendon and Rosemary A. Joyce, pp. 192–216. Blackwell Publishing, Oxford.

Joyce, Rosemary A., and Julia A. Hendon

2000 Heterarchy, History, and Material Reality: "Communities" in Late Classic Honduras. In *The Archaeology of Communities: A New World Perspective,* edited by Marcello A. Canuto and Jason Yaeger, pp. 143–160. Routledge Press, New York.

Lentz, David

1991 Maya Diets of the Rich and Poor: Paleoethnobotanical Evidence from Copán. *Latin American Antiquity* 2:269–287.

Lockhart, James

1992 *The Nahuas After the Conquest: A Social and Cultural History of the Indians of Central Mexico, Sixteenth Through Eighteenth Centuries*. Stanford University Press, Stanford.

Lohse, Jon C., and Fred Valdez Jr. (editors)

2004a *Ancient Maya Commoners*. University of Texas Press, Austin.

Lohse, Jon C., and Fred Valdez Jr.

2004b Examining Ancient Maya Commoners Anew. In *Ancient Maya Commoners,* edited by Jon C. Lohse and Fred Valdez Jr., pp. 1–21. University of Texas Press, Austin.

Lucero, Lisa J.

2003 The Politics of Ritual: The Emergence of Classic Maya Rulers. *Current Anthropology* 44:523–558

Manzanilla, Linda

2004 Social Identity and Daily Life at Classic Teotihuacan. In *Mesoamerican Archaeology,* edited by Julia A. Hendon and Rosemary Joyce, pp. 124–147. Blackwell Publishing, Oxford.

Marcus, George E.

1983 "Elite" as a Concept, Theory, and Research Tradition. In *Elites: Ethnographic Issues,* edited by George E. Marcus, pp. 7–27. University of New Mexico Press, Albuquerque.

Marcus, Joyce

2004 Maya Commoners: The Stereotype and the Reality. In *Ancient Maya Commoners,* edited by Jon C. Lohse and Fred Valdez Jr., pp. 255–283. University of Texas Press, Austin.

Martínez Hernández, Juan (editor)

1929 *Diccionario de Motul: Maya-Español.* Compañía Tipográfica Yucateca, S.A., Mérida.

Masson, Marilyn A., and Carlos Peraza Lope

2004 Commoners in Postclassic Maya Society: Social Versus Economic Class Constructs. In *Ancient Maya Commoners,* edited by Jon C. Lohse and Fred Valdez Jr., pp. 197–223. University of Texas Press, Austin.

Mathews, Jennifer P., and James F. Garber

2004 Models of Sacred Order: Physical Expression of Sacred Space Among the Ancient Maya. *Ancient Mesoamerica* 15:49–59.

McAnany, Patricia

1995 *Living with the Ancestors: Kinship and Kingship in Ancient Maya Society.* University of Texas Press, Austin.

2001 Perspectives on Actors, Gender Roles, and Architecture at Classic Maya Courts and Households. In *Royal Courts of the Ancient Maya,* Volume 1, *Theory, Comparison, and Synthesis,* edited by Takeshi Inomata and Stephen D. Houston, pp. 84–129. Westview Press, Boulder.

Plunket, Patricia (editor)

2002 *Domestic Ritual in Ancient Mesoamerica.* Monograph 46, Cotsen Institute of Archaeology. University of California, Los Angeles.

Reed, David M.

1998 Ancient Maya Diet at Copán, Honduras. Ph.D. dissertation, Pennsylvania State University. University Microfilms, Ann Arbor.

Resnick, Stephen, and Richard Wolff

1987 *Knowledge and Class.* University of Chicago Press, Chicago.

Saitta, Dean J.

1994 Agency, Class, and Archaeological Interpretation. *Journal of Anthropological Archaeology* 13:201–227.

1997 Power, Labor, and the Dynamics of Change in Chacoan Political Economy. *American Antiquity* 62:7–26.

Smith, Michael E.

1987 Household Possessions and Wealth in Agrarian States: Implications for Archaeology. *Journal of Anthropological Archaeology* 6:297–335.

1992 *The Aztecs.* Blackwell Publishers, Malden.

Stark, Barbara L., and Barbara Ann Hall

1993 Hierarchical Social Differentiation Among Late to Terminal Classic Residential Locations in La Mixtequilla, Veracruz, Mexico. In *Prehispanic Domestic Units in Western Mesoamerica,* edited by Robert S. Santley and Kenneth G. Hirth, pp. 249–273. CRC Press, Boca Raton.

Sugiyama, Saburo

2004 Governance and Polity at Classic Teotihuacan. In *Mesoamerican Archaeology,* edited by Julia A. Hendon and Rosemary A. Joyce, pp. 97–123. Blackwell Publishing, Oxford.

Tozzer, Alfred M.

1941 *Landa's Relación de las Cosas de Yucatán: A Translation*. Papers of the Peabody Museum of Archaeology and Ethnography, Volume 5, No. 3. Harvard University, Cambridge.

Tucker, Robert C. (editor)

1978 *The Marx-Engels Reader*. Second edition. W. W. Norton and Company, New York.

Weber, Max

1947 *The Theory of Social and Economic Organization*. Translated and edited by A. M. Henderson and Talcott Parsons. The Free Press, New York.

Webster, David, AnnCorinne Freter, and Nancy Gonlin

2000 *Copán: The Rise and Fall of an Ancient Maya Polity*. Case Studies in Archaeology Series, series editor Jeffrey Quilter. Harcourt College Publications, Fort Worth.

Willey, Gordon R., and Richard M. Leventhal

1979 Prehistoric Settlement at Copán. In *Maya Archaeology and Ethnohistory,* edited by Norman Hammond and Gordon R. Willey, pp. 75–102. University of Texas Press, Austin.

Wolf, Eric R.

1982 *Europe and the People Without History*. University of California Press, Berkeley.

Zaro, Gregory, and Jon C. Lohse

2005 Agricultural Rhythms and Rituals: Ancient Maya Solar Observation in Hinterland Blue Creek, Northwestern Belize. *Latin American Antiquity* 16:81–98.

COMMONER RITUAL AND IDEOLOGY IN ANCIENT MESOAMERICA

CHAPTER ONE

COMMONER RITUAL, COMMONER IDEOLOGY

(Sub-)Alternate Views of Social Complexity in Prehispanic Mesoamerica

JON C. LOHSE

INTRODUCTION

The purpose of this volume is to elucidate the roles of commoners in ancient Mesoamerica as active ideological agents who participated in numerous ways in religious expression and ritual practice. The lacunae in understanding these roles is somewhat understandable given that ritual, religion, and ideology cut across multiple avenues of research, creating a challenge to scholars seeking to understand the different ways in which members of societies express shared belief systems. Given, however, that non-elites are frequently omitted from hypotheses or conclusions regarding ritual behavior and religious expression, at least in any capacity beyond being modeled as inert supplicants (a conclusion strongly rejected by most contributors to this volume, also see L. Brown 2000, 2004; Hutson 2002; A. Joyce and Winter 1996; Kunen et al. 2002; Mathews and Garber 2004; and Plunket 2002a), it is imperative that the challenge of foregrounding their participation in these symbolic systems be taken up in a coherent and systematic fashion. At stake is a greater and probably more realistic understanding of how all individuals, elite and non-elite alike in Mesoamerica and far beyond, contributed to and participated in the regular (re-)constitution of social process.

Selecting ritual and ideology from the perspective of commoners, with implications for larger social contexts and bundled factional relations, as topics of study is timely. A great deal of attention has been turned in recent years to understanding ritual and ideology within complex and so-called egalitarian societies (select cross-cultural examples include Bell 1992, 1997; Blanton et al. 1996; Demarest and Conrad 1992; DeMarrais et al. 1996; Dietler and Hayden 2001; Earle 1997; Insoll 2004; Marcus and Flannery 2004; Plunket 2002b; Rappaport 1999; and Wolf 1999). Many of these studies impel and are motivated by agency-centered examinations that increasingly seek to situate elements of deliberate action within a multivocalic and polythetic prehistoric past (e.g., Brumfiel 1992; Dobres and Robb 2000; Hendon and Joyce 2004; Hutson 2002; A. Joyce et al. 2001; A. Joyce and Winter 1996; Love 1999; Robin 2002; Sheets 2000). Just as with other recent advances in subject-centered anthropological archaeology, the effort to understand the ideo-ritual role(s) of commoners in complex societies should not be considered as "adding commoners and stirring." As we question many of the underlying assumptions in research into these topics, serious and fundamental reworking of extant models of who controlled the past and by what means were resources—particularly of the "esoteric" type—allocated will be required. These issues lie at the very heart of organizational variation across all societies, past or present, complex or otherwise.

In this chapter, I seek to reconcile these frameworks, the study of ritual and ideology with agentive approaches to understanding motivated behavior, to advance our "common" understanding of how members of ancient societies, particularly those born or lived of non-elite standing, contended with the myriad tensions and forces that shaped their lives. Following chapters pursue a number of courses—some not necessarily in agreement with the ideas proposed here—to demonstrate aspects of ritual technology and ideological practice that are to be found in the material record of prehispanic Mesoamerican commoners. The data sets these chapters present are instrumental in helping renew and revise our view of many-stranded social relationships that hinged on unequal access to different kinds of goods, materials, resources, prestige, and perhaps ideas and information (see Preface). My own approach derives from an effort to find alternatives to the Dominant Ideology Thesis, which I argue directly or indirectly shapes most of the current scholarship regarding ritual performance and ideological motivation. Implicated are James Scott's (1985, 1990) notions of a Hidden Transcript and Social Resistance. I explore recent conceptualizations of power and the application of Structuration Theory (following Giddens 1979, 1984) to revise our understanding of the cause-and-effect relationship between commoners and elites. The significance of ritual and generative meaning, two related forces that served to cohere as well as distinguish social constituencies, are viewed from the perspective of collective remembrances (following Halbwachs 1941, 1952 [Coser 1992]). The result is a dynamic model of the ritualization of ideologically charged recursive relationships not simply between elites and non-elites themselves but between the organizational rules and expectations that shaped the negotiated relations between those categories and the variability they contain (see Preface). It is critical to note that this effort is *not* intended to place ancient commoners on equal footing with elites but rather to build a framework for examining the actions of both, particularly for commoners and particularly with respect to ideologically motivated ritual behavior, from a balanced perspective that fairly considers the contributions of all social elements in the constituted past.

SITUATING RELIGION, RITUAL, AND IDEOLOGY

The terms *religion, ritual,* and *ideology* are difficult to define with precision, and the many different approaches to their study reflect the diverse theoretical landscape that is one of the strengths of anthropological archaeology. Not all chapters in this volume employ these terms in the same ways; these discrepancies reflect the state of research in our discipline and individual perceptions and usages. Defining religion in particular proves evasive and I defer to Timothy Insoll (2004:7) who notes: "In many respects it [religion] is indefinable, being concerned with thoughts, beliefs, actions and material, and how these things are weighted. The important point to make is that regardless of all the complexities of definition which have been attempted—we have to recognize that religion also includes the intangible, the irrational, and the indefinable." Insoll (2004:figure 2) questions whether the analytical separation of religion from other "tangible" aspects of culture is appropriate (also Lansing 1991:5–8) and advocates recentralizing the religious condition of humanity in our overall

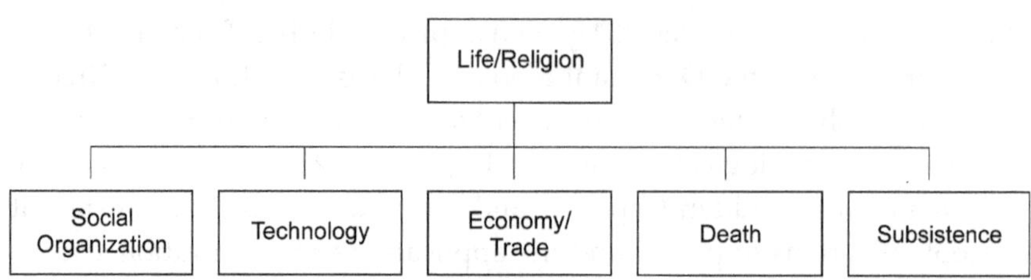

1.1. A view of the place of religion in archaeological models of historic and prehistoric societies (redrawn from Insoll 2004:figure 2).

conceptualization of the past (Figure 1.1). In general terms, religion refers to the supernatural, mythological, and mundane; spans temporal scales from the past through the present and into the future; and can apply to both the individual and the collective. Religion almost always, however, refers to an element of experience, expectation, or reality that lies outside the immediate control of humans (see Winter et al., Chapter 7, for a detailed discussion of Zapotec religious beliefs). Archaeologists are charged with discerning how different members of societies participated in these shared belief systems—quite clearly no easy task.

Ritual has been more concretely addressed in archaeological research. Joyce Marcus (1999:70–71), after Kent Flannery (1976), proposes a useful framework for studying ritual behavior, urging examiners to consider three components: *content,* referring to the subject of the ritual; *locus of performance,* referring to the place where rituals were carried out; and the *performers* of ritual. These elements and others have been considered in ethnoarchaeological studies of ritual practice that hold further potential to guide archaeological inquiry (e.g., L. Brown 2004; Deal 1988). Some of the chapters in this volume, such as Chapters 3, 4, 5, and 9, follow these guidelines, making considerable headway in elucidating the potential diversity of ritual technologies that are to be found in Mesoamerica. Understanding the purposes and motivations for ritual, however, represents an added challenge to archaeological investigations of its material residues. Evon Vogt (1993:7–8) echoes Edmund Leach (1966) and Clifford Geertz (1965) in considering ritual as symbolic behavior in the sense that it most typically stores and conveys information. Elements of this definition with beneficial implications for the current collection of studies are ritual's *informative* aspects—that is, its content, meaning, and representation through use of symbols—and *communicative* aspects. Symbols can be material or performative and include figurines, carved monuments, oral narratives and utterances, gestures, and even built space and landscapes (Robb 1998).

Like Vogt, Roy Rappaport sees ritual as a highly symbolic system of communication. Rappaport (1999:24), however, emphasizes ritual's active nature, defining it as "the performance of more or less invariant sequences of formal acts and utterances not entirely decoded by the performers." This observation suggests that all audiences and congregations witnessing ritual performances have some at least partial awareness and comprehension of the messages being conveyed and may at times even be key participants. He also considers the place of ritual in the enculturation process, arguing that it be considered as a *structure*, "that is, a more or less enduring set of relations among a number of general but variable features" (Rappaport 1999:3). He views ritual as the performative generation of meaning and information from which belief systems spring or on which they are founded. Although we might view the relationship between the act and the belief as being like that of the chicken and the egg, his point is both clear and profound: the performance (including use of material symbols) of ritual should occupy a central place in study not just of belief systems but also of the constitution of relations and processes of enculturation based on sets of knowledge that are passed on or reaffirmed from person to person or from one generation to the next. Within this framework, two variables in particular are important for archaeological study: unpacking the information content of symbolic communications and discerning the role(s) played by individuals in a diverse population.

Scholars have often drawn a close, although not precise, correspondence between ideology and religion, with religious and artistic expression as the most common examples of symbolic behavior. "Ideotechnic" artifacts (following Binford 1962) have included figurines, carvings, symbols of "natural agencies," and other difficult-to-interpret items. Ideology, in the past often termed a *worldview*, has historically been approached as but one of many components or subsystems of larger human-environment systems. Ideology/religion served to provide meaning for the surrounding social, natural, and supernatural realms (Robb 1998:334–337) but was seen as impossible for contemporary scholars to fully comprehend. Its perceived inaccessibility reduced ideo-religious behavior to epiphenomenon status (see Flannery 1972)—that is, acknowledged to have been important but diminished in priority alongside more tangible elements of the past such as economics and subsistence (Demarest 1992:6–7). When considered at all, ritual and religious behavior (here synonymous with ideology-as-worldview) was generally ascribed a functional role explaining order, coherence, and equilibrium among ancient social orders (Vayda 1968:x).

As the view of religion and its material expression—ritual—as shaping forces in human behavior has grown, ideology has become more widely perceived as not simply a shared belief system but rather communication-based strategies for maintaining the various social positions that archaeological subjects clearly held. Elites not only are believed to have manipulated meaning to underscore their paramount status but are often seen as the very source of ritual knowledge and overseers of most ceremonies. This position includes approaches that have been described as Marxist (e.g., Miller and Tilley 1984; Pearson 1982, 1984; Trigger 1991) and those that have not (e.g., Brumfiel 1998; Clark 1997; Demarest 1992; DeMarrais et al. 1996; Earle 1997; Freidel 1992; Inomata 2001; Peregrin 1991). One primary difference between these two positions is whether ideology (consisting of accessing and conveying esoteric information, conducting auspicious ceremonies, or maintaining contact with the divine) is viewed as naturalizing social distinction and unifying societies or serves to mask and obfuscate differences through deliberate intent, control, manipulation, and misinformation. Another significant difference is whether intentionality is attributed to the individual or the collective. David Freidel (1992), for example, argues for ideology as a unifying force in society, albeit one that is embedded primarily in and personified by rulers and exalted elites in their role as shamans facilitating intercommunication between the present and the Otherworld. In this usage ideological intent is manifest at the individual level for elites but on the collective level for non-elites.

In spite of these differences and at risk of oversimplification, I see these perspectives as comparable in terms of how our discipline has come to understand the roles of commoners. In both approaches, non-elites receive little attention as potential contributors in any meaningful sense to the maintenance of religious or social systems, institutions, and practices. Rather, non-elite involvement frequently is reduced to that of cultural dupes, or as "actors easily taken in by an ideology foisted upon them by the rich, famous, and powerful" (Clark 1996:52): ideology flows from or is maintained and manipulated by individual or small collectives of elites, whose names and identities are often known to archaeologists (in sharp contrast to the anonymous status of non-elites). In this sense it has mattered little whether commoners penetrate the layers of symbolic messaging; their involvement in these systems is rendered as mute, passive, or acquiescent. Although this conclusion is not universal among all current scholars of ritual and ideology, it can be fairly said that research has historically concluded very little regarding commoners, omitting any explanation of commoners' participation or implying an understanding derived exclusively from the roles of elites. One of this volume's goals is to begin exploring alternative approaches to theorizing the ritual and ideological roles of non-elite subjects in the past.

In *Huitzilopochtli's Conquest*, Elizabeth Brumfiel (1998:3) has offered a definition of ideology that allows us to move beyond (although not altogether depart from) notions of control, domination, and resistance, describing ideology as "a system of values and ideas that promotes social behavior benefiting some classes or interest groups more than others." This definition is well suited to examining the motivated behaviors of commoners and other subgroups that compose complex societies without imposing preconceptions about who did what to whom by what sleights of hand or controls over other social institutions (also Emerson 1997; Gilman 1989:68). In my own usage, *ideology* pertains to symbolic communication between parties (individuals or collectives) in ritualized practices for the purpose of shaping social relations. Other behavioral arenas beyond ritual—economic, political, subsistence—can also be, and frequently are, subsumed under the ideologic. Not all rituals are ideologically motivated and not all ideological practices project political agendas. There is a significant overlap of these ideas, however, that reflects the motivated actions of individuals or groups seeking to establish or reaffirm their identities in the context of larger social tensions and relationships. These motivated actions—*ideological practices* in my terminology—can both emphasize and minimize social differences. Opening up our understanding of these actions and the message content that underlies them to include more than dynamics of social control and maintenance of hierarchy and political status quo remains the challenge for archaeologists concerned with illuminating commoners' roles in the constitution of social relationships. This approach will be explored in further detail later in this chapter.

THE DOMINANT IDEOLOGY THESIS AND BEYOND

The predominating view of commoner involvement in ritual and ideological practice that I have described above conforms, intentionally or not, rather closely to the expectations of the Dominant Ideology Thesis (DIT), which was derived from Marxist models that describe some of the processes by which elites maintain control over society. As Nicholas Abercrombie and colleagues (1980) explain, in the DIT, beliefs are "materialized" by privileged members of society, often those with political, economic, and/or military power, who thereby control the message content of key symbols and social events to advance their own agendas. Followers remain largely unaware of the degree of their mystification and are generally incapable of any sort of self-awareness (without outside intervention) except in relation to their elite counterparts (see the subaltern historiographer Ranajit Guha's [1999:18–19] discussion of commoner "negative consciousness"). As an example, this position is endorsed by Michael Shanks and Christopher Tilley (1992:130), who correlate ideology with maintaining relations of inequality and argue: "[I]deology does not refer to a body of ideas, views, beliefs, held by a group of people, but is an aspect of a limited practice, an aspect of relations of inequality. Ideological practice misrepresents contradictions in the interests of the dominant group." Their position, that ideology is used to maintain inequality as elite actors mask imbalances manifest in material conditions, is a clear application of the DIT to the material and social past. When considering how the ritual and ideological status of commoners is treated, a careful reading of many current articles on this topic will reveal the degree to which some form of DIT serves as our discipline's prevailing framework in shaping discussion of these issues either directly, as in the case of Shanks and Tilley, or otherwise. Implications range from the psychological effect of being "common" to the contributions of non-elites to the process of developing political and social complexity. Two examples illustrate and substantiate these points.

Concerning the impact of low rank on members of the Early Formative Olmec community of San Lorenzo, John Clark (1997:217) has suggested, "The principal means of governing the commoners was to reiterate through ritual drama and oratory the *naturalness of class differences and of the superiority of nobles* and their rights to rule as entailed in creation myths, and to inspire a *sense of awe, and perhaps fear, for royal power*" (emphasis added). Referring to public works at that site, Clark (1997:219) continues, "The obvious exercise of discipline and power in projects involving hundreds of people at one time and in one place *would have generated its own self-evident truths of royal right and might,* and periodic projects would have kept these truths in the public eye" (emphasis added). Bruce Trigger (1991:125) similarly reasons that "by participating in erecting monuments that glorify the power of the upper classes, peasant laborers *are made to acknowledge their subordinate status and their sense of their own inferiority is reinforced*" (emphasis added). These statements, and the positions they reflect, hold extremely important implications for how the lived experiences of non-elites might be theorized by archaeologists. I do not suggest that processes of monumental constructions were not ideologically charged or that they did not underscore differences in rank or status in society, only that understanding the symbolic effects of public works on the daily lives of non-elites or considering how commoners might have experienced the fruits of their own efforts requires considerably broadening our theoretical perspectives. I discuss issues of monumental constructions and site planning and the question of whether builders were in reality alienated from their manual and material contributions in greater detail later.

In addition to understanding in fuller measure the daily psychological experiences of commoners, a second example illustrates the absence of non-elite contributions to the course of social development and the appearance and maintenance of systems of political complexity that were grounded largely in ideologically charged symbolic discourse:

> The internal and external forces leading to the rise of the Maya states are now totally open to debate. Future interpretations will need complex scenarios that combine some weak economic pressures for internal management originating from demography and warfare, but stimulated by both external influences and the class interests of emerging shamanistic leaders. This last ideological element was clearly reflected in Late Preclassic symbolic systems, architectural features, and artifacts that were later associated with the doctrines of sacred power of the Classic-period kings. At . . . early centers, the images and iconography of power already display the ruler's role as "axis mundi," the personified axis of the universe. . . . As we shall see, this form of divine royal kingship would guide the volatile history of the lowland Maya for the next thousand years. (Demarest 2004:87–88)

One implication of these statements is that non-elites, estimated to consist of between 80 and 98 percent of ancient populations, were largely unimportant to the rise and development of complex societies in which elaborated belief systems played a key role. Such propositions can be considered shortsighted at best. At worst, they are at risk of arguing from negative evidence precisely what contributions were made from all quarters of diverse populations at the inception of social and political complexity while denying any meaningful interrelatedness between rulers and their constituencies.

BEYOND DOMINATION: RECURSIVE RELATIONS, STRUCTURATION, AND MEMORY TRACES

In a significant departure from views of elite-dominated ideological practice, Scott (1976, 1985, 1990) has examined the negotiation between commoners and non-commoners over meaning and value, likening the exchange to a transcript. The part of this dialogue, Scott argues, that occurs in public forums is rarely complete for fear of reprisals, and much of subalterns' (following Guha 1988) expressions of their real value systems are conducted in private or take place in political peripheries, constituting a Hidden Transcript. These private practices are among many possible forms of social resistance, although nearly all are covert, secretive, small-scale, and anonymously conducted. Application of these ideas in Mesoamerica (Hutson 2002; A. Joyce et al. 2001; Joyce and Weller, Chapter 6) reveals some of the ways non-elites responded to their perceived subordination and has been instrumental in populating the ancient landscape with individuals capable of deliberate and premeditated action in response to their social realities.

Ranajit Guha (1999:11) has elaborated on Scott's transcript model, arguing that "subordination can hardly be justified as an ideal and a norm without acknowledging the fact and possibility of insubordination, so that the affirmation of dominance in the ruling culture speaks eloquently too of its Other, that is, resistance." If we acknowledge the roles played by non-elites in dialogue over religious meaning and ideological discourse, a key issue to resolve is the ways that elite and commoner behaviors modify and shape their counterparts. Such a dialectic approach requires closely examining the internal structure of social relations that unite people simultaneously across many different spatial scales of organization. As Randall McGuire (2002:12) describes the dialectic, "The relations are made up of contradictions that bind individuals and groups with opposing and conflicting interests together, and because small changes in any part of this social whole will alter the structure of relations, this whole is always in flux." Although the question of how classes affected each other has long been posed by social scientists—the social historian E. P. Thompson's (1963) examination of English "crowds" and their relationships to landowners, shopkeepers, and the ruling aristocracy is but one example—it is rarely expounded on by archaeologists (but see A. Joyce et al. 2001). To understand the recursive nature of class relationships, I turn to elements of Anthony Giddens's Structuration Theory.

Giddens (1979:64) defines *structuring properties* as "rules and resources recursively implicated in the reproduction of social systems." These elements include "(a) knowledge—as memory traces—of 'how things are to be done' on the part of social actors; (b) social practices organized through the recursive mobilization of that knowledge; [and] (c) capabilities that the production of those practices presupposes." Grounded in knowledge involving expectations of the future based on past experiences, structuring "rules" (which may be called on by all "competent" members of society) guide interaction between elites and non-elites around social values for how one is to be treated in both daily face-to-face associations and over longer periods. Did all commoners in all time periods universally accept the proposition of the elites' divine right to rule? To what degree was participation in such an ideologically driven political system dependent on or reinforced by the availability of material goods and resources? Under what conditions might a given status quo come under scrutiny, be modified, or even be rejected altogether? The expectations of various classes (or of groups within a social stratum) and the knowledge that informs them are embodied or ritualized in symbolic acts, utterances, gestures, performances, and the like. Recent research (Robb 1998:338) argues that the meanings of important symbols (of both the material and behavioral sorts) are not fixed but are situationally contested, conditioned, modified, appropriated, and exploited by individuals and factions. These various factions are integrated simultaneously across different scales and along different axes of society through often competing interests over material and nonmaterial resources as they respond to social, political, and environmental conditions (Brumfiel 1992). I echo Giddens's contention that most members of ancient societies were probably quite aware of this ongoing process and the significances behind the deployment of symbols and symbolic behavior. Giddens (1979:72) notes, "It is not a coincidence that the forms of social theory which have made little or no conceptual space for agents' understanding of themselves, and of their social contexts, have tended greatly to exaggerate the impact of dominant symbol systems or ideologies upon those in subordinate classes." In the case of complex societies consisting of elaborated and highly differentiated social roles, the kinds of expectations described previously are likely to undergo continual negotiation and formulation as rules of conduct are renewed over periods of time ranging from daily encounters to generations. Because of the context in which the Hidden Transcript took place and the recursive effects of commoner actions, including social resistance, on elite hegemonic strategies, the kinds of residential-scale investigations reported in many of the chapters in this volume (also Plunket 2002b) are central in helping to balance our awareness of ideologically motivated ritual practices conducted in the past.

In light of the foregoing discussions, however, it is important to consider just how far concepts of Hidden Transcripts and social resistance can take our understanding of commoner-elite dialogue. Scholars who view the "theoretical hegemony" (M. Brown 1996:730) of resistance as imperiling more balanced and inclusive models of the past (Hutson 2002; Ortner 1995) have urged caution in the application of these ideas. One alternative for adding flesh and tissue to the domination-resistance framework is offered in the diversification of the concept of power. Robert Paynter and Randall McGuire (1991), following Giddens (1979, 1984) and Daniel Miller and Christopher Tilley (1984), discuss the heterogeneity of power as having a transformative capacity to constructively intervene or negotiate as well as to thwart or negate. Archaeology has seen an increased awareness of "empowered" prehistoric and historic agents, including enslaved peoples (Thomas 1998), women (Gero and Conkey 1991; Gilchrist 1999; R. Joyce 2000a; Sweely 1999), and other previously marginalized people (our own efforts in this volume might also be placed into this category; also Lohse and Valdez 2004). An expanded definition of power, draped over and conforming to a polythetic past, is easily blended with the concept of pluralistic ideologies when we consider that the content of symbolic communication is known to have varied depending on the targeted audience and the objective (see Gonlin [Chapter 4] and Gossen and Leventhal [1993] for discussion of the parallel concept of religious pluralism). Brumfiel (1998), for example, describes how Aztec lords enacted symbolic behavior of one sort when attempting to build factions and support among peer or sub-elites while conveying messages of domination to subordinates (also see DeMarrais et al. 1996; Urban et al. 2002). Some of the chapters in this volume consider commoner circumstances and explore the formation of peer group solidarity, maintenance of localized identities, and expressions of communally shared beliefs at the scale of the individual or intimate family group. These responses each convey "power to" (versus "power over") in the transformative sense and have little to do with responding to elite-controlled ideological messaging.

Another alternative to binary approaches to ritual and ideological practice involves returning to Giddens's (1979:64) definition of structural properties as "knowledge—as memory traces—of how things 'are to be done.'" The study of collective memory, also called public or social memory (Hendon 2000; R. Joyce 2000b; Shackel 2001; Van Dyke and Alcock 2003), was pioneered by the Durkheim-influenced French sociologist Maurice Halbwachs. Halbwachs's conclusions are well suited to emphasizing organic aspects of social solidarity and continuity, apparently in contradistinction to more structural Marxist views on ideology and social relations. They can also be applied in an agency-oriented framework that allows scholars to understand commoner ritual and ideological behaviors in their own right as well as how they relate to larger, society-wide practices and discourses. The process of reconstituting the past centralizes questions such as what the past was like, whose recollection is valid, how it was experienced, and what it meant to different members of society (also see Van Dyke and Alcock 2003:2). Collective memory is held at both individual and group levels, although the former is contextualized into and framed by the latter. Halbwachs argued that "it is, of course[,] individuals who remember, not groups or institutions, but these individuals, being located in a specific group context, draw on that context to remember or recreate the past" (Coser 1992:23).

Two not necessarily exclusive forms of memory, historical and autobiographical memory, are outlined in Halbwachs's work. Historical memory "reaches the social actor only through written records and other types of records, such as photography. But it can be kept alive through commemorations, festival enactments, and the like" (Coser 1992:23). In contrast, autobiographical memory "is memory of events that we have personally experienced in the past. . . . It stands to reason, however, that autobiographical memory tends to fade with time unless it is periodically reinforced through contact with persons with whom one shared the experiences in the past" (Coser 1992:24). Many examples of each kind of memory can be found across Mesoamerica, from ritual enactments that reference cosmic creation events, such as the ballgame, to construction of monumental buildings and commemorating ancient deeds or ancestors (e.g., McAnany 1995). In pursuing an archaeology of commoner ritual and ideological behavior, it is necessary to not exclusively link historical memory with the actions of elites. The community-wide *guelaguetza* celebrations of reciprocal service and gift-giving in Oaxaca (Cohen 1999) provide but one example of how historical memory, emphasizing unity and solidarity but not leveling economic or status differences, can be shared collectively. Another example of historical memory as organized on a communal basis comes from the recent report of ballcourts in non-urban settings (R. Joyce and Hendon 2000; Walling et al. 2006), where they were apparently used without the direct involvement of ruling elites.

VARIATIONS ACROSS TIME AND SPACE IN MESOAMERICA

Brief perusals of the archaeological literature reveal significant differences in symbolic behavior and religious expression across Mesoamerica. At a low order of resolution, single-ruler polities found in the Eastern Lowlands seem fundamentally different from the corporate states of Central Mexico (Blanton et al. 1996). Clark (1997), for example, has argued that control over ritual and symbols of rulership and the divine, such as monolithic carved heads, thrones, and animal spirits, was a central element in the development and maintenance of inequality by ancient Olmec chiefs. This strategy appears quite different from that observed at Teotihuacan, where George Cowgill (1997:142) describes the ubiquity of composite censers in domestic contexts and their role in private rituals honoring the dead. These censers were mass-produced in a state-sponsored workshop near the Ciudadela, and their distribution may have served as a sort of state-regulated currency that played an instrumental role in the private expression of religious beliefs (see Barba et al., Chapter 3, and Manzanilla 2004 for additional treatment of domestic ritual at Teotihuacan).

A similar centralizing role could well have been served by the Postclassic Ehecatl/Quetzacoatl cult at Cholula in the Puebla Valley. Geoffrey McCafferty (Chapter 8) notes that images of the Wind God, identified as the patron deity of that community, are rarely reported in private, domestic contexts. Those living at or making pilgrimages to the site to participate in the *tecuhtli* ceremony granting divine authority to rulers and lineage heads were united by common identity, at least temporarily, despite differences in ethnicity or local religious custom (Pohl 1999:169–170). Although individual rulers of the Olmec chiefdoms and Maya polities appear to have been recognized and endowed with supernatural roles, Central Mexican society, at least as seen at Teotihuacan and Cholula, seems to have tended toward a corporate disposition (see Sugiyama 2004), a situation that surely had implications for the role of commoners in ritual behavior. Chapters 3 and 8, therefore, are central in balancing our understanding of the collective, corporate ideologies at Teotihuacan and Cholula and recognizing the scalar differences in ritual practice from the private domestic to the public polity.

Can these differences be ascribed to nonparallel evolutionary trajectories of different forms of complexity or to environmental variation between the Eastern Lowlands and Central Highlands? Or do they describe fundamental shifts in the basis of social, political, and ideological organization? Cowgill (1997:137) notes: "Whether or not impersonality and multiplicity were deliberately encouraged by state policy, they are themes that pervaded all classes and social sectors. No evidence of resistance or dissent has been recognized so far." Gabriela Uruñuela and Patricia Plunket (Chapter 2; also Plunket and Uruñuela 2002) make significant contributions to understanding the nature of Late Formative to Early Classic Central Mexican socioreligious constitution by examining ritual practice at the Formative period dispersed village of Tetimpa, one of many settlements whose inhabitants may have relocated to nearby urban centers such as Cholula or Teotihuacan after the eruption of the volcano Popocatépetl in the first century A.D. Studies like Uruñuela and Plunket's, as well as those in Chapters 3 and 8, are valuable in helping archaeologists understand fundamental differences between Central Mexico and the Eastern Lowlands by providing some historical context for the formation of urbanized, corporate centers and balancing our view of past religious life by adding household contexts to those from site centers. In this vein, research seeking out evidence for the kinds of "fear" and "awe" of royal power that Clark (1997) predicts in low-status households at San Lorenzo would seem critical for demonstrating more clearly and precisely the nature of social differentiation as it was expressed in ritual behavior in Early Formative societies. Without such balancing perspectives, conclusions about the effect of royal power on everyday constituencies seem premature.

APPLYING THE FRAMEWORK: MONUMENTAL ARCHITECTURE, SYMBOLIC ANALYSES, AND BALANCED PERSPECTIVES

Monumental architecture provides one opportunity to consider these topics in developing an archaeology of commoner ritual and ideology. Monumental architecture is frequently identified as a means of expressing or maintaining power in society (Trigger 1991), whether that society is corporate and "faceless" or networked and centered on individual elite agents. Open plazas served as stages for public ritual events, as well as informal socializing and economic exchange via occasional markets (Hirth 1998; Smith 1999), and large buildings often provided mural space for iconographic displays of elite messages regarding absolute power, perhaps even over life and death. Coordinating the labor required for their construction is argued to have further symbolized power and underscored status differences that began to develop as societies became increasingly complex, as discussed previously in this chapter.

Consequently, we can and should scrutinize the underlying, fundamental assumptions concerning the relationships among social labor, symbolic communication, and ideologies of power and domination or resistance. Regarding monumental architecture, these large constructions surely required coordinated labor from large numbers of people. Such efforts were probably more effective and efficient through some form of centralized management, and there is little doubt that laborers involved in these efforts must have recalled the tedious conditions under which those efforts took place. Stratigraphic sections, however, reveal that these monuments rarely appeared in a single event but were built in phases over a number of years or even centuries. Once established, they remained part of a highly symbolic and constantly evolving landscape representing collective efforts from multiple quarters. As part of community-wide historical memories (in the Halbwachsian sense) to which their own efforts and the efforts of their forbears contributed (making these constructions also part of multiple autobiographical histories), it is not likely that the generations of commoners who gave their time and labor experienced these constructions as entirely oppressive and subordinating (Hutson 2002:66). Moreover, the frequent integration of symbols intimately familiar to commoners, such as the thatched huts adorning numerous buildings across the Yucatán (Figure 1.2), into architectural veneers implies an effort by at least some building designers to appeal to commonly held ideas and shared values. No evidence indicates that these ideas and the ritual practices behind them were appropriated by elites. Rather, many of the monumental constructions that define urban zones appear to have been designed and positioned for public appreciation, understanding, and engagement.

These examples illustrate a number of salient points. First, multiple processes can be simultaneously involved in monumental constructions and other forms of community-scale symbolic behavior (Hutson 2002:65–66). Second, these processes may have changed through time across Mesoamerica (e.g., Urban and Schortman 1996). Third, monumental constructions may have been experienced differently by those who contributed their labor and other areas of expertise. Finally, we should be careful not to draw oversimplistic conclusions about relationships between elite

1.2. Thatched huts as decorative elements on public architecture. Structure 2 at Chicanná, Campeche, México, top, and the Arch at Labná, Yucatán, México, bottom (redrawn from Marquina 1951:figure 230).

control over ritual and cosmology, labor, and social power (see discussion by Saitta [1997]).

From the perspective of symbolic behavior and generated meaning, analyses of monumental site plans reveal how space was often designed and constructed to facilitate traffic and permit gatherings of large groups, thereby embracing and encompassing populations at an experiential level (e.g., Ashmore 1991; Ashmore and Sabloff 2002), at least during certain periods (see Joyce and Weller, Chapter 6, for a discussion of changes in site access and implications for commoner-elite relations). Site plans often reveal deeply rooted religious beliefs that structured lived space and social action in ancient Mesoamerica. The quadripartition of space and of the World Tree uniting three planes of existence pervade Mesoamerican belief systems (Coggins 1980; Mathews and Garber 2004; Wagner 2000). According to ethnographic sources, four cardinal places together with a central element make up a quincuncial whole that is replicated at a number of different scales (Hanks 1990; Vogt 1969). In ancient times, the practice conditioned the layouts of certain monumental structures, at least at some site centers (Ashmore 1991; Ashmore and Sabloff 2002; Mathews and Garber 2004; Sugiyama 1993; Wagner 2000:290–291), and even political regions (Marcus 1993). In this sense, "reading" monumental or political landscapes provides a way for archaeologists to understand certain foundational themes of a particular society's worldview.

In the absence of complementary data from a variety of social contexts, knowledge of the cosmic order can easily be described as "esoteric" or "restricted" in access, supporting inferences of elite ideological hegemony. One of the earliest documented expressions of a quadripartitioned Mesoamerican universe, however, was actually recorded in Oaxaca at San José Mogote's Household C3, dating to 1150–850 B.C. Shallow depressions, each painted a color corresponding to Zapotec notions of the four world corners, are believed to have been associated with women's divination rituals (Marcus 1999:80). Additional color-specific symbolism at the domestic scale is reported by Cynthia Robin (2002), whose excavations at Chan Nòohol near Xunantunich, Belize, revealed a Late Classic cache of four colored river cobbles positioned at cardinal points around a greenstone celt on top of a small, capped chultun beneath a house floor. Directionality, color symbolism, and cardinality were clearly not the exclusive purview of elite ideologists but rather were symbolically charged beliefs that were broadly understood by all Mesoamericans.

Another example of how the analysis of household data balances our view of common (and commoner) ritual practice comes from Dos Hombres in northwestern Belize (see Figure 0.1). Work at two residential groups, Operations 19 and 25 (Lohse 2001), revealed evidence suggesting that during the Late Classic period (ca. A.D. 600–850; see Figure 0.2), the plans of some house lots were partly conditioned by principles of cardinality, thereby mirroring practices noted in many site centers. With respect to the layouts of site plans discussed by Wendy Ashmore (1991), three key traits are relevant for recognizing cardinal patterning at the domestic level. First, each architectural unit that constituted a significant part of a site's plan, such as a plaza-focused cluster of buildings, provided a space for community members to come together to perform and share social functions. Analogs at the household level would be activity areas such as middens, gardens, and ancillary structures for kitchens or storage. Second, although components of the site may be representative of cardinal elements, the overall layout is often asymmetrical. Thus, a certain amount of geographic imprecision was acceptable to achieve a symbolically laden plan. Finally, all four cardinal places often are not discernable through mapping or excavation. Perhaps it is the case that certain components were left incomplete or were represented by natural features such as depressions for reservoirs or "vacant" terrain. Archaeologists working with household-scale data should maintain a similar degree of flexibility when attempting to interpret the oftentimes depauperate material records from residences that may have been inhabited only a generation or two.

The Operation 19 house group at Dos Hombres consists of two domestic ruins on a low (less than one meter) basal platform. Evidence of patterned off-mound activities include a refuse midden approximately fifteen meters west of the platform, a series of boulders thirty meters to the south that is taken to represent the southern houselot boundary, and the surface find of a limestone metate approximately twenty meters north of the platform (Figure 1.3). Excavations adjacent to the metate recovered artifacts and fauna, including more than 100 freshwater *jute* shells, a food source for the ancient Maya, suggesting this area was associated with food processing. Although no artifacts were recovered to the south or east of the group, these vast expanses of vacant space could easily have been used for domestic gardening.[1] A small burial crypt was uncovered beneath the center of the northern building; profiles show that this crypt did not intrude through the plaster floor but was constructed at the same time as the platform. This modest burial feature and its stratigraphic relationships with the construction sequence of the platform and Structure 1 indicate the significance of having a dedicatory ritual deposit in the virtual center of this house group and surrounding yard before construction was completed.

The Operation 25 house group consists of three medium-sized (approximately five by eight meters) mounds and a much smaller, open construction on a moderate-size platform located at the base of a steep escarpment

1.3. Artist's reconstruction (looking northwest) of Operation 19 houselot, based on archaeological data recovered during excavations (garden to south and pathways are inferred), Dos Hombres, Belize (after drawing by William R. Bowman).

(Figure 1.4). Off-mound excavations to the south revealed an elaborate subsurface feature designed to regulate levels of soil moisture throughout the year, signaling the location of a kitchen garden (Lohse and Findlay 2000). Interpreted as a possible kitchen, a buried plaster floor with a circular cut containing burned carbon was exposed behind or west of the platform. Although no strong evidence of patterned activity was recovered north of the platform, the low mound on the east side of the platform seems to have been used as a storage area or perhaps a small domestic shrine, as this construction was covered with hundreds of fragments of large utilitarian storage jars. Excavations into the platform center yielded evidence of ritual behavior in the form of an enigmatic plaster "patch"

1.4. Artist's reconstruction (looking northwest) of Operation 25 houselot, based on archaeological data recovered during excavations, Dos Hombres, Belize (after drawing by William R. Bowman).

lying directly atop bedrock for which no functional interpretation can be given. As with the burial at Operation 19, it is significant that this plaster was deposited prior to the construction of the residential platform, clearly indicating that this central element was of importance to the ancient inhabitants of this group.

Based on these data, occupants of Operations 19 and 25 house groups seem to have structured their domestic spaces—including investing symbolic meaning in ritual deposits prior to residence construction—according to fundamental beliefs held across Mesoamerica about the order of the cosmos. I am not arguing that religious principles structured all houselots in the Maya area, but evidence suggests that some houselots were structured by these principles. Reasons why other households at Dos Hombres were not certainly warrants consideration. As with Household C3 at San José Mogote, beliefs expressed through the daily practice of structuring living space help demonstrate the richness of domestic ritual behavior as well as the degree to which this knowledge permeated society. These examples, and also the case from Chan Nòohol, imply that *some* commoners had a deep and fundamental awareness of cosmological symbolism and were free to engage in certain practices such as rituals of divination or recreation. Such expressions have more to do with "power to" than "power over" and are crucial to balancing site-center or elite-focused data and for negating the idea that such esoteric ideas and information were under the exclusive purview of elites.

SUMMARY AND CONCLUSIONS

Concepts of collective memory and pluralistic definitions of power and ideology offer viable yet under-explored alternatives to the DIT and related models in explaining the role of ritual behavior and symbolic expression in complex societies. The examples I have offered do not speak of commoner empowerment per se, nor do they necessarily have anything to do with resistance. As do the following chapters, these examples amply demonstrate that there are no underlying, universal principles we can use to explain the dialogue between commoners and non-commoners with respect to religious beliefs and ideological messages of power, resistance, acquiescence, accommodation, or faction-building. Rather, these case studies show that ritual practice varied widely within each social stratum, depending on a number of factors, including the intended audience and the message content of that ritual. Further, we can see that many of these beliefs were actually shared between commoners and non-commoners, allowing us to move far beyond dualistic top-down or bottom-up models of negotiated ideology.

Because the public transcript between commoners and non-commoners over how and where ideas are expressed is not always complete as fossilized in the archaeological record, investigations conducted at the household level and in areas peripheral to political centers are absolutely critical to documenting the full nature of this dialogue. When identified by archaeologists, ritual behaviors of commoners in both household and larger community-wide contexts reveal a strong fluency with fundamental religious and symbolic information (Mathews and Garber 2004:56). These behaviors also imply flexibility in responding to different circumstances as well as engaging in and contributing to the ideological reconstitution of society from an active, agentive perspective. Important differences surely existed between rulers and other community members, but these distinctions are most likely to be understood only through practice-based approaches that foreground structuring rules and symbolic communications between (and within) social factions, and that illustrate how diverse constituencies differentially participated in the regular reconstitution of those rules.

A balanced framework that considers evidence from multiple social contexts and employs expanded, pluralistic definitions of power and ideology based on shared common experiences and motivations—as well as unitary and distinguishing ones—reveals that different interests in society were negotiated daily within the context of deeply structured belief systems, yielding rich cultural diversity through time and across the geographic space of Mesoamerica. Archaeologists' ability to break down the ideological content of messages conveyed through materialized beliefs and ritual behavior in both elite and non-elite contexts means that it is no longer appropriate to speak of a "dominant" ideology or consider ideology solely as emanating from exalted individuals. Instead, we are positioned to consider how different ideologies and ritual practices were motivated by a host of altogether other ends.

ACKNOWLEDGMENTS

This chapter has benefited tremendously from the comments of Elizabeth Brumfiel, Nancy Gonlin, Joyce Marcus, Mark Merher, Darrin Pratt, and three anonymous reviewers. The Blue Creek Regional Political Ecology Project provided support for the illustrations prepared by William Bowman. I alone, however, am responsible for errors or inadequacies in the chapter.

NOTE

1. William Doolittle (1992:82) reports that modern-day houselot gardens in northwestern Mexico are most frequently located to the south of houses. Even in the more southerly latitude of northwestern Belize, this location gives the advantage of more consistent sunlight exposure throughout the year.

REFERENCES CITED

Abercrombie, Nicholas, Stephen Hill, and Bryan S. Turner

1980 *The Dominant Ideology Thesis.* George Allen and Unwin, London.

Ashmore, Wendy
1991 Site-Planning Principles and Concepts of Directionality Among the Ancient Maya. *Latin American Antiquity* 2:199–226.

Ashmore, Wendy, and Jeremy A. Sabloff
2002 Spatial Order in Maya Civic Plans. *Latin American Antiquity* 13:201–215.

Bell, Catherine
1992 *Ritual Theory, Ritual Practice.* Oxford University Press, Oxford.
1997 *Ritual Perspectives and Dimensions.* Oxford University Press, Oxford.

Binford, Lewis R.
1962 Archaeology as Anthropology. *American Antiquity* 28:217–225.

Blanton, Richard E., Gary M. Feinman, Stephen A. Kowalewski, and Peter N. Peregrine
1996 A Dual-Processual Theory for the Evolution of Mesoamerican Civilization. *Current Anthropology* 37:1–14.

Brown, Linda A.
2000 From Discard to Divination: Demarcating the Sacred Through the Collection and Curation of Discarded Objects. *Latin American Antiquity* 11:319–333.
2004 Dangerous Places and Wild Spaces: Creating Meaning with Materials and Space at Contemporary Maya Shrines on El Duende Mountain. *Journal of Archaeological Method and Theory* 11:31–58.

Brown, Michael F.
1996 On Resisting Resistance. *American Anthropologist* 98:729–734.

Brumfiel, Elizabeth M.
1992 Breaking and Entering the Ecosystem: Gender, Class, and Faction Steal the Show. *American Anthropologist* 94:551–567.
1998 Huitzilopochtli's Conquest: Aztec Ideology in the Archaeological Record. *Cambridge Archaeological Journal* 8:3–13.

Clark, John E.
1996 Comments. *Current Anthropology* 37:51–52.
1997 The Arts of Government in Early Mesoamerica. *Annual Review of Anthropology* 26:211–234.

Coggins, Clemency Chase
1980 The Shape of Time: Some Political Implications of a Four-Part Figure. *American Antiquity* 45:727–739.

Cohen, Jeffery H.
1999 *Cooperation and Community: Economy and Society in Oaxaca.* University of Texas Press, Austin.

Coser, Lewis A. (editor and translator)

1992 *Maurice Halbwachs: On Collective Memory*. University of Chicago Press, Chicago.

Cowgill, George L.

1997 State and Society at Teotihuacan, Mexico. *Annual Review of Anthropology* 26:129–161.

Deal, Michael

1988 Recognition of Ritual Pottery in Residential Units: An Ethnoarchaeological Model of the Family Altar Tradition. In *Ethnoarchaeology Among the Highland Maya of Chiapas, Mexico*, edited by Thomas A. Lee Jr. and Brian Hayden, pp. 61–89. Papers of the New World Archaeological Foundation 56. Brigham Young University, Provo.

Demarest, Arthur A.

1992 Archaeology, Ideology, and Pre-Columbian Cultural Evolution: The Search for an Approach. In *Ideology and Pre-Columbian Civilizations*, edited by Arthur A. Demarest and Geoffrey W. Conrad, pp. 1–13. School of American Research Press, Santa Fe.

2004 *Ancient Maya: The Rise and Fall of a Rainforest Civilization*. Cambridge University Press, New York.

Demarest, Arthur A., and Geoffrey W. Conrad (editors)

1992 *Ideology and Pre-Columbian Civilizations*. School of American Research Press, Santa Fe.

DeMarrais, Elizabeth, Luis Jaime Castillo, and Timothy Earle

1996 Ideology, Materialization, and Power Strategies. *Current Anthropology* 37:15–31.

Dietler, Michael, and Brian Hayden (editors)

2001 *Feasts: Archaeological and Ethnographic Perspectives on Food, Politics, and Power*. Smithsonian Institution Press, Washington, D.C.

Dobres, Marcia-Anne, and John Robb (editors)

2000 *Agency in Archaeology*. Routledge Press, New York.

Doolittle, William E.

1992 House-Lot Gardens in the Gran Chichimeca: Ethnographic Cause for Archaeological Concern. In *Gardens of Prehistory: The Archaeology of Settlement Agriculture in Greater Mesoamerica*, edited by Thomas W. Killion, pp. 69–91. University of Alabama Press, Tuscaloosa.

Earle, Timothy

1997 *How Chiefs Come to Power: The Political Economy in Prehistory*. Stanford University Press, Stanford.

Emerson, Thomas E.

1997 Cahokian Elite Ideology and the Mississippian Cosmos. In *Cahokia: Domination and Ideology in the Mississippian World,* edited by Timothy R. Pauketat and Thomas E. Emerson, pp. 190–228. University of Nebraska Press, Lincoln.

Flannery, Kent V.

1972 The Cultural Evolution of Civilizations. *Annual Review of Ecology and Systematics* 3:399–426.

Flannery, Kent V. (editor)

1976 *The Early Mesoamerican Village.* Academic Press, New York.

Freidel, David A.

1992 *Ahau* as Idea and Artifact in Classic Lowland Maya Civilization. In *Ideology and Pre-Columbian Civilizations,* edited by Arthur A. Demarest and Geoffrey W. Conrad, pp. 115–133. School of American Research Press, Santa Fe.

Geertz, Clifford

1965 Religion as a Cultural System. In *Anthropological Approaches to the Study of Religion,* edited by Michael Banton, pp. 1–46. Frederick A. Praeger, New York.

Gero, Joan M., and Margaret W. Conkey (editors)

1991 *Engendering Archaeology: Women and Prehistory.* Basil Blackwell, Cambridge.

Giddens, Anthony

1979 *Central Problems in Social Theory: Action, Structure and Contradictions in Social Analysis.* University of California Press, Berkeley.

1984 *The Constitution of Society: Outline of a Theory of Structuration.* Polity Press, Cambridge.

Gilchrist, Roberta

1999 *Gender and Archaeology: Contesting the Past.* Routledge Press, New York.

Gilman, Antonio

1989 Marxism in American Archaeology. In *Archaeological Thought in America,* edited by C. C. Lamberg-Karlovsky, pp. 63–73. Cambridge University Press, Cambridge.

Gossen, Gary H., and Richard M. Leventhal

1993 The Topography of Ancient Maya Religious Pluralism: A Dialogue with the Present. In *Lowland Maya Civilization in the Eighth Century A.D.,* edited by Jeremy A. Sabloff and John S. Henderson, pp. 185–217. Dumbarton Oaks, Washington, D.C.

Guha, Ranajit

1988 Preface. In *Selected Subaltern Studies,* edited by Ranajit Guha and Gayatri Chakravorty Spivak, pp. 35–36. Oxford University Press, Oxford.

1999 *Elementary Aspects of Peasant Insurgency in Colonial India.* Duke University Press, Durham.

Halbwachs, Maurice

1941 *La topographie légendaire des évangiles en terre sainte: Étude de mémoire collective.* Universitaires de France, Paris. Republished in *Maurice Halbwachs: On Collective Memory,* edited and translated by Lewis A. Coser, 1992. University of Chicago Press, Chicago.

1952 *Las cadres sociaux de le mémoire.* Presses Universitaires de France, Paris. Republished in *Maurice Halbwachs: On Collective Memory,* edited and translated by Lewis A. Coser, 1992. University of Chicago Press, Chicago.

Hanks, William F.

1990 *Referential Practice: Language and Lived Space Among the Maya.* University of Chicago Press, Chicago.

Hendon, Julia A.

2000 Having and Holding: Storage, Memory, Knowledge, and Social Relations. *American Anthropologist* 102:42–53.

Hendon, Julia A., and Rosemary A. Joyce (editors)

2004 *Mesoamerican Archaeology.* Blackwell Publishers, New York.

Hirth, Kenneth G.

1998 The Distributional Approach: A New Way to Identify Marketplace Exchange in the Archaeological Record. *Current Anthropology* 39:451–476.

Hutson, Scott R.

2002 Built Space and Bad Subjects. *Journal of Social Archaeology* 2:53–80.

Inomata, Takeshi

2001 The Power and Ideology of Artistic Creation: Elite Craft Specialists in Classic Maya Society. *Current Anthropology* 42:321–349.

Insoll, Timothy

2004 *Archaeology, Ritual, Religion.* Routledge Press, New York.

Joyce, Arthur A., Laura Arnaud Bustamante, and Marc N. Levine

2001 Commoner Power: A Case Study from the Classic-Period Collapse on the Oaxaca Coast. *Journal of Archaeological Theory and Method* 8:343–385.

Joyce, Arthur A., and Marcus Winter

1996 Ideology, Power, and Urban Society in Pre-Hispanic Oaxaca. *Current Anthropology* 37:33–47.

Joyce, Rosemary A.

2000a *Gender and Power in Prehispanic Mesoamerica.* University of Texas Press, Austin.

2000b Heirlooms and Houses: Materiality and Social Memory. In *Beyond Kinship: Social and Material Reproduction in House Societies,* edited by Rosemary A. Joyce and Susan D. Gillespie, pp. 189–212. University of Pennsylvania Press, Philadelphia.

Joyce, Rosemary A., and Julia A. Hendon

2000 Heterarchy, History, and Material Reality: "Communities" in Late Classic Honduras. In *The Archaeology of Communities: A New World Perspective,* edited by Marcello A. Canuto and Jason Yaeger, pp. 143–160. Routledge Press, New York.

Kunen, Julie L., Mary Jo Galindo, and Erin Chase

2002 Pits and Bones: Identifying Maya Ritual Behavior in the Archaeological Record. *Ancient Mesoamerica* 13:197–211.

Lansing, J. Stephen

1991 *Priests and Programmers: Technologies of Power in the Engineered Landscape of Bali.* Princeton University Press, Princeton.

Leach, Edmund

1966 Ritualization in Man in Relation to the Symbolic Representation of Time. In *Rethinking Anthropology,* pp. 124–136. The Athlone Press, London.

Lohse, Jon C.

2001 The Social Organization of a Late Classic Maya Community: Dos Hombres, Northwestern Belize. Ph.D. dissertation, University of Texas at Austin. University Microfilms, Ann Arbor.

Lohse, Jon C., and Patrick N. Findlay

2000 A Classic Maya House-Lot Drainage System in Northwestern Belize. *Latin American Antiquity* 11:175–185.

Lohse, Jon C., and Fred Valdez Jr. (editors)

2004 *Ancient Maya Commoners.* University of Texas Press, Austin.

Love, Michael

1999 Ideology, Material Culture, and Daily Practice in Pre-Classic Mesoamerica: A Pacific Coast Perspective. In *Social Patterns in Pre-Classic Mesoamerica,* edited by David C. Grove and Rosemary A. Joyce, pp. 127–153. Dumbarton Oaks, Washington, D.C.

Manzanilla, Linda

2004 Social Identity and Daily Life at Classic Teotihuacan. In *Mesoamerican Archaeology,* edited by Julia A. Hendon and Rosemary Joyce, pp. 124–147. Blackwell Publishing, Oxford.

Marcus, Joyce

1993 Ancient Maya Political Organization. In *Lowland Maya Civilization in the Eighth Century A.D.*, edited by Jeremy A. Sabloff and John S. Henderson, pp. 111–183. Dumbarton Oaks, Washington, D.C.

1999 Men's and Women's Ritual in Formative Oaxaca. In *Social Patterns in Pre-Classic Mesoamerica*, edited by David C. Grove and Rosemary A. Joyce, pp. 67–96. Dumbarton Oaks, Washington, D.C.

Marcus, Joyce, and Kent V. Flannery

2004 The Coevolution of Ritual and Society: New C^{14} Dates from Ancient Mexico. *Proceedings of the National Academy of Sciences* 101(52):18257–18261.

Marquina, Ignacio

1951 *Arquitectura Prehispanica*. Memorias del Instituto Nacional de Antropología e Historia, Mexico, D.F.

Mathews, Jennifer P., and James F. Garber

2004 Models of Sacred Order: Physical Expression of Sacred Space Among the Ancient Maya. *Ancient Mesoamerica* 15:49–59.

McAnany, Patricia A.

1995 *Living with the Ancestors: Kinship and Kingship in Ancient Maya Society*. University of Texas Press, Austin.

McGuire, Randall H.

2002 *A Marxist Archaeology*. Percheron Press, New York.

Miller, Daniel, and Christopher Tilley (editors)

1984 *Ideology, Power, and Prehistory*. Cambridge University Press, Cambridge.

Ortner, Sherry B.

1995 Resistance and the Problem of Ethnographic Refusal. *Comparative Studies in Society and History* 37:173–193.

Paynter, Robert, and Randall H. McGuire

1991 The Archaeology of Inequality: Material Culture, Domination, and Resistance. In *The Archaeology of Inequality*, edited by Randall H. McGuire and Robert Paynter, pp. 1–27. Basil Blackwell, Cambridge.

Pearson, Michael Parker

1982 Mortuary Practices, Society and Ideology: An Ethnoarchaeological Study. In *Symbolic and Structural Archaeology*, edited by Ian Hodder, pp. 99–113. Cambridge University Press, Cambridge.

1984 Social Change, Ideology and the Archaeological Record. In *Marxist Perspectives in Archaeology*, edited by Matthew J. Spriggs, pp. 59–71. Cambridge University Press, Cambridge.

Peregrin, Peter

1991 Some Political Aspects of Craft Specialization. *World Archaeology* 23: 1–11.

Plunket, Patricia

2002a Introduction. In *Domestic Ritual in Ancient Mesoamerica,* edited by Patricia Plunket, pp. 1–9. Monograph 46, Cotsen Institute of Archaeology. University of California, Los Angeles.

Plunket, Patricia (editor)

2002b *Domestic Ritual in Ancient Mesoamerica.* Monograph 46, Cotsen Institute of Archaeology. University of California, Los Angeles.

Plunket, Patricia, and Gabriela Uruñuela

2002 Shrines, Ancestors, and the Volcanic Landscape at Tetimpa, Puebla. In *Domestic Ritual in Ancient Mesoamerica,* edited by Patricia Plunket, pp. 31–42. Monograph 46, Cotsen Institute of Archaeology. University of California, Los Angeles.

Pohl, John M.D.

1999 *Exploring Mesoamerica: Places in Time.* Oxford University Press, New York.

Rappaport, Roy A.

1999 *Ritual and Religion in the Making of Humanity.* Cambridge University Press, Cambridge.

Robb, John E.

1998 The Archaeology of Symbols. *Annual Review of Current Anthropology* 27:329–346.

Robin, Cynthia

2002 Outside of Houses: The Practices of Everyday Life at Chan Nòohol, Belize. *Journal of Social Archaeology* 2:245–268.

Saitta, Dean J.

1997 Power, Labor, and the Dynamics of Change in Chacoan Political Economy. *American Antiquity* 62:7–26.

Scott, James C.

1976 *The Moral Economy of the Peasant.* Yale University Press, New Haven.

1985 *Weapons of the Weak: Everyday Forms of Peasant Resistance.* Yale University Press, New Haven.

1990 *Domination and the Arts of Resistance.* Yale University Press, New Haven.

Shackel, Paul A.

2001 Public Memory and the Search for Power in American Historical Archaeology. *American Anthropologist* 103:655–670.

Shanks, Michael, and Christopher Tilley

1992 *Re-Constructing Archaeology: Theory and Practice.* Second edition. Routledge Press, New York.

Sheets, Payson

2000 Provisioning the Ceren Household: The Vertical Economy, Village Economy, and Household Economy in the Southeastern Maya Periphery. *Ancient Mesoamerica* 11:217–230.

Smith, Michael E.

1999 On Hirth's Distributional Approach. *Current Anthropology* 40:528–530.

Sugiyama, Saburo

1993 Worldview Materialized in Teotihuacan, Mexico. *Latin American Antiquity* 4:103–129.

2004 Governance and Polity at Classic Teotihuacan. In *Mesoamerican Archaeology,* edited by Julia A. Hendon and Rosemary A. Joyce, pp. 97–123. Blackwell Publishing, Oxford.

Sweely, Tracy L. (editor)

1999 *Manifesting Power: Gender and the Interpretation of Power in Archaeology.* Routledge Press, New York.

Thomas, Brian W.

1998 Power and Community: The Archaeology of Slavery at the Hermitage Plantation. *American Antiquity* 63:531–551.

Thompson, E. P.

1963 *The Making of the English Working Class.* Victor Gollancz, London.

Trigger, Bruce G.

1991 Monumental Architecture: A Thermodynamic Explanation of Symbolic Behaviour. *World Archaeology* 22:119–132.

Urban, Patricia, and Edward Schortman

1996 Comment on Playing with Power: Ballcourts and Political Ritual in Southern Mesoamerica. *Current Anthropology* 37:501–502.

Urban, Patricia, Edward Schortman, and Marne Ausec

2002 Power Without Bounds? Middle Preclassic Political Developments in the Naco Valley, Honduras. *Latin American Antiquity* 13:131–152.

Van Dyke, Ruth M., and Susan E. Alcock

2003 Archaeologies of Memory: An Introduction. In *Archaeologies of Memory,* edited by Ruth M. Van Dyke and Susan E. Alcock, pp. 1–13. Blackwell Publishing, Oxford.

Vayda, Andrew P.

1968 Foreword. In *Pigs for the Ancestors: Ritual in the Ecology of a New Guinea People,* by Roy A. Rappaport, pp. ix–xiii. Yale University Press, New Haven.

Vogt, Evon Z.

1969 *Zinacantan: A Maya Community in the Highlands of Chiapas.* The Belknap Press of Harvard University Press, Cambridge.

1993 *Tortillas for the Gods: A Symbolic Analysis of Zinacanteco Rituals.* New edition. University of Oklahoma Press, Norman.

Wagner, Elizabeth

2000 Maya Creation Myths and Cosmography. In *Maya: Divine Kings of the Rainforest,* edited by Nikolai Grube, pp. 281–293. Könemann, Cologne.

Walling, Stanley, Peter Davis, Jonathan Hanna, Leah Matthews, Nahum Prasarn, and Christine Taylor

2006 Residential Terracing, Water Management, Matrix Analysis, and Suburban Ceremonialism at Chawak But'o'ob, Belize: Report of the 2005 Rio Bravo Archaeological Survey. In *Programme for Belize Archaeological Project: Report of Activities from the 2005 Field Season,* edited by Fred Valdez Jr., pp. 41–88. Occasional Papers, Number 6. Mesoamerican Archaeological Research Laboratory, University of Texas at Austin.

Wolf, Eric R.

1999 *Envisioning Power: Ideologies of Domination and Crises.* University of California Press, Berkeley.

CHAPTER TWO

TRADITION AND TRANSFORMATION

Village Ritual at Tetimpa as a Template for Early Teotihuacan

GABRIELA URUÑUELA AND PATRICIA PLUNKET

INTRODUCTION

Fifty years ago Robert Redfield divided the educated elite and the illiterate peasants into two categories when he wrote of the "great tradition of the reflective few, and [the] . . . little tradition of the largely unreflective many" (1956:41–42). Although he perhaps envisioned more of a continuum than an opposition, during the past few decades anthropological thought has favored a paradigm rooted in the interaction between these extremes, an intricate and complex interplay between local village religiosity and the more formal and grandiose manifestations of citified state religion (McAnany 2002; Smith 2002). In this chapter, we explore this relationship by contrasting data from the rural setting of Tetimpa in southwestern Puebla, Mexico, with that from the urban context of Teotihuacan, Mexico (Figures 0.1 and 2.1).

Although Tetimpa was not divided into classes of commoners and elites, its Late and Terminal Formative occupation coincided with the

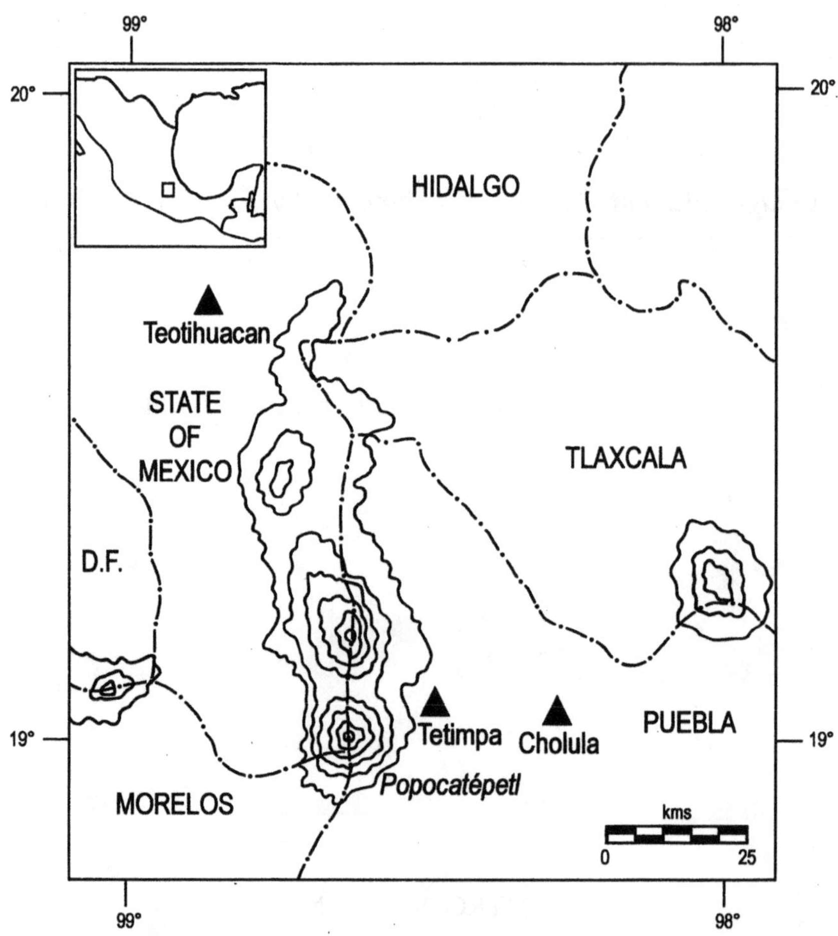

2.1. *Map showing sites mentioned in Chapter 2.*

emergence of stratified societies in centers like Cholula and Teotihuacan (Figure 0.2). Many of the original founders and subsequent immigrants who constituted these cities' populations probably came from settlements similar to Tetimpa, and thus we should expect to find significant patterns of rural life and belief embedded in the urban social and political structures. As Catherine Bell (1997:210) has observed, the continuity of ritual traditions under circumstances of shifting social realities provides the illusion of an enduring community and the legitimacy of age. Our study focuses on how and why certain elements of Formative village ritual served as the conceptual basis for generating both state and domestic canons at Classic period Teotihuacan.

At many Formative sites in the Central Highlands of Mesoamerica, later occupations significantly altered earlier archaeological deposits. At Tetimpa, however, a first century A.D. Plinian eruption of the Popocatépetl volcano covered the area with pumitic ash, which preserved the evidence of the contemporary setting and also protected earlier contexts from further human disturbance (Plunket and Uruñuela 1998a), thus providing a unique opportunity to study Late and Terminal Formative village life. Over the past ten years we have accumulated information on thirty-one different building compounds—which include household units, detached kitchens, and ritual structures—in addition to the surrounding agricultural fields, providing an ample database that allows us to solidly identify patterns of ritual behavior. The evidence from Tetimpa's houses provides fertile ground for exploring the roots of commoner ritual and ideology in later state societies since it affords a backdrop of beliefs, activities, and structures that must have played a significant part in the creation of the emergent ritual systems of class-structured urban societies.

The houses of Tetimpa consist of three wattle-and-daub rooms, each built on top of its own individual *talud-tablero* platform arranged around a patio (Figure 2.2). Detached kitchens use the same modular system (Flannery 2002) but are limited to one or two structures. The smaller, lateral buildings of the tripartite houses were probably used as kitchens and sleeping spaces, but the center room appears to have had a primarily ritual function: it is always the largest; its doorway is substantially wider, providing a view of the inside from the courtyard; and when ritual items, like censers and altars, are found outside the patio, they always occur here (Uruñuela and Plunket 1998:12). The majority of the burials, and in particular the most important interments, were placed under the floor of the central room, although occasionally they were deposited in the other platforms. Ritual was also conducted at the center of the patio, which is at least marked minimally by a large rounded cobble, although more often a formal shrine is present.

To illustrate their pattern and variation within the village, as well as their articulation with data from Teotihuacan, we have chosen three aspects of Tetimpa's domestic ritual and ideology: the *talud-tablero* platform, the mortuary pattern, and the patio shrines. At Tetimpa, these three elements coexisted as coherent parts of a single system; however, their incorporation into both private commoner and public state contexts at

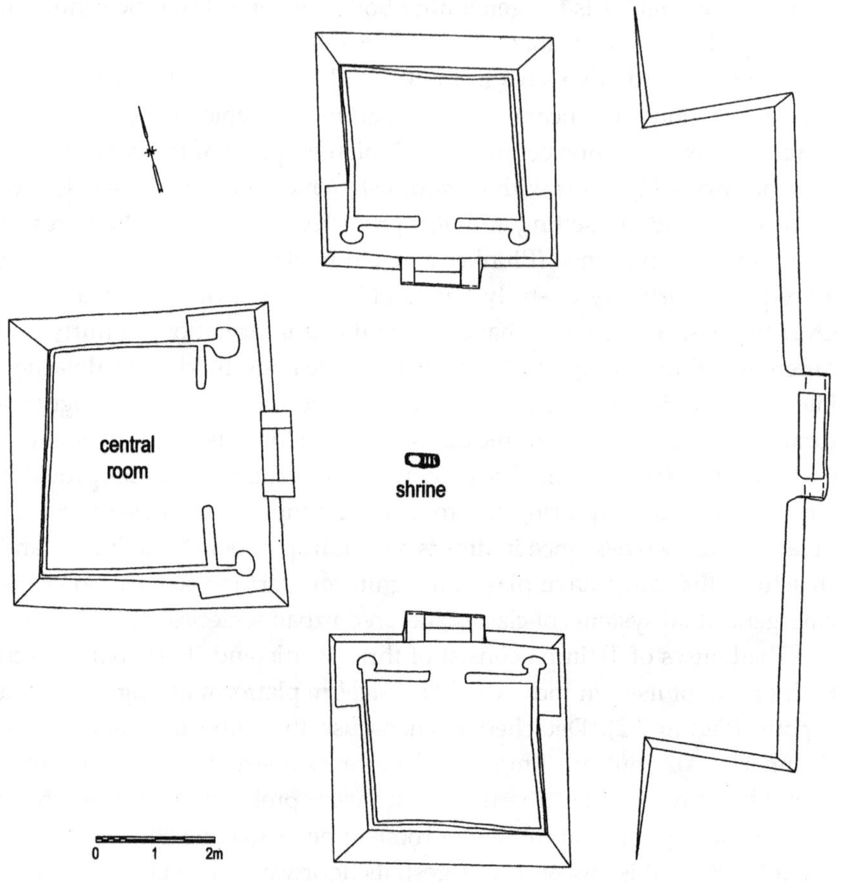

2.2. *Typical house layout at Tetimpa in Puebla, Mexico.*

Teotihuacan reveals a separate history of adaptation, elaboration, and possible resignification.

DOMESTIC RITUAL AND IDEOLOGY AT TETIMPA: DEEP STRUCTURES FOR TEOTIHUACAN

As in many lineage-based societies, the basic elements of Tetimpa's ritual system express the genealogical concerns associated with ancestor veneration (McAnany 1995). The tablero used to elaborate the façade of each stone-faced platform is of no practical utility. Indeed, these one- to two-meter-high platforms have no apparent functional value in the well-

2.3. Small Tetimpa talud-tablero platform with vestiges of wattle-and-daub walls (a rectangular sub-floor storage pit is visible to one side of the building).

drained piedmont of the Sierra Nevada except as repositories for the dead. Platforms grew in size as new floors were placed to seal graves excavated into existing surfaces so that structure height became a reliable measure of genealogical depth and continuity. Given that these platforms served as domestic burial grounds, the tablero embellishment should be viewed as part of a composite symbolic structure—in essence, an interface dividing the quarters of deceased family members located within the sloping basal walls from those of their living descendants who occupied the polished mud floors on the surface of the horizontal panel (Plunket and Uruñuela 2000).

Every platform at Tetimpa employed the *talud-tablero* system (Figure 2.3). Urban Teotihuacan adopted this ancient symbolic device, whose origins on the eastern side of the Sierra Nevada date back to ca. 300 B.C. (García Cook 1984), standardizing its proportions and enhancing the tablero with a thin stone frame. It was used on most of the city's buildings with two important exceptions: the pyramids of the Sun and the Moon (Figure 2.4). It may have been impossible to attach proportionally appropriate tableros to the huge taluds of these structures, but their absence on these monuments suggests that they were symbolically distinct from other buildings. At both

2.4. Talud-tablero platforms around the Moon Plaza at Teotihuacan, Mexico, with the Pyramid of the Sun rising in the background.

pyramid complexes the smaller anterior platforms (known as *adosadas*) do employ this device and it might be argued that this abbreviated use was meant to convey the same meaning for the larger monument behind. In the case of the Pyramid of the Moon, however, the tableros on the anterior platform were late additions (Cabrera and Sugiyama 1999:28), which may indicate a functional shift for the structure between the third and fourth construction stages. If the tablero was indeed an interface between the terrestrial surface and the underworld, then the earliest versions of these two pyramidal structures presumably embody a distinct symbolism not apparent in village domestic ritual systems.

During the first century A.D., Teotihuacan witnessed the arrival of approximately 50,000 people (Sanders 1981:table 6.2), most of whom came from the southern and eastern areas of the Basin of Mexico. Our dating of the massive Plinian eruption of the Popocatépetl volcano to this time period suggests that the eruption itself and its long-term environmental consequences along the Sierra Nevada were a major catalyst for these population movements (Plunket and Uruñuela 2002a). Perhaps not coincidentally, this same kind of demographic implosion is also apparent at Cholula, on the other side of the volcano in the western Puebla Valley.

Both Teotihuacan and Cholula were emerging urban centers that had to incorporate vast numbers of migrants over a relatively short period of time, and it seems likely that each manipulated existing ritual traditions as part of a set of political strategies devised to deal with the dramatically changing social and environmental contexts.

Most of the refugees must have come from villages like Tetimpa, small-scale societies where daily life and ritual activity were structured by the organizational principles of kinship and descent. If the *talud-tablero* architectural device both manifested and reinforced these principles, its use in Teotihuacan would have helped affirm and maintain individual family, lineage, clan, or "house" identities. The rapid population influx involving unrelated groups from many different settlements, however, may have precipitated the development of supra-kin mechanisms of integration, including a state ideology that could be relevant to a large, heterogeneous population. These new institutions required the creation of symbolically original public architectural programs that would be "kin neutral" and hierarchically superior to the exclusionary genealogical structures that divided the city's 90,000 inhabitants. The pyramids of the Sun and Moon must have formed part of this new supra-kin state ideology, a point to which we will return later.

The second element of Tetimpa's ancestor-focused ritual system is its selective domestic burial program. We have discussed this program in detail elsewhere (Uruñuela and Plunket 2002), so here we only present the most relevant aspects. From a demographic perspective, the number of skeletons within each house is insufficient to account for all family members' burial during the length of occupation (16 to 19 skeletons per compound for a time span of up to 300 years), but it would account for at least one burial per generation. The individuals placed within the platforms are adults, but on those rare occasions when infants or children are present (at most three per house), they are found in the courtyard. Eight out of every nine adults are males, placed in chronologically sequenced graves, each one resulting in the laying of a new floor. Most of these interments, especially the more elaborate ones, are located within the central platform. Four out of every five men are accompanied by ceramic vessels, whereas only one of every four women is, and non-adults lack these items entirely. Certain mortuary goods, particularly the censers for domestic ritual, occur exclusively with males.

We believe the best explanation for this patterned selectivity, which determined who was inhumed in the house and in which part of it, as well as the preponderance of adult male remains, may be that Tetimpa was organized into segmentary lineages with a strong patrilineal bias—that is, a hierarchical society where household heads had the prerogative of being interred within the domestic domain. The inclusion of a few women might reflect a certain flexibility that allowed females with special characteristics or even peculiar forms of death to be admitted to that privileged space. Similarly, the occasional non-adult burials might evince distinctive social identities that separated them from the many infants, children, and even adults who were deposited elsewhere or perhaps given alternate mortuary treatments. Their selection might manifest their position as potential family heads who died prematurely yet still retained the right to be buried within the house they otherwise would have owned someday; their placement in the patio, outside the platforms, might be related to the fact that they never fulfilled their roles as biological ancestors. In any event, the majority of the burials within the residential space are adult males, most of which, and certainly the more elaborate, are beneath the floors of the central room where their descendants apparently gathered for commemorative ceremonies.

The predominance of adult male interments, although not as striking as at Tetimpa, is also well documented at Teotihuacan (e.g., Cid and Torres 1999; González and Salas 1999; Manzanilla et al. 1999; Sempowski 1999; Spence and Gamboa 1999; Storey and Widmer 1999), as is the fact that the quantity of burials registered in the city is not sufficient to account for the number of people who lived there. For instance, recently published data (Manzanilla and Serrano 1999) indicate that a total of 1,647 skeletons have been reported from Teotihuacan, an exceptionally small sum when one considers that Martha Sempowski (1999:473) calculated that each apartment compound with a 400-year occupation should yield the remains of between 1,000 and 1,600 individuals. Thus, in general terms, we can identify another continuity between Tetimpa and Teotihuacan in their selective treatment of the dead.

But there are also some differences. At Tetimpa most burials are in the central platform, although a few occur under the lateral rooms. Even among those selected to be inhumed under the central room, there is variability since, although most were placed in simple pits, a few were interred in tombs (Uruñuela and Plunket 2001). These variations indicate that other factors beyond the familial role were recognized in the way these important individuals, perhaps household heads or senior lineage members, were treated at death, factors that might include differential wealth between generations or disparities in age, experience, personality, skill, knowledge, and personal achievements of the deceased (Joyce and Grove 1999:3; Uruñuela and Plunket 2002:28).

These depositional differences are more curtailed at Teotihuacan. With the exception of those in the foreign barrios (e.g., Cabrera 1999:511–512; Millon 1973:41–42; Paddock 1983; Spence 1989, 1992; Spence and Gamboa 1999), tombs are not characteristic of Teotihuacan domestic space, although a few have been reported (Linné 1934:45, figure 16; 54; 1942:110–111, figures 185 and 186, 125–126; Séjourné 1959:60). The vast majority of the dead were interred in simple pits or sometimes inside altars (Cabrera 1999:510; Martínez and González 1991; Rattray 1997; Sánchez 1989:373–375). We suspect that the development of supra-kin state ideology sought to minimize the differential individual celebration of distinguished household heads. Those distinctions that survived can be detected in the variable quantities of mortuary offerings (Sempowski 1987:127), but the extra effort to build special deposits at the domestic level was discontinued.

The third element to compare between Tetimpa and Teotihuacan is the shrines that mark the center of the patio as a pivotal location for ritual practice. At Tetimpa these are linked to the buried ancestors by the presence of concentrations of the same gravel-sized stones used to line the funerary deposits, suggesting that these pebbles are symbolically related to the dead (Figure 2.5). The shrines themselves are usually composed of one to three larger stones, most of which are carved as anthropomorphic heads, snakes, or felines. These may be representations of lineage founders or possibly natural forces associated with particular lineages (e.g., Marcus 1999; Plunket and Uruñuela 2002b).

Only five shrines were actual models of the volcano, but sub-floor chimneys occur underneath each stone even in the absence of the volcano imagery, suggesting that their smoke was equivalent to the frequent plumes of ash and vapor expelled by the mountain. This configuration leaves no doubt that Popocatépetl was a major factor in village ideology and expands the ritual reference beyond the immediate lineage to include the forces of nature. Like the chimneys, the crater of the volcano is a portal to the underworld: it is the navel, the place of origin, from which extend the four world quarters (Nicholson 1971:403) and the central fifth direction that defines the vertical connection between underworld, earth, and sky (Reilly 1995). These shrines tie Tetimpa's lineages to a greater cosmological order, twining the venerated past that represented the biological and social roots of each family with the contradictory forces of nature in

2.5. Anthropomorphic sculptures crowning a volcano effigy shrine with concentration of gravel-sized stones.

a challenging present, manifested in an active volcano that is potentially destructive at the same time that it amasses the clouds that provide life-giving rain.

This dual focus of Tetimpa's domestic cult is evident in other contexts (Uruñuela and Plunket 2003). In one of the thirty-one building groups we have explored (Operation 19), which was probably a senior lineage house, a small *talud-tablero* altar was constructed against the back wall of the central room (Figure 2.6). Fifteen individuals were buried under the floors of this room, most of them facing east toward this altar. In the same room, within the fill that covered the altar to raise the floor level after some kind of destructive event, two decapitated skulls were placed facing in the direction of the volcano, which rises against the western horizon (Figure 2.7). This arrangement is not fortuitous. Buried ancestors tended to face the altar that venerated their memory, whereas the decapitated individuals, perhaps sacrificial victims from local raiding ventures, were linked in some way to the greater meaning of the volcano. This contrasting orientation was also found in an anomalous burial placed in front of a communal ceremonial structure to the south of this senior lineage house. Once again, the context was associated with either the destruction or termination of

2.6. Interior talud-tablero altar of a central room (Unit 3, Operation 19), with an earlier burial in front (20 cm scale), Tetimpa, Puebla.

the building. A flexed male was placed facing east in a shallow pit excavated into the compacted surface, and on top of his head and shoulders were two decapitated heads, both facing west toward the volcano.

At Teotihuacan the central placement of patio shrines was maintained (Angulo 1987:280–283). Many families, however, were now grouped in apartment compounds that shared one large ritual patio (Barba et al., Chapter 3; Manzanilla 2002), whereas at Tetimpa each family had its own house, patio, and shrine. In each case, ritual activity took place in open yet private space. The ritual patios at Teotihuacan's apartment compounds are usually limited on three sides by rooms that differ from those that enclose other types of courtyards in these multifamily dwellings (Angulo 1987:279). At Tetimpa only the central room and the center of the patio, which are spaces that could have easily accommodated all family members, appear to have been used for cult activities. But at Teotihuacan the greater number of people concentrated in each apartment compound would have required more ample areas for communal activities, and it is likely that the main patio and all of its surrounding rooms provided the requisite space for the enactment of the compound's ritual.

2.7. Two decapitated skulls placed in the fill used to cover the altar shown in Figure 2.6, Tetimpa, Puebla.

But how was the greater cosmological order incorporated into the domestic venue at Teotihuacan? The patio altars in the city's compounds are not volcano effigies but rather miniature temples with *talud-tablero* façades (Figure 2.8). Although much more elaborate, they are reminiscent of the altar inside the central room at the senior lineage house at Tetimpa. Thus, it may be that this type of altar, previously used in interior spaces in the most important houses of large villages, was transferred to the center of the ritual patios of Teotihuacan's residential units, where they are sometimes associated with burials (Cabrera 1999:510; Sánchez 1989:373–375), in order to provide a common genealogical symbol for the inhabitants of each compound. At Tetimpa, only one patio shrine consists of a miniature *talud-tablero* platform.

Although the volcano imagery is not apparent in the apartment compounds, it may have been used as a template for the monumental architecture generated by the newly emergent state ideology. The idea that pyramids represented sacred mountains—cultural replicas of sacred geography—has been widely discussed in the literature (e.g., Broda 1987; Manzanilla 2000; Matos 1999; Reilly 1999; Schele and Mathews 1998). Sigvald Linné (1934:32–33) suggested that the Pyramid of the Moon is a

2.8. Courtyard altar at the Tetitla apartment compound at Teotihuacan, Mexico.

facsimile of the Cerro Gordo that emerges behind it, a reference to the cosmological relations between the pyramid-mountain and the celestial realms to the north (Sugiyama 1993:121). But what about the Pyramid of the Sun?

Teotihuacan's population consisted of a great number of groups that arrived during a short period of time from many towns and villages. Both René Millon (1981:217) and William Sanders and his colleagues (1979:107) have promoted models of political coercion by the fledgling Teotihuacan state to explain the depopulation of the Basin of Mexico during the Terminal Formative. This top-down view, however, denies the participation of more than 100 settlements, including 10 regional centers (Sanders et al. 1979:183), in decision-making processes involved in the relocation of perhaps 50,000 people. We believe that the massive eruption of Popocatépetl (with a Volcanic Explosivity Index of 6 [Siebe 2000:61]) during the first century A.D. and its devastating consequences over a vast area may provide a better explanation for these population movements. In this context, the public promotion of the veneration of a particular ancestral line would have been a divisive factor within the increasingly heterogeneous city. Instead, the emerging state required symbols that could be shared by all members of society, a common cause that may have been provided by the volcanic event.

In a city so architecturally symmetrical, the enormous mass of the Pyramid of the Sun stands alone on the east side of the Avenue of the Dead. Looking southeast from the Plaza of the Moon, the Pyramid of the Sun rises in the same direction as Popocatépetl. Echoing Doris Heyden (1975), Saburo Sugiyama (1993:120) suggests that the Pyramid of the Sun with its east-west-oriented cave might have been conceived as the entrance to the Underworld from which human beings first emerged. It would have been a fortunate decision to intertwine the image of the huge smoking mountain that changed the destiny of many of Teotihuacan's inhabitants with the concept of universal human origins, thereby avoiding any exclusionary genealogical references.

SUMMARY AND CONCLUSIONS

Domestic ritual in Mesoamerica so often has been ignored in favor of the grander ceremonialism of institutionalized religion (Lohse, Chapter 1). Redfield's influence is seen in the implicit belief that household or village ritual was merely a diminutive, impoverished, informal, crude, and subordinate copy of urban elite performances. But Tetimpa serves as a reminder that ideas are part of daily life and the complex give-and-take between different social orders and levels, and they cannot be divided easily into categories that belong to the "reflective few" or to the "unreflective many." Formative village ritual derived its patterns from genealogy and cosmology. Its variations expressed individual family history in addition to changing local conditions and outside relations. Emerging state religions built on the foundations of existing belief and practice in order to provide a credible continuity with past rites and a convincing coherence with contemporary community life (Bell 1997:203). State power was consolidated by relying on certain key ancestral beliefs for basic organizational structures while other deeply rooted concepts were modified, elaborated, and dramatized to create a higher level of community integration, sometimes transforming them beyond recognition.

We might imagine that as the dispersed residential patterns of segmentary lineages and other types of kin groupings at villages like Tetimpa were consolidated and compacted into the urban spaces of Teotihuacan, certain alterations and adjustments were inevitable. Although expressions of lin-

2.9. Papier-maché volcano effigy at the base of the Volador pole set up for the Altixcáyotl dance festival in Atlixco, Puebla, Mexico, in 1996 (photo courtesy of Eduardo Merlo).

eage and its attendant rituals were maintained to a large degree in the city's apartment compounds, this type of organization probably also permeated the new state ideology. Teotihuacan's negation of individual identity within its government resulted in the widespread acceptance of a model of corporate rule (e.g., Cowgill 1997; Pasztory 1997) although the precise nature of the political apparatus remains enigmatic. Collectivity seems to be manifested in the repetition of the Three Temple Complexes along the Street of the Dead, and indeed Annabeth Headrick (1999) has suggested that these architectural groups, identical in layout to the houses of Tetimpa (Plunket and Uruñuela 1998a), may have been used as lineage halls to house and venerate the bundled remains of ancestors prior to cremation. Therefore, the Three Temple Complexes of Teotihuacan are essentially an elaboration of the same basic concepts that generated the Tetimpa houses, and their appearance in the ceremonial center of the city suggests that they were built to accommodate an emergent, genealogically rooted political elite.

State ideologies came and went, as did the institutions that relied on them, but the basic premises that generated them are still found. Tetimpa's volcano effigies were not a concept foreign to indigenous peoples at the time of the Conquest. Once made of mud, these effigies were later made from amaranth dough (*tzoalli*) for the feasts of Tepeilhuitl and Atemoztli, which celebrated the high mountains and the rain deities associated with them (Sahagún 1969:199–201, 214–216). During the last decade of the twentieth century, as Popocatépetl entered into a new phase of eruptive activity, the volcano effigies reappeared once more, only now made of papier-maché, to be used in traditional dance festivals (Figure 2.9) held in the towns along the eastern flank of the volcano (Plunket and Uruñuela 1998b).

ACKNOWLEDGMENTS

We would like to thank the Mesoamerican Research Foundation, the Sistema de Investigación Ignacio Zaragoza, the Consejo Nacional de Ciencia y Tecnología, and the Instituto de Investigación y Posgrado of the Universidad de las Américas in Puebla for their generous support of our research at Tetimpa. The Consejo Nacional de Arqueología of the Instituto Nacional de Antropología e Historia granted the official permit for this project and has provided assistance and advice that are much appreciated. We are indebted to the editors, Nancy Gonlin and Jon Lohse, for kindly inviting us to contribute to this volume and for their careful revision of the manuscript.

REFERENCES CITED

Angulo, Jorge

1987 Nuevas consideraciones sobre los llamados conjuntos departamentales especialmente Tetitla. In *Teotihuacan: Nuevos datos, nuevas síntesis, nuevos problemas*, edited by Emily McClung and Evelyn C. Rattray, pp. 275–315. Instituto de Investigaciones Antropológicas, Universidad Nacional Autónoma de México, México City.

Bell, Catherine

1997 *Ritual: Perspectives and Dimensions*. Oxford University Press, New York.

Broda, Johanna

1987 Templo Mayor as Ritual Space. In *The Great Temple of Tenochtitlan: Center and Periphery in the Aztec World*, edited by Johanna Broda, Davíd Carrasco, and Eduardo Matos, pp. 61–123. University of California Press, Berkeley.

Cabrera, Rubén

1999 Las prácticas funerarias de los antiguos teotihuacanos. In *Prácticas funerarias en la Ciudad de los Dioses: Los enterramientos humanos de la antigua Teotihuacan*, edited by Linda Manzanilla and Carlos Serrano, pp. 503–539. Instituto de Investigaciones Antropológicas, Universidad Nacional Autónoma de México, México City.

Cabrera, Rubén, and Saburo Sugiyama

1999 El Proyecto Arqueológico de la Pirámide de la Luna. *Arqueología* 21: 19–33.

Cid, Rodolfo, and Liliana Torres

1999 Los entierros del occidente de la ciudad. In *Prácticas funerarias en la Ciudad de los Dioses: Los enterramientos humanos de la antigua Teotihuacan*, edited by Linda Manzanilla and Carlos Serrano, pp. 285–344. Instituto de Investigaciones Antropológicas, Universidad Nacional Autónoma de México, México City.

Cowgill, George L.

1997 State and Society at Teotihuacan, Mexico. *Annual Review of Anthropology* 26:129–161.

Flannery, Kent V.

2002 The Origins of the Village Revisited: From Nuclear to Extended Households. *American Antiquity* 67:417–433.

García Cook, Ángel

1984 Dos elementos arquitectónicos "tempranos" en Tlalancaleca, Puebla. *Cuadernos de Arquitectura Mesoamericana* 2:28–32.

González, Luís Alfonso, and María Elena Salas

1999 Los entierros del centro político-religioso y de la periferia de Teotihuacan de la Temporada 1980–1982. In *Prácticas funerarias en la Ciudad de los Dioses: Los enterramientos humanos de la antigua Teotihuacan*, edited by Linda Manzanilla and Carlos Serrano, pp. 219–246. Instituto de Investigaciones Antropológicas, Universidad Nacional Autónoma de México, México City.

Headrick, Annabeth

1999 The Street of the Dead . . . It Really Was: Mortuary Bundles at Teotihuacan. *Ancient Mesoamerica* 10:69–85.

Heyden, Doris

1975 An Interpretation of the Cave Underneath the Pyramid of the Sun in Teotihuacan, Mexico. *American Antiquity* 40:131–147.

Joyce, Rosemary A., and David C. Grove

1999 Asking New Questions About the Mesoamerican Pre-Classic. In *Social Patterns in Pre-Classic Mesoamerica*, edited by Rosemary A. Joyce and David C. Grove, pp. 1–14. Dumbarton Oaks, Washington, D.C.

Linné, Sigvald

1934 *Archaeological Researches at Teotihuacan, México*. The Ethnographical Museum of Sweden, Publication 1, Stockholm.

1942 *Mexican Highland Cultures: Archaeological Researches at Teotihuacan, Calpulalpan and Chalchicomula in 1934–35.* The Ethnographical Museum of Sweden, Publication 7, Stockholm.

Manzanilla, Linda

2000 The Construction of the Underworld in Central Mexico. In *Mesoamerica's Classic Heritage: From Teotihuacan to the Aztecs,* edited by Davíd Carrasco, Lindsay Jones, and Scott Sessions, pp. 87–116. University Press of Colorado, Boulder.

2002 Living with the Ancestors and Offering to the Gods: Domestic Ritual at Teotihuacan. In *Domestic Ritual in Ancient Mesoamerica,* edited by Patricia Plunket, pp. 43–52. Monograph 46, Cotsen Institute of Archaeology. University of California, Los Angeles.

Manzanilla, Linda, Mario Millones, and Magalí Civera

1999 Los entierros de Oztoyahualco 15B: N6W3. In *Prácticas funerarias en la Ciudad de los Dioses: Los enterramientos humanos de la antigua Teotihuacan,* edited by Linda Manzanilla and Carlos Serrano, pp. 247–283. Instituto de Investigaciones Antropológicas, Universidad Nacional Autónoma de México, México City.

Manzanilla, Linda, and Carlos Serrano (editors)

1999 *Prácticas funerarias en la Ciudad de los Dioses: Los enterramientos humanos de la antigua Teotihuacan.* Instituto de Investigaciones Antropológicas, Universidad Nacional Autónoma de México, México City.

Marcus, Joyce

1999 Men's and Women's Ritual in Formative Oaxaca. In *Social Patterns in Pre-Classic Mesoamerica,* edited by David C. Grove and Rosemary A. Joyce, pp. 67–96. Dumbarton Oaks, Washington, D.C.

Martínez, Enrique, and Alfonso González

1991 Una estructura funeraria teotihuacana. In *Teotihuacan 1980–1982: Nuevas interpretaciones,* edited by Rubén Cabrera, Ignacio Rodríguez, and Noel Morelos, pp. 327–333. Instituto Nacional de Antropología e Historia, México City.

Matos, Eduardo

1999 The Templo Mayor of Tenochtitlan: Cosmic Center of the Aztec Universe. In *Mesoamerican Architecture as a Cultural Symbol,* edited by Jeff Kowalski, pp. 198–219. Oxford University Press, New York.

McAnany, Patricia A.

1995 *Living with the Ancestors: Kinship and Kingship in Ancient Maya Society.* University of Texas Press, Austin.

2002 Rethinking the Great and Little Tradition Paradigm from the Perspective of Domestic Ritual. In *Domestic Ritual in Ancient Mesoamerica,* edited by Patricia Plunket, pp. 115–119. Monograph 46, Cotsen Institute of Archaeology. University of California, Los Angeles.

Millon, René

1973 *Urbanization at Teotihuacán, Mexico,* Volume 1. University of Texas Press, Austin.

1981 Teotihuacan: City, State, and Civilization. In *Handbook of Middle American Indians: Archaeology, Supplement I,* edited by Jeremy Sabloff, pp. 198–243. Victoria R. Bricker, general editor. University of Texas Press, Austin.

Nicholson, Henry B.

1971 Religion in Pre-Hispanic Central Mexico. In *Handbook of Middle American Indians,* Volume 10, *Archaeology of Northern Mesoamerica,* Part 1, edited by Gordon F. Ekholm and Ignacio Bernal, pp. 395–446. Robert Wauchope, general editor. University of Texas Press, Austin.

Paddock, John

1983 The Oaxaca Barrio at Teotihuacan. In *The Cloud People,* edited by Kent V. Flannery and Joyce Marcus, pp. 170–175. Academic Press, New York.

Pasztory, Esther

1997 *Teotihuacan, an Experiment in Living*. University of Oklahoma Press, Norman.

Plunket, Patricia, and Gabriela Uruñuela

1998a Preclassic Household Patterns Preserved Under Volcanic Ash at Tetimpa, Puebla, Mexico. *Latin American Antiquity* 9:287–309.

1998b Appeasing the Volcano Gods. *Archaeology* 51:36–42.

2000 Paisaje y cosmología: Las casas de Tetimpa, Puebla, México. Paper presented at the 50th Congreso Internacional de Americanistas, Warsaw.

2002a To Leave or Not to Leave: Human Responses to Popocatépetl's Eruptions in the Tetimpa Region of Puebla, Mexico. Paper presented at the 67th Annual Meeting of the Society for American Archaeology, Denver.

2002b Shrines, Ancestors and the Volcanic Landscape at Tetimpa, Puebla. In *Domestic Ritual in Ancient Mesoamerica,* edited by Patricia Plunket, pp. 31–42. Monograph 46, Cotsen Institute of Archaeology. University of California, Los Angeles.

Rattray, Evelyn C.

1997 *Entierros y ofrendas en Teotihuacan: Excavaciones, inventario, patrones mortuorios.* Instituto de Investigaciones Antropológicas, Universidad Nacional Autónoma de México, México City.

Redfield, Robert

1956 *Peasant Society and Culture.* University of Chicago Press, Chicago.

Reilly, F. Kent

1995 Art, Ritual, and Rulership in the Olmec World. In *The Olmec World: Ritual and Rulership,* edited by Jill Guthrie, pp. 27–45. The Art Museum, Princeton University, and Harry N. Abrams, New York.

1999 Mountains of Creation and Underworld Portals. In *Mesoamerican Architecture as a Cultural Symbol,* edited by Jeff Kowalski, pp. 14–39. Oxford University Press, New York.

Sahagún, Fray Bernardino de

1969 [1569] *Historia general de las cosas de Nueva España.* Editorial Porrúa, México City.

Sánchez, José

1989 Las unidades habitacionales en Teotihuacan: El caso de Bidasoa. Unpublished licenciatura thesis. Escuela Nacional de Antropología e Historia, México City.

Sanders, William

1981 Ecological Adaptation in the Basin of Mexico: 23,000 B.C. to the Present. In *Handbook of Middle American Indians: Archaeology, Supplement I,* edited by Jeremy Sabloff, pp. 147–197. Victoria R. Bricker, general editor. University of Texas Press, Austin.

Sanders, William, Jeffrey Parsons, and Robert Santley

1979 *The Basin of Mexico: Ecological Processes in the Evolution of a Civilization.* Academic Press, New York.

Schele, Linda, and Peter Mathews

1998 *The Code of Kings: The Language of Seven Sacred Maya Temples and Tombs.* Scribner, New York.

Séjourné, Laurette

1959 *Un palacio en la Ciudad de los Dioses: Exploraciones en Teotihuacan, 1955–1958.* Instituto Nacional de Antropología e Historia, México City.

Sempowski, Martha L.

1987 Differential Mortuary Treatment: Its Implications for Social Status at Three Residential Compounds in Teotihuacan, Mexico. In *Teotihuacan: Nuevos datos, nuevas síntesis, nuevos problemas,* edited by Emily McClung and Evelyn C. Rattray, pp. 115–131. Instituto de Investigaciones Antropológicas, Universidad Nacional Autónoma de México, México City.

1999 The Potential Role of Human Interment in Household Ritual at Tetitla. In *Prácticas funerarias en la Ciudad de los Dioses: Los enterramientos hu-*

manos de la antigua Teotihuacan, edited by Linda Manzanilla and Carlos Serrano, pp. 473–502. Instituto de Investigaciones Antropológicas, Universidad Nacional Autónoma de México, México City.

Siebe, Claus

2000 Age and Archaeological Implications of Xitle Volcano, Southwestern Basin of Mexico City. *Journal of Volcanology and Geothermal Research* 104:45–64.

Smith, Michael E.

2002 Domestic Ritual at Aztec Provincial Sites in Morelos. In *Domestic Ritual in Ancient Mesoamerica,* edited by Patricia Plunket, pp. 93–114. Monograph 46, Cotsen Institute of Archaeology. University of California, Los Angeles.

Spence, Michael

1989 Excavaciones recientes en Tlailotlacan, el barrio oaxaqueño de Teotihuacan. *Arqueología* 5:81–104.

1992 Tlailotlacan: A Zapotec Enclave in Teotihuacan. In *Art, Ideology and the City of Teotihuacan,* edited by Janet C. Berlo, pp. 59–88. Dumbarton Oaks, Washington, D.C.

Spence, Michael W., and Luis Manuel Gamboa

1999 Mortuary Practices and Social Adaptation in the Tlailotlacan Enclave. In *Prácticas funerarias en la Ciudad de los Dioses: Los enterramientos humanos de la antigua Teotihuacan,* edited by Linda Manzanilla and Carlos Serrano, pp. 173–201. Instituto de Investigaciones Antropológicas, Universidad Nacional Autónoma de México, México City.

Storey, Rebecca, and Randolph J. Widmer

1999 The Burials of Tlajinga 33. In *Prácticas funerarias en la Ciudad de los Dioses: Los enterramientos humanos de la antigua Teotihuacan,* edited by Linda Manzanilla and Carlos Serrano, pp. 203–218. Instituto de Investigaciones Antropológicas, Universidad Nacional Autónoma de México, México City.

Sugiyama, Saburo

1993 Worldview Materialized in Teotihuacan, Mexico. *Latin American Antiquity* 4:103–129.

Uruñuela, Gabriela, and Patricia Plunket

1998 Áreas de actividad en unidades domésticas de Tetimpa, Puebla. *Arqueología* 20:3–19.

2001 ¿"De piedra ha de ser la cama . . ."? Las tumbas en el Formativo de Puebla-Tlaxcala y la Cuenca de México, a partir de la evidencia de Tetimpa, Puebla. *Arqueología* 25:3–22.

2002 Lineages and Ancestors: The Formative Mortuary Assemblages of Tetimpa, Puebla. In *Domestic Ritual in Ancient Mesoamerica,* edited by Patricia Plunket, pp. 21–30. Monograph 46, Cotsen Institute of Archaeology. University of California, Los Angeles.

2003 Testimonios de diversos tipos de abandono en Tetimpa, Puebla. *Trace* 43:84–96.

CHAPTER THREE

COMMONER RITUAL AT TEOTIHUACAN, CENTRAL MEXICO

Methodological Considerations

Luis Barba, Agustín Ortiz, and Linda Manzanilla

INTRODUCTION

Prehispanic societies were integrated by different means. No one can doubt that ritual was one of the main integrative mechanisms, because it "links generations, unites men from different descent groups, unites women from different families, [and] connects the living to their ancestors" (Marcus 1998:1). As Marcus puts it, ritual is important in creating public spaces and structures but is also visible in the domestic domain. In village societies, women played an important role in domestic ritual (Marcus 1998), but in urban societies other participants were added to domestic ritual not only to communicate with the ancestors but also to offer special ceremonies and goods to the gods in ways that were sometimes dictated by the state (Manzanilla 2002).

One of the most outstanding urban developments of Classic Mesoamerica was Teotihuacan, a huge, planned, multiethnic metropolis in

Central Mexico (Figures 0.1 and 0.2) (Millon 1973). The importance of religion in this city can be assessed in different scales: the state religion is evident in the huge plazas (squares) and temples in the city's center, in the processions of priests and other officers portrayed in the mural paintings, and in the representations of the deities (in sculpture, battlements, vases, mural paintings, etc.). There seem to have been barrio temples that integrated people of particular sectors of the city. And the last scale is the domestic realm, where altars and temples were set in ritual courtyards and where ceremonies for the ancestors and deities, as well as termination rituals, may be traced (Manzanilla 2002).

Joyce Marcus (1998:11) distinguishes three components in ritual: the *content* (the subject matter), the *locus* of performance (specific places where ancient rites were performed), and the *performers*. (See also chapter 4). To assess the locus of performance and the objects involved in domestic ritual as well as other activity areas in Classic period apartment compounds at Teotihuacan, Mexico, we designed an interdisciplinary strategy that took into consideration chemical traces of activities preserved in plastered floors, as well as paleobiological macroremains, microscopic evidence (e.g., chemical compounds, pollen, phytoliths), architectural and funerary data, and distributions of artifacts and debris on floors of the Oztoyahualco (15B:N6W3) compound (Figure 3.1) (Barba et al. 1987; Manzanilla 1988–1989, 1993, 1996; Manzanilla and Barba 1990). Here, we consider ritual ceremonies as individual or group acts of a symbolic nature, which are repeated according to a set of rules. The same ritual ceremony may include prayers, sermons, taboos, games, immolations, sacrifices, magic, or mythical representations (Cazeneuve 1972). Such repeated activities leave their mark on the archaeological record.

Experience (Barba et al. 1997) has demonstrated that floors made with lime plaster preserve chemical residues, providing evidence that can reveal ancient human activities. The contaminating liquids (blood, sweat, food, etc.) that were repeatedly spilled on the floors during rituals allow us to chemically identify the areas where the activity took place and characterize the perishable materials used.

It is important to mention that most of our chemical analyses in archaeological sites have been oriented toward the study of domestic activities. The interpretations in these cases have been based on ethnographic analogies and ethnoarchaeological experiments in which food production, storage, and consumption activity areas, as well as rest and high traffic areas, have been determined (Barba 1986; Barba and Ortiz 1992; Barba et

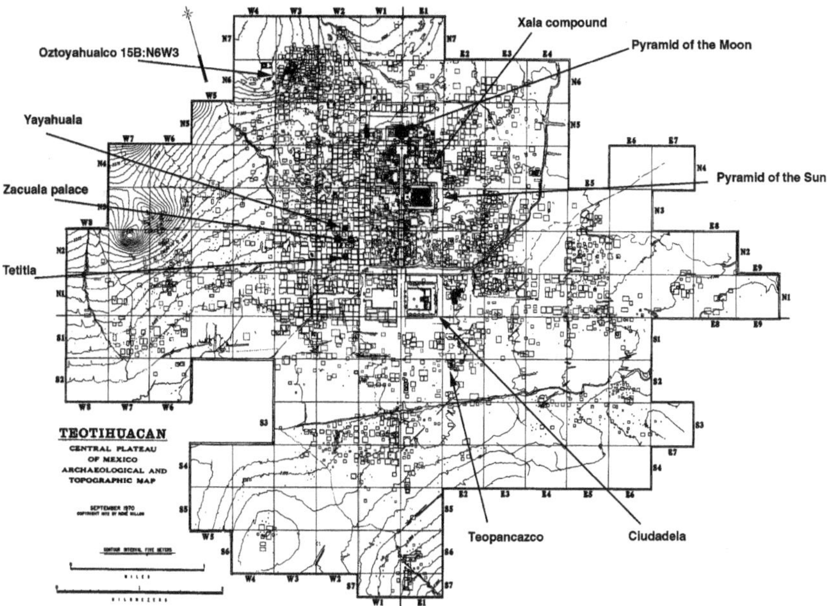

3.1. Location of the Oztoyahualco compound in the Classic city of Teotihuacan, Mexico.

al. 1995). A few examples of the use of this method for the study of ancient ritual follow.

Research on ritual activities in archaeological sites was carried out on floors of the Satunsat building, at Oxkintok in Yucatán, Mexico, to study a non-domestic archaeological structure (Ortiz and Barba 1992). Its architecture and associated archaeological material revealed that this building was devoted to initiation rituals, star observation, and time measurement (Rivera and Ferrándiz 1989:72–75).

Its floors were systematically sampled and chemical results revealed very low phosphate values, totally different from the concentrations usually found in the household, confirming it was a non-domestic building (Ortiz and Barba 1992:124). Absence of phosphate precisely under Burial 1 at Room 6—in contrast with previous experiences with chemical residues in shaft tombs, where we found chemical residues produced by body decay (Barba, Linares et al. 1991; Ortiz 1996)—confirmed the hypothesis that it was a secondary burial, with bones exhumed from another place and carefully positioned on top of the floor, generating an event different from the original use of the structure (Ortiz and Barba 1992:124).

In 1987, a small ritual structure was excavated in downtown Mexico City. This structure was an Aztec altar used around A.D. 1440, during the first developmental stages of Tenochtitlan, the Aztec capital. Based on the results of the chemical analyses, it was concluded that this structure played a role in the installation ceremony rituals of the Moyotlan neighborhood, close to the Great Temple of Tenochtitlan, and was used for community rituals later in time.

The altar, or *momoztli,* at the corner of Palma and Venustiano Carranza streets in downtown Mexico City must be considered a sanctuary in the core of a cluster of domestic units where people once carried out daily ceremonies. Based on descriptions of ritual festivities and analytical chemical results, Fernando Getino and Agustín Ortiz (1997:128) suggested that evidence for a termination ritual marking the end of the structure's use was recovered; specifically two human burials, sacrificed birds, and pottery were interred just after the large flood during Ahuízotl's reign. They were contaminated by organic materials, primarily copal resins and blood spilled after the bird sacrifice. In addition, it was possible to recognize the difference between the sumptuous ceremonies performed at the Main Temple of Tenochtitlan and the modest rituals carried out by people in their own neighborhoods, both of which were part of an institutionalized religion (Getino and Ortiz 1997:134).

One of the most successful studies of ritual activities was performed at the Hall of the Eagles at the Great Temple of Mexico-Tenochtitlan. The chemical analysis of almost 500 samples of the splendidly preserved hall floor offered evidence to reconstruct some of the ritual activities. The distribution map of chemical residues showed that the floor areas close to the altars had high concentrations of residues, especially fatty acids. Unexpectedly, significant amounts of carbohydrates and protein residues were concentrated on the floors just in front of the doorways. There are clear differences between residues found at the altars and those found in front of the access, suggesting different materials were involved in rituals. Some of the fatty acid concentrations in front of the main altar were identified as copal residues by gas chromatography (Barba et al. 1996). This research put together archaeological, iconographic, and ethnohistorical data, permitting us to define the functions of this Mexica building, its religious significance, and some of the materials involved in the rituals performed on its surfaces, such as blood, pulque, and copal (Barba et al. 1997).

RITUAL SPACES IN APARTMENT COMPOUNDS

In Classic Teotihuacan, ritual areas in apartment compounds may be represented by ritual courtyards, shrines, rooms, and temples adjoining them. Each nuclear family may have had a ritual courtyard, but the family group as a whole may have gathered in the most important courtyard of the compound to share particular cult activities (Manzanilla 1993). Central shrines are often found in the main ritual courtyards, and portable temple models may be used as a substitute in secondary and tertiary ritual courtyards (see Manzanilla 1993:88, 175, 152, 163; Manzanilla and Ortiz 1991).

As a part of a comparative architectural study at the Tetitla, Zacuala, and Yayahuala apartment compounds, Laurette Séjourné classifies courtyard types according to shape of portico (square or rectangular) and number of sides (two, three, or four) (1966:31). One of the types she mentions is the temple courtyard surrounded by temple platforms. As an example she points out the central courtyard of Zacuala, which was entered through four porticoes. Similarly, in Tetitla the courtyard was reached using four small stairs, and in Yayahuala it was surrounded by platforms on three sides and was open to the east with some wide steps. Her classification system includes a courtyard type with an angled portico. She also notes exceptions, such as Zacuala's porticoes without an inner room or Yayahuala's lack of porticoes. In addition, she identifies the gallery courtyard with atrium at Zacuala and Tetitla, where the open space has a central pillar with columns that supported the roof (Séjourné 1966:33).

Jorge Angulo's criteria for courtyard and open space classification are based primarily on their size and position in the apartment compound and function as meeting places, distribution and transit areas, and illumination and open areas adjoining porticoes and rooms. Following Angulo's classification, the largest courtyards might be regarded as central plazas, the medium-size courtyards can be classified as distribution courtyards, whereas the smallest should be considered as water mirrors or impluvia. The last category includes isolated open areas, considered to be backyards (Angulo 1987:280).

Séjourné mentioned that Zacuala contained thirteen courtyards with 843 m^2 of open spaces, with 1,200 m^2 of interior rooms and 1773 m^2 of intermediate spaces with columns supporting roofs. The main courtyard at Zacuala measured 19 by 18 m. Tetitla boasted thirty courtyards, five of which were true open spaces for lighting.

Finally, Yayahuala had one entrance courtyard plus twenty-two more, sixteen of which were grouped in just half of the total surface. This arrangement led Séjourné to suggest that the complex grew up without prior planning. The main courtyard measured 16 by 19 m and was surrounded by three temples, the largest being the one to the west. After analyzing the location, size, and architecture of the courtyards, she concludes that Tetitla was associated with mid-status individuals, whereas Zacuala and Yayahuala are identified with high- and utilitarian-status individuals, respectively (Séjourné 1966:31).

NON-ROOFED AREA COMPARISON

Among the excavated apartment compounds at Teotihuacan, at least four compounds might be considered barrio centers. All of them have features—their large courtyard sizes, altars, and temples—that distinguish them from the rest of the domestic units. Instead of the previously mentioned criteria, we found that the non-roofed area percentage may be a better indicator of the ritual significance. We calculated the ratio between courtyard area and total area and came up with the following order: La Ventilla (92–94 Front A) 33 percent, Zacuala 18.5 percent, Xolalpan 17 percent, Teopancazco 17.2 percent, Oztoyahualco (15B:N6W3) 11.7 percent, Tetitla 10 percent, Yayahuala 8.4 percent, and Tlamimilolpa 2 percent.

The four apartment compounds with the lowest non-roofed area percentages display more domestic traits. Oztoyahualco has only four courtyards, two of which are 27 m^2, and the smallest is only 6 m^2. The average size is almost 20 m^2, and the non-roofed area is barely 79 m^2. Tetitla's largest courtyard is 125 m^2, the smallest is only 17 m^2, and the average of its seven courtyards is 55 m^2. In this group of domestic compounds, Yayahuala has only six courtyards, the largest of which is 168 m^2, the smallest of which is 10 m^2, and the average size is 45 m^2. The total non-roofed area is 269 m^2. Finally, the Tlamimilolpa apartment compound includes fourteen courtyards, but the largest is only 7 m^2 and the smallest is roughly 2 m^2, with an average size of 4 m^2. This apartment compound is very large, but it seems to have more light cubes than courtyards, since the total open area is only 59 m^2.

When we focus on the surface of the main courtyards, it is clear that the main courtyard (C41) at Oztoyahualco (15B:N6W3) is average size and has almost the same dimensions as another courtyard in the compound (C25). Nevertheless, it has been identified as the most prominent courtyard because it has mural paintings, an altar, and a centralized chemical enrichment pattern.

ALTARS

The courtyards with buildings resting on the platforms always have a central small-scale temple (Séjourné 1966:159). In addition to the altar in the main courtyard, Yayahuala has another one with stairs and set in a small courtyard to the west, where two burials with rich offerings were found (see McCafferty, Chapter 8, for a discussion of altars at Cholula).

Two altars were found at La Ventilla (92–94 Front A), one made of stone, with circles sculpted on the *tablero* frame with a red panel resembling that of Yayahuala. The second altar has a big hole in the upper part, suggesting that an element of the altar is missing (Séjourné 1966:168).

Tetitla exhibits three altars: one in the main courtyard, another made of stone to the north of the compound, and finally a brazier-altar in the western courtyard that is a 1 x 1 m stone box sunk 60 cm into the floor (Séjourné 1966:167). The altar at the main courtyard covered another in a better conservation state. Its excavation provided information about the small wall that surrounds the upper part of this ceremonial table, which mimics something like a box and resembles the previously mentioned stone box at Tetitla and another at Atetelco (Séjourné 1966:168).

Surprisingly, the main courtyard at Zacuala does not have a floor or altar and none of the twelve courtyards has an altar or stairs. In another building to the south, however, an almost complete altar was uncovered (Séjourné 1966:167).

At Oztoyahualco 15B:N6W3, we found one fixed altar in C41a, but in this compound the use of small-scale model altars in the courtyards was the norm. Most of them were recovered during excavation (see discussion below).

THE OZTOYAHUALCO COMPOUND

Each one of the families living at Oztoyahualco seems to have chosen a particular god as its patron (Figure 3.2). These deities range from the state god Tlaloc, to middle-range gods (such as the Fire God [Huehueteotl] or the Butterfly God), to patron gods (such as the rabbit) (Manzanilla 1993:164, 524). These gods are represented in a variety of ways, including small sculptures, pottery vessels, incised or modeled decorations on pottery, and figurines. Spatial patterning seems to have been established for the disposition of functional sectors, which extended beyond the framework of nuclear families (Ortiz 1990). Thus, in general, storage zones were found to the west, with those for refuse to the south, and funerary areas

3.2. Patron family gods related to the domestic hierarchy at Teotihuacan: Tlaloc in the upper registers, Huehueteotl and the Butterfly God in the middle, and a rabbit in the lower register.

were concentrated in the middle of the eastern sector (although exceptions exist), with neonate burials located primarily on a north-south band in the eastern third of the compound.

Individual household sectors within the compound could be isolated by taking into consideration the circulation alleys or access points (Sanders 1994:19 et seq.) and mapping the different food preparation and consumption loci for each nuclear household. The Oztoyahualco 15B:N6W3 compound had three loci that we suggest were related to three households (Manzanilla 1996; Ortiz 1990; Ortiz and Barba 1993). Each apartment included a zone for food preparation and consumption, sleeping quarters, storage areas, sectors for refuse, courtyards for cult activities, and funerary areas (Figure 3.3). Additionally, there were zones in which the entire family group or compound group (i.e., all the households in an apartment compound; see Sempowski 1994:9–10) gathered to share activities, particularly those related to ritual and perhaps those related to raising domestic animals.

We suspect that members of different household units participated in specialized activities related to the larger urban setting. In the compound we studied, the whole compound group probably specialized in the stucco plastering of neighboring three temple plazas and perhaps other structures at Oztoyahualco. Some stucco mixtures with polishers had been left in rooms where burial pits were going to be covered again and may be evidence of rapid abandonment. Other evidence shows concentrations of obsidian blades that are associated with stone hammers, large pottery

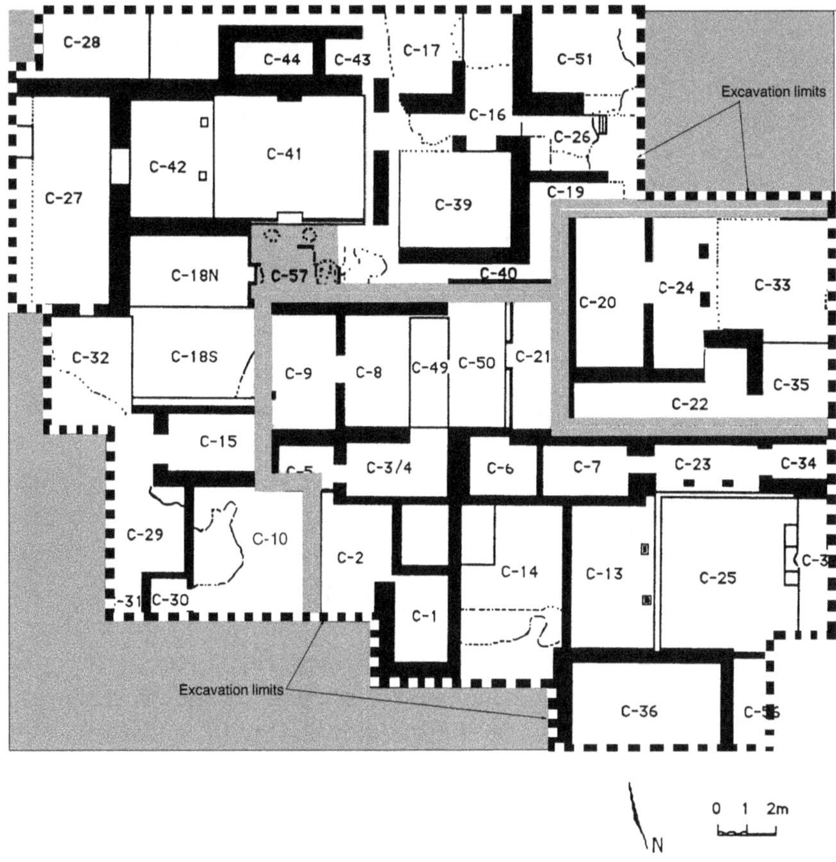

3.3. Three household sectors within the Oztoyahualco compound, Teotihuacan, Mexico.

plates, metates, and mortars on top of floors. Three north-south-aligned magnetic dipoles, carbonate, and high pH spots were found some meters to the west of the compound (Barba and Ortiz 1993; Lizárraga and Ortiz 1993; Manzanilla 1993; Ortiz 1990). Other compound groups in the city seem to have been similarly devoted to specific industries, such as ceramic crafting of certain wares, textile manufacture, obsidian or lapidary working, or even painting.

ARCHAEOLOGICAL INDICATORS OF DOMESTIC RITUAL

Domestic cult at Teotihuacan may be divided into three main categories: domestic ritual in courtyards, funerary cults, and abandonment rites

(Manzanilla 2002). We should envision domestic cult as the main low-level integrative device that the state used to integrate progressively larger social units, such as household groups, barrios, districts, and the city itself.

In Teotihuacan, domestic ritual is related particularly to ritual courtyards for each household in each apartment compound (Manzanilla 1993; Sanders 1966), which may comprise a central altar, a small temple or sanctuary, and connecting rooms. Zacuala, Yayahuala, and Tepantitla had their temples set to the east of the main courtyard. At Zacuala, the temple was substantial, with a portico, two inner rooms, and a roof decorated with merlons (Séjourné 1966:118–126). At Yayahuala, the temple was large enough to be interpreted as a likely neighborhood temple (Séjourné 1966:213). Elements related to domestic ritual—such as Tlaloc vases (related to burials or to abandonment rites), Huehueteotl sculptures, theater-type censers, *talud-tablero* temple models, *candeleros,* puppet figurines, and other artifacts—disappear from the archaeological record after the fall of the city (Cowgill 1997). They normally appear in ritual courtyards or the connecting rooms. Household 3 at Oztoyahualco 15B:N6W3 was the richest in burials and was related to Tlaloc symbolism. Artifacts such as Tlaloc vases, figurines, and representations in handled covers were found throughout this part of the compound. *Candeleros* and figurines are also found at other Classic period Mesoamerican sites south of Teotihuacan in the Maya region, such as Copán (Gonlin, Chapter 4) and the Naco Valley, Honduras (Douglass, Chapter 5).

At the ritual courtyard C25, a set of objects common to other ritual courtyards was recovered, including a sectional temple model (Manzanilla and Ortiz 1991), theater-type censer plaques (Manzanilla 2000a), three portrait figurines, two puppet figurines, *candeleros,* stone balls and hemispheres, a stucco polisher, as well as portable stoves and indications of fire burning (Figure 3.4) (Manzanilla 1993:140–152). This courtyard had a sanctuary to the east (C37), which had fragments of puppet figurines as well.

The second ritual courtyard (C33) had a complete portable basalt temple model with a rabbit sculpture, two puppet figurines, two *candeleros,* and two stucco polishers. In the southwest corner near the temple model, fire burning was indicated by the presence of blackened stucco and three-pronged portable stoves (Manzanilla 1993:163–164). Near this courtyard, Portico 24 and Room 20 had high pH values, indicating some ritual use of this space as well (Ortiz and Barba 1993:637). Fire burning related to blackened floors and theater-type censers was also noted by Séjourné (1966:165)

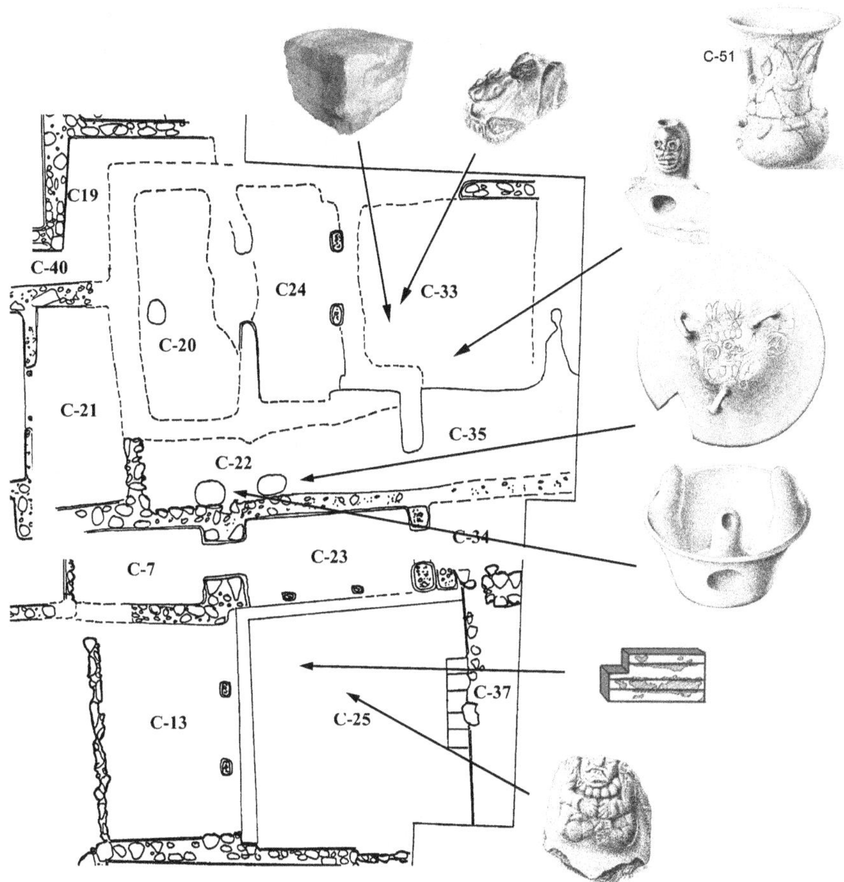

3.4. Ritual elements found in and around ritual courtyards C33 and C25 of the Oztoyahualco compound, Teotihuacan, Mexico.

in ritual courtyards at Zacuala, Yayahuala, and Tetitla. William Sanders (1966:138) has suggested that rooms bordering ritual courtyards with altars at Maquixco, Mexico, may have served to store religious paraphernalia. We propose that some of the preparations for ritual activities actually took place in similar rooms (C20 and C24) at Oztoyahualco 15B:N6W3. It is usual that altars in ritual courtyards may house important burials containing jadeite, slate, marine shells, miniature vases, *floreros,* and other objects (Sánchez Alaniz 2000).

Some activity areas related to ritual preparation were detected around Oztoyahualco's main ritual courtyard (C41). A small temple model was found in C44, and in the corner of C9 (just to the south of the sanctuary) a concentration of fifty-eight obsidian fragments, a basalt hammer, and a limestone half sphere (with radial cutting marks probably made by the continuous cutting of rabbit and hare legs) were found (Hernández 1993; Manzanilla 1993). There were also numerous funerary (for newborn babies) and offering pits, often with flowers or grasses, particularly in the eastern half of the compound. The northeastern household (n. 3) had most of the burials and also the greatest amount of foreign fauna (a jaguar's fang, a bear's paw, and other remains) (Manzanilla 1996:242).

Huehueteotl sculptures are often found in ritual courtyards (Linné 1934:48) or the eastern rooms of apartment compounds (Manzanilla 1993). At Oztoyahualco 15B:N6W3, we found fragments of the brazier in the eastern sector. At Teopancazco, a complete sculpture of the Fire God was found in a western inner room (C17) and had been thrown from its pedestal and was lying facedown on the floor (Manzanilla 2002).

Theater-type censers (Manzanilla 2000a) were used profusely at the Xolalpan apartment compound, where they were found in the altar and in a western courtyard (Linné 1934:48), and at the Tlamimilolpa compound, where they were gathered around Burial 4 and kept dismantled in caches, ready for ritual use (Linné 1942:141). In the Oztoyahualco compound, a remarkable dismantled theater-type censer was found in Burial 8 (Manzanilla and Carreón 1991). Decorated tripods, which are common at Xolalpan and Tlamimilolpa, are very rare, but still present, at Oztoyahualco 15B:N6W3. Such tripods were recently found in the remains of a termination ritual (Late Tlamimilolpa/Early Xolalpan) at Teopancazco (Manzanilla 2000b, 2003).

Lineage gods were patrons of particular families, and above them probably stood neighborhood and occupational deities, the gods of specific priestly groups, and state deities, such as Tlaloc, as patron of the city (López Austin 1989; Manzanilla 1993). Tlaloc vases are often found in domestic cult and are associated with burials (i.e., Oztoyahualco 15B:N6W3, Xolalpan, Tetitla, Zacuala Patios, La Ventilla [Linné 1934:70; Manzanilla 1993; Sempowski 1987:126]) or abandonment rites (i.e., Teopancazco [Manzanilla 2002]).

In sum, ritual courtyards in apartment compounds seem to have been gathering places for one or all of the households in the compound, particularly those groups centered on patron gods. Ritual was one of the main integrating activities inside the compounds, promoting group cohesion and solidarity.

METHODOLOGY AND ASSUMPTIONS

Several types of floors can be observed in Mesoamerica. Of this assortment, the stuccoed floors are the most suitable for the study of activity areas because of the way they were constructed. For this research, it is essential to assume that the floor had a homogeneous composition from the moment of its construction. Thus, human activities modify such homogeneity by leaving specific chemical residues (Lazos 1997).

In the Oztoyahualco (15B:N6W3) apartment compound, samples were taken from plastered floors using an electric drill with a concrete point to produce dust from a hole 2 cm in diameter and 2 cm in depth. The samples were bagged and labeled, registering the sampling point on a map of the unit. Chemical analyses were carried out at the UNAM's Archaeological Prospecting Laboratory to determine carbonate, phosphate, fatty acid, and protein residue content in addition to pH values, following the procedures established in the *Manual de técnicas microquímicas de campo para la arqueología* (Barba, Rodríguez et al. 1991).

The use of chemical indicators for the study of activity areas is based on the following assumptions (Barba and Lazos 2000):

(1) When an activity takes place, some liquid residues may be spilled on the surface and, sometimes, depending on the characteristics (porosity) of this surface, the residues could be absorbed. For that reason, a differential enrichment of the floor could be observed depending on the distribution and diversity of the activities that took place in a particular room.

(2) Once the compounds that are by-products of human activities have been incorporated into the ground, they are subject to chemical laws controlled by factors such as pH, EH, ion concentration in solutions, the speed and direction of water movement in the profiles, and the time of abandonment. All these factors determine the possibility of chemical indicators to survive over long periods of time, and this result is more apparent in lime plaster floors than in earth floors and soils.

(3) By chemical analyses of floor samples, it is possible to identify and evaluate the presence and the spatial distribution of several indicators. Some residues were produced by specific activities. Thus, by their characterization, it could be possible to identify the function of the place.

(4) The comparative study of materials in ancient domestic units, as well as previous studies of modern households, offers the possibility of interpretation in archaeological terms.

The differential chemical enrichment of floors depends on the following four criteria (Ortiz 1990). First, the type of activity (e.g., production, use-consumption, storage, or waste) will leave particular signatures. Second, the continuity, intensity, and duration of the activity will affect the chemical signature. Third, changes in the spatial distribution of the activity will determine the strength of the signature and the distribution of it. And fourth, differential use of the same area (both contemporary and after) will affect the signature.

With respect to the chemical enrichment of lime plastered floors, it must be considered that instead of dealing with soils and sediments, we are dealing with a stucco floor, which is a porous archaeological material. In this case, there are no soil processes such as lixiviation, oxidation, depletion, and migration. This artificial surface was prepared with overlapping layers of mud mixed with gravel, a base of lime mixed with sand, and finally a thin layer of a lime-enriched finish coat. This arrangement of layers prevents the vertical movement of water, and the way lime is produced—by burning limestone fragments—ensures the removal of most organic remains, producing a "clean" surface from the chemical point of view.

The systematic grid sampling of the floors and the chemical analysis provide information about the concentration of residues found in the floor, enabling the reconstruction of the enrichment patterns. These patterns have been interpreted as revealing human activities through the comparison with recognizable patterns found in previous ethnoarchaeological studies.

It is impossible to identify for sure any human activity just by analyzing some chemical residues in floors, since it has to be considered that different activities can produce the same chemical concentration of one chemical compound or element. Nevertheless, our laboratory has chosen an integrative approach to optimize the interpretation opportunities; thus, the spatial association of different chemical residues and diagnostic archaeological materials provides a better probability of interpreting the actual activities that produced the chemical enrichment.

The analytical techniques employed and the goals of these studies do not attempt to interpret small differences in concentrations. Our approach focuses on large concentrations of chemical residues since they reveal activities that must have been important because they were carried out on a daily basis for a long time or once involved large amounts of material residues. In addition, we deal with chemical enrichment patterns comprising not just a few samples but hundreds of samples surveying the whole occupation surface.

The analysis of chemical residues provides information concerning the places where some human activities were carried out and, as a consequence, about the way the spaces were used in ancient times. It is well-known that most of the archaeological materials are not found in primary contexts. On the other hand, the concentration of chemical residues does not undergo displacement; thus, there is a high probability that the place where a high chemical concentration is found was where a given activity produced signatures on a particular section of the floor. The risk, therefore, is not that the residue will be wrongly associated with a given place but that the residue will be misinterpreted as signifying a different activity, and this problem is especially true in courtyards, which are likely to be areas with multiple uses and many overlapping patterns.

RESULTS

During the 1970s and 1980s, inorganic analyses of floor samples were undertaken (Ortiz 1990), but the organic analyses presented here are more recent. The distribution map of these chemical indicators furnishes information concerning the enrichment patterns on the floor surface. The interpretation of these patterns in terms of ritual activities and their relationship to other archaeological evidence is one of the goals of this research. Results of the analysis of the Oztoayahualco compound are presented here.

Because most of the architectural surfaces are covered by lime plaster in Teotihuacan, the low concentration of carbonates in floors suggests either intense surface wear without later renovation or poor construction quality. At Oztoyahualco 15B:N6W3, high concentrations of carbonates have been associated with polishers and ready-to-use plaster on top of the floors. We observed that the central part of the domestic compound shows better flooring, which has been interpreted as higher construction quality or perhaps flooring repaired after long-term use. Rooms in the periphery tend to have lower carbonate values.

The high content of sodium and potassium hydroxides in ash produces a sizable increase in pH values in some parts of the floors. As a consequence, the pH level may be an indirect indicator of burning areas. At Oztoyahualco, the high values of pH suggest the disposal of ashes on their surface. Some of them resulted from food preparation, but others, especially in patios, seem to be related to ritual activities. Phosphates are frequently related to food preparation and consumption. In this case, some high concentrations are also found in courtyards and it is possible that they are more related to ritual activities.

Food preparation and consumption areas have a higher content of protein residues than do other areas, but specific areas of the courtyards also show higher concentrations of protein residues. Fatty acids related to protein residues are produced by the decay of resins, fats, and oils and are often associated with areas of food preparation and consumption. More important for our goals, however, are the concentrations of these acids in some courtyards close to the places where braziers were found. This protein residue may be from the ritual use of copal, a substance with high concentrations of fatty acids.

Courtyard C41a

This courtyard is special since it was the only one with a permanent centered altar. Unfortunately the Xolalpan floor was damaged and during excavation it was removed to expose the floor C41. Nevertheless, it was sampled and analyzed like the others. The results showed a band of higher values to the north of the altar. Approximately in the same place, we found low phosphate values, whereas higher values were found at the southwestern corner of the altar. Pattern distribution of chemical indicators suggests that the southern part of the altar was used more intensively than the northern part (Figure 3.5).

Courtyard C41

The central distribution of high carbonate values in this red courtyard, along with the high phosphate concentrations surrounding the low values in the central portion of the courtyard (also enriched with fatty acids and residues derived from ancient proteins placed in both sides—north and south—of the central area), suggests the setting of ritual activities was a mobile altar at the center of the patio (Figure 3.6). In this case, domestic activities are not represented in the distribution of chemical residues. There are interesting correspondences among phosphates, protein residues, and fatty acids just in the doorway between C27 and C42. Because C27 has been defined as a storage room, this area could be considered a possible preparation area for the rituals carried out at the courtyard.

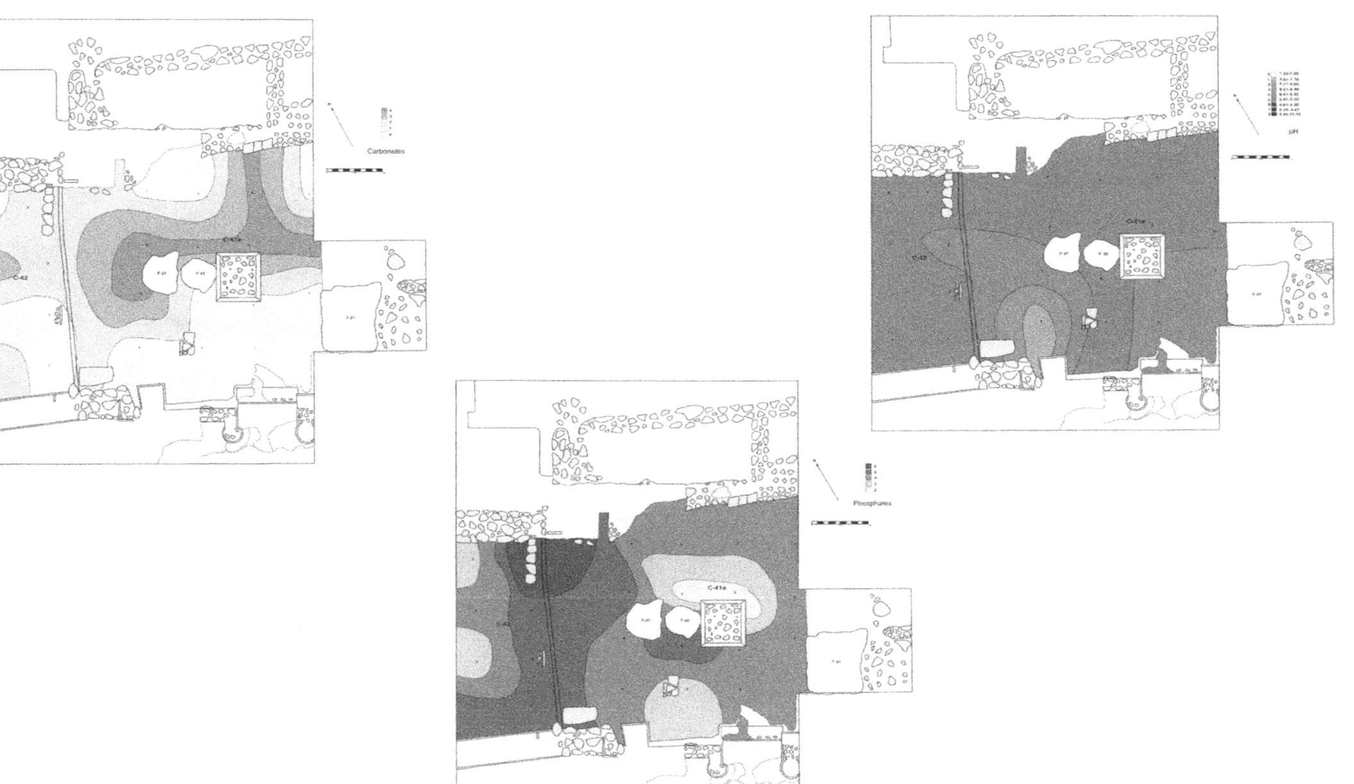

3.5. *Chemical residues at Xolalpan floor C41a, Oztoyahualco, Teotihuacan, Mexico.*

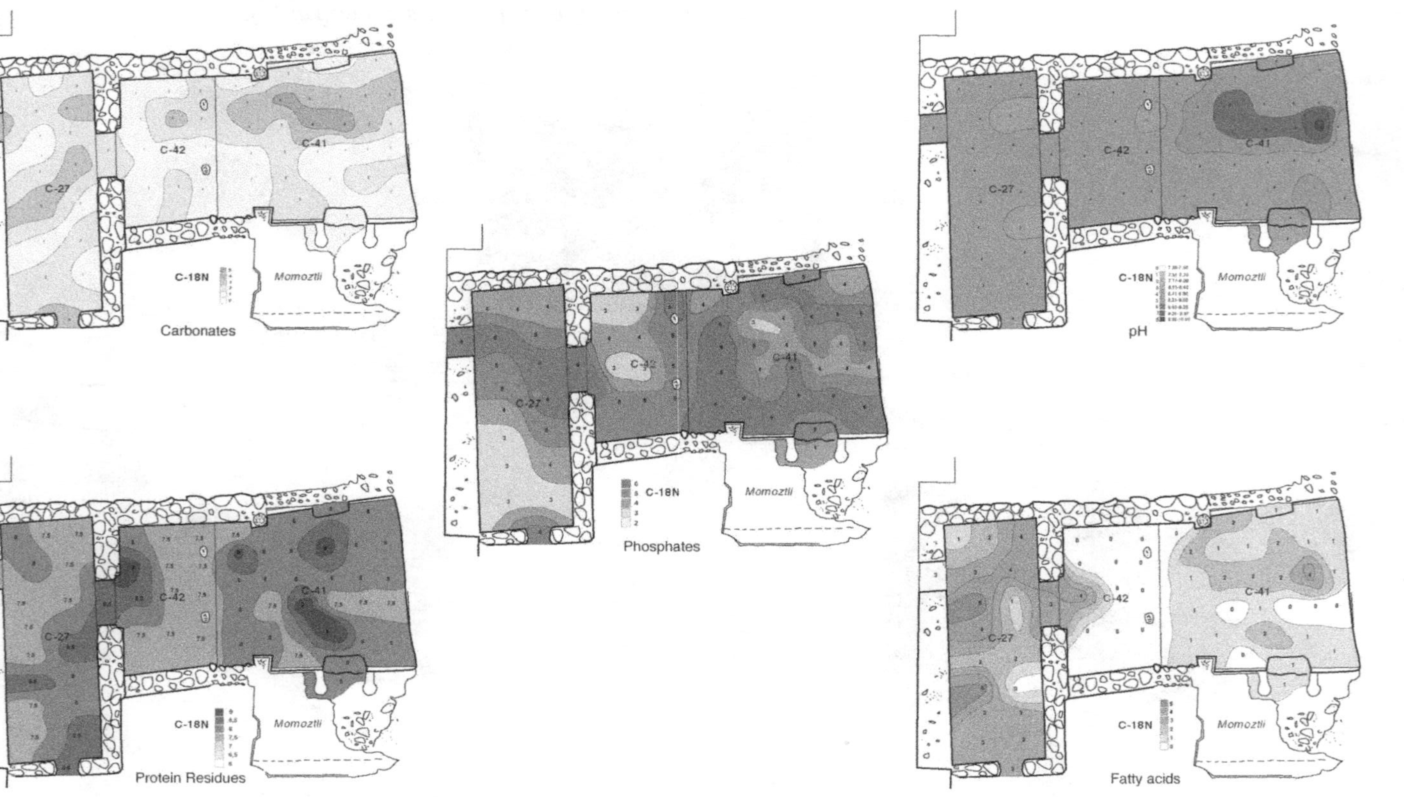

3.6. Chemical residues at courtyard C41, Oztoyahualco, Teotihuacan, Mexico.

Courtyard 25

At this courtyard, the maximum carbonate values are located in the northern and western parts, just in the place where a theater-type censer was found. Meanwhile, the maximum pH values are just overlapping, with a concentration low in carbonates and high values of phosphate, protein residues, and fatty acids. The enrichment pattern suggests that some activities—perhaps rituals—were carried out at the central part, possibly close to a mobile altar placed on top of F36. Some other high phosphate values are at the northwestern sector at room C7 and in the southern part of C13. The northern and western limits of the courtyard have the highest values of protein residues and fatty acids, displaying markedly similar patterns, suggesting the use of the double step to execute some specific activities while seated (Figure 3.7).

Courtyard 33

Some low carbonate values suggest the more intense use of the courtyard area. Maximum pH values can be found at the center and southwestern corner beside most of the surface of C20. Highest phosphate concentrations were found in the southern portion of the courtyard. Room C20's pH and protein residue patterns are remarkably similar, suggesting important activities occurred here, too. High values of fatty acids overlap with high concentrations of phosphates and protein residues in the southern and northern limits of the courtyard. In this case the central enrichment is absent and the high residue enrichment found at room C22 suggests the presence of a food preparation area. In this case, the patterns are mixed and it is more feasible that both domestic and ritual activities are represented (Figure 3.8).

Summary and Conclusions

In and around the courtyards of Oztoyahualco 15B:N6W3, activity areas related to ritual preparation may be present, as identified by several archaeological indicators. Some courtyards have burned incense in theater-type censers or sectional temple models. Radial cutting marks on limestone half spheres suggest that the activity of cutting rabbit and hare limbs may have taken place (Hernández 1993; Manzanilla 1993). The use of fire and the throwing of ashes may be indicated by chemical signatures, and the use and consumption of organic materials took place as well (Manzanilla 1993).

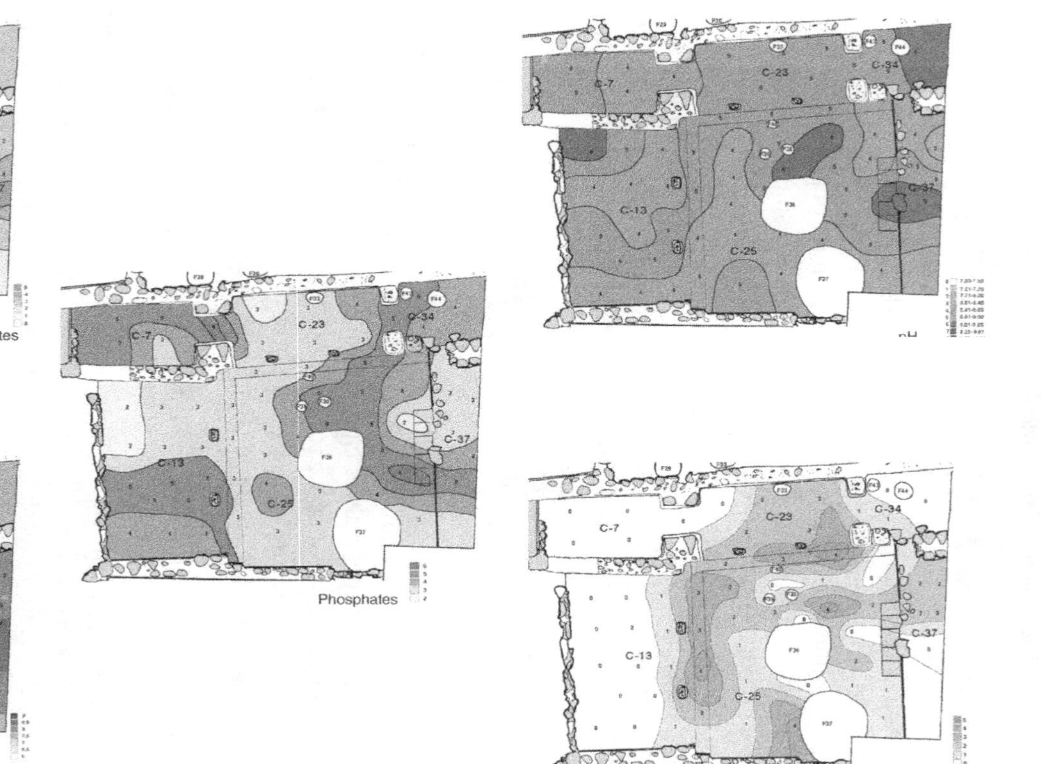

3.7. Chemical residues at courtyard C25, Oztoyahualco, Teotihuacan, Mexico.

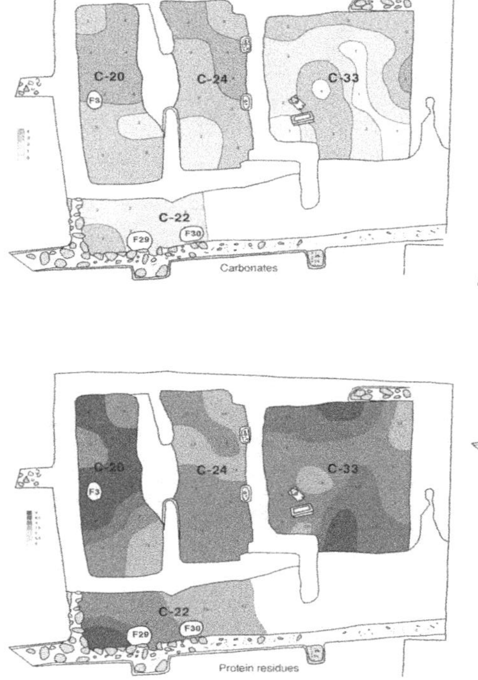

3.8. Chemical residues at courtyard C33, Oztoyahualco, Teotihuacan, Mexico.

Courtyard C25 was identified as the ritual space of Family Unit 2. During the excavation of this courtyard, a portable altar was found, and the surrounding area has high concentrations of chemical residues. Other important rituals were performed in rooms C20, C24, and C33, which are part of the Family Unit 3 apartment. All of them display well-preserved floors. Room C20 shows high pH values and protein residues and has been interpreted as an area of ritual preparation for the ceremonies performed at courtyard C33. On the floor of courtyard C33, a portable altar and a zoomorphic representation of a rabbit directly corresponded to high concentrations of all chemical indicators.

In regard to the study of ritual activities, chemical evidence in the courtyards of the domestic compounds was recovered. The most significant was the Red Courtyard (C41) with relicts of mural painting in the eastern wall. This courtyard is connected to the sanctuary to the south, forming a significant ritual complex. During the excavation process, in the upper layer of the same courtyard (C41a), a Late Xolalpan central altar was found. Taking into consideration that some portable altars have been excavated in other patios, it is possible that one of these altars was at the center of the Red Courtyard during the Late Tlamimilolpa phase, and the activities performed around it produced chemical distribution patterns in its center (Figure 3.9).

A large concentration of ritual materials in the western portion of the Oztoyahualco compound (specifically in C18) is particularly interesting (Figure 3.10). This room may be interpreted as a storeroom because ritual elements (censer plaques, *candeleros*, figurines, Copa Ware vessels) as well as foreign materials (Thin Orange pottery) were found. It is located directly in contact with the sanctuary (C57) and the Red Courtyard (C41), through a passage closed in Late Xolalpan times. This storage sector may be interpreted as the place where ritual paraphernalia was stored.

After carefully reviewing the relationship among architecture, chemical residues, and archaeological materials found in courtyards, we can be certain that ritual activities were performed in the courtyards, sometimes at the center and sometimes at one of the sides, leaving archaeological traces and chemical residues as evidence of the type of activities performed. There also is a clear indication, however, that other domestic activities were mainly carried out in courtyards C33 and C25.

It is interesting to note that the hierarchical organization of the households within this apartment compound is also seen in ritual: the largest ritual courtyard is related to the household bearing Tlaloc (the state god)

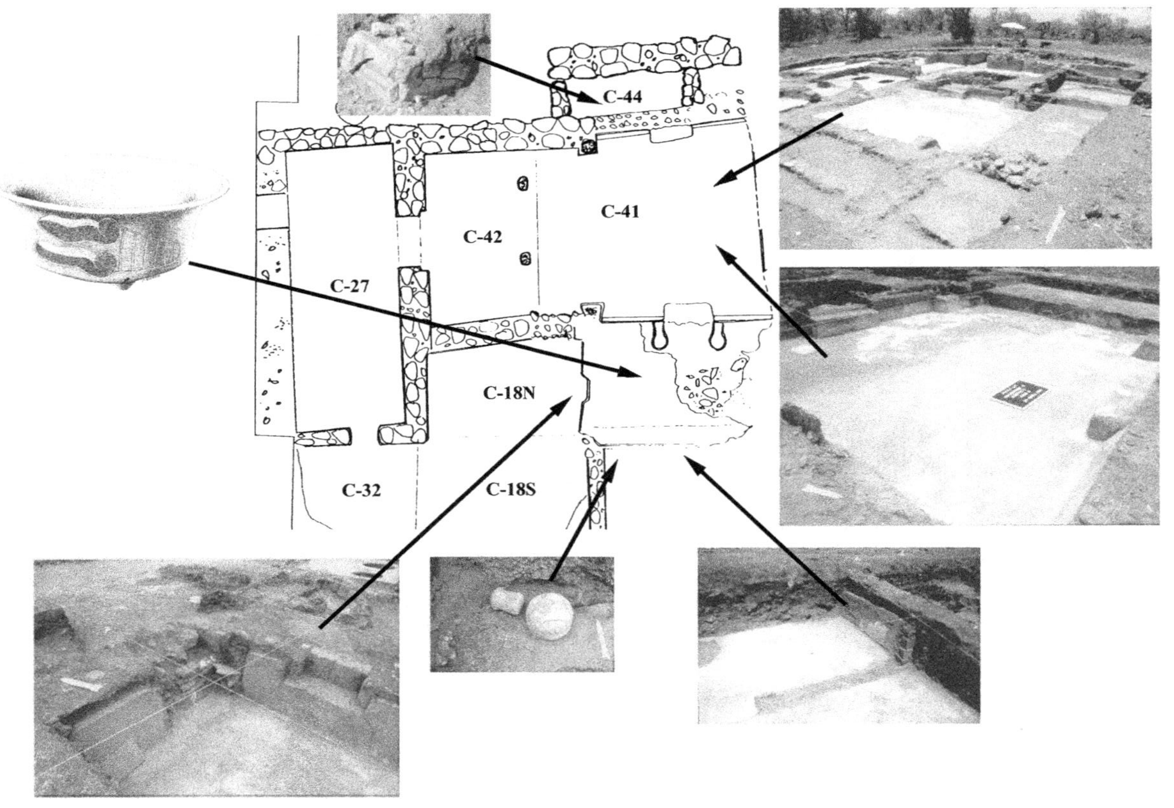

3.9. Ritual elements in and around main ritual courtyard C41 in the Oztoyahualco compound, Teotihuacan, Mexico.

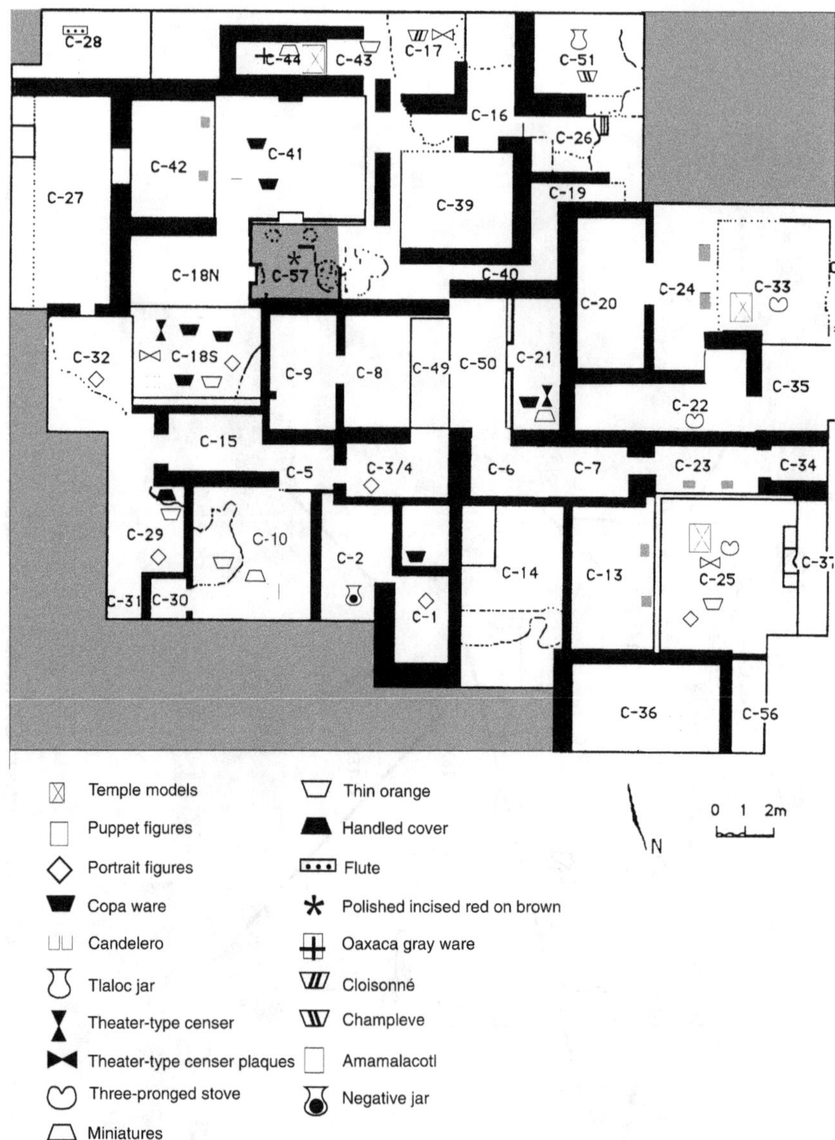

3.10. Ritual elements in the Oztoyahualco compound, Teotihuacan, Mexico.

symbols, as well as to the largest amount of foreign materials, whereas the other courtyards show rituals related to the rabbit and other domestic gods.

REFERENCES CITED

Angulo Villaseñor, Jorge

1987 Nuevas consideraciones sobre Tetitla y los llamados conjuntos departamentales. In *Teotihuacan: Nuevos datos, nuevas síntesis, nuevos problemas,* edited by Emily McClung and Evelyn Rattray, pp. 275–315. Universidad Nacional Autónoma de México, México.

Barba, Luis

1986 La química en el estudio de áreas de actividad. In *Unidades habitacionales mesoamericanas y sus áreas de actividad,* edited by Linda Manzanilla, pp. 21–39. Universidad Nacional Autónoma de México, México.

Barba, Luis, and Luz Lazos

2000 Chemical Analysis of Floors for the Identification of Activity Areas: A Review. *Antropología y Técnica* 6:59–70.

Barba, Luis, Luz Lazos, Agustín Ortiz, Karl Link, and Leonardo López Luján

1997 La arquitectura sagrada y sus dioses: Estudio geofísico y químico de la Casa de las Águilas, Tenochtitlan, Mexico. *Revista de Arqueología Española.* Año XVIII (October):44–53.

Barba, Luis, Eliseo Linares, and Guillermo Pérez

1991 Estudio químico de tumbas saqueadas. *Revista Mexicana de Estudios Antropológicos* 36:9–24.

Barba, Luis, Beatriz Ludlow, Linda Manzanilla, and Raúl Valadez

1987 La vida doméstica en Teotihuacán: Un estudio interdisciplinario. *Ciencia y Desarrollo* 77:21–32.

Barba, Luis, and Agustín Ortiz

1992 Análisis químico de pisos de ocupación: Un caso etnográfico en Tlaxcala, México. *Latin American Antiquity* 3:63–82.

1993 Capítulo XII. Superficie-excavación: Evaluación del sector estudiado a través de los restos excavados. In *Anatomía de un conjunto residencial teotihuacano en Oztoyahualco,* Volume 2, *Los estudios específicos,* edited by Linda Manzanilla, pp. 595–616. Universidad Nacional Autónoma de México, Mexico City.

Barba, Luis, Agustín Ortiz, Karl F. Link, Leonardo López Luján, and Luz Lazos

1996 The Chemical Analysis of Residues in Floors and the Reconstruction of Ritual Activities at the Templo Mayor, Mexico. In *Archaeological Chemistry: Organic, Inorganic and Biochemical Analysis,* edited by Mary Virginia Orna, pp. 139–156. Chemical Society of America, Washington, D.C.

Barba, Luis, Fabienne Pierrebourgh, Claudia Trejo, Agustín Ortiz, and Karl Link

1995 Activités humaines reflétées dans les sols d'unités d'habitation contemporaine et préhispanique du Yucatan (Mexique): Études chimiques ethnoarchéologiques et archéologiques. *Revue d'Archéométrie* 19:79–95.

Barba, Luis, Roberto Rodríguez, and Jose Luis Córdova

1991 *Manual de técnicas microquímicas de campo para la arqueología.* Universidad Nacional Autónoma de México, México City.

Cazeneuve, Jean

1972 *Sociología del rito.* Amorrortu, Buenos Aires.

Cowgill, George L.

1997 State and Society at Teotihuacan, Mexico. *Annual Review of Anthropology* 26:129–161.

Getino, Fernando, and Agustín Ortiz

1997 La actividad ritual a nivel de barrio: El momoztli de Palma y Venustiano Carranza. *Arqueología* 18, segunda época (July–December):119–138.

Hernández, Cynthia

1993 Capítulo VII. La lítica. In *Anatomía de un conjunto residencial teotihuacano en Oztoyahualco,* Volume 1, *Las Excavaciones,* edited by Linda Manzanilla, pp. 388–467. Universidad Nacional Autónoma de México, México.

Lazos, Luz

1997 Estudio para el análisis químico sistemático de pisos arqueológicos. Master's thesis in Chemical Sciences, Facultad de Química, Universidad Nacional Autónoma de México, México City.

Linné, Sigvald

1934 *Archaeological Researches at Teotihuacan, Mexico.* Publication 1, Ethnographic Museum of Sweden, Stockholm.

1942 *Mexican Highland Cultures: Archaeological Researches at Teotihuacan, Calpulalpan and Chalchicomula in 1934–35.* Publication 7, Ethnographical Museum of Sweden, Stockholm.

Lizárraga, Yara, and Agustín Ortiz

1993 Capítulo VIII. Hacia una reinterpretación de los pulidores de estuco. In *Anatomía de un conjunto residencial teotihuacano en Oztoyahualco,* Volume 1, *Las excavaciones,* edited by Linda Manzanilla, pp. 468–493. Universidad Nacional Autónoma de México, México City.

López Austin, Alfredo

1989 La historia de Teotihuacan. In *Teotihuacan,* pp. 13–35. El Equilibrista, Citicorp/Citibank, Mexico.

Manzanilla, Linda

1988–1989 The Study of Room Function in a Residential Compound at Teotihuacan, Mexico. In *Origini, Giornate in onore di Salvatore Maria Puglisi* 14:175–186.

1996 Corporate Groups and Domestic Activities at Teotihuacan. *Latin American Antiquity* 7:228–246.

2000a Fuego y regeneración: Los incensarios teotihuacanos y su simbolismo. *Revista Precolombart* 3:21–33.

2000b Noticias. Hallazgo de dos vasijas policromas en Teopancazco, Teotihuacan. *Arqueología Mexicana* VIII:80.

2002 Living with the Ancestors and Offering to the Gods: Domestic Ritual at Teotihuacan. In *Domestic Ritual in Ancient Mesoamerica,* edited by Patricia Plunket, pp. 43–52. Monograph 46, Cotsen Institute of Archaeology. University of California, Los Angeles.

2003 Teopancazco: Un conjunto residencial teotihuacano. *Arqueología Mexicana. Teotihuacan: Ciudad de misterios,* XI (64):50–53

Manzanilla Linda (editor)

1993 *Anatomía de un conjunto residencial teotihuacano en Oztoyahualco,* Volume 1, *Las excavaciones.* Universidad Nacional Autónoma de México, Mexico City.

Manzanilla, Linda, and Luis Barba

1990 The Study of Activities in Classic Households. Two Case Studies from Coba and Teotihuacan. *Ancient Mesoamerica* 2:299–307.

Manzanilla, Linda, and Emilie Carreón

1991 A Teotihuacan Censer in a Residential Context: An Interpretation. *Ancient Mesoamerica* 2:299–307.

Manzanilla, Linda, and Agustín Ortiz

1991 Los altares domésticos en Teotihuacan, hallazgo de dos fragmentos de maqueta. *Cuadernos de Arquitectura Mesoamericana* 13:11–13.

Marcus, Joyce

1998 *Women's Ritual in Formative Oaxaca: Figurine-Making, Divination, Death and the Ancestors.* Memoirs of the Museum of Anthropology No. 33, University of Michigan, Ann Arbor.

Millon, René

1973 *Urbanization at Teotihuacan, Mexico,* Volume 1, *The Teotihuacan Map Text.* University of Texas Press, Austin.

Ortiz, Agustín

1990 Oztoyahualco: Estudio químico de los pisos estucados de un conjunto residencial teotihuacano para determinar áreas de actividad. Thesis in Archaeology, Escuela Nacional de Antropología e Historia, Mexico City.

1996 Estudio químico del piso de la tumba tres de Bolaños. Paper presented in the IV Coloquio de Occidentalistas. Instituto Cultural Cabañas, Guadalajara, Mexico.

Ortiz, Agustín, and Luis Barba

1992 Estudio químico de los pisos del Satunsat, en Oxkintok, Yucatán. *Oxkintok* 4:119–126.

1993 Capítulo XII. La química en el estudio de áreas de actividad. In *Anatomía de un conjunto residencial teotihuacano en Oztoyahualco,* Volume 1, *Las excavaciones,* edited by Linda Manzanilla, pp. 617–660. Universidad Nacional Autónoma de Mexico, Mexico City.

Rivera, Miguel, and Francisco Ferrándiz

1989 Excavaciones en el Satunsat. *Oxkintok* 2:63–75.

Sánchez Alaniz, José Ignacio

2000 *Las unidades habitacionales en Teotihuacan: El caso de Bidasoa.* Serie Arqueología, Colección Científica 421. Instituto Nacional de Antropología e Historia, Mexico.

Sanders, William T.

1966 Life in a Classic Village. In *Teotihuacan: XI Mesa Redonda,* pp. 123–143. Sociedad Mexicana de Antropología, Mexico City.

1994 *The Teotihuacan Valley Project: Final Report.* Volume 3, *The Teotihuacan Occupation of the Valley.* Part 1. *The Excavations.* Occasional Papers in Anthropology 19. Matson Museum of Anthropology, Pennsylvania State University, University Park.

Séjourné, Laurette

1966 *Arquitectura y pintura en Teotihuacán.* Siglo XXI, Mexico City.

Sempowski, Martha L.

1987 Differential Mortuary Treatment: Its Implications for Social Status at Three Residential Compounds in Teotihuacan, Mexico. In *Teotihuacan: Nuevos datos, nuevas síntesis, nuevos problemas,* edited by Emily McClung de Tapia and Evelyn Childs Rattray, pp. 115–131. Universidad Nacional Autónoma de México, Mexico City.

1994 Part I. Mortuary Practices at Teotihuacan. In *Mortuary Practices and Skeletal Remains at Teotihuacan,* by Martha Sempowski and Michael W. Spence, pp. 1–311. Urbanization at Teotihuacan, Mexico, Volume 3, edited by René Millon. University of Utah Press, Salt Lake City.

CHAPTER FOUR

RITUAL AND IDEOLOGY AMONG CLASSIC MAYA RURAL COMMONERS AT COPÁN, HONDURAS

NANCY GONLIN

INTRODUCTION

The most visible remains of Central America's and Mexico's Classic Maya (A.D. 250–900) culture are the stone temples towering amidst jungle overgrowth, grand palaces, tombs laden with exotic objects, elaborate sculptures, and hieroglyphs, all of which in some way relate to ancient ideologies and worldviews. One rarely conjures up the remains of a humble household when asked to visualize the Classic Maya. Presumably, contained in these monuments of the past is abundant evidence for the multiple perspectives of elites during Classic times (e.g., Miller and Martin 2004; inter alia). The majority of people, however, fulfilled productive and supportive roles within society, primarily as laborers living in small abodes on the outskirts of site cores. These are the people to whom archaeologists frequently refer as "commoners." Given the grandiose nature of many Classic Maya ruins, it may not be apparent that such elaborate displays may be viewed from the perspective of commoners as well, or that much information about the past is encoded in the housemounds of the masses.

The various types of ideologies—such as political, religious, and gender—overlap each other and are inherently intertwined. Although this volume focuses primarily on religious ideologies, we realize that the separation of these spheres is not possible. Several approaches may be taken to investigate ancient ideology and its expression in ritual. For a comprehensive understanding of complex societies, the material record of various factions needs to be examined. What types of evidence exist that reveal the rituals and ideology of people of differing social statuses? Was there a dominant ideology to which all members of society subscribed, and if so, what was the extent and nature of their participation? How is this dominant ideology, if it existed, manifested archaeologically across the social spectrum? These issues can be effectively addressed by examining the remains of households from all levels of society, from the smallest, most inconspicuous vestiges of a farming household to a palace inhabited by royal heirs. This chapter presents a case study of rural commoner ritual and ideology from the Classic Maya site of Copán, Honduras (Figures 0.1 and 0.2), which has been extensively surveyed, tested, and excavated by many researchers throughout the past several decades. Three recent publications conveniently summarize much of these efforts (Andrews and Fash 2005; Fash 2001; Webster et al. 2000). The term *commoner ritual* is used to refer to those practices in which low-ranking members of the polity participated. As described later, there were several loci for the implementation of such traditions and varying degrees of participation.

The role of household archaeology in the study of ritual and ideology is indispensable, as it provides the tool to seek answers to the questions posed above. It creates a window through which one may peer at private rituals, whether they occurred in royal abodes or field huts. Contributors to this volume and others (e.g., Plunket 2002) have working assumptions that domestic rituals did indeed exist, that they relate to a perceivable ideology, and that the remains of these rituals, and hence ideology, are recoverable in the archaeological record. Fortunately for the archaeologist, rituals, as the observable manifestations of nonmaterial culture in ethnographic circumstances, often have material components, such as the use of particular places, particular artifacts, and particular people. Joyce Marcus (1996, 1999) labels these dimensions "loci," "content," and "performance," respectively. (See also Chapter 3.) I use the term *content* in an archaeological context (i.e., artifacts, features, or place), rather than in an ethnographic sense as defined by Marcus, who states, "*Content* refers to the subject matter of the ritual" (1999:70). The symbolic information contained in such material remains allows us to compare content and context to make statements about ideological realms of culture.

These places, artifacts, and people may be ordinary in nature until they are transformed to the sacred realm to serve loftier purposes. For example, a house is the location for the everyday activities of cooking and craft-making yet also functions in ritual contexts as a shrine. The ubiquitous obsidian blade serves equally well for food processing as it does for bloodletting. Pine has multiple uses (Morehart et al. 2005). Context is all important. The heads of households performed political, social, and economic functions while perhaps simultaneously serving as ritual heads. The roles of places, things, and people vary with the demands of the household and society. As Jon Lohse comments in Chapter 1, many advances are being made in finding the evidence of commoner ritual throughout Mesoamerica. Once the data have been collected and analyzed, we then can evaluate the elements that are held in common between disparate members of society and those which are idiosyncratic in nature, leading us to an enriched understanding of social complexity and a comprehension of contemporaneous multiple ideologies.

A DEFINITION OF "COMMONER" AT COPÁN, HONDURAS

From numerous investigations conducted at Copán, it is apparent that the region had a long history of occupation, beginning in the Early Preclassic (Rayo phase) 3,000 years ago (Figure 0.2). The focus here is primarily on the part of the Coner phase settlement, spanning A.D. 650–900, known as the Late Classic. Variation in settlement remains at Copán have been categorized into a five-tier hierarchy[1] of sites. (Unlike at other Maya sites, individual groups at the site of Copán are also called "sites.") The site core containing the monumental temples, palaces, stelae, and altars is referred to as the Main Group and is the only Type 5 site (Figure 4.1). The Main Group along with the densely packed remains of urban neighborhoods (Las Sepulturas and El Bosque) around it is collectively called the Urban Core. Type 4 and Type 3 sites are classified as "elite" habitations and their remains are concentrated in the Urban Core and Copán Pocket (the largest tract of rich agricultural lands in which the Urban Core is situated [Webster et al. 2000]). Corbelled vaulting, sculpture, and high platforms made of

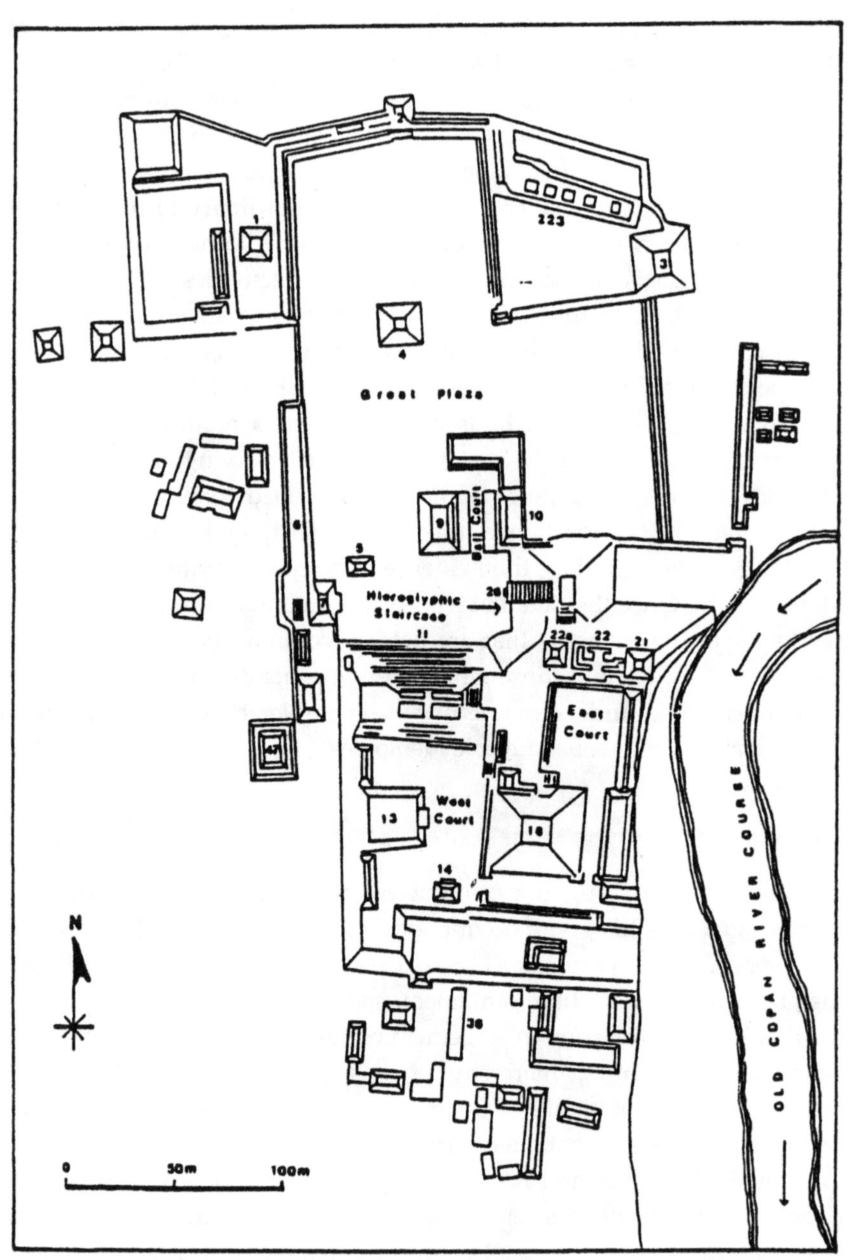

4.1. The Classic Maya center of Copán, Honduras. The monumental architecture is commonly referred to as the Main Group. Note the location of the Great Plaza, where polity-wide congregations likely assembled (after original by A. Freter).

finely cut stone characterize the elite architecture at Copán. Commoner groups, known as Type 2 and Type 1 sites, have been excavated in the Urban Core, outside of the Urban Core in the Copán Pocket, and in the hinterlands of Copán, beyond the Copán Pocket (Canuto 2002; Fash 1985; Freter 1988; Gonlin 1993; Hendon 1987; Mallory 1981; Murillo 1983; Pohl 1994; Webster and Gonlin 1988; Whittington 1985; Willey et al. 1994).

Although Type 2 sites are generally larger than Type 1 sites in terms of numbers of structures and plazas, these two types of sites are more alike than they are different. Both characteristically have cobble construction with low substructure platform height. From a sample of twenty Type 1 structures that were wholly intact, the average dimensions are 5 x 5.7 m with a substructure height of 0.46 m (Gonlin 1993:table 5.5). In rural areas, architectural features such as dressed stone, internal stone divisions, and plaster are typically absent, although these features may be present in urban Type 1 and Type 2 units. Both types of sites are definitively associated with commoner status, as evidenced by other methods of analyses apart from architecture. Human burial, paleopathological, and nutritional analyses, along with statistical studies of artifact distributions, confirm that there is not only a qualitative but, indeed, a quantitative difference between "commoner" (i.e., Types 1 and 2) sites and "elite" (i.e., Types 3 and 4) sites at Copán (Gonlin 1993; Hendon 1991; Lentz 1991; Whittington 1989; Willey and Leventhal 1979). The typology is an oversimplification of past complexity, but it serves well as a heuristic device. There are multiple lines of evidence to support the use of these subdivisions while recognizing the variety that exists within each category.

Geographically speaking, the occupation of the hinterlands is dominated by commoner sites where the majority of the farming population resided. Additionally, commoners were known to have lived at higher-ranking "elite" sites (i.e., those classified as Types 3 and 4), where small structures are found on the edges of palace-type buildings. For this chapter data are derived primarily from excavations that took place during David Webster's Rural Sites Project in 1985 and 1986, which focused on rural Type 1 sites located outside of the Copán Pocket (Figure 4.2). These sites represent some of the smallest, most unprepossessing Late Classic structures that have been excavated completely in the Maya Lowlands within the framework of household archaeology. As our understanding of the rural segment of Classic Maya culture increases, we are in a better position to speak of the complexity that characterized such settlement and to appreciate its diversity (see Iannone and Connell 2003).

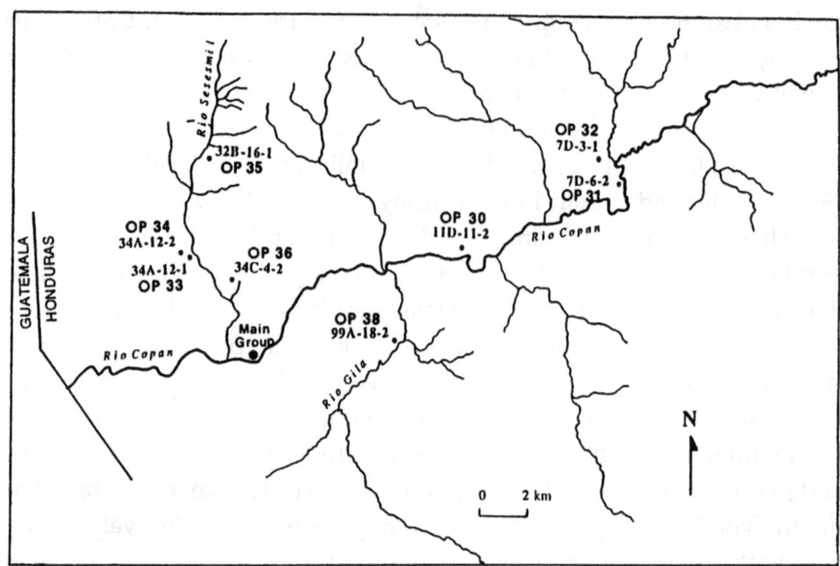

4.2. The location of completely excavated rural Type 1 sites in the Copán Valley, Honduras, by Webster's Rural Sites Project, 1985–1986.

WHERE COMMONER RITUALS TRANSPIRED: THE "LOCI" OF PERFORMANCE

In what contexts did rituals in which commoners participated occur in the Classic Maya world? For Copán, we may generally speak of three different scales of organization that most likely crosscut the Late Classic social spectrum. These three scales, or loci of performance following Marcus (1999), although in this case also denoting levels of social organization, focus on the built environment.[2] First, there were events that had a bearing on the polity as a whole. One venue may have been the Main Group, where majestic ceremonies involving kings and queens would likely have been performed. The Great Plaza of Copán has often been interpreted as the gathering place for ceremonial events for the entire polity, which likely consisted of as many as 25,000 to 30,000 people at its peak (Webster and Freter 1990; Webster et al. 1992). The birth of an heir, the accession of a new king, a royal marriage, the ballgame, or rituals for a bountiful harvest may have been occasions for celebrations that included all members of society. Structures around the Great Plaza have a series of bleacher-like steps that could have been used as reviewing stands for those who came to witness and partake in the events of the day. Throughout Copán's history, access to this area does not seem to have been restricted (see Joyce and Weller, Chapter 6), and the area as a whole remained quite public in nature. The buildings in the site core were constructed by all factions of society through commoner labor (Abrams 1994) and elite management and could symbolize the incorporation of the people. Built throughout the city's history, the massive structures could symbolize the efforts and skills of the ancestors of the commoners. Surely, some of the rural inhabitants participated in some capacity in these public festivities, which may have featured royal bloodletting. The readily identifiable symbols of Maya cosmovision would have been there for all to see. Although these community-wide festivities functioned to unite all inhabitants of the Copán polity, at the same time they would have underscored the extreme economic and social differences among the people. When standing in the Great Plaza, an individual is physically and metaphorically at the bottom, with those in control in the temples and palaces situated above. It is at such gatherings that commoners would have been most vulnerable to dominant ideologies of the state. Whether commoners and elites conceived of these rituals in a similar fashion can only be conjectured, but it is not likely given their different conditions in life.

The second level for ritual participation by Maya commoners is at the scale of the corporate group or lineage. Many large Type 3 or 4 sites at Copán (i.e., primarily associated with elite occupation) may have served as residences for lineage heads or other elites and also housed attached commoners. Lineage organization at Copán (Diamanti 1991; Fash 1983; Sanders 1989) integrated rural inhabitants, who may have been members of core lineages and commoners living in elite compounds, and formed a community of people linked through affinal and consanguineal ties. Ritual activity at the lineage level is a step below polity-wide ceremonies and a step above independent household activities. The celebration of auspicious occasions relating to rites of passage, such as birth, marriage, and death, perhaps took place at the residence of the lineage head. These nobles may have called on their kinspeople for contributions of labor and food, and at propitious times these kinsfolk may have been integrated for momentous ceremonies. Economic, social, political, and religious ties bound the urban kinsfolk to their rural lineage members.

The third level of ritual activity is represented by the Classic Maya household. The practice of household ritual was present at all levels of society, from the independent, small, isolated rural farmsteads to the grand palaces of site cores. For commoners, ample evidence demonstrates that outlying residents had their own ceremonies, festivities, and religious practices that reflected both their ideologies and possible pan-polity ideologies. For various reasons, commoner practices were most effectively expressed within the domestic compound, a point elaborated on later. The remains of ancient households are most readily identified by the architectural ruins and artifacts left behind. The household, however, is inclusive of the surrounding gardens and fields, which may have served as extramural loci for ritual performance. A discussion of domestic architecture as it relates to ritual and ideology, burials (or "content," per Marcus), and artifacts and ecofacts (also "content") thought to be specifically related to ritual will be discussed later to elaborate on ritual activity at the household level.

DOMESTIC ARCHITECTURE IN COMMONER HOUSEHOLD RITUALS

Although functional categorization of architecture is an oversimplification of actual use, the terms employed by archaeologists, and Mayanists in particular, warrant consideration here (see Gonlin 2004 for a fuller treatment of these functional categories). For the ancient Maya, it is well accepted that structures were living ritual entities, yet there are those buildings in particular that stand out to archaeologists as having a "ritual" purpose because of their architectural features and associated artifacts (Gonlin 1993, 2004; Hendon 1987, 1989). The type of structure usually referred to as a temple (*oratorio*) or shrine is identified architecturally as having had a small, sometimes perishable, superstructure perched atop a high square stone substructure. Ritual structures are most often situated on the east side of the courtyard. Artifacts are few in comparison with residences and those found often relate to ritual activities (a tautological relationship!), and there are no middens. Caches and burials are rarely associated with ritual structures, and benches, if present, are small. Buildings with exclusively ritual functions have not been identified in rural Copán commoner groups (Gonlin 1993, 2004), but Marcello Canuto (2002) has recorded ritual structures in the rural neighborhoods of Los Achiotes and El Raizal, none of which are explicitly associated with a Type 1 domicile. Even in Copán's elite urban neighborhoods, structures used solely for ritual are not commonly found in every single compound (Hendon 1987). Differential use of space may have to do with energy procurement and status in both rural and urban contexts, rather than with differences in household activities per se, as Marshall Becker (1986) has found to be the case at Tikal. These functional categories that we impose on the complex past do not always serve us well.

Family shrines are recorded for the modern Maya, but they are not necessarily enclosed in separate facilities. The shrine is often located against one of the walls of the house; hence, the term *household worship* is appropriate for the scale and nature of ritual activity. This pattern would seem to hold for the Copán rural commoner Type 1 sites, where the distribution of "ritual" objects does not coincide with any particular building on a site, and for some higher-ranking sites at Copán as well. Almost all refuse around structures would be labeled "domestic" in nature, reaffirming the use of a building as a house, kitchen, and/or storehouse. Each of these structures, however, may have occasionally served ritual purposes as well, and the functional divisions are not as distinct as we may assume. The conflation in the use of space inevitably occurred as dwellings became shrines on auspicious occasions.

Michael Deal's (1987) work with the Highland Maya shows that the family altar is the focus of household ritual. From ethnohistoric sources (Deal 1987:177), Deal notes that "native-priests and nobility had private oratories within their household compound, while few poorer families could afford them." Modern family altars within domiciles are constructed of perishable material, as is much of the associated paraphernalia. If similar materials were used in archaeological contexts, recovery of such ritual areas will be extremely challenging.

Ritual structures or shrines in small groups have been defined at other Classic Maya sites such as Ceren (Brown and Gerstle 2002), Cobá (Manzanilla 1987), and Tikal (Haviland 1985), as well as from Copán's urban neighborhoods (Hendon 1987). From the sample of excavated rural Type 1 sites at Copán, the structure that appears most "ritual" in terms of its architecture is located at Site 11D-11-2 in the El Jaral part of the Copán Valley. This courtyard group of five buildings is one of the larger rural Type 1 sites excavated in the valley and has a history spanning from at least the seventh through the tenth centuries A.D. On top of an earlier building called Structure 1-sub sits a small, compact, nearly square building measuring 3.8 x 3.65 m with a height of 1.2 m (Figure 4.3). The remains of a censer and a frog effigy (described later) were found adjacent to Structure 1, on the terraces of Structure 1-sub. Both buildings were trenched, but caches or burials were not recovered in either and the associated middens reflect domestic activities. The orientation of Structure 1 on the eastern side of the courtyard with an opening to the west, combined with its size and

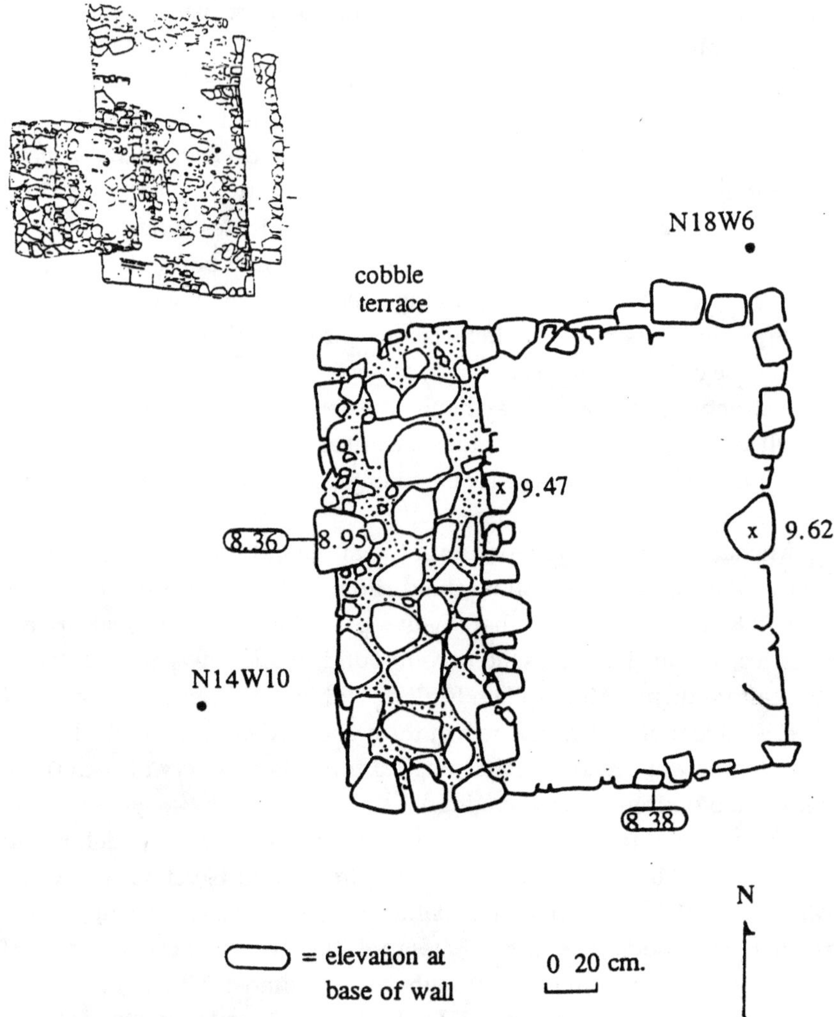

4.3. Plan map of a possible ritual structure in the Copán Valley, Honduras, at Site 11D-11-2. Structure 1 and 1-sub make up a residence, with Structure 1 the possible ritual structure (after original by D. Webster).

shape, is indicative of a special-use building, but this special use may not have excluded routine activities. It is interesting to note that Structure 1 was likely built during the later years of 11D-11-2's occupation. Following Arthur Joyce and Errin Weller (Chapter 6), it may be that these commoners were expressing their "resistance" in a more visible fashion during the decline of the Copán kingdom.

Can energetic requirements of construction really account for the differences in the use of space? It does not seem that energetic analyses provide a sufficient answer to explain the lack of separate ritual structures at commoner residences, given the fact that, on average, a small (5 x 5.6 m) wattle-and-daub building with a low (0.47 m) cobble platform took the equivalent of fifty-four person-days for construction at Copán (Gonlin 1993:445; see Abrams 1994, for a full explanation of energetic studies). This estimate indicates that the time and energy required for construction were minimal. Were rural commoners not "allowed" to construct their own temples/shrines, or was it a matter of choice? Did they prefer to keep the practice of their rituals inconspicuous and confined to the interiors of their own homes? Or were ritual structures built of entirely perishable materials, leaving no trace in the archaeological record? It may be that what we call "houses" were indeed ritual structures to the inhabitants, regardless of other domestic functions (Gillespie 2000).

THE "CONTENT" OF LATE CLASSIC COMMONER RITUALS

According to Marcus (1999:70), "*Content* refers to the subject matter of the ritual," such as a burial ceremony. We must do our best to reconstruct these practices from artifacts. Gary Gossen and Richard Leventhal (1993) have interpreted the remains of incense burners, household altars, figurines, and family shrines that are found in direct association with residential structures as evidence for the existence of localized cults, and they advocate a position of religious pluralism for the Classic Maya. In order to further understand the content of rituals, this analysis will look at burials, caches, artifacts, and ecofacts to reveal ritual activities throughout the Copán Valley.

Late Classic Burial Patterns at Rural Copán Type 1 Sites

Classic Maya burials throughout the lowlands are most commonly sought within structures or along plaza-facing walls in domestic compounds. Numerous burials were recovered in this fashion in Copán's urban neighborhoods for both high- and low-status occupants (Diamanti 1991; Whittington 1989). This burial pattern does not prevail in rural areas outside of the Copán Pocket at Type 1 sites. From AnnCorinne Freter's work (1988) in rural parts of the Copán Valley, less than 5 percent of the 169 tested sites yielded burials. One might conclude that rural inhabitants rarely buried their dead. Freter's testing project, however, was not designed to excavate the customary burial locations. This conclusion, among others (Gonlin 1996), was examined with full-scale excavations of eight rural Type 1 sites (Gonlin 1993; Webster and Gonlin 1988). Only two of the eight sites contained burials of the simple pit variety, confirming Freter's original work. Many explanations exist for the lack of burials, some of which will be considered below, after detailing those sites that did contain interments.

Inhabitants who lived at Site 34A-12-2 in the northern Sesesmil drainage and at Site 99A-18-2 in the southern Rio Gila drainage (see Figure 4.2) chose to inter their dead within the immediate vicinity of the household in the customary locations within structures or alongside retaining walls. A number of the burials at Site 34A-12-2 were those of children and, hence, were individuals who had not attained full adult status. Collectively, sixteen individuals were recovered, and most burials had some type of grave offering. Several burials were marked by stones to denote their locations. A few of the graves included entire ceramic vessels; however, this type of offering was rare. More often, broken artifacts, such as potsherds, were recovered in the burial fill, items that could have originated from secondary sources. At least eight individuals were buried at Site 99A-18-2, representing women and children, some of whom had grave offerings. The placement of offerings is consistent with the Maya belief in the afterlife, but the paucity of offerings should not be interpreted as a paucity of beliefs. Low-status burials are often compared with elite and royal burials and are described as materially lacking, which they are. It is unknown, however, what perishables, if any, may have been included in the pits and what rituals accompanied a Maya burial of any status. Clearly, some rural inhabitants had revered family members, or ancestors, as Patricia McAnany (1995:160–162) refers to them. These burials and their associated constructions may symbolize the rights and obligations of those who lived, a sense of place, and a continuity of genealogy (McAnany and Plank 2001:91). Such burials may also have been part of termination rituals, as suggested by David Freidel and Linda Schele (1989) and James Brady and Wendy Ashmore (1999:134).

Other rural commoners obviously handled their dead differently since no remains have been found at the majority of rural Type 1 sites tested or excavated. There are many possible scenarios. Other forms of burial, such as cremation, may have been carried out, but at present there is no evidence to support this hypothesis. Alternatively, the dead may have been buried at the household of the lineage head where control of the land was reinforced by the symbolic act of burial. This practice, if it existed, would be difficult to determine archaeologically, although there are ethnographic counterparts for its existence in the Old World (i.e., Goddard 1965). It also would have profound implications for land tenure and ownership, lineage control, and rural autonomy. Another possibility is that perhaps no one died during his or her residency of the groups' short-lived occupations. Or, if they did, the living householders took the remains of their ancestors with them from location to location as they moved around to better farm the landscape. It is also possible that areas outside of the structural remains of households were used for burials, such as cemeteries (see McCafferty, Chapter 8, for a discussion of this practice at Cholula, Mexico). At the present time, I do not believe we fully understand the variety of interment practices employed by the Late Classic Maya at Copán. It is, however, possible that the lack of remains at some rural Copán sites may signal a tradition unique to some rural inhabitants during this time period. Maya archaeologists need to consider that other locations may have been used to bury the dead, places that we have not yet conceived. Instead of looking in areas where elite burials are typically recovered, we should reorient our efforts to determine where non-elites typically buried their dead.

Caches and Cists

Caches are defined as "[i]ntentionally hidden objects or groups of objects [and t]hose that by content, grouping, or context appear to have a votive, dedicatory, or ceremonial function" (Jones 2001:87). Caches are found in domestic and non-domestic contexts as well as commoner and elite habitations and temples throughout Mesoamerica. In the Copán polity, for example, at the base of the Hieroglyphic Stairway (Structure 10L-26) underneath an altar, a deposit was uncovered containing "a lidded ceramic censer containing two jadeite pieces, a lanceolate flint knife, a shell, some ash and carbon, and some stingray and sea urchin spines. Carefully placed next to the ceramic vessel were three elaborately chipped eccentric flints" (Fash 1991:147). John Fox (1994) has studied Mesoamerican ballcourts and their caches, noting that the placement and control of those caches reveal crucial information about their meaning. These types of deposits may represent a single episode of behavior that relates to either dedication or termination, since the artifacts placed within these caches are removed from daily use. Our knowledge of the distribution of caches is necessarily focused on those material remains that have survived through the centuries, such as ceramic vessels or stone tools. Caches that consisted of only perishable materials are not usually archaeologically recoverable, reflecting a bias in the archaeological record.

Domestic caches may represent prerequisites for proper living, keeping in mind that the ritual/residential dichotomy does not in fact exist when we speak of Maya buildings. As more houses have been excavated, archaeologists have come to realize that the dedicatory deposit is a common feature of "domestic" architecture (Coe 1965). Diane Chase and Arlen Chase (1998) discuss the architectural context of caches at Caracol, Belize, and note the chronological change from ritual deposits found in centrally located monumental architecture during the Classic period to deposits found in domestic contexts located throughout the community prevalent during the Postclassic period. At Copán, caches have been recovered from dynastic and post-dynastic periods and from monumental and domestic contexts alike.

Offerings are common at domestic groups at Copán in both rural and urban residential locations. For example, Leventhal (1983:61) recorded a cached offering in one of the residences in Sepulturas, part of the Urban Core of Copán. An example from the rural commoner sites is that of a polychrome Copador vessel unearthed in the substructure of Site 7D-6-2's Structure 2, located in the Rio Amarillo area. Such offerings have been variously interpreted. From evidence at the site of Mayapan, Ledyard Smith (1962) argues that they represent the growing importance of family group worship during the Late Postclassic period. Linda Manzanilla (1987) records cists and caches at Classic Cobá and interprets them as construction offerings.

Caches are not common at every rural Type 1 residence in this Copán sample. Of the eight sites excavated, three contained caches. One cache was found at each of these sites 7D-6-2, 7D-3-1 (described later), and 34C-4-2. Caches are not present in every structure within a group. More commonly, only one of the buildings contains a cache. The location of buildings that contain caches varies, with caches found in buildings to the south, north, and west of the plaza, but not east of the plaza. The most common cached object is a polychrome ceramic vessel, some of which may be standing upright, whereas others are placed upside down. Two of the caches (7D-6-2, 7D-3-1) were found inside the centers of structures, and the third (34C-4-2) was located just north of the north retaining wall. If those structures containing the caches are the oldest within their respective groups, then

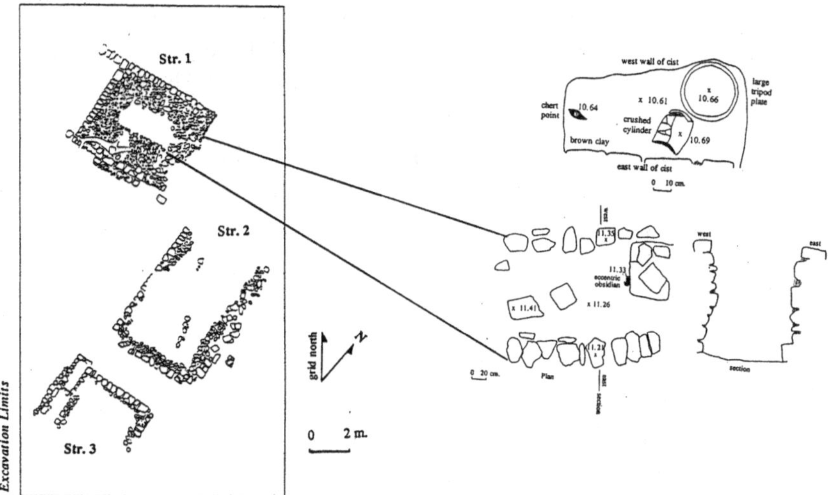

4.4. Site 7D-3-1, Copán Valley, Honduras; the cist inside Structure 1, containing ceramics, an eccentric, a spear point, and a tiny piece of jade (after original by D. Webster).

successive inhabitants may not have had to repeat such activities since they had already been performed.

One of the more elaborate caches was found at Site 7D-3-1, a three-mound group in the Rio Amarillo part of the Copán polity, which is twenty-one kilometers from the Main Group. The buildings in this group are rather unprepossessing, but Structure 1 contained a cist with cached objects. The low substructure of Structure 1 was constructed of carefully chosen cobbles arranged neatly to form an even outward line in the shape of a square measuring 4.5 meters on a side. A wattle-and-daub superstructure most likely sat atop the substructure. On the floor of the building is a capping of small cobbles placed closely together and covering the entire surface, except for a 1 x 2 m rectangular section in the middle of the structure. It is here that the inhabitants constructed a stone cist in the center of Structure 1 and placed several offerings inside it (Figure 4.4). The cist was built of several courses of rough masonry on its east and west walls and measured 70 cm high. The north and south walls were built of clay. The fill of this feature consists of hard reddish brown clay with a capping of the same material over the cist. Five artifacts were recovered: a fishhook-shaped obsidian eccentric from the surface; and from the base of the cist, two complete ceramic vessels, a 10 cm long chert spear point, and a small, extremely thin piece of jade. One of the vessels is a Caterpillar plate, about

30 cm in diameter, and is so badly eroded that no paint remains on its surface. The other vessel, a Copador cylinder, was found to the southwest of the plate on its side with its mouth toward the east. The cylinder is 16 cm high and 15 cm in diameter, with little of its paint preserved. It is unknown if the vessels had contained food offerings or cremations.

Stone cists such as these are also known to exist in low-status structures in Copán's Urban Core and outside of this area in the Copán Pocket (Fash 1983, 1985). They have been variously interpreted as burial chambers that were never used or those that were used but had their contents removed at a later date. From the architectural clues present on Structure 1 at Site 7D-3-1, it appears that the cist may have been built during the building's initial construction, and the stratigraphic profile confirms that it was not disturbed after construction. It is unknown if this cist was originally built to serve as a burial chamber, as it appears that it was used as a depository for heirlooms.

Ethnographic examples of house dedication ceremonies are plentiful in the literature (Freidel et al. 1993; Vogt 1998) and help explain these ancient deposits. With regard to the Yucatec Maya, Robert Wauchope (1938: 143) records that

> when a house is completed a hole is dug in the center of the floor and in it are placed some holy water, a sacrificed chicken, and some silver. Prayers are then offered for the safety of the house and its occupants. Incense is burned in the hole in order that the smoke may drive away evil spirits. The cache in the floor is then sealed with marl and earth. The same thing is done when the first mainpost hole is dug.

Likewise, Robert Redfield and Alfonso Villa Rojas (1934:146–147) make note of a new-house ceremony at Chan Kom, Yucatán. Rather than caching objects, sacrificial food and drink are offered to the house framing. This type of ceremony would not leave material evidence behind for the archaeologist. In some highland Mexican villages of the Tzotzil, a new-house ceremony is performed by offering food and drink to the earth or earth lord. According to Robert Laughlin (1969:179), "A rooster, a pig head, a pig's head and intestines, a sheep head or even a whole sheep may be buried in the center of the floor and cane liquor and chicken broth are poured on the roof and in the corners to 'tame' the house."

Not all rural commoner households constructed cists or cached offerings, and not all evidence has withstood the ravages of time. Variability in these practices may indicate variability in the conception of the house and its proper functioning, or the lack of durable goods as offerings may be an indicator of the choice of commoners or the dire economic circumstances of some commoners. Elite and royal members shared this aspect of house dedication ceremonies with commoners, with many partaking in a tradition that crosscut social differences. It is unknown if all commoners, or other members of society, shared the tradition of house dedication through the use of perishable goods, or if valuable cached objects were removed upon abandonment.

Ritual Artifacts: Censers, Figurines, and Candeleros in Commoner Rituals

Artifacts commonly thought to relate to religious ritual include censers, figurines, and *candeleros,* all of which have been recovered in both rural and urban areas of Copán. Censers, or *incensarios,* are vessels that are typically used to burn incense made of copal or other substances. They are not numerous in the Copán polity, judging by the percentage of rim sherds. At low-status rural sites, censer rims number less than 1 percent on average of total rims (Gonlin 1993); for urban groups, the percentage of rims ranges anywhere from 2 to 6 percent of the total (Diamanti 1991). Their limited but consistent presence, however, indicates that censers were part of a necessary "ritual kit" (see Douglass, Chapter 5) in all areas of the Copán Valley. Copal resin, blood-stained bark paper, or dried-up leaves could be offered to the deities for nourishment. Substances that produced smoke would provide visual evidence of offerings. Censers, censer stands, and incense have been recovered throughout the Maya Lowlands. For example, Roberto López Bravo (2004:256) reports on censer stands from Palenque that provided the opportunity for "heads of families [to] communicate with venerated ancestors, without the intervention of specialized priests."

Figurines have long been associated with ritual behavior, although other interpretations of their function are offered by Geoffrey McCafferty (Chapter 8) and Jan Olson (Chapter 9), depending on recovery of context. They are found throughout Mesoamerica in wide geographical and chronological contexts, from the Formative period Olmec on the Gulf Coast (Grove 1984), the Classic Zapotecs of Oaxaca (Marcus 1996), the Classic Teotihuacanos (Barba et al., Chapter 3), at Postclassic Cholula (McCafferty, Chapter 8), to the Aztecs of Postclassic times (Olson, Chapter 9). Figurines may come in human, animal, or deity form, but their specific use is unknown. They are rare artifacts in rural Copán, but are relatively common at the Classic Maya site of Piedras Negras (Kovak 2002). Only five figurines have been recovered from the eight complete excavations of rural Type 1 sites, and they are present only at the largest of these Type 1 sites, indicating variation in the distribution of this type of artifact. Julia Hendon's (2003) study on figurines from Copán's high-status neighborhood of Las Sepulturas, however, reveals a different distribution. From the excavations of thirteen groups, 511 whole or partial figurines were recovered (Hendon 2003:29). These mold-made figurines, some of which are whistles, may have originated in the complex polities in northeastern Honduras, where such figurines and whistles are common to all peoples (Hendon 2003:32; also see Douglass, Chapter 5). Does the near absence of figurines at low-status rural sites signal that householders were restricted in how they communed with their ancestors, as Marcus (1996:290) suggests for Zapotec households of Oaxaca? Or did Maya commoners at Copán commune some other way? If figurines were an important ritual component to all people in the Copán Valley, perishable materials, such as wood or corn dough, may have been used to manufacture such items (Hendon 2003:30), rather than the more durable materials of clay or stone.

Candeleros are found at most rural Type 1 sites but in low numbers. These small vessels, less than 6 cm tall with one or two holes poked in the top, may have been used to burn some substance in a ritual context and are also common to Copán's urban domestic compounds. *Candeleros* are found outside of the Maya area at Naco, Honduras. Given the context and smoke marks on them, Patricia Urban and Ellen Bell (1993:269) interpret them as "items of family-based ritual." John Douglass (Chapter 5) expands on the interpretation of *candeleros* from Naco with some interesting insights on form and function. The presence of "ritual" artifacts (censers, figurines, *candeleros*) in both low-status and high-status groups at Copán may indicate that these paraphernalia constituted elements of ritual behavior for Classic Copán and that access to these articles was not entirely restricted to elites, although the poorest of the poor may not have had the means to acquire or produce such goods, or even the desire to do so.

A number of unique artifacts provide clues about rural commoner beliefs, perhaps more so than those described previously. Several artifacts stand out as highly significant to the pursuit of understanding commoner ritual. Small sculptures, a mirror, bark beaters, and food remains, although rare, are not unknown at rural commoner sites, and are discussed in detail later.

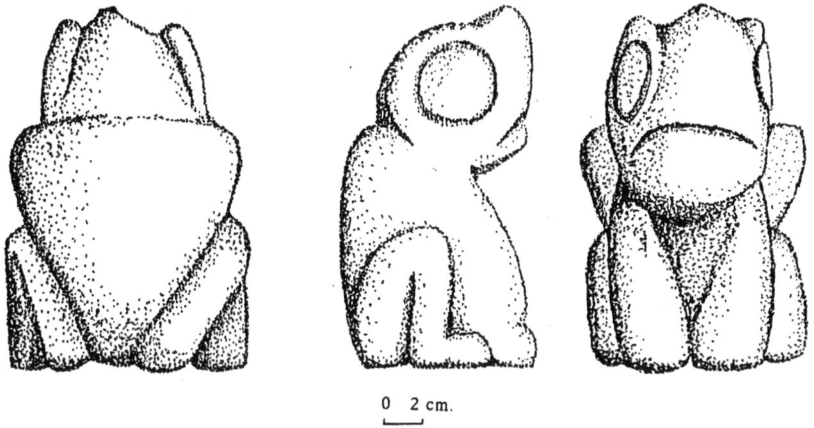

4.5. Frog/toad sculpture in green tuff recovered from Structure 1-sub, Site 11D-11-2, Copán Valley, Honduras (after original by D. Webster).

Small Sculptures in Commoner Rituals

Small sculptures of toads or frogs were recovered from two different sites in the rural area, one at 11D-11-2 in the El Jaral area (Figure 4.5) and another at 7D-3-1 in Rio Amarillo, both of which date to the peak of Copán's population during the eighth century A.D. Frogs or toads are pictured on Maya vessels (Benson and Griffin 1988) and in Maya codices (Tozzer and Glover 1910). They are especially prominent at Copán and are featured in the Main Group at Sepulturas (Willey et al. 1994:348) and at a site in the rural Copán Pocket, locally known as El Sapo ("the Toad") because of its amphibian petroglyphs. Bell (2002:96) reports that a carved stone monument associated with the Margarita tomb in the Main Group holds the inscription *Siyah K'ak'*, which possibly translates to "Smoking Frog," which relates to a warlord from Teotihuacan noted at Tikal in the fourth century. The "upended frog glyph" noted by Tatiana Proskouriakoff (1961:231) is used to denote the birth date of a noble. Toad/frog iconography has a wide geographic distribution in Mesoamerica, appearing at sites such as Teotihuacan (Manzanilla 2000), Monte Albán (Winter et al., Chapter 7), the Aztec Templo Mayor (Moctezuma 1999), Cholula (McCafferty, Chapter 8), Izapa and Cacaxtla (Miller and Taube 1993), as well as a lengthy temporal span from Formative to Postclassic times and beyond (Manzanilla 2000).

The Maya may have put these batrachian creatures to many uses, which Emery (2001) describes. Frogs may have been a part of ancient diets as meat for stews and tamales. Toads have long been associated with shamanistic rituals; one particular species, *Bufo marinus,* is noted for its hallucinogenic properties (Davis and Weil 1992), although Peter Furst (2001:374) rules out this species for "ecstatic-visionary purposes" because of the extreme toxicity of its secretions. Herpetological fauna, including frogs, toads, and snakes, all had ceremonial importance and strong symbolism associated with rain, fertility, and water (see Winter et al., Chapter 7, and McCafferty, Chapter 8), and not just for elites.

Modern Maya perform rites using frogs or toads, as recorded by Redfield and Villa Rojas (1934:138–143) at Chan Kom. Frogs and toads figure prominently in agricultural rituals of ethnographically known Chorti (Girard 1949:604–609), and there is an association between the fiesta dedicated to Itzamná, the rain deity, and the toad. As retold by Elizabeth Benson and Gillet Griffin (1988:338, 340):

> During the explicit prayer for rain, four boys performing as frogs were tied to the altar, a bound wooden structure. An impersonator of the chief Chac (rain god) was carried to a cleared space called the *chun-ca'an,* meaning "trunk of heaven." Here, while the boys imitated the chirping of frogs, the Chac impersonator occasionally rose and emitted a sound imitating the rumbling of thunder. Along with the scaffold form of the altar and the bound individuals, the Chan Kom *ch'a-chaac* ceremony seems to have retained much of the prehispanic symbolism associated with the Classic Pax God. The frogs and growling sound recall the jaguar attributes of the deity; moreover, the Chac impersonator is placed in the space termed the "trunk of heaven," thus, in effect, becoming both the tree and the god.

The amphibian counterpart of the jaguar is the toad (Benson and Griffin 1988:342–343), which may represent birth or water symbolism, as its depiction on stelae from Piedras Negras suggests. Thus, accession glyphs and the renewal of the agricultural cycle are linked iconographically, perhaps symbolizing the importance of the cyclical nature of the kingdom. The scaffold ceremony or human sacrifice marks the beginning of the planting season and was an auspicious event in Classic times. Blood from the victim represents the raindrops. Sacrificial ceremonies may have been performed during late winter or early spring, when planting was started.

Given the obvious ties among toads/frogs, the agricultural cycle, fertility, birth, and rain, it is not surprising that batrachian sculptures were found in the rural area of Copán and particularly at two farmstead sites dating to the peak population of the valley. As representations of rain or fertility, these two small sculptures may have been placed on the family shrine and their namesakes called on to ensure a bountiful crop or plentiful rain. Davíd Carrasco (1990:99) notes, "All the Maya, but especially the peasants, worshipped the chacs, who were associated with the four world directions from which flowed the rain that nurtured the fields and trees." Frogs may have figured prominently in shamanistic rituals of the local group. The recovery of frog/toad sculptures in rural Copán, their presence in urban and royal areas of the polity, and their widespread distribution in Mesoamerica may speak of widely held, long-lasting beliefs.

Water symbolism was not only significant to the farming populations of Maya polities but crucial to the ruling lineages that were associated with aqueous symbols (Davis-Salazar 2003). Recently, a case has been made for water control's role in the collapse of the Classic Maya. In Lisa Lucero's (2002:822) model, "Creating and controlling critical resources in the form of water-management systems in conjunction with the use of integrative strategies such as ceremonies provided a powerful, centripetal political tool for Maya rulers of regional centers." Evidence from rural households given previously suggests that elite control of such symbols was not exclusive, even though the types of symbols may have differed. Karla Davis-Salazar (2003) finds the water-lily motif to be prevalent in elite contexts among both royals and non-royals of Copán's Urban Core, but this motif has not been recovered in low-status rural domiciles. Even though Lucero (2002:820) claims that minor centers did not contain water imagery, perhaps more intensive household excavations would reveal a wider distribution than what is presently known. Furthermore, research by Estella Weiss-Krecji and Thomas Sabbas (2002) demonstrates the possibility that the control of water may have been at the household level, or, as suggested by Davis-Salazar (2003), it may have been at the community level.

In addition to the two small frog sculptures, a finely executed miniature stone sculpture of an altar (Figure 4.6) was recovered from one of the largest Type 1 sites in the valley, Site 34C-4-2. The altar's dimensions are 17 x 9.5 x 9 cm high. Obviously in a secondary context, this sculpture was apparently tossed or had fallen in the fill of the plaza in front of the southern structure (Structure 3). One can imagine its use in ritual within a household context, as it would have provided a smooth flat surface on which to place offerings. Alternative interpretations of this artifact are that it represents a house or a bench, or that it is some kind of grinding platform.

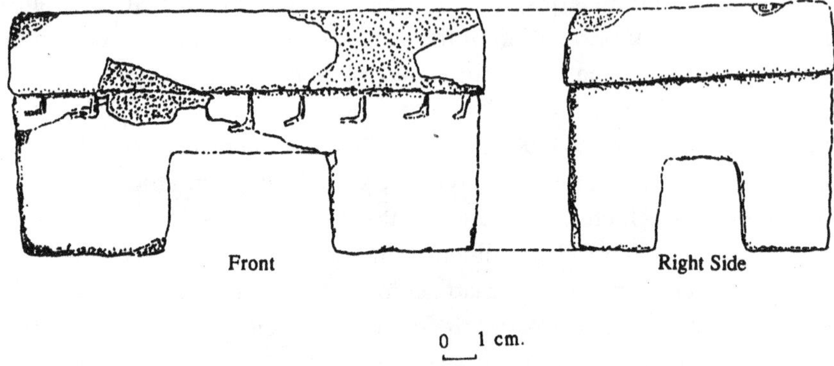

4.6. Drawing of the miniature altar recovered in front of Structure 3, Site 34C-4-2, Copán Valley, Honduras (after original by D. Webster).

Its similarity to carved stone benches, like the one found in Sepulturas at Plaza A of 9N-8 (Webster 1989), must be considered in analyzing the function of this small carving. Similar artifacts recovered from Sepulturas Type 2 and Type 3 groups (Willey et al. 1994:260–261) are labeled "stone tables" and are thought to have functioned in some ritual capacity. These stone tables sometimes have burning marks on the top surface, and one was recovered as one of nine objects in a domestic cache with polished black stones. One of the stone tables in this collection shows evidence for grinding, indicating that it functioned as a mortar.

Mirrors in Commoner Ritual

At Site 7D-3-1, where one of the frog effigies and a cist were recovered, a polished mirror was also found. It is a small round object composed of some type of iron-bearing mineral and is one of the few mirrors found at Copán, although they are not entirely unknown. A pyrite mirror was reclaimed from the Margarita tomb on Copán's acropolis (Bell 2002:99). A few mirrors (seven or eight) were recovered from Harvard's excavations in the Sepulturas urban zone (Willey et al. 1994:251) from Type 1, 2, and 3 sites, further indicating that their distribution is not limited to elite or royal contexts. Mirrors are also recovered at other Maya sites. One such object was found in the recent excavations at Piedras Negras (Webster 2001) associated with a sweatbath, and several mirrors were found at Structure M8-4 at Aguateca, prompting archaeologists there to nickname that structure "The House of the Mirrors" (Inomata et al. 2002).

Mirrors are associated with rulership as well as divination (Pohl and Pohl 1983:51; Taube 1992:30), and they are equated with supernatural caves, as both mirrors and caves are portals to another world (Brady and Ashmore 1999:137). Mirrors have been used for centuries by ancient Mesoamericans to decorate the body (Joyce 2001). Their purpose of observing oneself must also be considered.

Bark Beaters in Commoner Rituals

Bark beaters, used in the manufacture of paper, are distributed widely in time and space throughout Mesoamerica. Paper is portrayed iconographically in elite Maya art (Schele and Miller 1986) for use in the scribal arts, bloodletting ceremonies, and cloth manufacture. Although not ubiquitous, bark beaters have been recovered at Copán from both elite (Willey et al. 1994) and non-elite domiciles (Gonlin 1993). As Patricia McAnany and Shannon Plank (2001:92) so aptly state, "What cannot be determined at this time is whether the produced paper was used for household records, worn, ritually burned, traded, or 'offered' as tribute to a local ruler." Rural Copán commoners may very well have participated in bloodletting rituals in much the same fashion as their elite counterparts. The equipment for such activities, obsidian blades and bark beaters (as symbols of paper), are recovered at some, but not all, households. Three rural commoner residences in different parts of the Copán Valley (7D-3-1, 32B-16-1, and 34C-4-2) produced one bark beater each. There is no reason to assume rural commoners were not the consumers of these objects since they were the ones controlling the productive technology. Inter-household exchange may have been necessary for polity-wide distribution of paper and cloth. The uneven distribution of bark beaters may signal different ritual practices, clothing, economic activities, or ancient curation of such valuable artifacts among households of the polity, or it simply may reveal differences in modern recovery processes.

Food in Commoner Rituals

Food remains provide additional clues about potential ritual practices. The use of intoxicants in ritual has a long global history from ancient to modern times and particularly in Mexico and Central America (Bruman 2000). Fermented beverages, plant hallucinogens, intoxicating snuff, and intoxicating enemas were all methods used for achieving altered states

(Furst 2001). It is well-known that the "Mexican Indians also practiced ritual intoxication with alcohol made from fermented fruits, maize, honey, and sap (distillation was unknown anywhere in the Americas prior to the Spanish invasion)" (Furst 2001:371). Farther south in the Copán region, a variety of plants existed that could provide the ingredients for intoxicating beverages. Maize can be fermented by a number of methods and a form of fermented maize may have been a beverage consumed by people of all statuses in Maya society, based on the recovery of *Zea mays* remains at all types of sites throughout the Copán polity. However, the archaeobotanical remains of maize at Copán (Lentz 1991) and from isotope studies, which show a high degree of maize consumption (Reed 1998:43–44), do not reveal whether Copanecos were consuming tortillas or beer since the stable isotope ratios are not affected by food preparation (Marino and DeNiro 1987). The production of wine may have been possible by using wild grapes (Lentz 1991) or coyol (Bruman 2000; McKillop 1996), both of which have been recovered in rural Copán. It is known that coyol palms were found throughout the Copán Valley (Lentz 1990) as evidenced by the recovery of coyol nut fragments and nutting stones (Gonlin 1993, n.d.). The sap from which coyol wine is made may also have been collected and processed. Alcohol or other substances may have been a desired or even essential ingredient for ritual performance among Copán commoners.

The shells of the *jute* snail (*Pachychilus*) provide us with an example that ties together two loci of ritual performance, the homestead and the cave. Although caves are not explicitly discussed in this chapter, they may have figured importantly in commoner and elite rituals alike (Brady and Prufer 2005). Recent work by Halperin and colleagues (2003) has shown that although *jute* subsistence uses are well documented (Healy et al. 1990), ritual uses of *jutes* have been less discussed. In a survey of the southern Maya Lowlands, numerous caves are reported to contain deposits of *jutes*. Their presence may be accounted for by the fact that, after consumption in the household, they were deposited within the cave to return them to Mother Earth. Alternatively, *jute* consumption may have occurred in the caves themselves. *Jutes* are also found in association with burials and may have served as food for the dead in the afterlife (Halperin et al. 2003:216). The activity of secondary deposition of *jute* shells in caves may account for the pattern observed at rural Copán, where some commoner households contained abundant *jute* remains (386 *jutes* at 34A-12-2 and 676 *jutes* at 99A-18-2), whereas other households contained very few (2 *jutes* at 11D-11-2 and 3 *jutes* at 34A-12-1) or none (7D-6-2, 7D-3-1, 34B-16-1, 34C-4-2).

Alternatively, this distribution may represent differences in procurement and consumption.

SUMMARY OF THE "CONTENT" OF LATE CLASSIC RURAL MAYA COMMONER RITUALS

Much of the above artifactual evidence relates to three main subjects of rituals. According to McAnany and Plank (2001:table 4.2), ritual practices essential to a household are divided into three categories: mortuary/ancestor, "house" dedication, and agricultural/calendrical. The evidence for such household activities exists at all social levels in Classic society, perhaps indicating the strength of shared traditions not only within the Copán polity but across the Maya Lowlands as well. Those ritual practices for which little importance is assigned at the household level—but which are important in the royal courtyards of the Maya according to McAnany and Plank—include succession/heir designation, military/ballgame exercises, and territory delimitation (on a polity-wide scale, as opposed to the delineation of space at the household level). Yet, it is clear from discussions of the distributions of some artifacts (e.g., censers, *candeleros*, and frog images) that ritual paraphernalia was shared throughout Copán society, perhaps indicating some shared beliefs.

THE "PERFORMERS" OF RURAL MAYA COMMONER RITUALS

The "performers" (following Marcus 1999:71) of household rituals in Copán's countryside would most likely have been all the members of the household, but individuals would have participated in different capacities, depending on age, gender, ability, and status. Surely there was a division of labor along the lines of gender for ritual performances and differences between men and women in the perception of such activities. Household heads, whether male or female, may have held a special position in the group, as variations in status characterized the family grouping. One would expect that household heads led ritual proceedings. They may have been the keepers of ritual paraphernalia and the decision-makers as to what times were best for the performance of certain rituals. This information would have been passed down in the enculturation process to younger family members. Household heads may have been the ones chosen to be buried within the compound or, alternatively, at another sacred location (since many low-status rural sites did not contain burials). Differences in gendered activities varied by status, with royal and elite women most likely performing different tasks than commoner women. A similar situation prevailed for men as well. It is not necessary, or may not even be appropriate, to interpret the ritual roles of commoner men and women from portrayals of royal men and women, since it is likely that both genders participated in ritual activities and that each likely had their own ideologies as well.

Paraphrasing Gabrielle Vail and Andrea Stone (2002:224), information provided by Colonial documents in the Yucatán and from ethnographic accounts of the Maya suggests that old women (i.e., postmenopausal) were particularly instrumental in the performance of public ritual, being allowed to dance and conduct certain ceremonies. Women of productive age, sexually and economically speaking, likely contributed to rituals in the provision of food and drink (Joyce 1993; McCafferty, Chapter 8; Pohl 1991), if not in a more public capacity.

Shamans may have been either men or women perceived to have special powers. Although it is not known for certain if any of the rural inhabitants who lived in the Copán countryside were indeed shamans, the remains of the mirror found at Site 7D-3-1 perhaps provide a small hint that some may have been. The possible ritual structure at Site 11D-11-2 may provide additional clues to where some shamanistic ceremonies were performed.

The role of children in rituals is still unknown for the Late Classic Maya, but it is likely they were both active and passive participants, with various roles depending on the occasion. Presumably, young Maya farming children most often accompanied their parents, who would have been responsible for their socialization into appropriate ritual behaviors, whether these activities occurred within the confines of their own courtyard, at the courtyard of the lineage head in the Urban Core, or in the Great Plaza in the Main Group. The ethnographic account by Benson and Griffin (1988) cited previously and recent ethnographic work by Karen Kramer (1998) on Maya children indicate that children were indeed vital actors in ritual performance. Children at times may have been the objects of ritual for events such as naming ceremonies or those rituals involving rites of passage into adulthood.

The men and women central to commoner ritual behavior were not confined to household members alone. As previously stated in the discussion of the loci of ritual performance, commoners likely participated in polity-wide festivities run by kings and queens and also in large corporate group functions headed by elite men and women. In other words, commoners invited people of varying statuses to share in their ritual lives.

SUMMARY AND CONCLUSIONS

One of the most productive paths by which to understand ancient ritual and ideology is to undertake analyses of household remains. In this manner, people of all social levels can be considered in reconstructions of past belief systems. At Copán, where a rich body of data exists across a wide spectrum both socially and geographically, this approach has been particularly fruitful. The evidence that exists to reveal the rituals, and hence ideology, of the past is more abundant than what one might initially suppose for the commoners of Copán. When households of various statuses can be compared, patterns of consumption are revealed that indicate whether particular artifacts are exclusive to one group or another. Additionally, for many people throughout the world, past and present, the landscape beyond their abodes figures prominently in ritual behavior. Although this chapter has not dealt with natural features imbued with symbolic significance, such as caves or mountaintops, features on the landscape provide information pertaining to ideologies that are equally important (see Uruñuela and Plunket, Chapter 2, and Douglass, Chapter 5; Brady and Prufer 2005). Other parts of the built environment besides domiciles, such as agricultural fields, likely served as loci for ritual activity (McAnany 1995).

There are many lines of evidence to suggest that the low-status rural inhabitants of the Copán kingdom enjoyed a rich ritual life and were active participants in their own spiritual well-being. Some commoners and elites had access to the same ritual paraphernalia, such as *candeleros* and censers, and likely had similar ceremonies pertaining to house dedications, ancestor worship, and agriculture. Or phrased another way, one could potentially see the same kinds of ritual activities occurring in both low- and high-status households. Dominant themes at Copán, such as frog iconography, crossed into royal and commoner and urban and rural realms alike. The consumption of particular foodstuffs, such as *jutes* or alcoholic beverages, likewise extended across the social spectrum. As integral parts of the polity, commoners would have had ample reason, above and beyond economic gain or obligations, to journey to the site core to witness historical events and to partake in lineage ceremonies. These two levels of interaction fall outside the geographic locale of the commoner household but constituted part of the ideological makeup of the common people. The presence of burials, caches, effigies, and artifacts such as censers, figurines, and *candeleros*, although recovered in lower numbers than in higher-ranking urban groups, may indicate similar patterns of behavior and belief for some commoner inhabitants. We do not know, however, if these behaviors and beliefs were identical and exactly to what extent rural commoners subscribed to some predominating ideology. Architectural analysis shows that the location of ritual activities may not have been as compartmentalized as it was in Copán's Urban Core, a difference that may be more indicative of status differences than other sociocultural factors. The material record seems to support two views: (1) shared practices that transcended social boundaries at Copán, and (2) idiosyncratic practices observed on the domestic level. Not all commoner households shared equally in all material remains, suggesting diversity of practices and expression within this varied group of people. Variations in the material record, such as architecture, burials, and distributions of artifacts and features, suggest that Classic Maya commoners at Copán were not a monolithic entity, nor were they simply mimicking elite patterns of behavior and thought. Their decision to partake in those traditions within their own households indicates a connection to the wider Maya culture of Copán while simultaneously creating unique practices imbued with meanings known only to them. At Copán, where household assemblages are similar from urban to rural areas, from elite to commoner households, it is not surprising to find that material evidence of ancient rituals, and hence ideologies, crosscut society. The degree to which commoners at Copán were influenced or dominated by a "dominant ideology" may be debated, depending on whether one focuses on the material similarities or the differences. Shared beliefs hold together any society, but identifying whether those beliefs are forced on members or are readily accepted and used to benefit all individuals can provide information about commoners and elites alike.

ACKNOWLEDGMENTS

I gratefully acknowledge the thoughtful advice of Trina Ballard, John G. Douglass, Jon Lohse, David M. Reed, K. Viswanathan, and David Webster, all of whom have greatly improved this chapter. Many thanks to the anonymous reviewers who helped me reorient this contribution to address more substantial questions. I am grateful for the support of Bellevue Community College and, in particular, my colleagues in the Social Science

Division; Frances J. Peppard's and Pamela Quinter's technical expertise; and Benayah Israel's interlibrary loan skills. Darrin Pratt at the University Press of Colorado was instrumental in making this chapter a worthy contribution, and Laura Furney at UPC is a copy editor extraordinaire. Gratitude to the Instituto Hondureño de Antropología for allowing me to present material on Copán.

NOTES

1. Copán's site hierarchy, detailed by Gordon Willey and Richard Leventhal (1979), is given briefly as follows. The "Main Group" in the Copán Pocket where the monumental remains of palaces, temples, ballcourts, and grand plazas are located is referred to as a Type 5 site. There is only one such site in the settlement hierarchy. The elite Type 4 sites are those that have several courtyard groupings of structures, some of which may have a height of 10 m or more; remains of sculpture may be present as well as corbelling and dressed stone. Type 4 sites are primarily located near the Main Group in the Copán Pocket, the largest alluvial deposit in the valley. The elite Type 3 sites may have 6 or more structures arranged around 1 to 3 courtyards, with mound height less than 5 m, and dressed stone and vault stones are likely present. Both Type 3 and Type 4 sites also contain less elaborate architecture similar to that found in Type 1 and Type 2 sites that are thought to have been lived in or used by commoners. Type 2 sites typically have 6 to 8 mounds arranged in 1 or 2 courtyards. Mound height is less than 5 m and construction may include dressed stone with cobbles. Type 1 sites are by far the most numerous and typically have 3 to 5 mounds around a single courtyard. Remains are less than 1 m in height and cobble construction predominates, although dressed stone may be present. Freter (1988:75) has added the category of "aggregate site" to connote Type 1 structures that have no formal courtyard arrangement and no presence of dressed stone. In this analysis, aggregate sites are combined with Type 1 sites. Type 1 and Type 2 sites represent the remains of independent commoner habitations. Single mound sites may be the remains of large, tall temple buildings or small isolated field huts. In addition, artifact scatters are labeled as non-mound sites.

2. The caves at Copán, known as locations of ritual activities, have been investigated by many researchers, from the earliest (Gordon 1896) to more recent (Brady 1995; Brady and Prufer 2005; Rue et al. 1989). Although caves have great importance and multiple meanings to Mesoamericans in general (Brady 1988; Vogt 1981), they are not the specific focus of analysis in this chapter. Classic Maya commoner rituals probably also occurred in other locales, such as agricultural fields, mountaintops, or gravesides, as noted for the sixteenth-century Zapotec by Marcus (1996:287).

REFERENCES CITED

Abrams, Elliot

1994 *How the Maya Built Their World: Energetics and Architecture*. University of Texas Press, Austin.

Andrews, E. Wyllys, and William L. Fash (editors)

2005 *Copán: The History of an Ancient Maya Kingdom*. School of American Research, Santa Fe.

Becker, Marshall Joseph

1986 Household Shrines at Tikal, Guatemala: Size as a Reflection of Economic Status. *Revista Española de Antropología Americana* 14:81–85.

Bell, Ellen E.

2002 Engendering a Dynasty: A Royal Woman in the Margarita Tomb, Copán. In *Ancient Maya Women*, edited by Traci Ardren, pp. 89–104. Altamira Press, Walnut Creek.

Benson, Elizabeth, and Gillet G. Griffin (editors)

1988 *Maya Iconography*. Princeton University Press, Princeton.

Brady, James E.

1988 The Sexual Connotation of Caves in Mesoamerican Ideology. *Mexicon* 10:51–55.

1995 A Reassessment of the Chronology and Function of Gordon's Cave #3, Copán, Honduras. *Ancient Mesoamerica* 6:29–38.

Brady, James E., and Wendy Ashmore

1999 Mountains, Caves, Water: Ideational Landscapes of the Ancient Maya. In *Archaeologies of Landscape: Contemporary Perspectives*, edited by Wendy Ashmore and A. Bernard Knapp, pp. 124–145. Blackwell, Oxford.

Brady, James E., and Keith M. Prufer (editors)

2005 *In the Maw of the Earth Monster*. University of Texas Press, Austin.

Brown, Linda A., and Andrea I. Gerstle

2002 Structure 10: Feasting and Village Festivals. In *Before the Volcano Erupted: The Ancient Ceren Village in Central America*, edited by Payson Sheets, pp. 97–103. University of Texas Press, Austin.

Bruman, Henry J.

2000 *Alcohol in Ancient Mexico*. University of Utah Press, Salt Lake City.

Canuto, Marcello A.

2002 A Tale of Two Communities: Social and Political Transformation in the Hinterlands of the Maya Polity of Copán. Ph.D. dissertation, University of Pennsylvania. University Microfilms, Ann Arbor.

Carrasco, Davíd

1990 *Religions of Mesoamerica: Cosmovision and Ceremonial Centers*. Waveland Press, Prospect Heights.

Chase, Diane Z., and Arlen F. Chase

1998 The Architectural Context of Caches, Burials, and Other Ritual Activities for the Classic Period Maya (as Reflected at Caracol, Belize). In *Function and Meaning in Classic Maya Architecture,* edited by Stephen D. Houston, pp. 299–332. Dumbarton Oaks, Washington, D.C.

Coe, William R.

1965 Caches and Offertory Practices of the Maya Lowlands. In *Handbook of Middle American Indians,* Volume 2, *Archaeology of Southern Mesoamerica,* Part 1, edited by Gordon R. Willey, pp. 462–468. Robert Wauchope, general editor. University of Texas Press, Austin.

Davis, Wade, and Andrew T. Weil

1992 Identity of a New World Psychoactive Toad. *Ancient Mesoamerica* 3:51–59.

Davis-Salazar, Karla

2003 Late Classic Water Management and Community Organization at Copán, Honduras. *Latin American Antiquity* 14:275–299.

Deal, Michael

1987 Ritual Space and Architecture in the Highland Maya Household. In *Mirror and Metaphor: Material and Social Constructions of Reality,* edited by Daniel W. Ingersoll and Gordon Bronitsky, pp. 171–198. University Press of America, Lanham.

Diamanti, Melissa

1991 Domestic Organization at Copán: Reconstruction of Elite Maya Households Through Ethnographic Models. Ph.D. dissertation, Pennsylvania State University. University Microfilms, Ann Arbor.

Emery, Kitty

2001 Fauna. In *Archaeology of Ancient Mexico and Central America: An Encyclopedia,* edited by Susan Toby Evans and David L. Webster, pp. 255–265. Garland Publishing, New York.

Fash, William L., Jr.

1983 Maya State Formation: A Case Study and Its Implications. Ph.D. dissertation, Harvard University. University Microfilms, Ann Arbor.

1985 Excavations at CV-16. Manuscript on file, Department of Anthropology, Pennsylvania State University, University Park.

1991 *Scribes, Warriors, and Kings: The City of Copán and the Ancient Maya.* Thames and Hudson, London.

2001 *Scribes, Warriors, and Kings: The City of Copán and the Ancient Maya.* Revised edition. Thames and Hudson, London.

Fox, John Gerard

1994 Putting the Heart Back in the Court: Ballcourts and Ritual Action in Mesoamerica. Ph.D. dissertation, Harvard University. University Microfilms, Ann Arbor.

Freidel, David, and Linda Schele

1989 Dead Kings and Living Temples: Dedication and Termination Rituals Among the Ancient Maya. In *Word and Image in Maya Culture: Explorations in Language, Writing, and Representation,* edited by William F. Hanks and Don S. Rice, pp. 233–243. University of Utah Press, Salt Lake City.

Freidel, David, Linda Schele, and Joy Parker

1993 *Maya Cosmos: Three Thousand Years on the Shaman's Path.* William Morrow and Company, New York.

Freter, AnnCorinne

1988 The Classic Maya Collapse at Copán, Honduras: A Regional Settlement Perspective. Ph.D. dissertation, Pennsylvania State University. University Microfilms, Ann Arbor.

Furst, Peter

2001 Intoxicants and Intoxication. In *Archaeology of Ancient Mexico and Central Mexico: An Encyclopedia,* edited by Susan Toby Evans and David L. Webster, pp. 371–375. Garland Publishing, New York.

Gillespie, Susan D.

2000 Maya "Nested Houses": The Ritual Construction of Place. In *Beyond Kinship: Social and Material Reproduction in House Societies,* edited by Rosemary A. Joyce and Susan D. Gillespie, pp. 135–160. University of Pennsylvania Press, Philadelphia.

Girard, Rafael

1949 *Los Chortis ante el problema Maya, Tomo 11.* Impreso en las Editorial Cultura, T. G., S. A. Guatemala, No. 96. Mexico, D.F.

Goddard, S.

1965 Town-Farm Relationships in Yorubaland: A Case Study from Oyo. *Africa* 35:21–29.

Gonlin, Nancy

1993 Rural Household Archaeology at Copán, Honduras. Ph.D. dissertation, Pennsylvania State University. University Microfilms, Ann Arbor.

1996 Methodological Analysis of the Copán Testing Program. In *Arqueología Mesoamericana: Homenaje a William T. Sanders,* edited by Alba Guadalupe

Mastache, Jeffrey R. Parsons, Robert S. Santley, and Mari Carmen Serra Puche, pp. 231–252. Instituto Nacional de Antropología e Historia, Mexico, D.F.

2004 Methods for Understanding Classic Maya Commoners: Structure Function, Energetics, and More. In *Ancient Maya Commoners*, edited by Jon Lohse and Fred Valdez Jr., pp. 395–446. University of Texas Press, Austin.

n.d. Production and Consumption in the Countryside: A Perspective from Late Classic Commoner Households at Copán, Honduras. In *Ancient Households of the Americas: Conceptualizing What Households Do*, edited by John G. Douglass and Nancy Gonlin. University Press of Colorado, Boulder, forthcoming.

Gordon, George B.

1896 *The Prehistoric Ruins of Copán, Honduras*. Memoirs of the Peabody Museum, Harvard University, Volume 1, No. 1, Cambridge.

Gossen, Gary H., and Richard M. Leventhal

1993 The Topography of Ancient Maya Religious Pluralism: A Dialogue with the Present. In *Lowland Maya Civilization in the Eighth Century A.D.*, edited by Jeremy A. Sabloff and John S. Henderson, pp. 185–217. Dumbarton Oaks, Washington, D.C.

Grove, David C.

1984 *Chalcatzingo: Excavations on the Olmec Frontier*. Thames and Hudson, London.

Halperin, Christina T., Sergio Garza, Keith M. Prufer, and James E. Brady

2003 Caves and Ancient Maya Ritual Use of *Jute*. *Latin American Antiquity* 14:207–219.

Haviland, William A.

1985 *Excavations in Small Residential Groups of Tikal: Groups 4F-1 and 4F-2*. University Museum, University of Pennsylvania, Philadelphia.

Healy, Paul F., Kitty Emergy, and Lori Wright

1990 Ancient and Modern Maya Exploitation of the *Jute* Snail (*Pachychilus*). *Latin American Antiquity* 1:170–183.

Hendon, Julia A.

1987 The Uses of Maya Structures: A Study of Architecture and Artifact Distribution at Sepulturas, Copán, Honduras. Ph.D. dissertation, Harvard University. University Microfilms, Ann Arbor.

1989 Elite Household Organization at Copán, Honduras: Analysis of Activity Distribution in the Sepulturas Zone. In *Households and Communities, Proceedings of the 21st Annual Chacmool Conference*, edited by Scott MacEachern, David J.W. Archer, and Richard D. Garvin, pp.

371–380. The Archaeological Association of the University of Calgary, Calgary.

1991 Status and Power in Classic Maya Society: An Archaeological Study. *American Anthropologist* 93:894–918.

2003 In the House—Maya Nobility and Their Figurine-Whistles. *Expedition* 45:28–33.

Iannone, Gyles, and Samuel V. Connell (editors)

2003 *Perspectives on Ancient Maya Rural Complexity*. Monograph 49, Cotsen Institute of Archaeology. University of California, Los Angeles.

Inomata, Takeshi, Daniela Triadan, Erick Ponciano, Estela Pinto, Richard E. Terry, and Markus Eberl

2002 Domestic and Political Lives of Classic Maya Elites: The Excavation of Rapidly Abandoned Structures at Aguateca, Guatemala. *Latin American Antiquity* 13:305–330.

Jones, Christopher

2001 Caches. In *Archaeology of Ancient Mexico and Central America: An Encyclopedia,* edited by Susan Toby Evans and David L. Webster, pp. 87–88. Garland Publishing, New York.

Joyce, Rosemary

1993 Women's Work: Images of Production and Reproduction in Prehispanic Southern Central America. *Current Anthropology* 34:255–274.

2001 Negotiating Sex and Gender in Classic Maya Society. In *Gender in Prehispanic America: A Symposium at Dumbarton Oaks 12 and 13 October 1996,* edited by Cecelia F. Klein, pp. 109–141. Dumbarton Oaks, Washington, D.C.

Kovak, Amy

2002 Children's Toys or Important Ritual Objects? Figurines from Piedras Negras, Guatemala. Paper presented at the 67th Annual Meeting of the Society for American Archaeology, Denver.

Kramer, Karen

1998 Variation in Children's Work Among Modern Maya Subsistence Agriculturalists. Ph.D. dissertation, University of New Mexico. University Microfilms, Ann Arbor.

Laughlin, Robert M.

1969 The Tzotzil. In *Handbook of Middle American Indians,* Volume 7, *Ethnology,* edited by Evon Z. Vogt, pp. 152–194. University of Texas Press, Austin.

Lentz, David

1990 *Acrocomia mexicana*: Palm of the Ancient Mesoamericans. *Journal of Ethnobiology* 10:183–194.

1991 Maya Diets of the Rich and Poor: Paleoethnobotanical Evidence from Copán. *Latin American Antiquity* 2:269–287.

Leventhal, Richard M.

1983 Household Groups and Classic Maya Religion. In *Prehistoric Settlement Patterns: Essays in Honor of Gordon R. Willey*, edited by Evon Z. Vogt and Richard M. Leventhal, pp. 55–76. University of New Mexico Press and Peabody Museum of Archaeology and Ethnology, Harvard University, Cambridge.

López Bravo, Roberto

2004 State and Domestic Cult in Palenque Censer Stands. In *Courtly Art of the Ancient Maya*, edited by Mary Miller and Simon Martin, pp. 256–258. Fine Arts Museum of San Francisco, San Francisco.

Lucero, Lisa J.

2002 The Collapse of the Classic Maya: A Case for the Role of Water Control. *American Anthropologist* 104:814–826.

Mallory, John K., III

1981 Especializacion economica en el Valle de Copán: Excavaciones en "El Duende." *Yaxkin* 4:171–178.

Manzanilla, Linda (editor)

1987 *Cobá, Quintana Roo: Análisis de dos unidades habitacionales Mayas*. Instituto de Investigaciones Antropológicas, Serie Antropologica 82. Universidad Nacional Autónoma de Mexico, D.F.

2000 The Construction of the Underworld in Central Mexico. In *Mesoamerica's Classic Heritage: From Teotihuacan to the Aztecs*, edited by Davíd Carrasco, Lindsay Jones, and Scott Session, pp. 87–116. University Press of Colorado, Boulder.

Marcus, Joyce

1996 The Importance of Context in Interpreting Figurines. *Cambridge Archaeological Journal* 6:285–291.

1999 Men's and Women's Ritual in Formative Oaxaca. In *Social Patterns in Pre-Classic Mesoamerica*, edited by David C. Grove and Rosemary A. Joyce, pp. 67–96. Dumbarton Oaks, Washington, D.C.

Marino, B. D., and M. J. DeNiro

1987 Isotopic Analysis of Archaeobotanicals to Reconstruct Past Climates: Effects of Activities Associated with Food Preparation on Carbon, Hydrogen, and Oxygen Isotope Ratios of Plant Cellulose. *Journal of Archaeological Science* 14:537–548.

McAnany, Patricia A.

1995 *Living with the Ancestors: Kinship and Kingship in Ancient Maya Society*. University of Texas Press, Austin.

McAnany, Patricia A., and Shannon Plank

2001 Perspectives on Actors, Gender Roles, and Architecture at Classic Maya Courts and Households. In *Royal Courts of the Ancient Maya,* Volume 1, *Theory, Comparison, Synthesis*, edited by Takeshi Inomata and Stephen D. Houston, pp. 84–129. Westview Press, Boulder.

McKillop, Heather

1996 Prehistoric Maya Use of Native Palms: Archaeobotanical and Ethnobotanical Evidence. In *The Managed Mosaic: Ancient Maya Agriculture and Resource Use,* edited by Scott L. Fedick, pp. 278–294. University of Utah Press, Salt Lake City.

Miller, Mary, and Simon Martin

2004 *Courtly Art of the Ancient Maya*. Fine Arts Museum of San Francisco, San Francisco.

Miller, Mary, and Karl Taube

1993 *An Illustrated Dictionary of the Gods and Symbols of Ancient Mexico and the Maya*. Thames and Hudson, New York.

Moctezuma, Eduardo Matos

1999 The Templo Mayor of Tenochtitlan: Cosmic Center of the Aztec Universe. In *Mesoamerican Architecture as a Cultural Symbol,* edited by Jeff Karl Kowalski, pp. 198–219. Oxford University Press, New York.

Morehart, Christopher T., David L. Lentz, and Keith M. Prufer

2005 Wood of the Gods: The Ritual Use of Pine (*Pinus spp.*) by the Ancient Lowland Maya. *Latin American Antiquity* 16:255–274.

Murillo, Saul

1983 Excavaciones en Sepulturas del Complejo Tipo 9M-24. Manuscript on file, Department of Anthropology, Pennsylvania State University, University Park.

Plunket, Patricia (editor)

2002 *Domestic Ritual in Ancient Mesoamerica*. Monograph 46, Cotsen Institute of Archaeology. University of California, Los Angeles.

Pohl, Mary Deland

1991 Women, Animal Rearing, and Social Status: The Case of the Formative Period Maya of Central America. In *The Archaeology of Gender,* edited by Dale Walde and Noreen D. Willows, pp. 392–399. University of Calgary, Calgary.

1994 Appendix D: Late Classic Maya Fauna from Settlement in the Copán Valley, Honduras: An Assertion of Social Status Through Animal Consumption. In *Ceramics and Artifacts from Excavations in the Copán*

Residential Zone, edited by Gordon R. Willey, Richard M. Leventhal, Arthur A. Demarest, and William L. Fash Jr., pp. 459–476. Papers of the Peabody Museum of Archaeology and Ethnology, No. 80. Harvard University, Cambridge.

Pohl, Mary, and John Pohl

1983 Ancient Maya Cave Rituals. *Archaeology* 36:28–32, 50–51.

Proskouriakoff, Tatiana

1961 The Lords of the Maya Realm. *Expedition* 4:229–238.

Redfield, Robert, and Alfonso Villa Rojas

1934 *Chan Kom: A Maya Village*. Carnegie Institution of Washington Publication 448. Washington, D.C.

Reed, David M.

1998 Ancient Maya Diet at Copán, Honduras. Ph.D. dissertation, Pennsylvania State University. University Microfilms, Ann Arbor.

Rue, David J., AnnCorinne Freter, and Diane A. Ballinger

1989 The Caverns of Copán Revisited: Preclassic Sites in the Sesesmil River Valley, Copán, Honduras. *Journal of Field Archaeology* 16:395–404.

Sanders, William T.

1989 Household, Lineage, and State at Eighth-Century Copán, Honduras. In *The House of the Bacabs, Copán, Honduras,* edited by David Webster, pp. 89–105. Studies in Pre-Columbian Art and Archaeology, No. 29. Dumbarton Oaks, Washington, D.C.

Schele, Linda, and Mary Ellen Miller

1986 *The Blood of Kings: Dynasty and Ritual in Maya Art*. Kimball Art Museum, Fort Worth.

Smith, A. Ledyard

1962 Residential and Associated Structures at Mayapan. In *Mayapan, Yucatan, Mexico,* edited by H.E.D. Pollock, Ralph L. Roys, Tatiana Proskouriakoff, and A. Ledyard Smith, pp. 165–320. Carnegie Institution of Washington Publication 519. Washington, D.C.

Taube, Karl Andreas

1992 *The Major Gods of Ancient Yucatan.* Studies in Pre-Columbian Art and Archaeology No. 32. Dumbarton Oaks, Washington, D.C.

Tozzer, Alfred M., and Allen M. Glover

1910 *Animal Figures in the Maya Codices.* Papers of the Peabody Museum of American Archaeology and Ethnology, Volume 4, No. 3. Harvard University, Cambridge.

Urban, Patricia, and Ellen Bell

1993 Comments on Women's Work: Images of Production and Reproduction in Prehispanic Southern Central America by Rosemary Joyce. *Current Anthropology* 34:268–269.

Vail, Gabrielle, and Andrea Stone

2002 Representations of Women in Postclassic and Colonial Maya Literature and Art. In *Ancient Maya Women*, edited by Traci Ardren, pp. 203–228. Altamira Press, Walnut Creek.

Vogt, Evon Z.

1981 Some Aspects of the Sacred Geography of Highland Chiapas. In *Mesoamerican Sites and World Views*, edited by Elizabeth P. Benson, pp. 119–138. Dumbarton Oaks, Washington, D.C.

1998 Zinacanteco Dedication and Termination Rituals. In *The Sowing and the Dawning*, edited by Shirley Boteler Mock, pp. 21–39. University of New Mexico Press, Albuquerque.

Wauchope, Robert

1938 *Modern Maya Houses: A Study of Their Archaeological Significance.* Carnegie Institution of Washington Publication 502. Washington, D.C.

Webster, David

2001 A Rural Sweat Bath at Piedras Negras, Guatemala. Paper presented at the 66th Annual Meeting of the Society for American Archaeology, New Orleans.

Webster, David (editor)

1989 *The House of the Bacabs, Copán, Honduras*. Studies in Pre-Columbian Art and Archaeology, No. 29. Dumbarton Oaks, Washington, D.C.

Webster, David, and AnnCorinne Freter

1990 The Demography of Late Classic Copán. In *Precolumbian Population History in the Maya Lowlands*, edited by T. Patrick Culbert and Don S. Rice, pp. 37–62. University of New Mexico Press, Albuquerque.

Webster, David, AnnCorinne Freter, and Nancy Gonlin

2000 *Copán: The Rise and Fall of an Ancient Maya Kingdom*. Harcourt College Publishers, Fort Worth.

Webster, David, and Nancy Gonlin

1988 Household Remains of the Humblest Maya. *Journal of Field Archaeology* 15:169–190.

Webster, David, William T. Sanders, and Peter van Rossum

1992 A Simulation of Copán Population History and Its Implications. *Ancient Mesoamerica* 3:185–197.

Weiss-Krecji, Estella, and Thomas Sabbas

2002 The Potential Role of Small Depressions as Water Storage Features in the Central Maya Lowlands. *Latin American Antiquity* 13:343–357.

Whittington, Stephen L.

1985 Site report of 3O-7. Manuscript on file, Department of Anthropology, Pennsylvania State University, University Park.

1989 Characteristics of Demography and Disease in Low Status Maya from Classic Period, Copán, Honduras. Ph.D. dissertation, Pennsylvania State University. University Microfilms, Ann Arbor.

Willey, Gordon R., and Richard M. Leventhal

1979 Prehistoric Settlement at Copán. In *Maya Archaeology and Ethnohistory,* edited by Norman Hammond and Gordon R. Willey, pp. 75–102. University of Texas Press, Austin.

Willey, Gordon R., Richard M. Leventhal, Arthur A. Demarest, and William L. Fash Jr.

1994 *Ceramics and Artifacts from Excavations in the Copán Residential Zone.* Papers of the Peabody Museum of Archaeology and Ethnology, Volume 80. Harvard University, Cambridge.

CHAPTER FIVE

SMOKE, SOOT, AND CENSERS

A Perspective on Ancient Commoner Household Ritual Behavior from the Naco Valley, Honduras

JOHN G. DOUGLASS

INTRODUCTION

Across time and space in Mesoamerica, household ritual behavior has been viewed as an important facet of everyday life. Research, however, has primarily focused on elite ritual behavior, with little attention paid to ritual behavior of commoner households. This chapter examines household-level ritual behavior at Late Classic (A.D. 600–950) rural and urban households identified in the Naco Valley of northwest Honduras, including the context of household ritual in the surrounding landscape (Figures 0.1 and 0.2). I begin with a discussion of ritual landscapes, followed by a brief summary of past research in the Naco Valley. Next, I describe specific artifact categories normally associated with commoner household ritual activity and discuss inferences about ritual behavior and the underlying ideology associated with these activities that can be derived from the archaeological distribution of these artifacts. In addition, this case study offers important insight into the separate, yet parallel, ideologies and ritual behaviors of commoners and elites in southeastern Mesoamerica.

RITUAL PATTERNS AND IDEOLOGY— RITUAL LANDSCAPES DEFINED

The concept of landscapes as an archaeological category has seen a tremendous increase in interest by anthropological archaeologists during the past decade (Adler 1996; Anschuetz et al. 2001; Aston 1997; Dunning et al. 1999; Holliday 1992; Kirch and Hunt 1997; Knapp and Ashmore 1999; Varien 1999; Young 2000). Certainly, landscapes have been identified and defined in different fashions since the rise of modern archaeology. Early on, landscapes were defined almost strictly in a physical way. For example, Gordon Willey, in his landmark settlement pattern study of the Viru Valley, Peru, argued that, in prehistoric societies, people placed themselves on the physical landscape based on the natural ecology and cultural norms (Willey 1953:1). Settlement pattern studies many times tended to focus on the relationship between humans and physical features on the landscape. More recent paradigms in anthropology and archaeology, however, have taken a much more sophisticated view of this relationship. Landscape is much more than the physical backdrop for human actions; rather, it is "an entity that exists by virtue of its being perceived, experienced and contextualized by people" (Knapp and Ashmore 1999:1). The concept of ritual and sacred landscapes is discussed in detail here because it is directly connected with commoner household ritual behavior. Following Kurt Anschuetz and colleagues (2001:160–161), four essential assumptions are associated with the concept of landscapes.

1. Landscapes are much more than physical environs; rather, they are created by an interaction between cultural norms and peoples' responses to these norms in their surrounding natural settings.
2. Landscapes are constructs of culture; the surrounding physical environment has special meaning projected on it by the daily interactions of people.
3. Landscapes are an interface for human activity; humans live and work in the same landscape those cultural norms and constructions have created.
4. The conceptual construction of landscapes is a dynamic one; from culture to culture, across time and space, each community will attribute its own meaning and significance to the surrounding anthropogenic landscape.

In other words, landscapes are socially constructed, dynamic media for social interaction that contain both the physical environment and anthropogenic meaning. Communal and personal histories and knowledge all help create this landscape. Yet, just as histories and knowledge change, the cultural meaning may change from occupation to occupation; Parcero Oubina and colleagues (1998) have referred to this phenomenon as "re-writing" landscape.

Sacred and ritual landscapes are important aspects of this overall conception. I follow Evon Vogt's (1981:119) definition of sacred landscape as "a geographical place . . . visited and prayed to in the rituals of the people." The creation of a sacred landscape can be realized by something as simple as burying ancestors in a household crypt, thus creating a genealogy of place (McAnany 1995), or something as complex as constructing monumental architecture or creating settlement patterns that express the spatial order of ritual features (Ashmore 1991). Through the creation of a ritual landscape, humans occupying an area legitimize their claim to land. Sacred and ritual landscapes often are constructs reflecting overarching conceptions of the universe.

The concept of a mountain as an axis mundi, connecting the Underworld and heavens together with the terrestrial world, has both chronological and geographical depth in Mesoamerica (Manzanilla 2000; Schele 1995; Vogt 1981, 1992). The concept of axis mundi is an important one that is shared by many cultures and appears in a variety of forms around the globe (Eliade 1957, 1964, 1976). Generally, this axis mundi is conceived of as a central pivotal point in a universe or world, however that universe or world is conceptualized (Eliade 1976:24–25). A physical or spiritual connection between the underworld, the terrestrial world, and the heavens is a pan-cultural phenomenon that is particularly pronounced in ancient and contemporary Mesoamerican cultures. As Mircea Eliade (1976:26) reminds us, cosmic symbolism is found in the very structure of everyday situations and habitations.

Mountains and temples both illustrate this principle of axis mundi (see Uruñuela and Plunket, Chapter 2). Related to the Mesoamerican concept of a World Tree (see Lohse, Chapter 1), the concept of three planes of existence (Underworld, terrestrial world, and heavens) is a pervasive one. As Linda Schele and David Freidel (1990:66–67) describe it, the World Tree's "trunk went through the Middleworld; its roots plunged to the nadir in the watery Underworld region of the Otherworld, and its branches soared to the zenith in the highest layer of the heavenly region of the Otherworld."

They continue (Schele and Freidel 1990:67) that "this axis could be materialized at any point in the natural or human-made landscape."

Elites create sacred spaces and landscapes, harnessing the labor of subordinates to the fashioning of axis mundi, through the construction of such monuments as temples and ballcourts. As far back as Olmec society, temples have been interpreted as metaphors to sacred mountains and, thus, entrances to both the Underworld (through caves) and the heavens as they reach upward (Schele 1995; Reilly 1999). In addition, hills and caves have been interpreted as analogies for fertility and water (Taube 1986, 1995). For example, the Pyramid of the Sun at Teotihuacan was constructed with earthen fill that Linda Manzanilla (2000:98–99) believes may be related to fertility and sacred geography. The creation of caves beneath the Pyramid of the Sun offers additional evidence to support this interpretation.

Rulers across time and space in ancient Mesoamerica used these types of analogies to create a physical axis mundi in everyday, visible architecture at civic ceremonial centers (see Brady and Ashmore 1999:132–136). At Copán, analogies to temples as sacred mountains are easily visible via the numerous stone sculptures of *witz* (mountain) monsters (Stuart 1987; see also Schele and Freidel 1990:figure 2.7) on the sides of temples. These temples were artificial mountains. In addition, the west court of Copán's acropolis contains sculpture alluding to this place as an aquatic setting, an allusion to supernatural realms (Miller 1984).

Of central concern here are commoner households. How did ritual traditions of commoner households fit into these larger overarching ancient Mesoamerican traditions? Certainly, it is clear that elites used these concepts and belief systems to create a sacred landscape that supported their power by creating monumental architecture and restricting access to sacred knowledge. Did commoner households identify with a similar worldview and belief system? Did commoner households have independent access to the supernatural?

THE LATE CLASSIC NACO VALLEY

The Naco Valley encompasses 96 km^2 along the central portion of the Rio Chamelecon (Figures 0.1 and 5.1). A number of small hills dot the otherwise level valley floor, which sits approximately 100–200 m above sea level (Urban 1986). The mountains surrounding the Naco Valley have moderate to steep slopes, but to the north the Sierra de Omoa rises dramatically.

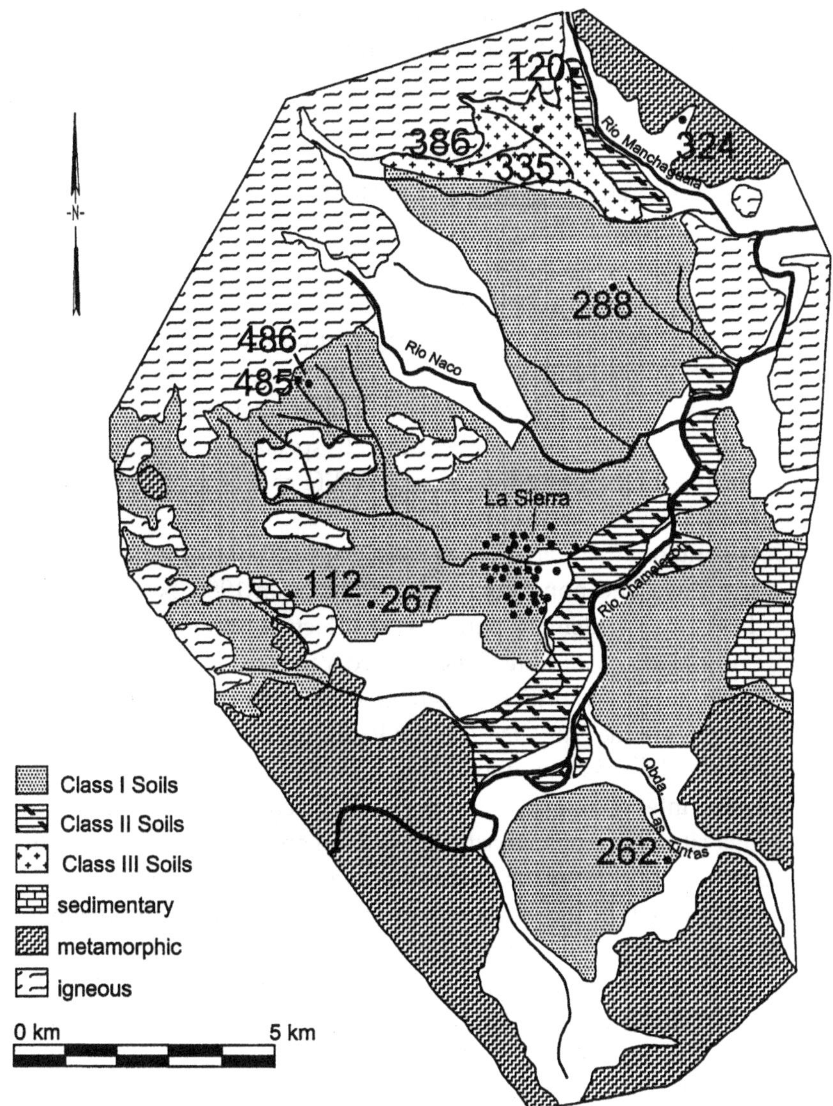

5.1. Map of the Naco Valley, Northwest Honduras (originally published as Douglass 2002: figure 1.1, reprinted courtesy of the University Press of Colorado).

Research since 1975 has documented occupation in the valley from the Middle Formative (1000–400 B.C.) to the Spanish Conquest (Henderson et al. 1979; Schortman and Urban 1994; Schortman et al. 2001; Wonderley 1981, 1986) (Figure 0.2). By the Early Classic (A.D. 300–600), population was increasing and the emerging capital of the polity, La Sierra, was founded. By the Late Classic period, population and political organization were at a zenith in the valley. The settlement system in the Naco Valley during this period was a primate one, with La Sierra functioning as the primary center. La Sierra contained 468 structures, over ten times the number of structures found in the second largest center in the valley. Although population in the valley may have been drawn to this large center for economic or religious reasons, this eclipsing of the next largest site in the settlement hierarchy strongly suggests forced settlement (de Montmollin 1989). La Sierra's regal-ritual site core, containing monumental architecture, open plazas, and a ballcourt, is evidence of an elite politico-religious rulership. In addition, the presence in the site core of at least two kilns and numerous structures containing remains of craft specialization suggests that elites controlled a portion of the economic life as well (see Connell 2002; Schortman et al. 2001).

Occupants of the Naco Valley had political and economic contact with both Maya and non-Maya areas (Schortman 1986; Schortman and Urban 1994). The settlement patterns, architecture, material culture, and presumably ideology of Late Classic Naco Valley populations, however, were clearly non-Mayan (Schortman 1986; Schortman and Urban 1994). Although elites in the Late Classic Naco Valley emulated Maya elite behavior, politically this was an independent, non-Maya polity. Strong evidence for trade and interaction between elites in the Naco Valley and those at lowland Maya sites like Copán exists (Schortman and Urban 1994), but elites at La Sierra created local traditions. For example, as Edward Schortman and colleagues (2001:321) have recently illustrated, crab and bird motifs together on ceramics may have been emblems of a social identity for the entire polity. The non-Maya regions in southeastern Mesoamerica, such as the adjoining La Venta and Florida valleys (Inomata and Aoyama 1996; Nakamura 1994; Nakamura et al. 1992; Schortman and Nakamura 1991), the middle Ulua drainage (Ashmore et al. 1987; Schortman and Urban, eds., 1994; Schortman et al. 1986), and the Sula Plain (Henderson 1981; Joyce 1991, 1993), all clearly were distinct cultures, both ethnically and politically. However, members of these societies, especially local elites, emulated certain lowland Maya practices and belief traditions. Some of these practices, as current research has shown, appear to have been variations on pan-Mesoamerican traditions (e.g., Schortman and Urban 1994). For example, the arrangement of the ballcourt at La Sierra appears to emulate that found at the nearby Maya site of Copán (see Gonlin, Chapter 4, for discussion of Copán), as do iconographic architectural elements identified from the polity's capital, such as sculpture of an apparent elite wearing head garb, which is similar to sculpture found at Copán (Schortman and Urban 1994).

Although elites did live outside the capital, the rural areas of the Naco Valley were primarily inhabited by members of commoner agrarian households. In this chapter, commoner households are thought of as being the primary rural inhabitants in the valley. When discussing household ritual behavior, it is helpful to identify and view households as "activity groups" (Ashmore and Wilk 1988:3; see also Wilk 1990). Certainly, in the case of settlement pattern data, the clustering of residential and multi-use structures into small, nucleated groups suggests joint activities. In sum, this settlement form suggests cooperative behavior that may represent the maximal overlap of household functions (Wilk 1990). The term *commoner* may represent something slightly different from author to author in this volume. For the purposes of this chapter, I am discussing agrarian households that differed in kind from elites primarily in access to economic, social, and political spheres. For example, commoner households in the rural sectors of the Late Classic Naco Valley generally had less access to valuables, such as imported or elaborately decorated ceramics, and they occupied smaller houses than groups residing at La Sierra (see Douglass 2002:figures 6.2–6.4).

Households at the Late Classic polity's capital, La Sierra, appear to have had greater access to goods and belief systems than those in rural areas did. High-ranking elites at La Sierra enjoyed a belief system that sanctified rulership and power over the majority and offered privileges that were not available to all valley inhabitants. Elites utilized public rituals to codify their power and create a monopoly on the disbursement of the most powerful ritual knowledge (Demarest 1992; see Lohse, Chapter 1). Certainly, not all elites in the Naco Valley were rulers nor were there only elites residing at La Sierra, and some households in the rural sectors had strong connections with La Sierra. Several rural sites in the Naco Valley, including Sites 426 and 428 (see Schortman et al. 2001), for example, contain residential architectural features rarely found outside the capital. Such similarities may suggest political ties to La Sierra elites. Nonetheless, magnates residing in the valley's hinterlands were different from high-ranking and ruling elites at La Sierra in their relative power, wealth, and prestige.

MATERIAL CULTURE OF HOUSEHOLD RITUAL

A number of material traits related to commoner household ritual behavior, such as *candeleros* and *incensarios,* qualify some of the differences between elite and commoner household ritual behavior in the Late Classic Naco Valley. These ubiquitous ritual-related items were recovered from household or specialized contexts in both rural and urban sectors of the valley. Both elites and commoners used these objects to interact with the sacred and ritual landscape that both physically and conceptually surrounded them.

CANDELEROS

Candelero is an enigmatic artifact class that varies a great deal across commoner households. These vessels generally are low ceramic forms that have from one to more than twenty narrow (ca. 1–2 cm) chambers (Urban and Bell 1993:269) (Figure 5.2). Although there is variety in the shape of these perforations, at least some appear to have been produced by an individual sticking a finger directly into the clay. The simpler forms of this artifact class do not appear to have required specialized labor and could have been easily produced by individual households (Schortman and Urban, eds., 1994:72). There is a broad range in the degree of finishing of these items, but the most common motifs are incised parallel lines, *chevrons* and X's (Urban and Bell 1993:269). I use the term *enigmatic* for *candeleros* because it is unclear how these vessels functioned. Many of the chambers have burn marks on the interiors near vents, indicating the igniting of copal, pitch, or other types of resin within them. In the middle Ulua drainage, *candeleros* appear to have functioned similarly because they show signs of smoke residue (Urban and Smith 1987).

Candeleros are found in a variety of contexts, including commoner households. They are usually found in the general mix of terminal occupation refuse within and around household structures but only rarely appear in caches (see Gonlin, Chapter 4, for different data on caches from the Copán Valley). The fragmentary nature of many suggests they were used and then discarded. If *candeleros* were used in household ritual activity, as is suggested by their archaeological context, then they also may have served in private rituals (Schortman and Urban, eds., 1994:76; Urban and Bell 1993:269; see also Widmer and Storey 1993:91–92 for a similar argument).

5.2. Late Classic multi-chamber candelero *from Honduras (photo courtesy of the Naco Valley Archaeological Project).*

Figurines and Whistles

Figurines and related whistles (single-tone) and *ocarinas* (multi-tone whistles) are a well-described class of artifacts in the Late Classic Naco Valley (Bell 1991). Generally, these items are solid or hollow-bodied ceramic forms created entirely by using molds (Urban and Bell 1993:269). In the adjoining Sula Plain, these types of artifacts have been analyzed to study gender imagery (Joyce 1993).

The functions of figurines, whistles, and *ocarinas* are highly debated, as has been discussed at length by both Jan Olson and Geoffrey McCafferty in this volume. At the time of Spanish Conquest of central Mexico, figurines were ubiquitous household items but, as such, were not well documented by the Spanish outside of a few references (Charlton 1994:203–204). In the Late Classic Naco Valley, figurines were plentiful and found in both elite and commoner households. As with *candeleros*, they are generally found (with a few notable exceptions) within terminal occupation household debris rather than in caches or other specialized contexts. This issue of context is an important one when determining function (Marcus 1996). Remains of figurines and *ocarinas* are generally fragmentary, although the rare whole artifact may be uncovered. Whistles and *ocarinas* appear similar in form to figurines but produce sounds. Music has been documented to have played an important part in ritual behavior in many times and places in Mesoamerica, especially in the neighboring Maya culture area (Healy 1988).

The fragmentary nature of figurines, whistles, and *ocarinas* in household refuse contexts suggests that they were consumed on a regular basis. Although some foci of figurine and *ocarina* production appear to have been at the polity capital of La Sierra, many rural households in the valley have evidence for figurine production in the form of figurine molds. When molds are recovered, however, they are usually found in very low numbers (for details of these molds, see Schortman et al. 2001:table 1). The wide availability and high rate of consumption of figurines, along with their general lack of specialized contexts, suggest that they may have functioned as household-level deities (Widmer and Storey 1993:91–92). Many households, then, may have produced and used figurines regularly. Certainly, not all households were self-sufficient in figurine manufacture, but it appears likely that they were easily obtained. Although I do not believe that they were used daily, as Randolph Widmer and Rebecca Storey (1993) have argued for households at Teotihuacan, they certainly were a common aspect of household life.

Incensarios

Incensarios, or censers, are another ubiquitous artifact class found in commoner household contexts within the Late Classic Naco Valley. There are four general categories of censers: lids, prongs, ladles, and modeled (see Schortman and Urban, eds., 1994:70–72 for a complete description). Lid censers are simple, shallow plates with crosshatched incised designs on their convex surface, whereas prong censers are shallow plates with plain or modeled conical elements protruding up from their rims. Ladle censers are shallow bowls, often with perforated bases and an attached strap or tube handle (Figure 5.3). All three of these censer categories show evidence of burning, which was sometimes intense. These three types are commonly found in commoner household contexts and appear to have been used in household-level ritual activity. It is extremely rare to find these types of censers whole; as with *candeleros* and figurines, their archaeological contexts suggest they may have been smashed after use.

Modeled censers, in contrast, are much more ornate than prong, ladle, and lid censers and are not often found in commoner household

5.3. Late Classic ladle censer from Honduras (photo courtesy of the Naco Valley Archaeological Project).

contexts. This type of censer is usually a tall cylinder with an inverted rim (Schortman and Urban, eds., 1994:71). The exterior of this censer type is normally embellished with modeled designs that often employ complex anthropomorphic and zoomorphic designs. Found primarily within the polity's capital of La Sierra, modeled censers appear to be associated with heavily ritualized activities, including the use of *Spondylous* shell and other exotic materials not commonly found in rural areas (Schortman and Urban 1991:81–82).

ELITE AND COMMONER RITUAL ACTIVITY ASSESSED

Based on the discussion thus far, several points can be made about the nature of commoner household ritual behavior in the Naco Valley. First, it seems apparent that every commoner household possessed a ritual "kit," or assemblage, that generally included items such as figurines, whistles, *ocarinas*, *candeleros*, and several types of censers. Second, these items generally were goods that could be easily replaced if damaged. The ubiquity of many of these household items suggests that household members used these items on a regular basis. Third, households across the Late Classic

Naco Valley had the ability to readily replace many of these items. Simple forms of *candeleros*, for example, did not require specialized craft skills beyond firing the product. Although not all household excavations have yielded figurine/*ocarina* molds, they are found in many commoner household contexts, albeit usually in small quantities (see Schortman et al. 2001 for specific data). Censer production would have required more specialized skills than the other ritual artifact categories, but if rural households were able to produce ceramics, they had the technology and skill to produce censers. Some of these items, then, such as *candeleros*, could have been produced by numerous households in the valley, whereas other forms of ritual items could have been produced by those households that had the skills related to ceramic production. I am not suggesting that every household produced at least a part of their ritual assemblage; rather, these data indicate that elites at La Sierra did not control the production of commoner household ritual goods.

Some distinctions between rituals performed by commoner and elite households, however, are evident. Commoner household activities tend to be private affairs conducted within specific domestic contexts. This statement does not mean, however, that all commoner household rituals in the Naco Valley were entirely private; it is reasonable to assume that some, if not many, household rituals included extrahousehold members. What is meant here is that commoner household rituals appear to be much less public than those performed by elites, as will be discussed later. Similar patterns have been seen in other areas of southeast Mesoamerica, including the lower Motagua Valley (Schortman 1984). In contrast, ritual activity in elite contexts at La Sierra appears to be a much more public event. Modeled censers appeared to have been restricted to some extent (Schortman and Urban, eds., 1994:198); although primarily found at La Sierra, modeled censers have been infrequently recovered from non-elite, even rural, settings. La Sierra's rulers conducted public rites not only using restricted items, including modeled censers, but also performing them in special purpose monumental edifices, such as temples and the ballcourt. I agree with Edward Schortman and Patricia Urban (eds., 1994) in their assessment that by restricting access to certain types of ritual goods to specific groups, elites were able to restrict access to sacred knowledge and thus sanctify their power over commoners. Elites, through architecture and relatively elaborate ritual paraphernalia, created and monopolized certain sacred spaces and ritual observances. In this way, they transformed the landscape and materialized sacred spaces within it. Thus, ruling elites were poised to continue their leadership through certain rituals and support their power base (see Lohse, Chapter 1).

Similarly, one must also consider other types of goods that are not as readily identifiable in the archaeological record. Production of paper, as evidenced by the presence of bark beaters, appears to have been undertaken by a few commoner households within rural areas of the Late Classic Naco Valley. In and of itself, the presence of bark beaters at these rural sites is a bit of an oddity. One of the functions of bark paper was as a surface for writing, but there is no evidence of a written language in the Late Classic Naco Valley (but see Gonlin, Chapter 4, for other alternatives). Perhaps some of this paper, along with other goods, could have been traded to neighboring areas, such as Copán. A more likely use for this paper, however, may have been bloodletting. It is unclear, given the distribution of bark beaters and the dearth of paper in the archaeological record, exactly who may have used this paper in ritual. During the sixteenth century, Bishop de Landa wrote that bloodletting was a behavior conducted by elites and commoners. If both commoner and elite households used paper for bloodletting, elites may have used paper with associated items that had a more restricted access. For example, elites may have used this paper to collect let blood and then burned it in a ceramic receptacle or in *Spondylous* shell. *Spondylous* shell, like modeled censers, has a highly restricted distribution in the Naco Valley and appears to be related to elite ritual activity primarily at La Sierra.

SUMMARY AND CONCLUSIONS

This chapter has outlined the principal types of ritual activity performed by commoner households in the Late Classic Naco Valley and identified specific differences between ritual activity undertaken by commoner and elite households. Commoner households primarily performed localized, household-based rituals within the confines of their residential compounds. All commoner households appear to have had a shared ideology related to these daily activities, as displayed by the presence of similar ritual assemblages across the valley. Many of these ritual artifacts appear to have been produced and used by the same commoner households. Elite households did perform some rituals that were similar to those performed by commoner households; that is, they both burned incense or other material in ceramic vessels. Some may interpret that these rituals were more similar than different, with elites able to burn incense in fancier censers than commoners. The data, however, suggest that elite households at the primate center of La Sierra performed ritual activities that were different in quantity and kind from those performed by commoner rural households (Urban 2001). As discussed previously, elites created ritual paraphernalia and artificial monuments that guaranteed paramount monopolies over the power conjured within these artificial creations.

Commoners, because they lack the material resources to fabricate the dramatic expressions of the sacred that elites possess, use what they can to interact with the supernatural. Manipulating ritual objects that are easily fashioned and establishing ritual sites on potential features on the landscape offer opportunities for commoners to interact in the same ritual sphere as elites but through easily reproduced and accessed resources. As a result, sacred spaces and ritual paraphernalia can be accessed by virtually all members of society. In sum, then, elites appear to have had the ability to create artificial metaphors to sacred landscape through monumental architecture and restricted ritual knowledge, whereas commoners did not. Commoners maintain some autonomy in their independent access to the supernatural through their ritual tool kits and replication of sacred landscape via the natural terrain surrounding them, whereas elites are simultaneously working to maintain exclusive control of the sacred. Both commoners and elites hold similar ideologies, yet they express these views in different, although somewhat parallel, venues. In many cases, the nature of commoner household ideology is difficult to determine based on the dearth of remains. This discussion, however, offers insight into the worldview of Late Classic Naceños, both elite and commoner.

ACKNOWLEDGMENTS

I thank Nan Gonlin and Jon Lohse for inviting me to participate in the session at the 2002 Society for American Archaeology annual meeting in Denver, as well as this subsequent volume. Both Jon and Nan have been immensely patient with me as I have tried (and failed) to meet deadlines. I appreciate their useful criticism of an earlier draft of this chapter. I have been pondering issues of commoner household ritual behavior over the past few years and am pleased to have an opportunity to share some of these ideas. This research could not have been undertaken without the generous support of Edward Schortman and Patricia Urban, the directors of the Naco Valley Project. Pat and Ed have opened up all the project's data and analysis to me, for which I am grateful. Data used in portions of this chapter were funded by a number of different granting agencies to the Naco Valley Project, including the National Science Foundation, National Geographic Society, and the National Endowment for the Humanities. Comments and encouragement by Nan Gonlin, Jon Lohse, Pat Urban, Ed Schortman, Karl Taube, Wendy Ashmore, Jill Onken, and an anonymous reviewer have all made this chapter much stronger. I am thankful to Jill Onken for her wonderful wordsmith abilities; my thoughts are presented much more clearly as a result of her help. Of course, any lapses of logic or bizarre twists of judgment are entirely my own responsibility.

REFERENCES CITED

Adler, Michael

1996 Land Tenure, Archaeology, and the Ancestral Pueblo Social Landscape. *Journal of Anthropological Archaeology* 15:337–371.

Anschuetz, Kurt F., Richard H. Wilshusen, and Cherie L. Scheick

2001 An Archaeology of Landscapes: Perspectives and Directions. *Journal of Archaeological Research* 9:157–211.

Ashmore, Wendy

1991 Site-planning Principles and Concepts of Directionality Among the Ancient Maya. *Latin American Antiquity* 2:199–226.

Ashmore, Wendy, Edward Schortman, Julie Benyo, Jason Weeks, and Sylvia Smith

1987 Ancient Society in Santa Barbara, Honduras. *National Geographic Research* 3:232–354.

Ashmore, Wendy, and Richard R. Wilk

1988 Household and Community in the Mesoamerican Past. In *Household and Community in the Mesoamerican Past,* edited by Richard R. Wilk and Wendy Ashmore, pp. 1–27. University of New Mexico Press, Albuquerque.

Aston, Mick

1997 *Interpreting the Landscape: Landscape Archaeology and Local History*. Routledge, London.

Bell, Ellen

1991 The Figurine and Ocarina Assemblages of the Naco Valley, Northwestern Honduras. Honors thesis, Department of Anthropology and Sociology, Kenyon College, Gambier.

Brady, James, and Wendy Ashmore

1999 Mountains, Caves, Water: Ideational Landscapes of the Ancient Maya. In *Archaeologies of Landscape: Contemporary Perspectives,* edited by Wendy Ashmore and A. Bernard Knapp, pp. 124–148. Blackwell Publishers, Malden.

Charlton, Cynthia

1994 Plebeians and Patricians: Contrasting Patterns of Production and Distribution of Aztec Figurines and Lapidary Industries. In *Economies and Polities in the Aztec Realm,* edited by Mary Hodge and Michael E. Smith, pp. 195–219. Institute for Mesoamerican Studies, State University of New York, Albany.

Connell, Samuel V.

2002 Getting Close to the Source: Using Ethnoarchaeology to Find Ancient Pottery Making in the Naco Valley, Honduras. *Latin American Antiquity* 13:401–417.

de Montmollin, Olivier

1989 *The Archaeology of Political Structure: Settlement Analysis in a Classic Maya Polity.* Cambridge University Press, Cambridge.

Demarest, Arthur A.

1992 Archaeology, Ideology and Pre-Columbian Cultural Evolution: The Search for an Approach. In *Ideology and Pre-Columbian Civilizations,* edited by Arthur A. Demarest and Geoffrey W. Conrad, pp. 1–13. School of American Research Press, Santa Fe.

Douglass, John G.

2002 *Hinterland Households: Rural Agrarian Household Diversity in the Naco Valley, Honduras.* University Press of Colorado, Boulder.

Dunning, Nicholas, Vernon Scarborough, and Fred Valdez Jr.

1999 Temple Mountains, Sacred Lakes, and Fertile Fields: Ancient Maya Landscapes in Northwestern Belize. *Antiquity* 73:650–660.

Eliade, Mircea

1957 *The Sacred and the Profane: The Nature of Religion.* Harcourt, Brace and World, New York.

1964 *Shamanism: Archaic Techniques of Ecstasy.* Bollingen Series 76. Princeton University Press, Princeton.

1976 *Occultism, Witchcraft and Cultural Fashions: Essays in Comparable Religion.* University of Chicago Press, Chicago.

Healy, Paul

1988 Music of the Maya. *Archaeology* 41:24–31.

Henderson, John (editor)

1981 *Archaeology in Northwest Honduras: Interim Reports of the Proyecto Arqueológica Sula,* Volume 1. Intercollege Program in Archaeology, Cornell University, Ithaca.

Henderson, John, Ilene Wallace, Anthony Wonderley, and Patricia Urban

1979 Archaeological Investigations in the Valle de Naco, Northwest Honduras: A Preliminary Report. *Journal of Field Archaeology* 6:169–192.

Holliday, Vance T.

1992 *Soils in Archaeology: Landscape Evolution and Human Occupation.* Smithsonian Institution, Washington, D.C.

Inomata, Takeshi, and Kazuo Aoyama

1996 Central-Place Analysis in the La Entrada Region, Honduras: Implications for Understanding the Classic Maya Political and Economic Systems. *Latin American Antiquity* 7:291–312.

Joyce, Rosemary

1991 *Cerro Palenque: Power and Identity on the Maya Periphery.* University of Texas Press, Austin.

1993 Women's Work: Images of Production and Reproduction in Pre-Hispanic Southern Central America. *Current Anthropology* 34:255–274.

Kirch, Patrick, and Terry L. Hunt (editors)

1997 *Historical Ecology in the Pacific Islands: Prehistoric Environmental and Landscape Change.* Yale University Press, New Haven.

Knapp, A. Bernard, and Wendy Ashmore

1999 Archaeological Landscapes: Constructed, Conceptualized, Ideational. In *Archaeologies of Landscape: Contemporary Perspectives,* edited by Wendy Ashmore and A. Bernard Knapp, pp. 1–32. Blackwell Publishers, Malden.

Manzanilla, Linda

2000 The Construction of the Underworld in Central Mexico. In *Mesoamerica's Classic Heritage: From Teotihuacan to the Aztecs,* edited by Davíd Carrasco, Lindsay Jones, and Scott Sessions, pp. 87–116. University Press of Colorado, Boulder.

Marcus, Joyce

1996 The Importance of Context in Interpreting Figurines. *Cambridge Archaeological Journal* 6:285–291.

McAnany, Patricia

1995 *Living with the Ancestors: Kinship and Kingship in Ancient Maya Society.* University of Texas Press, Austin.

Miller, Mary E.

1984 The Meaning and Function of the Main Acropolis, Copán. In *The Southeast Classic Maya Zone,* edited by Elizabeth Boone and Gordon R. Willey, pp. 149–94. Dumbarton Oaks, Washington, D.C.

Nakamura, Seiichi

1994 Desarrollo y decaimiento en la periferia de Copán. *Annals of Latin American Studies* 14:39–95.

Nakamura, Seiichi, Kazuo Aoyama, and Eiji Uratsuji

1992 *Investigación arqueológica en La Entrada, Copán, Primera Fase.* Instituto Hondureño de Antropología e Historia, Servicio de Voluntarios Japoneses para la Cooperación con el Extranjero, San Pedro Sula, Honduras.

Parcero Oubina, Cesar, Felipe Criado Boado, and Manuel Santos Estevez

1998 Rewriting Landscape: Incorporating Sacred Landscapes into Cultural Traditions. *World Archaeology* 30:159–178.

Reilly, F. Kent, III

1999 Mountains of Creation and Underworld Portals: The Ritual Function of Olmec Architecture at La Venta, Tabasco. In *Mesoamerican Architecture as a Cultural Symbol,* edited by Jeff Karl Kowalski, pp. 14–39. Oxford University Press, New York.

Schele, Linda

1995 The Olmec Mountain and Tree of Creation in Mesoamerican Cosmology. In *The Olmec World: Ritual and Rulership,* edited by Michael Coe, pp. 105–117. The Art Museum, Princeton University, Princeton.

Schele, Linda, and David Freidel

1990 *A Forest of Kings: The Untold Story of the Ancient Maya.* William Morrow and Company, New York.

Schortman, Edward

1984 Archaeological Investigations in the Lower Motagua Valley, Izabal, Guatemala: A Study in Monumental Site Function and Interaction. Ph.D. dissertation, University of Pennsylvania. University Microfilms, Ann Arbor.

1986 Interaction Between the Maya and Non-Maya Along the Late Classic Southeast Maya Periphery: The View from the Lower Montagua Valley, Guatemala. In *The Southeast Maya Periphery,* edited by Patricia Urban and Edward Schortman, pp. 114–137. University of Texas Press, Austin.

Schortman, Edward, and Seiichi Nakamura

1991 A Crisis of Identity: Late Classic Competition and Interaction in the Southeast Maya Periphery. *Latin American Antiquity* 2:311–336.

Schortman, Edward, and Patricia Urban

1994 Living on the Edge: Core/Periphery Relations in Ancient Southeastern Mesoamerica. *Current Anthropology* 35:401–430.

Schortman, Edward, and Patricia Urban (editors)

1991 Sociopolitical Hierarchy and Craft Production: The Economic Bases of Elite Power in a Southeast Mesoamerican Polity. Manuscript on file at Kenyon College, Gambier.

1994 Sociopolitical Hierarchy and Craft Production: The Economic Bases of Elite Power in a Southeast Mesoamerican Polity, Part 3, The 1992 Season of the Naco Valley Archaeological Project. Manuscript on file at Kenyon College, Gambier.

Schortman, Edward, Patricia Urban, Wendy Ashmore, and Julie Benyo

1986 Interregional Interaction in the Southeast Maya Periphery: The Santa Barbara Archaeological Project, 1983–84 Seasons. *Journal of Field Archaeology* 13:259–272.

Schortman, Edward, Patricia Urban, and Marne Ausec

2001 Politics with Style: Identity Formation in Prehispanic Southeastern Mesoamerica. *American Anthropologist* 103:312–330.

Stuart, David

1987 *Ten Phonetic Syllables*. Research Reports on Ancient Maya Writing, 14, Center for Maya Research, Washington, D.C.

Taube, Karl

1986 The Teotihuacan Cave of Origin: The Iconography and Architecture of Emergence Mythology in Mesoamerica and the American Southwest. *Res* 12:51–83.

1995 The Rainmakers: The Olmec and Their Contribution to Mesoamerican Belief and Ritual. In *The Olmec World: Ritual and Rulership*, edited by Michael Coe, pp. 83–105. The Art Museum, Princeton University, Princeton.

Urban, Patricia

1986 Systems of Settlement in the Precolumbian Naco Valley, Northwestern Honduras. Ph.D. dissertation, University of Pennsylvania. University Microfilms, Ann Arbor.

2001 Hierarchy and Decentralization: The Transition from the Classic Middle Preclassic Political Developments in the Naco Valley, Honduras. *Latin American Antiquity* 13:131–152.

Urban, Patricia, and Ellen Bell

1993 Comments on Women's Work: Images of Production and Reproduction in Pre-Hispanic Southern Central America. *Current Anthropology* 34:268–269.

Urban, Patricia, and Sylvia Smith

1987 The Incensarios and Candeleros of Central Santa Barbara: Distributional and Functional Studies. In *Interaction on the Southeast Mesoamerican Frontier: Prehistoric and Historic Honduras and El Salvador,* edited by Eugenia Robinson, pp. 267–279. BAR International Series 327, Oxford.

Varien, Mark

1999 *Sedentism and Mobility in a Social Landscape.* University of Arizona Press, Tucson.

Vogt, Evon

1981 Some Aspects of Sacred Geography of Highland Chiapas. In *Mesoamerican Sites and World Views,* edited by Elizabeth Benson, pp. 119–142. Dumbarton Oaks, Washington, D.C.

1992 The Persistence of Maya Traditions in Zinacantan. In *The Ancient Americas: Art from Sacred Landscapes,* edited by Richard Townsend, pp. 60–69. Art Institute of Chicago, Chicago.

Widmer, Randolph, and Rebecca Storey

1993 Social Organization and Household Structure of a Teotihuacan Apartment Complex: S3W1:33 of the Tlajinga Barrio. In *Prehispanic Domestic Units in Western Mesoamerica: Studies of the Household, Compound and Residence,* edited by Robert S. Santley and Kenneth G. Hirth, pp. 87–104. CRC Press, Boca Raton.

Wilk, Richard R.

1990 The Built Environment and Consumer Decisions. In *Domestic Architecture and the Use of Space,* edited by Susan Kent, pp. 34–42. Cambridge University Press, Cambridge.

Willey, Gordon R.

1953 *Prehistoric Settlement Patterns in the Viru Valley, Peru.* Bulletin No. 155, Bureau of American Ethnology, Washington, D.C.

Wonderley, Anthony

1981 *Late Postclassic Occupations at Naco, Honduras.* Latin American Studies Program Dissertation Series 86. Cornell University, Ithaca.

1986 Naco, Honduras: Some Aspects of Late Precolumbian Community on the Eastern Maya Frontier. In *The Southeast Maya Periphery,* edited by Edward Schortman and Patricia Urban, pp. 313–332. University of Texas Press, Austin.

Young, Amy L.

2000 *Archaeology of Southern Urban Landscapes.* University of Alabama Press, Tuscaloosa.

CHAPTER SIX

COMMONER RITUALS, RESISTANCE, AND THE CLASSIC-TO-POSTCLASSIC TRANSITION IN ANCIENT MESOAMERICA

Arthur A. Joyce and Errin T. Weller

INTRODUCTION

Early Colonial period documents in Mesoamerica provide many examples of expressions of resistance and rebellion by indigenous peoples against Spanish colonial authorities (Jones 1989; Restall 1997; Terraciano 2001). Yet within these documents there are occasional references to the discontent of common people toward indigenous nobles who in some areas continued to exert considerable power over their subjects for centuries after the Conquest. For example, in the Maya *Book of Chilam Balam of Chumayel*, people are said to lament the hardships that a warlike leader imposes on subjects because of military drafts, famine, and strife resulting from frequent warfare (McAnany 1995:140–141; Roys 1967:103). Likewise, Kevin Terraciano (2001) reports the testimony of a woman named Catalina from Etlatongo, Oaxaca, during the Inquisition trial of Yanhuitlán in the 1540s. Catalina fled from the house of a male lord of Yanhuitlán where she was a servant because her seven-year-old sister was sacrificed for the health of the lord and Catalina feared she would be next. Terraciano (2001:272) argues: "Judging from their statements, many slaves failed to see the sacred qualities of human sacrifice. A slave named Juan suggested that sacrifices were at times little more than vengeful acts."

Although these colonial documents record a period of social disruption and discord resulting from the Spanish Conquest, we believe that expressions of resistance to political domination are a component of all complex societies characterized by institutionalized power differentials and therefore have a deep history in prehispanic Mesoamerica that likely conditioned (along with other aspects of daily life) commoners' "sense" of themselves (also see Brumfiel 1996; Hutson 2002; A. Joyce 2000; A. Joyce et al. 2001; R. Joyce 1993; Robin 1999).

In this chapter, we consider evidence for ritual expressions of resistance in prehispanic Mesoamerica (Figure 0.1), particularly during the Classic period collapse (ca. A.D. 700–1000) (Figure 0.2). We follow poststructuralist and feminist theorists who have increasingly developed a more contingent and fractured concept of society than traditional approaches in archaeology and social sciences as a whole (Bourdieu 1977; Butler 1993; Dirks 1994; Giddens 1979; Goldstein 2003; Scott 1990). All people are now recognized as having some power to produce or reproduce social systems and structure. Systems of political power result from social negotiations of all members of society so that domination is always contested to varying degrees. Although we recognize the complex and multifaceted ways in which all people contribute to social production and reproduction, we choose to focus this study on issues of resistance. Our focus does not imply that we view the agency of commoners as restricted only to resisting domination and we strongly reject the dominant ideology thesis (see M. Brown 1996; Hodder and Hutson 2003:96–99; Lohse, Chapter 1). We recognize that the lives of subordinate groups are rich and complex. As discussed by Arthur Joyce and his colleagues (2001; A. Joyce n.d.), resistance and other forms of engagement with domination are important forms of social production and are not simply reactions to a dominant ideology. The purpose of this chapter is to explore evidence of, as well as possible methods for, investigating resistance as one form of social production.

We choose to focus on the Classic period collapse because periods marked by the collapse of political institutions give commoners a greater opportunity to express more overtly and visibly resistance to domination even when not actively rebelling against those institutions. Because of the inconsistency of available data, this chapter does not attempt a comprehensive model of commoner resistance during the collapse. Instead, we explore two areas of investigation that we feel offer the potential to yield useful inferences on resistance. First, we consider evidence for the exclusion of commoners from ceremonies that embodied a public transcript of power (Scott 1990). As commoners were distanced and disengaged from state ceremonies, people may have more fully penetrated dominant ideologies and expanded modes of resistance. Second, we consider evidence for actual expressions of resistance both before the Conquest, when people were subject to the coercive sanctions of the Late Classic state, and after the collapse, when they were freer to express dissatisfaction with traditional symbols of rulership. We conclude that in many political centers commoners were excluded from state ceremonies toward the end of the Classic period. We find few clear indications of resistance prior to the collapse, although this may be a result of resistance having been expressed in less visible or disguised forms, or what James Scott (1990) has termed the "hidden transcript." Immediately after the collapse, however, evidence from several areas of Mesoamerica suggests the destruction and denigration of architecture and carved stone monuments that had been powerful symbols of rulership and ruling institutions. We argue that these practices reflect an earlier hidden transcript of resistance among many commoners that was expressed in more visible ways only after the decline of ruling institutions.

THEORETICAL PERSPECTIVE

In this chapter, we use a theoretical perspective based on practice theory (Bourdieu 1977; Giddens 1979, 1984; Ortner 1984; Sewell 1992) along with the work on subalterns by James Scott (1985, 1990) to examine resistance to state power during the Late Classic and Early Postclassic periods in Mesoamerica (also see A. Joyce et al. 2001). Following Anthony Giddens (1979:88–94), we define power as the transformative capacity of an agent to achieve an outcome, which can either reproduce or change social systems and structure. The transformative capacity of agents is determined by the compromise struck between their creativity, skill, and awareness of the world on the one hand and the cultural principles and the properties of resources that create asymmetries in access to resources on the other. Power, therefore, is a condition of social relations; all people have some power, even if it is in the form of passive resistance. Thus, the consequences of the actions of even the least powerful affect system and structure.

Power can be viewed as manifest in a continuum from more discursive to non-discursive forms. Drawing on the work of Antonio Gramsci (1971), several scholars have distinguished between hegemony, which includes the deeper and largely uncontested network of symbols, meanings, and actions, and ideology, which encompasses the more discursive beliefs and practices that legitimate the interests of particular social groups in relation to others (Comaroff and Comaroff 1991:19–27; Comaroff and Comaroff 1992:28–31; Goldstein 2003:35–37; Janusek 2004:12–16; also see Lohse, Chapter 1). The boundary between hegemony and ideology is fluid such that the internalized and naturalized aspects of a dominant discourse can be brought to light and contested. Successful ruling strategies promote cognitive resonance between people's lived experiences and the dominant discourse, driving aspects of the dominant ideology into the unexamined truths of hegemony. It is particularly during periods of historical upheaval, such as during the collapse of centralized political institutions, that aspects of hegemony may be discursively reexamined and the dominant ideology increasingly penetrated and questioned (Comaroff and Comaroff 1991:26; Janusek 2004:15–16; A. Joyce et al. 2001).

Research on politico-religious power in Mesoamerica has traditionally stressed elite ideologies and domination with little consideration of the role of commoners in political discourse. In contrast to traditional top-down models of power, this volume demonstrates the increasing recognition among Mesoamerican archaeologists that systems of political power that support inequality in complex societies result from social negotiations among all members of society (Ashmore et al. 2004; Brumfiel 1996; A. Joyce 2000; A. Joyce et al. 2001). Dominant ideologies are, therefore, historically constituted through the ongoing interaction of people of different social positions with varying dispositions and degrees of power. This model means that dominant ideologies are never simply imposed on commoners by elites; commoners as well as elites contribute to social processes. Joyce and his colleagues (2001) have argued that commoners contribute to dominant discourses through three overlapping forms of social interaction: engagement, avoidance (or independence; see later discussion), and resistance.

Engagement refers to the compromise achieved in a dominant discourse produced through the mutual engagement of elites and commoners with divergent interests and dispositions (e.g., Costin 1996; A. Joyce 2000; Pauketat 2000; Sheets 2000). Engagement acknowledges that although elites have more power in social interactions, commoners have some power to advance their interests and alternative readings of structural principles, including ideologies. Thus, elites cannot simply impose their will on commoners. A dominant discourse will always be to some degree an accommodation among people of different social positions.

Commoners also produce and reproduce alternative discourses and social practices that are largely independent of and do not directly engage or contest elite sources of power. Joyce and his colleagues (2001:369–370) termed this form of interaction "avoidance," but this implies a conscious intent to avoid elite power, an intent that is not always present when commoners act independently of dominant ideologies. Some commoners will often simply live far from political centers and other places where dominant ideologies are expressed in symbolism and practice so that their independence may not be the result of conscious intent to avoid domination. We therefore propose here a broader and more neutral term: *independence.* Commoners in rural communities often have a great deal of independence from regional elites in distant centers (Gonlin 1994; McAnany 1995; Mehrer 2000; Robin 1999). Alternative discourses and social practices can be conducted in separate spatial or symbolic realms that do not contribute significantly to the negotiation or contestation of dominant ideologies. These practices are often carried out in less visible settings, often in the houses of commoners away from the view of elites or their functionaries (Robin 1999). Finally, commoners may not have much involvement in the production or reproduction of a dominant ideology if it is largely constructed to engage other nobles (Abercrombie et al. 1980) so that commoners are excluded from ritual expressions of ideology (Brumfiel 1998). For example, Elizabeth Brumfiel (1998) argues that Aztec state ideology was designed to achieve unity among the nobility, whereas power over commoners was largely coercive with little apparent concern for whether people penetrated the dominant ideology.

Recent poststructuralist and feminist theory recognizes that subordinate groups, including commoners, always have some degree of penetration of dominant discourses that can be actualized as resistance (Butler 1993; Comaroff 1985; Giddens 1979:145–150; Goldstein 2003; Kertzer 1988; Scott 1985, 1990). In particular, James Scott (1985, 1990) has explored the ways in which non-elites express resistance to domination in a wide variety of forms, both discursively and non-discursively. Resistance can occur as active rebellion, although more often it is expressed in subtle forms that do not directly confront authority or that operate in ways that appear to reinforce dominant ideas and institutions. Commoners are often limited to expressing resistance in subtle hidden forms because of the possibility of reprisals by elites. Even under highly repressive forms of domination, however, commoners can at least express resistance passively, subtly, or privately. Under less repressive conditions, it is often still difficult to invest in and organize more overt and challenging forms of protest because subordinates are caught up in the daily struggle to make a living.

Scott (1990) terms these subtle and often less visible or disguised forms of resistance the "hidden transcript." Examples of hidden transcripts include private or concealed rituals that challenge or bypass authority, although these examples would overlap with what we have termed *independence.* Resistance also includes foot-dragging, or withholding payments to the state in the form of labor or resources (Dirks 1994; Giddens 1979:145–150; Scott 1990). Dominant ideologies always provide a framework in which subordinates can resist, such as by claiming that the ideologically constructed social contract has not been met by the elite (Scott 1976). Resistance via a dominant ideology can be more public since it does not appear to overtly challenge ideas that legitimate authority, providing subordinates more leeway to express resistance. Legal labor actions, appeals to rulers to curb exploitation by lesser nobles, and elite-sanctioned rituals of reversal are examples of resistance expressed through the symbolic language of domination (Kertzer 1988:144–150; Scott 1990). Scott (1990) argues that expressions of resistance via the principles of domination appear superficially to reinforce domination and so, although more visible to elites as social action, are still hidden as forms of resistance. Nevertheless, it is important to recognize that "hidden" forms of resistance contribute to social production and are not simply passive reactions to domination.

These hidden forms of resistance account, in part, for the absence of commoners in most considerations of power by both traditional social theorists and archaeologists (Janusek 2004; A. Joyce et al. 2001; Lohse, Chapter 1; Robin 1999). The expression of resistance in subtle, often disguised forms tends to create the historical impression that expressions of resistance by commoners are rare and that people have been duped by dominant discourses. The appearance of an uncontested domination is also a product of what Scott (1990) calls the "public transcript," where the dominant discourse is overwhelmingly represented in overt, public expressions of power in writing, architecture, art, and ritual performance. It is in the interest of elites to represent power as uncontested, and public performances of subordinates "will out of prudence, fear, and the desire to curry favor, be shaped to appeal to the expectations of the powerful" (Scott 1990:2). Rituals objectify and embody particular power relations and may create a degree of social cohesion and a shared corporate identity, but they also tolerate a considerable degree of resistance and negotiated appropriation (Bell 1992; Kertzer 1988). Expressions of resistance via the principles of a dominant ideology may also appear to be affirmations of that ideology, further reinforcing hegemonic appearances.

Since the hidden transcript of resistance is often carried out in private and disguised, its material expressions in the archaeological record are challenging to identify. Places in which expressions of resistance should be more common and overt will be distant or hidden from the view of elites or their functionaries (e.g., Brumfiel 1996; Casella 2001; Robin 1999; Scott 1985, 1990; Stein 1999), including household settings, peripheral communities, and the countryside (e.g., shrines, rituals in fields, forest poaching). During periods of rebellion and political upheaval, however, the hidden transcript often becomes public and resistance can be more enthusiastically and openly expressed (e.g., during the Pueblo Revolt of the 1680s in the American Southwest and the 1847 Caste War of Yucatán). Rebellions and periods marked by the collapse of established political orders allow commoners to express alternative discourses and the anger that is stifled by coercive and oppressive systems (A. Joyce et al. 2001; Scott 1990:213). Times of social and political upheaval also often compel people to reassess aspects of the world as hegemonically constituted and to increasingly penetrate the dominant ideology (Comaroff and Comaroff 1991). It is, therefore, periods of political upheaval and collapse that are most promising for observing the public expressions of commoner power in the form of resistance and outright rebellion. Prehispanic Mesoamerica's most dramatic period of political upheaval was the collapse of the centralized, urban states of the Classic period.

RESISTANCE AND THE CLASSIC-TO-POSTCLASSIC TRANSITION

The Late Classic period political landscape of Mesoamerica was dominated by powerful state polities with their political capitals located at urban centers such as Tikal, Teotihuacan, and Monte Albán. The power of Late Classic Mesoamerican nobles and the state institutions they controlled was based on a combination of religious authority, military coercion, and economic control (Chase and Chase 1992; Cowgill 1997; A. Joyce and

Winter 1996; Marcus and Flannery 1996:208–235; Sabloff and Henderson 1993; Scarborough 1998; Schele and Freidel 1990). These forms of state power were legitimated by religious beliefs, which were embodied in a wide range of public and private ceremonies sponsored, directly and indirectly, by the nobility. Religious practices that communicated ideological principles and power relations included a complex set of rituals involving sacrifice, shamanism, ancestor veneration, bloodletting, processions, divination, dance, dedicatory and termination rituals, and mortuary ceremonialism.

From approximately A.D. 700 to A.D. 1000, however, many Mesoamerican states collapsed. The specific timing, causes, histories, and consequences of the collapse varied across Mesoamerica. Most regions, however, experienced dramatic changes in political institutions and ruling ideologies, including the political fragmentation of polities, depopulation of many major cities, and the loss of power by ruling dynasties (Culbert, ed., 1973; Demarest et al. 1997; Diehl and Berlo 1989; Inomata 1997; Lucero 2002; Sabloff and Andrews 1986; Sabloff and Henderson 1993; Sharer 1994; Webster 2002). Some regions, such as the Copán Valley in Honduras and parts of the Petén lowlands, were largely depopulated (Culbert, ed., 1973; Sabloff and Andrews 1986; Sharer 1994; Webster 2002). Explanations for the collapse have varied from region to region but usually focus on some combination of warfare, landscape degradation, climate change, and internal political unrest. Several researchers have suggested that a rebellion by commoners may have been a major factor in the Classic period collapse (Millon 1988; Thompson 1954). At Teotihuacan, evidence for the destruction and looting of ritual objects, the burning of public buildings, and the defacement of monuments could have been the result of a commoner revolt, although other explanations, such as factional conflict or warfare, are also plausible (Manzanilla et al. 1996:247; Millon 1988). With the possible exception of Teotihuacan, however, we recognize little evidence at present for widespread commoner rebellions at the end of the Classic period.

Although outright rebellion was probably not a major factor in the collapse, we wish to explore whether changes in ruling institutions at the end of the Classic period and the collapse of those institutions by the Early Postclassic provided commoners with greater freedom to express independence from and resistance to dominant ideologies. We explore the relationship between commoners and dominant discourses in two ways. First, we consider evidence from the Late Classic period for the increasing exclusion of commoners from the "public transcript" of state-sponsored politico-religious ceremonies performed in public spaces that would have engaged people in ritual expression of state ideology (Kertzer 1988; Scott 1990). Although ceremonial expressions of state power do not necessarily diminish resistance, they can contribute to social cohesion and a corporate identity by creating a shared communal experience that celebrates the symbols and history of the state and its rulers. Public rituals also communicate the coercive power of the state in ways that tend to drive resistance into more hidden and disguised forms out of fear of reprisals. If state ceremonies excluded commoners, then we might expect that non-elites would have been increasingly distanced and disengaged from dominant ideologies. Disengagement from state ceremonies could have increased cognitive dissonance among commoners and led to the reopening of hegemonic ideas as well as the increasing penetration of the dominant ideology (Comaroff and Comaroff 1991:26; Janusek 2004:15–16). Since Mesoamerican nobles acted as intermediaries between commoners and the sacred realm (A. Joyce 2000; Schele and Freidel 1990), commoners may also have sought new ways to contact the Otherworld through domestic ritual (Brumfiel 1996; Plunket 2002; Weller 2002).

Second, we examine evidence for ritual expressions of the "hidden transcript" of resistance both before and after the collapse. We expect that identifying hidden transcripts of resistance before the collapse may prove difficult because they were probably often subtle, disguised, or hidden. This point is an important one and will be elaborated later. In addition, Mesoamerican archaeologists are only just beginning to explore the relationship between domestic rituals of commoners and state ceremonies sponsored by nobles (L. Brown 2000; Brumfiel 1996; Garber et al. 1998; Lucero 2003; McAnany 1995; Plunket 2002; Weller 2002). Expressions of resistance to ruling ideologies should be more overt and public immediately following the collapse of ruling institutions (A. Joyce et al. 2001). These post-collapse expressions of dissatisfaction with the Late Classic state reflect a response to a collective memory (Hendon 2000; Lohse, Chapter 1) of the experiences of domination, as well as a probable reassessment of hegemonic understandings, and are not examples of precisely what Scott (1990) characterized as the hidden transcript. We argue, however, that they are useful for providing indications that commoners penetrated dominant ideologies immediately prior to the collapse and that they probably were expressing resistance via a hidden transcript during the Late Classic. Overall, we hope that our examples provide some useful avenues of research to explore commoner resistance in ancient Mesoamerica.

COMMONERS AND THE PUBLIC TRANSCRIPT OF DOMINATION

We examine changes in the spatial layout of the ceremonial precincts of Classic period urban centers as a means of assessing the degree to which commoners were excluded from the public transcript of state power. Evidence from many of the major Classic period state-centers of Mesoamerica indicates that ceremonial precincts embodied politico-religious beliefs that legitimated authority (Ashmore 1991; Ashmore and Sabloff 2002; A. Joyce 2000; Koontz et al. 2001; Sugiyama 1993). The physical arrangement and symbolism of buildings, plazas, courtyards, roads, and other architectural features were important structural elements that channeled the movement and experiences of actors, especially during ritual performances. The ongoing use and alteration of monumental spaces in turn transformed the meanings they embodied. Researchers of architectural space have shown that by manipulating space through the erection of physical or symbolic barriers, elites can restrict interaction between members of different groups to times and places of their choosing so as to control both the content and presentation of social discourse (Hegmon et al. 2000; Hillier and Hanson 1984; Love 1999). In this section we argue that toward the end of the Classic period, ceremonial precincts in many cities were increasingly closed off and segmented in ways that intentionally or unintentionally restricted access by commoners. In several Late Classic cities, the ceremonial precincts also appear to have increasingly changed from public space to private ritual and residential spaces restricted to the elite (A. Joyce 2004).

Monte Albán, Mexico

In the Valley of Oaxaca, Mexico, the ceremonial precinct of the Zapotec capital of Monte Albán was the site's Main Plaza (Figure 6.1). The Main Plaza was a huge public plaza measuring roughly 300 m north-south by 150 m east-west (Acosta 1965). In its final form the Main Plaza complex was bounded on its north and south ends by high platforms supporting numerous public buildings. The eastern and western sides of the Main Plaza were defined by rows of monumental buildings; a third row of structures ran north-south through the center of the plaza. Like monumental spaces at other ceremonial centers in Mesoamerica (Ashmore 1991; Ashmore and Sabloff 2002; Sugiyama 1993), the Main Plaza complex was built as an axis mundi, creating a point of communication and mediation between the human world and the supernatural Otherworld (Gámez

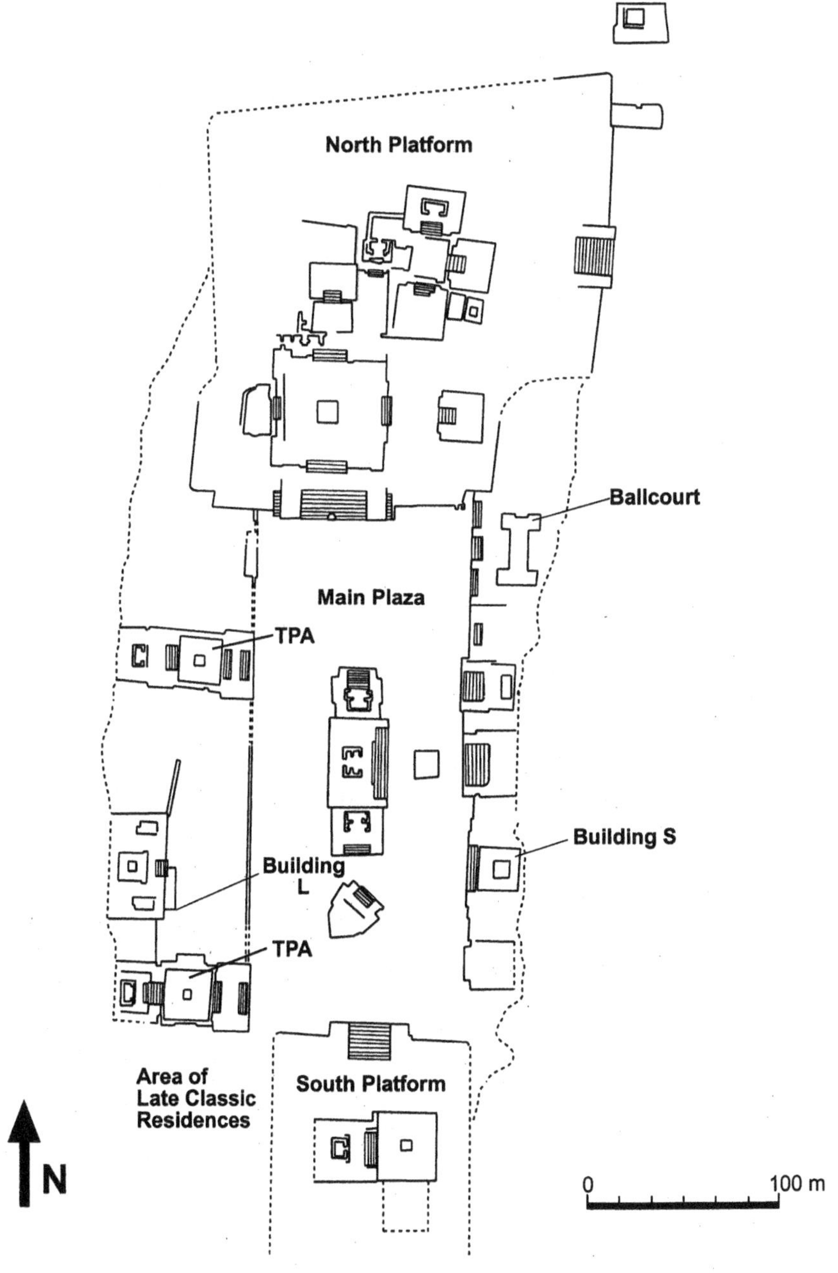

6.1. Plan of the Main Plaza at Monte Albán, Oaxaca, Mexico.

Goytia 2002; A. Joyce 2000, 2004). The archaeological evidence suggests that the Main Plaza was an arena where thousands of people participated in public rituals organized and led by the nobility (A. Joyce 2000, 2004; Marcus and Flannery 1996).

An analysis of the life history of Monte Albán's Main Plaza shows that through time the ceremonial precinct was increasingly closed off, thereby restricting and channeling traffic into the plaza. The Main Plaza was first constructed toward the end of the Middle Formative (ca. 500 B.C.) and at this time consisted only of its western row of buildings and the North Platform (A. Joyce 2004; Winter 2001). Until the Terminal Formative, the Main Plaza was therefore open on its eastern and possibly its southern sides, making activities on the plaza accessible to commoners living on the terraces below. During the Terminal Formative, early versions of the South Platform as well as the eastern and central row of structures were built. Access to the Main Plaza was further restricted during the Classic period by the construction of buildings that increasingly closed off access points to the plaza (Blanton 1978:63–66). By the Late Classic the only public entry points were narrow corridors on the northeastern and southeastern corners of the plaza.

The Main Plaza by the Late Classic period had become a focus of elite domestic activities and appears to have been less frequently used as an arena for large-scale public ceremonies (Hutson 2002; A. Joyce 2004; Winter 2001). Beginning with its initial construction around 500 B.C., elite residences had always been located near the Main Plaza, creating an elite ceremonial precinct. During the Late/Terminal Formative, elite residences were located on and around the North Platform but did not directly face onto the Main Plaza. Although elite residences continued to be concentrated around the North Platform, during the Early Classic a high-status residence was also built in the southwestern corner of the plaza just west of the South Platform. During the Late Classic at least ten residences were constructed in this area. Elaborate Late Classic palace complexes were also built directly facing each other on the southern end of the Main Plaza. One of these structures was Building S, the largest Late Classic palace identified at the site.

Another major change in spatial configuration during the Late Classic was the construction of two temple-patio-altar (or TPA) complexes on the west side of the Main Plaza, creating restricted ceremonial spaces. The TPA consists of a temple elevated on a platform that faces a patio with an altar in the center. Access to the TPA was usually restricted by building a wall around the patio or by constructing a sunken patio. This trend toward restricted ceremonial spaces is found in administrative centers throughout the valley (Kowalewski et al. 1989:262–263).

A shift away from large-scale public ceremonies and toward restricted, private ones is also indicated by a contextual analysis of monumental art (A. Joyce 2004). During the Late Classic most newly carved stones at Monte Albán and other sites in the valley were set in highly restricted locations, especially as carved lintels and doorjambs for tombs. Themes represented on carved stone monuments also changed during the Classic period. Public monuments erected on the Main Plaza during the Formative expressed themes of human sacrifice and warfare with few overt depictions of nobles. By the Late Classic, the most common type of carved stone depicted several generations of nobles, sometimes showing marriage scenes or rituals related to ancestor veneration. Another form of Late Classic elite art included painted murals found in the valley's most elaborate tombs, which depict scenes of ancestor veneration (Miller 1995). The data on both spatial organization of ceremonial space and the context and iconography of monumental art suggest that by the Late Classic, Monte Albán's nobles were less concerned with large-scale public ceremonies and more focused on rituals involving restricted audiences of other elites.

Caracol, Belize

Like Monte Albán, many lowland Maya political centers have evidence for the increasing restriction of commoners from expressions of the public transcript of domination during state rituals in ceremonial precincts. For example, at the massive city of Caracol in the Maya Mountains of Belize there is evidence that during the Late/Terminal Classic, rulers restricted non-elite access to ceremonial space (Chase and Chase 1985, 1987, 2001a, 2001b). The earliest public ceremonial space at Caracol dates to the Preclassic in the A-Group Plaza. By the Late Classic, the ceremonial emphasis shifted to the nearby B-Group Plaza, whereas the use of space in the ceremonial precinct, consisting of both the A-Group and B-Group plazas, was increasingly restricted (Chase and Chase 1985). During the Late and Terminal Classic, the entire site core—including both the A-Group Plaza and the B-Group Plaza—was effectively closed off. Access to the ceremonial precinct was through a number of causeways connected to elite residential groups. The increasingly restricted setting of elite ritual activities was exemplified by the Caana, or "Sky Place," in the B-Group Plaza.

The Caana is the largest structure at the site and includes a combination of palace rooms along with three temples surrounding a central court at the summit of the pyramid. Ritual activities associated with the summit temples and court would not have been visible from the plaza floor below. The huge Caana pyramid, therefore, supported a private temple complex whose usage was restricted to the ruling elite and whose modifications extend very late into the Late and Terminal Classic.

Xunantunich, Belize

The important Late/Terminal Classic Maya center of Xunantunich in western Belize provides additional evidence that access to the main ceremonial precinct was increasingly restricted at the end of the Classic period. In the Late Classic (ca. A.D. 700–850), the ceremonial center comprised Plazas AI and AII (Figure 6.2), an area dominated by the massive Castillo temple and accessed via multiple entranceways (Keller 1995; Leventhal 1996; Leventhal and Ashmore 2004; Yaeger 2003). During the Terminal Classic (ca. A.D. 850–1050), the ceremonial precinct as well as the site as a whole contracted to focus on Plaza AI (Figure 6.3), which remained the only public space at the site (Leventhal 1996:11).

The changes during the Late to Terminal Classic transition at Xunantunich are numerous and began with the abandonment of the site to the south of the Castillo. Access to the summit of the Castillo was restricted by an "audiencia building" (Structure A-1) that served both to shield sections of the structure from view and to physically restrict access (Leventhal 1996:11; Leventhal and Ashmore 2004:173). The main plaza area, composed of Plazas AI and AII, which during the Late Classic consisted of a single open space, was segregated in the Terminal Classic by the construction of Structure A-1. Structure A-1 limited access to the northern plaza to a narrow passage that effectively closed off the space immediately in front of the Castillo, which served to reduce public ritual space to the south section of the plaza. Structure A-1 also incorporated one side of an existing ballcourt (Ballcourt II) into its mass, further delineating two separate plaza spaces not only spatially but ideologically (Leventhal 1996:12). Additional private space was created by the construction of Structure A-16, consisting of a small, two-room superstructure surrounding a stela and altar. Structure A-16 removed the altar and stela from public view and further narrowed the passageway between the two plazas. Access to Plaza AII was then almost completely blocked by the dismantling of an earlier

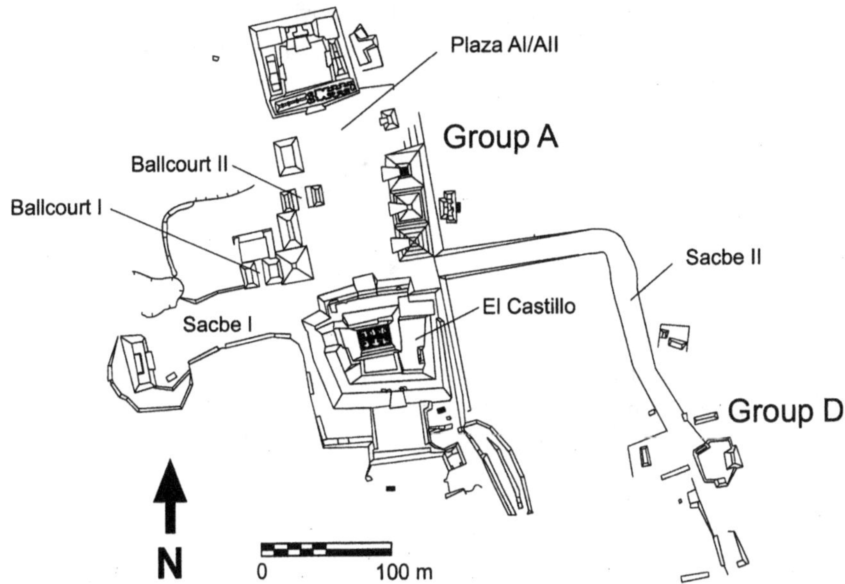

6.2. Plan of Xunantunich, Belize, Group A, Late Classic period (redrawn from Robin 1999: figure 4).

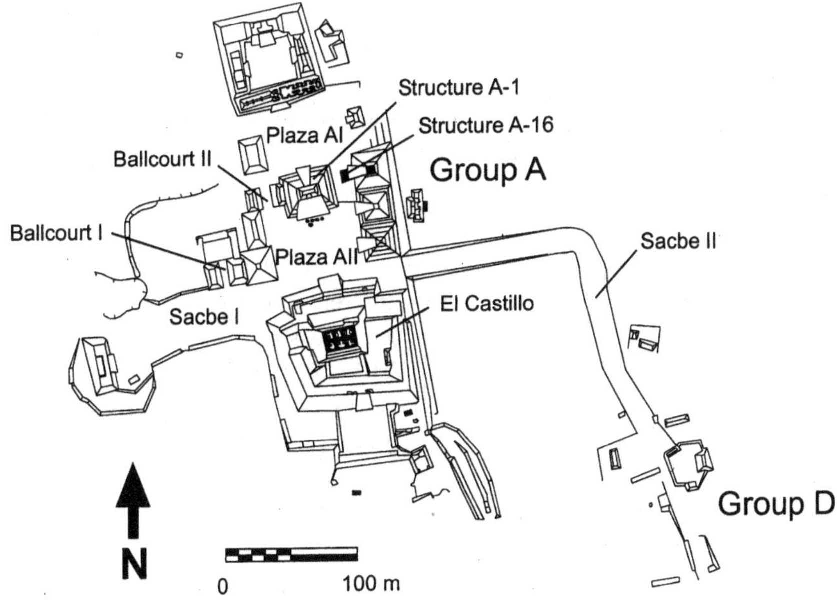

6.3. Plan of Xunantunich, Belize, Group A, Terminal Classic period (redrawn from Robin 1999:figure 7).

stairway and the construction of a wall. According to Richard Leventhal (1996:13), "Plaza AII is closed to the public and, we believe, is only accessed by the elite family and various family retainers and other elite individuals. Plaza AI remains the only area open to the public within the site core." Leventhal (1996:14) argues that by the end of the Terminal Classic, the ruling family of Xunantunich was physically separated from the surrounding community.

Altun Ha, Belize

Located in northern Belize, the site of Altun Ha was a major Maya political center from the Late Preclassic into the Early Postclassic period (Pendergast 1979, 1982, 1992). Excavations by David Pendergast identified the primary spaces for public ceremonies as the A and B plazas (Figure 6.4). Investigation of the construction history reveals a trend of increasing enclosure of these plaza spaces and the addition of elite residences in formerly ceremonial space.

In the Early Classic, the A Plaza witnessed an intensive phase of construction as the ceremonial space was defined (Pendergast 1979). Multiple access points from the north, east, and west were present, and inhabitants of the adjacent residential Zone C could move freely to and from the plaza. In the Late Classic, however, a construction program was initiated that gradually closed down major access points and served to divert the flow of foot traffic. One of the key changes was the addition of Structure A8 in an area that had previously been open plaza space, which effectively closed off access from Zone C. When Structure A8 was completed it was used for rituals, but this purpose soon changed as it was converted into an elite residence. Additional ceremonial structures were built that effectively shielded Structure A8 from the remainder of the plaza; the noble residents of Structure A8 had private access to these ritual buildings. As access to the plaza became more restricted, the plaza also assumed a more domestic function, as one of the last additions to the main plaza was Structure A7, another elite residence. Pendergast (1979:196) believes these additions are indicative of "increasing internalization and secretiveness" and signal the "start of an internalization process and of a widening gulf between ruler and populace." Similar trends toward restricted access and a shift from ceremonial to elite residential space are also apparent in the B Plaza (Pendergast 1982:142–144). When the construction history of the ceremonial precincts at Altun Ha is considered, it indicates an elite more di-

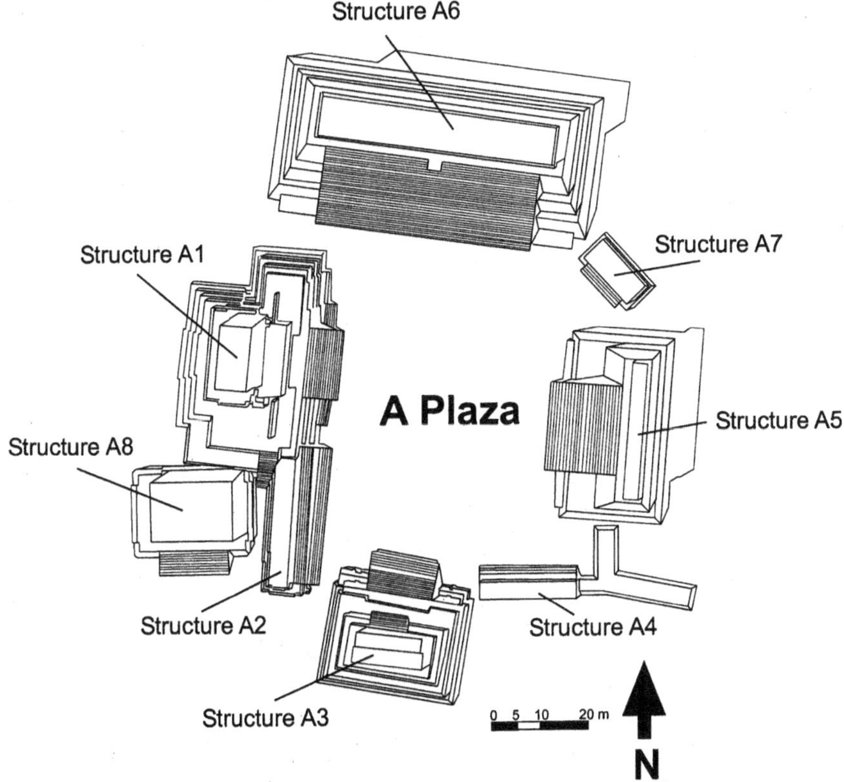

6.4. Plan of Altun Ha, Belize, A Plaza (redrawn from Pendergast 1979:figure 1).

rectly associating themselves with ceremonial spaces and buildings while increasingly restricting access by the populace.

A Summary of Archaeological Evidence

The detailed evidence from Caracol, Xunantunich, and Altun Ha reveals that the architectural changes of the Late/Terminal Classic increasingly excluded commoners from ceremonial precincts. Evidence from many other lowland Maya centers also suggests this trend. For example, during the Late Classic at Blue Creek in northwestern Belize, the site's core area was increasingly transformed from a public ceremonial space to a high-status residential zone (Lichtenstein 1996, 2000). At Baking Pot, a medium-sized center in western Belize, Late Classic nobles constructed Group II, a highly restricted ceremonial precinct formed by range structures, a ballcourt, and the largest pyramid at the site (Moore 1999; Willey et al. 1965). Access into this plaza was from only two points: a southern ballcourt and a causeway. Finally, at Tikal in the Petén lowlands of Guatemala, the eighth-century construction of Temples 1 and 2 significantly closed off the Great Plaza ceremonial precinct (Harrison 1999; Laporte 1993). At about the same time, the North Acropolis was closed off by the construction of several temples along its front.

The evidence from Oaxaca and parts of the Maya Lowlands suggests that at the end of the Classic period, commoners were being excluded from ceremonial precincts at many major political centers. These precincts had been places where both nobles and commoners participated in ritual expressions of the public transcript of domination during earlier periods. By the Late/Terminal Classic, however, monumental ceremonial precincts at these sites were increasingly restricted to private elite ritual and residential spaces. We should acknowledge, however, that our sample is limited to sites where detailed architectural histories are available. In addition, not all sites that we examined seemed to show this shift toward the closing off of ceremonial precincts and the exclusion of commoners. The available data from Teotihuacan (Millon 1973) and Copán (Fash 1991; Gonlin, Chapter 4), for example, do not suggest major changes in the accessibility of ceremonial space during the Late Classic. Nevertheless, it is our impression that by the Late Classic, ceremonial precincts at many sites in Mesoamerica were losing their public character. Commoners may have been largely excluded from ceremonial expressions of elite power, which could have provided them with the opportunity and perhaps the necessity to find alternative means to contact the sacred via local public and domestic rituals (Barba et al., Chapter 3). To the degree that ceremonial performances of commoners also expressed dissatisfaction with rulers as well as ruling institutions and ideologies, they would also represent a hidden transcript of resistance. In the next section we consider evidence for ritual expressions of a hidden transcript before and after the Classic period collapse.

THE HIDDEN TRANSCRIPT OF COMMONER RESISTANCE

Since hidden transcripts are often carried out in concealed locations or disguised as something other than resistance, we expect that their material expressions in the archaeological record will be challenging to identify. As discussed previously, we hypothesize that expressions of resistance should be more common and visible in households, peripheral communities, and the countryside, places that are distant or hidden from the view of elites or their functionaries. We have chosen to focus on the Classic period collapse since we suspect that during periods of rebellion and political upheaval, cognitive dissonance with the dominant discourse increases and the hidden transcript often becomes more public and should be more visible archaeologically. In this section, we consider evidence for expressions of resistance by commoners before and immediately after the collapse of Classic period states.

The increasing exclusion and disengagement of commoners from state ceremonies at the end of the Classic may have weakened their allegiance to state rulers, institutions, and symbols, leading to disaffection from the state actualized in independence from and perhaps resistance to domination. Unfortunately, several factors, in addition to the concealed and/or disguised nature of resistance, make hidden transcripts difficult to identify. Perhaps the most significant problem is that studies of the ritual practices of commoners are only just beginning in Mesoamerica (see reviews by L. Brown 2000; Johnston and Gonlin 1998; Lohse, Chapter 1; Plunket 2002; Robin 2003) and few studies trace changes through time in commoner ritual practices (Chase and Chase 1998:327; Garber et al. 1998; LeCount 2001). Another problem is the identification of rituals specifically as expressions of resistance.

Cynthia Robin (2003) has identified three primary types of commoner rituals in household studies: (1) burial and ancestor worship, (2) feasting, and (3) dedication and termination rituals (also see Gonlin, Chapter 4). Several researchers have pointed out the congruence between the ritual forms of commoners and elites (Garber et al. 1998; McAnany 1995; Robin 2001, 2003; Walker and Lucero 2000; Weller 2002; Yaeger 2002). Similarities in ritual practices across social classes, however, can be interpreted in several ways (Robin 1999). For example, elites may have appropriated traditional ritual forms found in domestic settings or commoners may have appropriated elite rituals. In the latter case, commoners could be resisting elite control over ritual authority, or they could be affirming a dominant ideology through domestic expressions of state rituals. Jon Lohse (Chapter 1) has suggested that commoners might use local rather than exotic materials in household activities and thereby reduce the degree of elite control on their lives. The use of local materials in commoner rituals (e.g., substituting local lithics for jade) could be an expression of independence from or resistance to elite power but could also be a result of the availability or cost of exotics (see Olson, Chapter 9). The political significance of differences in ritual forms between elites and commoners is also difficult to assess, although Rosemary Joyce (1993) has shown a divergence in state and popular imagery of women for the Classic Maya that could reflect resistance to dominant gender ideologies.

The most effective way of identifying ritual expressions of resistance would involve tracking changes in commoner ritual through time relative to elite expressions of dominant ideologies, especially toward the end of the Classic as ruling institutions begin to fail. One intriguing example of changes in ritual practices possibly linked to increasing commoner resistance during the Late Classic is found at Caracol. Diane Chase and Arlen Chase (1998) have found evidence for a shift in the context of caching practices from public architecture to domestic contexts during the Late Classic, concurrent with the increasing exclusion of commoners from public ceremonial spaces. They (1998:327) argue:

> Changes occur in the caching (and burial) patterns at Caracol. Ordered epicentral Late Preclassic/Early Classic caches are believed to have functioned in the sanctification of ritual space related to the territorial whole. This class of caches is associated only with public architecture through the Early Classic era. Late Classic offerings were both more varied and more decentralized. . . . The shift in cache emphasis from monumental architecture to domestic architecture seen at Caracol (and possibly at Altun Ha), however, is reflective of a continuity in caching practice documented for the Post-Classic period . . . the shift in placement of the most important ritual deposits of the Maya ultimately from epicentral monumental architecture to domestically linked architecture located throughout the community is clearly reflective of very different, but effective, strategies for dealing with a changing Maya world.

Data such as these are usually interpreted as expressions of the acceptance of a dominant ideology by common people (e.g., Chase and Chase 2004:141). We would like to raise the possibility that the increase in domestic ritual across the site of Caracol was the result of commoners' appropriation of formerly elite ritual practices and an expression of independence and perhaps resistance.

Archaeological evidence from Monte Albán also suggests the possibility of resistance by lesser nobles and/or commoners at the end of the Late Classic period. Archaeological data suggest that at this time the site's nobility were increasingly isolating themselves from the general population as people began to leave the city and ruling institutions failed

(Blanton 1978:100; Winter 2003). Many of Monte Albán's elite residences were abandoned or were rebuilt on a smaller, more modest scale. Several new high-status residences were built in the Main Plaza complex in very restricted locations often protected by walls. For example, a high-status residence was built on top of the nine-meter-high platform of Building L, which had previously supported a temple. The Building L residence was separated from the Main Plaza by an adobe wall built along the west side of the plaza, which was the latest construction detected on the Main Plaza. Another high-status house built at this time was located adjacent to the Late Classic TPA on the highest point of the North Platform. A diagonal adobe wall blocked the view of the residence from people on the flat area north of the ballcourt, which had been the major access point to the Main Plaza. Residences throughout the site became increasingly enclosed and inwardly focused during the Late Classic, perhaps because of rising social tensions and divisions, especially between competing nobles and/or commoners (Hutson 2002:68–69).

Despite these intriguing cases, few clear examples of Classic period resistance have been identified in the archaeological record. The emerging interest in commoner ritual, as exemplified by this volume, will undoubtedly provide additional evidence of hidden transcripts as well as new means of teasing out resistance from other ways in which commoners participated in the social negotiation of power.

Another promising approach to identifying resistance to the ruling ideas and institutions of the Classic period state is to consider the reaction of commoners to the collapse of these institutions. Archaeological, epigraphic, and iconographic data demonstrate that the political, economic, and military power of Classic period rulers in Mesoamerica was primarily legitimated through religious beliefs and practices (e.g., Ashmore and Sabloff 2002; Chase and Chase 1992; Joyce and Winter 1996; Martin and Grube 2000; McAnany 1995; Schele and Freidel 1990). As we discussed previously, the ceremonial precincts of political centers were axis mundi where nobles performed important state ceremonies. The coercive power of the nobility during the Classic period appears to have constrained the agency of commoners such that resistance may have been expressed as a hidden transcript that is difficult to identify archaeologically at this time. The threat of coercive sanctions, however, would have been lessened or eliminated after the collapse and people would then have been freer to overtly express their views concerning rulers and ruling institutions. It is also possible that the social upheaval of the collapse might have caused

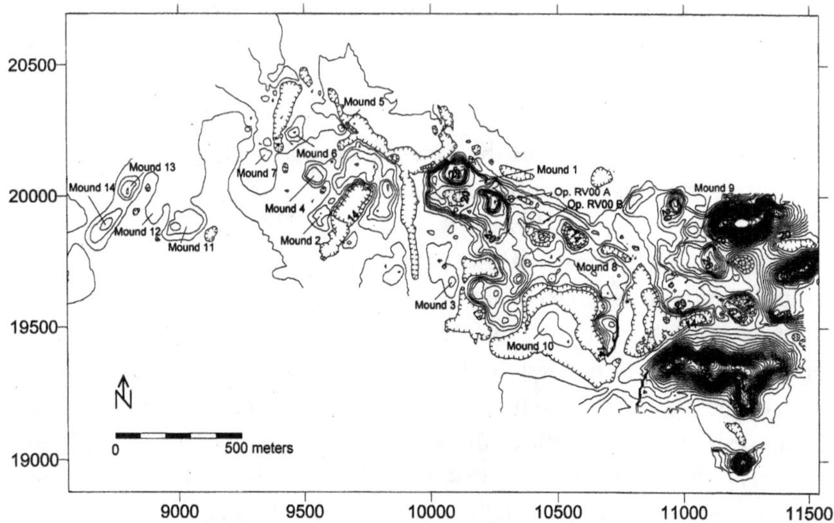

6.5. Plan of Río Viejo, Oaxaca, Mexico, showing mounds and locations of excavations in 2000.

people to reassess and question previously hegemonic aspects of the dominant discourse. Evidence that commoners destroyed and denigrated symbols of Classic period ruling institutions immediately following the collapse would suggest that even before the collapse, commoners had penetrated dominant ideologies and expressed resistance via a hidden transcript (A. Joyce n.d.; A. Joyce et al. 2001). Evidence for the denigration and destruction of state symbols has been recovered from coastal Oaxaca, the Maya Lowlands, and perhaps Teotihuacan.

In the lower Río Verde Valley on the Pacific coast of Oaxaca, archaeological research shows that during the Late Classic the region was the locus of a state polity with its capital at the urban center of Río Viejo (A. Joyce 1993, 1999; A. Joyce et al. 2001; Urcid and Joyce 2001). Late Classic Río Viejo covered 250 ha, with much of the site artificially raised above the floodplain by a series of large residential platforms (Figure 6.5). Río Viejo's Late Classic civic-ceremonial center was the huge acropolis designated Mound 1, which measured 350 x 200 m along its base. The acropolis supported two large substructures, reaching heights of 15 m above the floodplain. Evidence that Mound 1 was a locus of important public ceremonies includes the presence of three Late Classic carved stone monuments, a large public plaza, and a sunken patio. Excavations on Mound 1–Structure 2, the monumental substructure located on the eastern portion

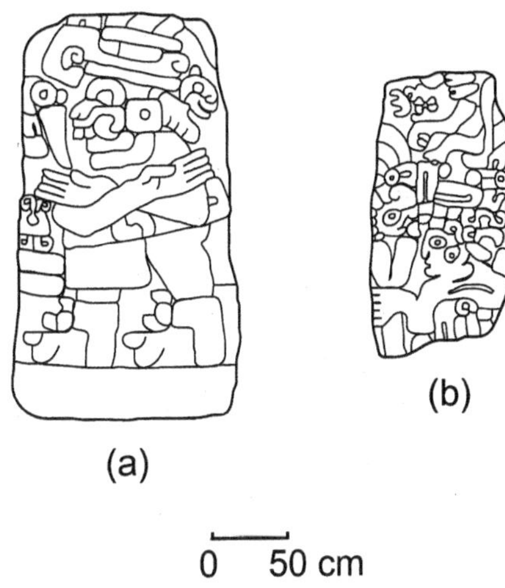

6.6. Carved stone monuments from Río Viejo, Oaxaca, Mexico (a = Monument 8; b = Monument 11).

of the acropolis, exposed the poorly preserved remains of a public building. A test excavation 50 m south of Mound 1 recovered thick deposits of sherds from fancy serving vessels, suggesting elite domestic activities or ceremonial feasting (A. Joyce 1991:480). A total of thirteen carved stone monuments has been dated stylistically to the Late Classic at Río Viejo (Urcid and Joyce 2001). Many of the carved stones depict nobles, probably rulers of Río Viejo, dressed in elaborate costumes and sometimes accompanied by a glyph that represents their calendrical name (Figure 6.6). Data from a full-coverage regional survey over 152 km^2 show that Río Viejo was the first-order capital of a seven-tiered settlement hierarchy (A. Joyce et al. 2001:352–353). The evidence from the lower Río Verde Valley shows that the Río Viejo polity shared many features with other Late Classic Mesoamerican states, including urbanism, monumental art and architecture, writing, the institution of kingship, craft specialization, and a settlement hierarchy with at least four levels (A. Joyce 1991, 1993, 1999; A. Joyce et al. 2001). The numerous carved stone monuments depicting individual rulers suggest an ideology that was focused on the institution of kingship and that sacrifice, ancestor worship, and genealogical ties were important elements of a dominant ideology.

The collapse of the Late Classic state in the lower Río Verde region is dated to approximately A.D. 800 (A. Joyce et al. 2001). The data from the lower Río Verde demonstrate that a major change in settlement patterns and sociopolitical organization occurred during the Early Postclassic period. The occupational area in the full-coverage survey zone declined from 605 ha in the Late Classic to 452 ha by the Early Postclassic, and the regional settlement hierarchy decreased from seven to four tiers. Río Viejo continued as a first-order center, although settlement at the site declined from 250 to 140 ha as another first-order center emerged at the site of San Marquitos. At Río Viejo, excavation data indicate a cessation of the construction of monumental buildings to house rulers and the ruling institutions of the state. The lack of monumental building activity is mirrored in a reduction in monumental art with only three stone monuments recorded at Río Viejo that are tentatively dated stylistically to the Early Postclassic and appear to represent deities rather than rulers (Urcid and Joyce 2001:211–212).

Large-scale horizontal excavations exposed two areas with the remains of Early Postclassic residences (A. Joyce et al. 2001; Joyce and King 2001). Operation A cleared 242 m^2 on Mound 1–Structure 2, the monumental substructure located on the eastern portion of the acropolis. Two structures were completely exposed as well as portions of three others. Operation B exposed portions of seven structures on Mound 8, approximately 180 m southeast of the acropolis. All of the Postclassic structures were low platforms, approximately 0.5 m high, and supported wattle-and-daub superstructures. The excavations yielded burials along with artifacts, features, and refuse that demonstrate the domestic function of these buildings. The size and form of the buildings in the two areas were virtually identical and the relatively modest architecture and burial offerings indicate commoner status. Similar structures have been observed and mapped on the surface over a broader area of Mound 8 (Joyce and King 2001). The excavations at Río Viejo, along with the regional survey data, suggest relatively little variation in wealth and power during the Early Postclassic.[1]

The Operation A excavations show that by the Early Postclassic, the acropolis at Río Viejo was no longer the civic-ceremonial center of the site but instead was a locus of commoner residences (Figure 6.7). The five low platforms exposed on the top of Mound 1–Structure 2 were densely packed, often with less than two meters separating structures. Three of the structures surrounded a central patio. The presence of commoner residences on the acropolis at Río Viejo shows that Early Postclassic people did not treat the earlier sacred spaces, objects, and buildings with the same reverence those places had been afforded in the Late Classic and earlier. This inference is reinforced by excavation data indicating that the stones used to construct the Early Postclassic platforms had been obtained by dismantling a Late Classic public building. In addition, at least five Late Classic carved stone monuments at the site were reused in later, probably Early Postclassic, walls. Excavations in Operation B recovered a fragment of a Late Classic period carved stone monument reutilized in an Early Postclassic wall (Joyce and King 2001). The fragment was the upper portion of the original monument and depicted the feathered headdress and

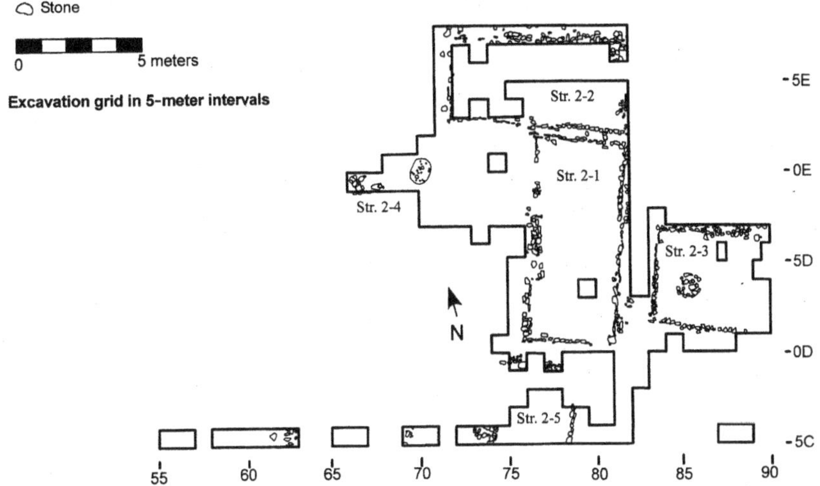

6.7. Plan of Op. RV00 A excavations, Río Viejo, Oaxaca, Mexico.

upper part of a noble's head. Prior to its placement in the wall of a commoner residence, this monument fragment had been utilized as a metate.

We find it highly unlikely that the stones from the public building and carved monuments were simply reused opportunistically for the construction of walls and a metate and that Early Postclassic people exhibited ignorance of or indifference to the earlier meanings of sacred objects and spaces.[2] Both operations exhibited stratigraphic continuity between Late Classic and Early Postclassic deposits and there were no indications of a hiatus in the occupation of these areas (Joyce and King 2001). Evidence from Mesoamerica and throughout the world shows that earlier meanings of monumental art and architecture continue to inform their reuse and reinterpretation for hundreds, and sometimes thousands, of years after their creation and initial use (Barrett 1999; Bender 1998; Bradley 1993, 1998). It is unlikely that only a few generations after the collapse of the Río Viejo state the earlier meaning of these portraits of rulers would have been lost and the stone they were made of would simply have been considered as convenient building materials. The occupation of the acropolis by commoners, the dismantling of public buildings, and the reuse of carved stone monuments for utilitarian purposes suggest the active destruction and denigration of earlier sacred spaces, objects, and buildings. We argue that the destruction, denigration, and reuse of these material symbols of the Late Classic state were based on a collective memory of the experiences of having lived under elite domination. By dismantling the public buildings of the Late Classic state to build their houses, commoners were re-inscribing the acropolis with markers of their identities as freed from the subjugation of the rulers and ruling institutions that were once housed in those buildings. Perhaps the most evocative symbol of this re-inscription was the symbolic act of grinding maize on the head of a Late Classic ruler.

In the southern Maya Lowlands evidence from several Late Classic political centers also suggests the destruction and denigration of the symbols of rulership during the collapse period. Evidence from Dos Pilas in the Petexbatun region of Guatemala suggests the active destruction of symbols of rulership immediately following the political collapse and the elite abandonment of the site (Palka 1997). In the period immediately after the collapse, local commoners continued to reside there. The post-collapse occupation consisted of continuity in some residences and occupation of formerly elite compounds by commoners. Some of the most striking examples of the destruction of earlier symbols of rulership include the intentional breaking of stone monuments and benches in the former residences of Maya elites at Dos Pilas. In Structure L4-41, fragments of carved stone monuments were recovered from wall fall, indicating they may have been reset into the walls after the collapse, similar to the Early Postclassic reuse of stone monuments at Río Viejo. Archaeological evidence also indicates that after the collapse, residents of Dos Pilas intentionally broke a hieroglyphic bench in Structure L4-41 and then dug a looter's pit over the noble burial interred beneath. Another hieroglyphic bench, destroyed in antiquity, was encountered in the Bat Palace at Dos Pilas. In Structure N5-21 another sculpted bench was dismantled and an intrusive non-elite burial was cut through the structure's plaster floor. In the El Duende pyramid a large block from the central staircase was removed and relocated to the stairway of another structure. Following the collapse of Dos Pilas, therefore, local people occupied elite areas of the site, looted materials (including tombs), smashed carved benches, and possibly broke a number of carved stone monuments.

Archaeological research at Xunantunich and its satellite communities of San Lorenzo and Chan Nòohol has shown that the first people to abandon the area during the collapse were mostly commoners, with elites generally holding out somewhat longer (Ashmore et al. 2004; LeCount et al. 2002; Robin 1999; Yaeger 2000). Research has found no evidence of mass death or environmental degradation that might have triggered the abandonment of the area. Instead, researchers suggest that the collapse of polities in the Petén heartland may have disrupted the external links that Xunantunich's nobles relied on for the symbolic and material resources that underwrote the power of the center's nobility. As the prestige and power of Xunantunich's nobles declined, people increasingly voted with their feet and left the area for nearby communities that had stronger ties to the growing political and economic networks linked to the Caribbean coast (Ashmore et al. 2004; Robin 1999:374). As the Xunantunich polity began to disintegrate during the Terminal Classic, nobles increasingly gifted decorated pottery to commoners (LeCount 1999), perhaps in an unsuccessful attempt to buy their allegiance. Yet at the nearby community of San Lorenzo, the remaining residents no longer used ties to the Xunantunich elite as a source of legitimating symbols (Ashmore et al. 2004:314).

Evidence from several other Classic period political centers also suggests the destruction and denigration of symbols of rulership immediately following the collapse. At Tikal, public buildings and palaces were used for refuse disposal, tombs and caches were looted, and stelae and altars were reused (Culbert 1973; Harrison 1999:192–198). Funerary practices at Tikal's Mundo Perdido changed during the ninth century from elite tombs to non-elite interments that were "intruded into earlier architectural elements, such as stairways and floors, or were simply laid under the rubble of fallen buildings" (Laporte 1993:312). During the ninth-century collapse, the residence of the royal family at Copán (Group 10L-2) and perhaps the entire Principal Group, as well as adjacent elite residential areas, were intentionally burned and destroyed (Andrews and Fash 1992). Several altars at Copán also were intentionally broken at this time. E. Wyllys Andrews and Barbara Fash (1992:86) argue that the destruction of the Principal Group was "almost certainly visited on an unwilling resident population by outsiders, either from within the Copán polity or from without." At Teotihuacan, people looted and destroyed ritual objects, set fire to public buildings, and defaced monuments (Cowgill 1997:156–157; Manzanilla et al. 1996:247; Millon 1988). Post-collapse changes in ritual paraphernalia in domestic courtyards at Teotihuacan may be related to the rejection of the state religion (Cowgill 1997:142; Manzanilla 2002:45). In the civic-ceremonial precinct of Altun Ha, trash was dumped in many buildings during or immediately following the collapse and a tomb was desecrated (Pendergast 1979:183, 199; 1982:144, 263).

SUMMARY AND CONCLUSIONS

Our goal in this chapter has been to explore ways in which resistance might be inferred from the archaeological record. We chose the Classic period collapse because any form of resistance is more likely to be visible when ruling institutions are collapsing even when resistance is not a major factor in political change. We have addressed resistance both directly, by exploring evidence for the expression of what Scott (1990) has termed the hidden transcript of resistance, and indirectly, by considering evidence for the exclusion of commoners from the public transcript of power, which may have fostered reassessments of hegemony and the penetration of dominant ideologies. What we have found is that resistance is difficult, although not impossible, to identify archaeologically. Given the available evidence, our conclusions must be considered tentative, although they hopefully provide some direction for exploring resistance in the archaeological record in general as well as for considering the role of commoner resistance specifically during the Classic period collapse.

The Late/Terminal Classic trend toward excluding commoners from ceremonial expressions of elite power would have distanced and disengaged non-elites from the public transcript of domination. Disengagement from state ceremonies could have increased cognitive dissonance among commoners and led to the reopening of hegemonic ideas as well as the increasing penetration of the dominant ideology. It is possible that the exclusion of commoners from state ceremonies could have been viewed as a violation of the moral responsibilities of the nobility (Jansen 2004). If nobles failed to meet their ritual obligations, commoners might have begun to find alternative means to contact the sacred.

Our data at present suggest the exclusion of commoners primarily from ceremonial precincts at major state centers, such as Monte Albán, Caracol, and Xunantunich. We hypothesize that under these circumstances people had the option to deepen their allegiance (and perhaps tribute) to local nobles in exchange for their ritual services. Commoners could also have increasingly contacted the sacred through their own ritual practices. To the degree that these changes in ritual practice expressed dissatisfaction with ruling elites and their ideologies, they would also constitute resistance. Although evidence from many parts of Mesoamerica suggests a weakening of the power of ruling elites toward the end of the Late Classic (Ashmore et al. 2004; Harrison 1999; Webster 2002; Webster et al. 2000), until the collapse commoners would have been subject to the coercive sanctions of the state. Resistance, therefore, was probably expressed as a hidden transcript in ways that were disguised, hidden, or couched in the symbolic language of domination.

At present, few examples of resistance have been identified in the archaeological record prior to the collapse. The lack of data for resistance could be the result of ancient people having been duped by a state ideology so that much of the dominant discourse was hegemonic in character. Overwhelming evidence from historically known societies shows, however, that domination is never complete and that there is always some degree of discursive penetration and resistance (e.g., Comaroff 1985; Jean Comaroff and Comaroff 1991; Dirks 1994; Goldstein 2003; Scott 1985, 1990). Instead, we suspect that the lack of evidence is a result of resistance having been expressed in hidden or disguised forms as well as the fact that commoner ritual and resistance have only been recognized as subjects of investigation for a relatively short time. Of course, concerted research into the lives of common people should provide new means of identifying resistance, especially through the study of ritual paraphernalia (e.g., censers and figurines) and ritual deposits (burials and caches). Undoubtedly, there are many forms of resistance, such as humor, sarcasm, and foot-dragging, that will be difficult or impossible to identify archaeologically. The most effective way to investigate hidden transcripts will involve tracking changes in state and commoner ritual to consider shifts in the degree of convergence or divergence in ritual practices, locations, and symbolic content (see Lohse, Chapter 1).

More overt and visible expressions of resistance are more likely to occur during and immediately following the collapse of ruling institutions. We have identified several examples of the destruction and denigration of state symbols immediately following the collapse that we argue reflect a collective memory of domination. In some cases these activities may have been the result of conflict and termination rituals that led to the collapse of these centers (Freidel 1998; Freidel et al. 1998). In most of the cases discussed here, however, the denigration of state symbols appears to have been at the hands of resident commoners who remained at these sites for at least a few years after the collapse. The data from Río Viejo, in particular, provide a strong case for resistance (A. Joyce et al. 2001).

This chapter represents only an initial exploration of resistance during the Classic-to-Postclassic transition. We conclude by suggesting a possible role for resistance in the collapse. In most regions of Mesoamerica, we find little evidence at present for social revolutions that triggered the collapse. The evidence in most of Mesoamerica suggests that the collapse occurred because of some combination of environmental degradation, climate change, warfare, factional competition, and the disruption of trade and alliance networks (Brenner et al. 2001; Cowgill 1997; Culbert, ed., 1973; Demarest et al. 1997; Lucero 2002; Sabloff and Andrews 1986; Sharer 1994; Webster 2002). We think it likely, however, that the disengagement of commoners from state ceremonies toward the end of the Classic period at least in some parts of Mesoamerica weakened their allegiance to the nobility, especially to ruling elites residing in polity centers. When the ruling institutions began to fail, regardless of the specific causes, commoners declined to support these institutions and their rulers. Commoners may have ceased paying tribute to nobles and in many cases, such as at Xunantunich, voted with their feet and abandoned the political centers. Our research suggests, therefore, that resistance contributed to the social conditions that led to the collapse. Regardless of their specific role in the collapse, it is important to recognize the contribution of commoners as well as nobles to social production and the negotiation of power in ancient Mesoamerica.

ACKNOWLEDGMENTS

We thank the Instituto Nacional de Antropología e Historia, especially the president of the Consejo de Arqueología, Joaquín García-Bárcena; and the directors of the Centro INAH Oaxaca, María de la Luz Topete, Ernesto González Licón, and Eduardo López Calzada, who have supported the research in the lower Río Verde Valley, Oaxaca. Funding for the field research in the lower Verde has been provided by grants from the following organizations: National Science Foundation (grants SBR-9729763 and BNS-8716332), Foundation for the Advancement of Mesoamerican Studies (#99012), National Geographic Society (grant 3767-88), Wenner-Gren Foundation (GR. 4988), Vanderbilt University Research Council and Mellon Fund, Fulbright Foundation, H. John Heinz III Charitable Trust, Explorers Club, Sigma Xi, University of Colorado, and Rutgers University. We thank Nancy Gonlin, Jon Lohse, and Payson Sheets for their comments on this chapter. We thank Jon Lohse and Nancy Gonlin for inviting us to participate in this volume. We also thank Chris Ward and Curtis Nepstad-Thornberry for drafting most of the figures.

NOTES

1. Early Postclassic evidence suggests only modest differences in wealth and power, which might suggest that the term *commoner* is inappropriate since inequality was minimal and there were no "elites" as defined by wealth differences. I argue, however, that the use of the term *commoner* is justified by the historical relations embodied in tradition and social memory, which would have reflected centuries of living under conditions of hierarchical political systems. It is also likely that the immediate descendants of Late Classic noble families continued to embrace an identity as nobles during the Early Postclassic even if these families were no longer distinguished by unusual wealth or political power. In other words, commoner and noble identities were not just a product of the economic relations of the time but were the result of historical relations embodied in people's dispositions.

2. Mesoamerican peoples have a strong indigenous historical tradition. Prehispanic Maya and Mixtec written texts recorded indigenous histories that referenced events occurring hundreds of years prior to the production of the text (Joyce et al. 2004; Martin and Grube 2000). Likewise, oral histories in indigenous Mesoamerican communities include social memories that reference places, people, and events of the prehispanic era.

REFERENCES CITED

Abercrombie, Nicholas, Stephen Hill, and Bryan S. Turner

1980 *The Dominant Ideology Thesis*. Allen and Unwin, London.

Acosta, Jorge G.

1965 Preclassic and Classic Architecture of Oaxaca. In *Handbook of Middle American Indians,* Volume 3, *Archaeology of Southern Mesoamerica,* Part 2, edited by Robert Wauchope and Gordon R. Willey, pp. 814–836. University of Texas Press, Austin.

Andrews, E. Wyllys, V, and Barbara W. Fash

1992 Continuity and Change in a Royal Maya Residential Complex at Copan. *Ancient Mesoamerica* 3(1):63–88.

Ashmore, Wendy

1991 Site-Planning Principles and Concepts of Directionality Among the Ancient Maya. *Latin American Antiquity* 2:199–226.

Ashmore, Wendy, and Jeremy Sabloff

2002 Spatial Orders in Maya Civic Plans. *Latin American Antiquity* 13:201–216.

Ashmore, Wendy, Jason Yaeger, and Cynthia Robin

2004 Commoner Sense: Late and Terminal Classic Social Strategies in the Xunantunich Area. In *The Terminal Classic in the Maya Lowlands: Collapse,*

Transition, and Transformation, edited by Don Rice, Prudence Rice, and Arthur Demarest, pp. 302–323. University Press of Colorado, Boulder.

Barrett, John C.

1999 The Mythical Landscapes of the British Iron Age. In *Archaeologies of Landscapes: Contemporary Perspectives,* edited by Wendy Ashmore and A. Bernard Knapps, pp. 253–265. Blackwell Press, Oxford.

Bell, Catherine

1992 *Ritual Theory, Ritual Practice.* Oxford Press, New York.

Bender, Barbara

1998 *Stonehenge: Making Space.* Berg Press, Oxford.

Blanton, Richard E.

1978 *Monte Albán: Settlement Patterns at the Ancient Zapotec Capital.* Academic Press, New York.

Bourdieu, Pierre

1977 *Outline of a Theory of Practice.* Cambridge University Press, Cambridge.

Bradley, Richard

1993 *Altering the Earth: The Origins of Monuments in Britain and Continental Europe.* The Rhind Lectures 1991–1992. Monograph Series No. 8. Edinburgh Society of Antiquaries of Scotland, Edinburgh.

1998 *The Significance of Monuments.* Routledge Press, London.

Brenner, Mark, David A. Hodell, Jason H. Curtis, Michael F. Rosenmeier, Michael W. Binford, and Mark B. Abbott

2001 Abrupt Climate Change and Pre-Columbian Cultural Collapse. In *Interhemispheric Climate Linkages,* edited by Vera Markgraf, pp. 87–103. Academic Press, San Diego.

Brown, Linda

2000 From Discard to Divination: Demarcating the Sacred Through the Collection and Curation of Discarded Objects. *Latin American Antiquity* 11:319–333.

Brown, Michael F.

1996 On Resisting Resistance. *American Anthropologist* 98:729–735.

Brumfiel, Elizabeth M.

1996 Figurines and the Aztec State: Testing the Effectiveness of Ideological Domination. In *Gender and Archaeology,* edited by Rita Wright, pp. 143–166. University of Pennsylvania Press, Philadelphia.

1998 Huitzilopochtli's Conquest: Aztec Ideology in the Archaeological Record. *Cambridge Archaeological Journal* 81:3–13.

Butler, Judith

1993 *Bodies That Matter: On the Discursive Limits of "Sex."* Routledge Press, New York.

Casella, Eleanor C.

2001 Landscapes of Punishment and Resistance: A Female Convict Settlement in Tasmania, Australia. In *Contested Landscapes: Movement, Exile, Place,* edited by Barbara Bender and Margot Winer, pp. 103–120. Oxford Press, Berg.

Chase, Arlen F., and Diane Z. Chase

1985 Private Versus Public Space at Caracol, Belize: Implications for Classic Maya Organization. Paper presented at the 83rd Annual Meeting of the American Anthropological Association, Washington, D.C.

1987 *Investigations at the Classic Maya City of Caracol, Belize: 1985–1987*. Pre-Columbian Art Institute, San Francisco.

2001a The Royal Court of Caracol, Belize: Its Palaces and People. In *Royal Courts of the Ancient Maya,* Volume 2, edited by Takeshi Inomata and Stephen D. Houston, pp. 102–137. Westview Press, Boulder.

2001b Ancient Maya Causeways and Site Organization at Caracol, Belize. *Ancient Mesoamerica* 12:273–282.

Chase, Diane Z., and Arlen F. Chase

1998 The Architectural Context of Caches, Burials, and Other Ritual Activities for the Classic Period Maya as Reflected at Caracol, Belize. In *Function and Meaning in Classic Maya Architecture,* edited by Stephen D. Houston, pp. 299–332. Dumbarton Oaks, Washington, D.C.

2004 Archaeological Perspectives on Classic Maya Social Organization from Caracol, Belize. *Ancient Mesoamerica* 15:139–147.

Chase, Diane Z., and Arlen F. Chase (editors)

1992 *Mesoamerican Elites: An Archaeological Assessment*. University of Oklahoma Press, Norman.

Comaroff, Jean

1985 *Body of Power, Spirit of Resistance.* University of Chicago Press, Chicago.

Comaroff, Jean, and John Comaroff

1991 *Of Revelation and Revolution: Christianity, Colonialism, and Consciousness in South Africa*. University of Chicago Press, Chicago.

Comaroff, John, and Jean Comaroff

1992 *Ethnography and the Historical Imagination*. Westview Press, Boulder.

Costin, Cathy L.

1996 Exploring the Relationship Between Gender and Craft in Complex Societies: Methodological and Theoretical Issues of Gender Attribution.

In *Gender and Archaeology,* edited by Rita Wright, pp. 111–140. University of Pennsylvania Press, Philadelphia.

Cowgill, George L.

1997 State and Society at Teotihuacan, Mexico. *Annual Review of Anthropology* 26:129–161.

Culbert, T. Patrick

1973 The Maya Downfall at Tikal. In *The Classic Maya Collapse,* edited by T. Patrick Culbert, pp. 63–92. University of New Mexico Press, Albuquerque.

Culbert, T. Patrick (editor)

1973 *The Classic Maya Collapse.* University of New Mexico Press, Albuquerque.

Demarest, Arthur A., Matt O'Mansky, Claudia Wolley, Dirk Van Tuerenhout, Takeshi Inomata, Joel Palka, and Hector Escobedo

1997 Classic Maya Defensive Systems and Warfare in the Petexbatun Region. *Ancient Mesoamerica* 8:229–253.

Diehl, Richard A., and Janet C. Berlo (editors)

1989 *Mesoamerica After the Decline of Teotihuacan,* A.D. *700–900.* Dumbarton Oaks, Washington, D.C.

Dirks, Nicholas B.

1994 Ritual and Resistance: Subversion as a Social Fact. In *Culture/Power/History,* edited by Nicholas Dirks, Geoff Eley, and Sherry Ortner, pp. 483–503. Princeton University Press, Princeton.

Fash, William L.

1991 *Scribes, Warriors and Kings: The City of Copan and the Ancient Maya.* Thames and Hudson, New York.

Freidel, David A.

1998 Sacred Work: Dedication and Termination in Mesoamerica. In *The Sowing and the Dawning,* edited by Shirley Boteler Mock, pp. 189–193. University of New Mexico Press, Albuquerque.

Freidel, David A., Charles K. Suhler, and Rafael Cobos Palma

1998 Termination Ritual Deposits at Yaxuna. In *The Sowing and the Dawning,* edited by Shirley Boteler Mock, pp. 135–144. University of New Mexico Press, Albuquerque.

Gámez Goytia, Gustavo

2002 El eje sagrado en Monte Albán: Elemento central de la arquitectura religiosa zapoteca. In *La religión de Los Binnigula'sa',* edited by Víctor de la Cruz and Marcus Winter, pp. 197–217. Fondo Editorial, IEEPO, Oaxaca.

Garber, James F., W. David Driver, Lauren A. Sullivan, and David M. Glassman
1998 Bloody Bowls and Broken Pots: The Life, Death, and Rebirth of a Mayan House. In *The Sowing and the Dawning,* edited by Shirley Boteler Mock, pp. 125–134. University of New Mexico Press, Albuquerque.

Giddens, Anthony
1979 *Central Problems in Social Theory.* University of California Press, Berkeley.
1984 *The Constitution of Society: Outline of the Theory of Structuration.* University of California Press, Berkeley.

Goldstein, Donna
2003 *Laughter out of Place: Race, Class, Violence, and Sexuality in a Brazilian Shantytown.* University of California Press, Berkeley.

Gonlin, Nancy
1994 Rural Household Diversity in Late Classic Copán, Honduras. In *Archaeological Views from the Countryside: Village Communities in Early Complex Societies,* edited by Glenn M. Schwartz and Steven E. Falconer, pp. 177–197. Smithsonian Institution Press, Washington, D.C.

Gramsci, Antonio
1971 *Selections from the Prison Notebooks.* International Publishers, New York.

Harrison, Peter D.
1999 *The Lords of Tikal: Rulers of an Ancient Maya City.* Thames and Hudson, London.

Hegmon, Michelle, Scott G. Ortman, and Jeannette L. Mobley-Tanaka
2000 Women, Men, and the Organization of Space. In *Women and Men in the Prehispanic Southwest: Labor, Power, & Prestige,* edited by Patricia L. Crown, pp. 43–90. School of American Research Press, Santa Fe.

Hendon, Julia
2000 Having and Holding: Storage, Memory, Knowledge, and Social Relations. *American Anthropologist* 102:42–53.

Hillier, Bill, and Julienne Hanson
1984 *The Social Logic of Space.* Cambridge University Press, Cambridge.

Hodder, Ian, and Scott R. Hutson
2003 *Reading the Past.* Third edition. Cambridge University Press, Cambridge.

Hutson, Scott R.
2002 Built Space and Bad Subjects: Domination and Resistance at Monte Albán, Oaxaca, Mexico. *Journal of Social Archaeology* 2:53–80.

Inomata, Takeshi
1997 The Last Days of a Fortified Classic Maya Center: Archaeological Investigations at Aguateca, Guatemala. *Ancient Mesoamerica* 8:337–352.

Jansen, Maarten

2004 La transición del Clásico al Posclásico: Una interpretación a partir de los Códices Mixtecos. In *Estructuras politicas en el Oaxaca antiguo: Memoria de la tercera mesa redonda de Monte Albán,* edited by Nelly M. Robles García, pp. 121–146. Instituto Nacional de Antropología e Historia, Mexico.

Janusek, John

2004 *Identity and Power in the Ancient Andes.* Routledge Press, New York.

Johnston, Kevin J., and Nancy Gonlin

1998 What Do Houses Mean? Approaches to the Analysis of Classic Maya Commoner Residences. In *Function and Meaning in Classic Maya Architecture,* edited by Stephen Houston, pp. 141–185. Dumbarton Oaks, Washington, D.C.

Jones, Grant

1989 *Maya Resistance to Spanish Rule: Time and History on a Colonial Frontier.* University of New Mexico Press, Albuquerque.

Joyce, Arthur A.

1991 Formative Period Occupation in the Lower Río Verde Valley, Oaxaca, Mexico: Interregional Interaction and Social Change. Ph.D. dissertation, Rutgers University. University Microfilms, Ann Arbor.

1993 Interregional Interaction and Social Development on the Oaxaca Coast. *Ancient Mesoamerica* 4:67–84.

1999 El Proyecto Patrones de Asentamiento del Río Verde. Report submitted to the Consejo de Arqueología, Instituto Nacional de Antropología e Historia, Mexico.

2000 The Founding of Monte Albán: Sacred Propositions and Social Practices. In *Agency in Archaeology,* edited by Marcia-Ann Dobres and John Robb, pp. 71–91. Routledge Press, London.

2004 Sacred Space and Social Relations in the Valley of Oaxaca. In *Mesoamerican Archaeology,* edited by Julia Hendon and Rosemary Joyce, pp. 192–216. Blackwell Press, Oxford.

2008 Domination, Negotiation, and Collapse: A History of Centralized Authority on the Oaxaca Coast. In *After Monte Albán: Transformation and Negotiation in Oaxaca, Mexico,* edited by Jeffrey Blomster, pp. 219–254. University Press of Colorado, Boulder.

Joyce, Arthur, Laura Arnaud Bustamante, and Marc N. Levine

2001 Commoner Power: A Case Study from the Classic Period Collapse on the Oaxaca Coast. *Journal of Archaeological Method and Theory* 84:343–385.

Joyce, Arthur A., and Stacie M. King

2001 Household Archaeology in Coastal Oaxaca, Mexico. Final report submitted to the Foundation for the Advancement of Mesoamerican Studies, Crystal River.

Joyce, Arthur A., and Marcus Winter

1996 Ideology, Power, and Urban Society in Prehispanic Oaxaca. *Current Anthropology* 37:33–86.

Joyce, Arthur A., Andrew Workinger, Byron Hamann, Peter Kroefges, Maxine Oland, and Stacie King

2004 Lord 8 Deer "Jaguar Claw" and the Land of the Sky: The Archaeology and History of Tututepec. *Latin American Antiquity* 15(3):273–297.

Joyce, Rosemary

1993 Women's Work: Images of Production and Reproduction in Prehispanic Southern Central America. *Current Anthropology* 34:255–274.

Keller, Angela H.

1995 Getting into Xunantunich: The 1995 Investigations of the Access Points and Accessibility of Xunantunich. Report on 1995 Investigations, Department of Archaeology, Belize.

Kertzer, David

1988 *Ritual, Politics, and Power.* Yale University Press, New Haven.

Koontz, Rex, Kathryn Reese-Taylor, and Annabeth Headrick

2001 *Landscape and Power in Ancient Mesoamerica.* Westview Press, Boulder.

Kowalewski, Stephen, Gary Feinman, Laura Finsten, Richard Blanton, and Linda M. Nicholas

1989 Monte Albán's Hinterland, Part II: Prehispanic Settlement Patterns in Tlacolula, Etla, and Ocotlán, the Valley of Oaxaca, Mexico. Memoirs of the University of Michigan Museum of Anthropology, Ann Arbor.

Laporte, Juan Pedro

1993 Architecture and Social Change in Late Classic Maya Society: The Evidence from Mundo Perdido, Tikal. In *Lowland Maya Civilization in the Eight Century* A.D., edited by Jeremy Sabloff and John Henderson, pp. 299–317. Dumbarton Oaks, Washington, D.C.

LeCount, Lisa

1999 Polychrome Pottery and Political Strategies in Late and Terminal Classic Lowland Maya Society. *Latin American Antiquity* 10:239–258.

2001 Like Water for Chocolate: Feasting and Political Ritual Among the Late Classic Maya at Xunantunich, Belize. *American Anthropologist* 103: 935–953.

LeCount, Lisa J., Jason Yaeger, Richard M. Leventhal, and Wendy Ashmore

2002 Dating the Rise and Fall of Xunantunich, Belize: A Late and Terminal Classic Lowland Maya Regional Center. *Ancient Mesoamerica* 13:41–63.

Leventhal, Richard M.

1996 The End at Xunantunich: The Architecture and Setting in the Terminal Classic. In 1996 Report on Excavations, Department of Archaeology, Belize.

Leventhal, Richard M., and Wendy Ashmore

2004 Xunantunich in a Belize Valley Context. In *The Ancient Maya of the Belize Valley: Half a Century of Archaeological Research,* edited by James F. Garber, pp. 168–179. University Press of Florida, Gainesville.

Lichtenstein, Robert J.

1996 The Structure 19 Courtyard. In 1999 Research and Field Season, Blue Creek, Belize, 1996 Site Report, edited by Thomas Guderjan, pp. 39–50, Department of Archaeology, Belize.

2000 *Settlement Zone Communities of the Greater Blue Creek Area.* Occasional Paper 2. Maya Research Program, Fort Worth.

Love, Michael

1999 Ideology, Material Culture, and Daily Practice in Pre-Classic Mesoamerica: A Pacific Coast Perspective. In *Social Patterns in Pre-Classic Mesoamerica,* edited by David C. Grove and Rosemary Joyce, pp. 127–154. Dumbarton Oaks, Washington, D.C.

Lucero, Lisa J.

2002 The Collapse of the Classic Maya: A Case for the Role of Water Control. *American Anthropologist* 104:814–826.

2003 The Politics of Ritual: The Emergence of Classic Maya Rulers. *Current Anthropology* 44:523–558.

Manzanilla, Linda

2002 Living with the Ancestors and Offering to the Gods: Domestic Ritual at Teotihuacan. In *Domestic Ritual in Ancient Mesoamerica,* edited by Patricia Plunket, pp. 43–52. Monograph 46, Cotsen Institute of Archaeology. University of California, Los Angeles.

Manzanilla, Linda, Claudia López, and AnnCorinne Freter

1996 Dating Results from Excavations in Quarry Tunnels Behind the Pyramid of the Sun at Teotihuacan. *Ancient Mesoamerica* 7:245–266.

Marcus, Joyce, and Kent Flannery

1996 *Zapotec Civilization.* Thames and Hudson, London.

Martin, Simon, and Nikolai Grube

2000 *Chronicle of the Maya Kings and Queens.* Thames and Hudson, London.

McAnany, Patricia A.

1995 *Living with the Ancestors.* University of Texas Press, Austin.

Mehrer, Mark W.

2000 Heterarchy and Hierarchy: The Community Plan as Institution in Cahokia's Polity. In *The Archaeology of Communities,* edited by Marcello Canuto and Jason Yaeger, pp. 44–57. Routledge Press, London.

Miller, Arthur G.

1995 *The Painted Tombs of Oaxaca, Mexico.* Cambridge University Press, Cambridge.

Millon, René

1973 *Urbanization at Teotihuacan, Mexico.* University of Texas Press, Austin.

1988 The Last Years of Teotihuacan Dominance. In *The Collapse of Ancient States and Civilizations,* edited by Norman Yoffee and George Cowgill, pp. 102–164. University of Arizona Press, Tucson.

Moore, Allan F.

1999 Microsettlement-Analysis in the Belize River Valley: Archaeological Investigations at Atalaya, a Formal Patio Group at Baking Pot. Ph.D. dissertation, Institute of Archaeology, University College London, London.

Ortner, Sherry B.

1984 Theory in Anthropology Since the Sixties. *Comparative Studies in Society and History* 26:126–166.

Palka, Joel

1997 Reconstructing Classic Maya Socioeconomic Differentiation and the Collapse at Dos Pilas, Petén, Guatemala. *Ancient Mesoamerica* 8:293–306.

Pauketat, Timothy R.

2000 The Tragedy of the Commoners. In *Agency in Archaeology,* edited by Marcia-Ann Dobres and John Robb, pp. 113–129. Routledge Press, London.

Pendergast, David

1979 *Excavations at Altun Ha, Belize, 1964–1970,* Volume 1. Royal Ontario Museum, Toronto.

1982 *Excavations at Altun Ha, Belize, 1964–1970,* Volume 2. Royal Ontario Museum, Toronto.

1992 Noblesse Oblige: The Elites of Altun Ha and Lamanai, Belize. In *Mesoamerican Elites: An Archaeological Assessment,* edited by Diane Chase and Arlen Chase, pp. 61–79. University of Oklahoma Press, Norman.

Plunket, Patricia (editor)

2002 *Domestic Ritual in Ancient Mesoamerica*. Monograph 46, Cotsen Institute of Archaeology. University of California, Los Angeles.

Restall, Matthew

1997 *The Maya World: Yucatec Culture and Society, 1550–1850*. Stanford University Press, Stanford.

Robin, Cynthia

1999 Towards an Archaeology of Everyday Life: Maya Farmers of Chan Nòohol and Dos Chombitos Cik'in, Belize. Ph.D. dissertation, University of Pennsylvania. University Microfilms, Ann Arbor.

2001 Peopling the Past: New Perspectives on the Ancient Maya. *Proceedings of the National Academy of Sciences of the United States of America* 98:19–21.

2003 New Directions in Classic Maya Household Archaeology. *Journal of Archaeological Research* 11:307–356.

Roys, Ralph

1967 *The Book of Chilam Balam of Chumayel*. University of Oklahoma Press, Norman.

Sabloff, Jeremy A., and Edward Wyllys Andrews V (editors)

1986 *Late Lowland Maya Civilization: Classic to Postclassic*. University of New Mexico Press, Albuquerque.

Sabloff, Jeremy A., and John S. Henderson (editors)

1993 *Lowland Maya Civilization in the Eighth Century A.D.* Dumbarton Oaks, Washington, D.C.

Scarborough, Vernon L.

1998 Ecology and Ritual: Water Management and the Maya. *Latin American Antiquity* 9: 135–159.

Schele, Linda, and David A. Freidel

1990 A *Forest of Kings: The Untold Story of the Ancient Maya*. William Morrow, New York.

Scott, James C.

1976 *The Moral Economy of the Peasant: Subsistence and Rebellion in Southeast Asia*. Yale University Press, New Haven.

1985 *Weapons of the Weak: Everyday Forms of Peasant Resistance*. Yale University Press, New Haven.

1990 *Domination and the Arts of Resistance*. Yale University Press, New Haven.

Sewell, William H.

1992 A Theory of Structure: Duality, Agency, and Transformation. *American Journal of Sociology* 98:1–29.

Sharer, Robert J.

1994 *The Ancient Maya.* Fifth edition. Stanford University Press, Stanford.

Sheets, Payson

2000 Provisioning the Ceren Household. *Ancient Mesoamerica* 11:217–230.

Stein, Gil J.

1999 *Rethinking World-Systems: Diasporas, Colonies, and Interaction in Uruk Mesopotamia.* University of Arizona Press, Tucson.

Sugiyama, Saburo

1993 Worldview Materialized in Teotihuacan, Mexico. *Latin American Antiquity* 4:103–129.

Terraciano, Kevin

2001 *The Mixtecs of Colonial Oaxaca.* Stanford University Press, Stanford.

Thompson, J. Eric S.

1954 *The Rise and Fall of Maya Civilization.* University of Oklahoma Press, Norman.

Urcid, Javier, and Arthur A. Joyce

2001 Carved Monuments and Calendrical Names: The Rulers of Río Viejo, Oaxaca. *Ancient Mesoamerica* 12:199–216.

Walker, William H., and Lisa J. Lucero

2000 The Depositional History of Ritual and Power. In *Agency in Archaeology,* edited by Marcia-Ann Dobres and John Robb, pp. 130–147. Routledge Press, London.

Webster, David L.

2002 *The Fall of the Maya: Solving the Mystery of the Maya Collapse.* Thames and Hudson, London.

Webster, David, AnnCorinne Freter, and Nancy Gonlin

2000 *Copán: The Rise and Fall of an Ancient Maya Kingdom.* Harcourt College Publishers, Fort Worth.

Weller, Errin T.

2002 Ancient Maya Elite-Commoner Ritual Interaction: Continuity or Disjuncture? Master's thesis, University of Colorado, Boulder.

Willey, Gordon R., William R. Bullard Jr., John B. Glass, and James C. Gifford

1965 *Prehistoric Maya Settlements in the Belize Valley.* Peabody Museum, Cambridge.

Winter, Marcus

2001 Palacios, templos y 1300 años de vida urbana en Monte Albán. In *Reconstruyendo la ciudad Maya: El urbanismo en las sociedades antiguas,* edited by Andrés Ciudad Ruiz, M. J. Iglesia Ponce de León, and M. del Carmen Martínez, pp. 253–301. Madrid, Sociedad Española de Estudios Mayas.

2003 Monte Albán and Late Classic Site Abandonment in Highland Oaxaca. In *The Archaeology of Settlement Abandonment in Middle America*, edited by Takeshi Inomata and Ronald W. Webb, pp. 103–119. University of Utah Press, Salt Lake City.

Yaeger, Jason

2000 Changing Patterns of Community Structure and Organization: The End of the Classic Period at San Lorenzo, Cayo District, Belize. Ph.D. dissertation, University of Pennsylvania. University Microfilms, Ann Arbor.

2002 Hinterland Ritual Practice and the Constitution of Classic Maya Households and Communities: Examples from the Upper Belize River Valley. Paper presented at the 100th Annual Meeting of the American Anthropological Association, New Orleans.

2003 Untangling the Ties That Bind: The City, the Countryside, and the Nature of Maya Urbanism at Xunantunich. In *The Social Construction of Ancient Cities*, edited by Monica L. Smith, pp. 121–155. Smithsonian Books, Washington, D.C.

CHAPTER SEVEN

SHRINES, OFFERINGS, AND POSTCLASSIC CONTINUITY IN ZAPOTEC RELIGION

Marcus Winter, Robert Markens, Cira Martínez López, and Alicia Herrera Muzgo T.

INTRODUCTION

One of the most drastic changes in prehispanic Mesoamerica occurred around A.D. 800 with the demographic and political decline of a number of the great Classic period centers: Teotihuacan in Central Mexico; Tikal, Palenque, and many others in the Maya area; and Monte Albán in Oaxaca (Figures 0.1 and 0.2). In the subsequent Early Postclassic period, new centers arose in some regions, such as Tula in Central Mexico and Chichén Itzá in the Maya area. In other regions, notably highland Oaxaca, populations remained relatively low during several centuries, and no large communities appeared until the Late Postclassic.

Why a large number of Classic centers collapsed and how the transition to the Postclassic occurred are perennial, unresolved questions for much of Mesoamerica (see Joyce and Weller, Chapter 6). This situation is particularly true in Oaxaca. Classic period Zapotec culture is known from

Monte Albán and other centers, such as Cerro de la Campana, Jalieza, and Lambityeco, whereas Late Postclassic Zapotec culture is well documented at Mitla, Yagul, and Zaachila in the highlands, as well as at Guiengola on the isthmus. When Spanish colonists arrived they found dozens of Zapotec communities flourishing in the Valley of Oaxaca, in the surrounding mountains to the north and south, and in the southern Isthmus of Tehuantepec to the southeast. Today in the state of Oaxaca there are more Zapotecs than any other ethnic or linguistic group. Nevertheless, the Early Postclassic remains an enigmatic period, poorly documented, but crucial for understanding cultural continuity between the great Classic centers and present-day groups. What happened to Classic Zapotec culture and how did it continue after the Classic period?

Excavations in the 1990s at Monte Albán and more recently at Macuilxóchitl provide new data on this period of change. Especially notable are deposits of artifacts used in ritual context. Here we describe these discoveries and discuss their implications for continuity and change in Zapotec religion between the Classic and Postclassic.

Monte Albán, in the center of the Valley of Oaxaca, was the largest community in the region from 500 B.C. to A.D. 800 and is well documented archaeologically (e.g., Blanton 1978; Winter 1994). Macuilxóchitl, about 25 km east of Monte Albán in the Tlacolula subvalley, was occupied at least from the Rosario phase (700 B.C.) to the present (Figure 7.1). Surface survey (Kowalewski et al. 1989) shows that during the Late Classic, Macuilxóchitl was the second or third largest community in the Valley of Oaxaca, covering several square kilometers, with a population of some 6,000 people (as compared with Monte Albán with an estimated population of 25,000). Residential terraces occur on the slopes of Cerro Danush and more than 150 mounds have been located on the flat alluvial areas along the river south of the hill. The excavated site of Dainzú (Bernal and Oliveros 1988) is an area of early occupation within the Macuilxóchitl site.

Chronological divisions of interest to this study are the Late Classic and Postclassic, including the Xoo phase (Late Classic), the Liobaa phase (Early Postclassic), and the Chila phase (Late Postclassic) (Figure 7.2). Xoo phase ceramics have been described in detail by Cira Martínez López and colleagues (2000), while Xoo, Liobaa, and Chila phase ceramics have been chronologically ordered and compared in a recent seriation by Robert Markens (2004). Our recent work at Macuilxóchitl has helped to further clarify differences between Liobaa and Chila phase domestic pottery.

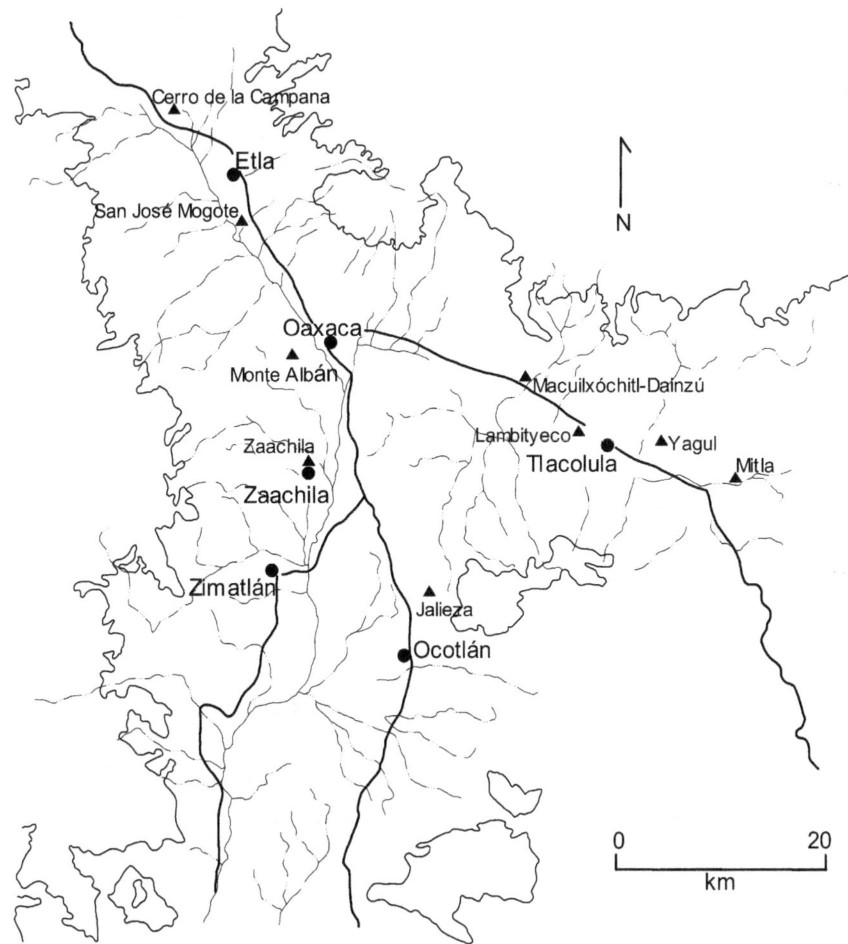

7.1. Map of the Valley of Oaxaca, Mexico, with sites mentioned in the chapter.

PREHISPANIC MESOAMERICAN RELIGION

Several previous studies of prehispanic Zapotec religion in Oaxaca either start from a general anthropological perspective and try to explain the specific (e.g., Drennan 1976; Flannery and Marcus 1976) or focus on particular artifacts, buildings, or features of religious import, such as temples or offerings, in order to characterize a specific culture (e.g., Gámez Goytia 2002; Herrera Muzgo Torres 2002; Martínez López 2002; Winter 2002). Here we prefer a historical perspective, which we believe provides fuller insights (see also Marcus and Flannery 1996; Urcid 2001). Based on

Years	Period		Phase
1600	Colonial		Convento
1521			
1400	Postclassic		Chila
1200			V
1000			Liobaa
800			
600	Classic		Late Xoo
			IIIB-IV
			Early Xoo
400			Pitao (Dxu' Complex) IIIA
200			Late Niza II
I AD / BC		Late	Early Niza
200			Pe
			I
400		Middle	Danibaan
600	Preclassic		Rosario

7.2. Chronological chart.

some general features known from Mesoamerican and Zapotec ethnographic data (rather than on general anthropological principles), we suggest a model geared to Oaxaca and the Zapotec and then evaluate the archaeological evidence in those terms. In this model, drawn in part from a recent ethnographic study by Alicia Barabas (2003) on sacred ethnoterritoriality in Oaxaca, we are specifically interested in rituals that might account for the material evidence found in the archeological record.

The work of Barabas (2003) fits within the recent current of research concerned with ritual landscapes. Using as a point of departure the premise that societies define their territory culturally (e.g., Carrasco 1990; Koontz et al. 2001), researchers involved in this enterprise have identified the core organizing principles used to structure the natural and built environment among ancient and contemporary ethnic groups. Archaeologists employing this line of inquiry have identified measurements, corresponding to the calendrical cycles common to Mesoamerican peoples, manifest spatially in the layouts of, for example, Teotihuacan (Sugiyama 2004) and Monte Albán (Peeler and Winter 1992–1993, 1995). Others have recognized the long enduring model among Mesoamerican peoples of conceiving hills and temple platforms as sacred mountains embodying the bounty of the natural world (Carrasco 1990; Joyce 2000; Reilly 1999; Schele 1996; Schele and Guernsey Kappelman 2001), and it is here in particular that the work of Barabas (2003) fits.

Following Barabas, our model includes the following points. First, notable geographical features in the natural world are attributed significance by cultural constructs. Natural features are inhabited by beings or spirits (*dueños,* literally "owners") or guardians, some possibly equivalent to prehispanic Zapotec gods (Smith Stark 2002). Thus, springs, caves, and rocks as well as the earth are sacred. Mountains have special importance and sacred mountains are conceived of as places of richness and plenty or maintenance (*mantenimiento*), as sources of water and thus fertility (the *altepetl* of Central Mexico), and with caves as entrances to the Underworld. Sacred mountains mark the territorial limits of many communities; emblem mountains (Barabas 2003) may stand as symbolic centers for an entire ethnic group of several communities, as does Zempoaltépetl for the Mixe.

Second, actions between humans and the supernaturals or spirits are based on reciprocity, or what Barabas (2003) calls the ethic of giving (*ética del don*): humans petition the gods for health, well-being, and sustenance and reciprocate with offerings to complete the action. Humans are thus intimately connected with the environment, described by John Monaghan (1995) as covenants with the earth and rain (see also Joyce 2000). This culturally constructed world can be kind and bountiful or dangerous, depending, in part, on whether one follows the correct procedures of interchange and obtains the gods' approval.

Third, spirits, guardians, or *dueños* are not only present in natural features but in all lived-in spaces, from the house and courtyard to community buildings, cornfields, and environmental features beyond (cf. Greenberg 2001). All are loci where rituals may be carried out for the protection and benefit of the inhabitants. Rituals today performed by any adult member of a community might include burning candles, placing food and drink out for the gods, and offering words of supplication. A shaman or part-time religious practitioner might act as facilitator and intermediary in the ceremony.

Barabas (2003), especially concerned with rites related to territory, describes several types of rituals that are practiced by Oaxacan groups and that have general characteristics that may be useful for evaluating the archaeological data. These rituals are life-cycle rites related especially to birth and death; propitiatory rites, which include petitions for rain, good crops, health, and fertility; divinatory rites, which involve prognostications for results of petitions; commemoration rites to offer thanks; and therapeutic rites, such as ritual cleansing or bathing in preparation for other rituals.

ZAPOTEC RELIGION

Before turning to the Early Postclassic data, let us look at some aspects of Zapotec religion, especially from the Classic period, to set the context for the Early Postclassic changes and to see how Zapotec religion fits the Mesoamerican concept mentioned above.

Monte Albán, the earliest urban center in Oaxaca (and perhaps Mesoamerica), can be conceptualized as a sacred mountain in Barabas's (2003) terms. Springs were present on the slopes (some still exist today) and a small pond or pool of water apparently existed, at least seasonally, in what is now the southwest corner of the Main Plaza. Water still accumulates here in the rainy season, and excavations years ago revealed a layer of clay at the base of a depression about three meters below the surface. Natural openings, both cracks in the rock and small hollows, exist at Monte Albán, including one under the North Platform on the north side of the Sunken Patio. These cavities may have been considered entrances to the Underworld.

Some of these features were enhanced by construction (Figure 7.3). The Danzantes Wall was built on the west side of the pool. It is possible that the pool was used in conjunction with rituals carried out in this part of the plaza. Later, in the Early Nisa phase, a square open cistern was constructed on the east side of the Main Plaza, perhaps as a substitute for the pool and possibly serving a similar ritual purpose. Water symbolism was common at Monte Albán in early times. Ceramic effigy vessels depict fish, ducks, and frogs (Danibaan phase); ceramic figurines represent frogs and river otters (Early Nisa phase); and water glyphs occur on ceramic boxes (Nisa phase). Numerous tunnels were constructed in the Danibaan, Pe, and Nisa phases. Many functioned as drains as well as passageways, and they also may have been conceived as entrances to the Underworld.

The quadripartite cosmos was expressed architecturally in the layout of the Main Plaza and the Sunken Patio, both with four sides oriented to the cardinal directions. This conceptualization was mirrored in houses at Monte Albán and their central patios oriented east-west/north-south. Later construction, both public and domestic, followed this same pattern.

From early times the Main Plaza was imbued with the sacred through the use of calendrical proportions in the architecture: temporal cycles (260, 365, and 584 days) were translated into spatial proportions in architectural elements (Peeler and Winter 1992–1993). Mound J was a calendrical temple (Peeler and Winter 1995) associated with zenith passage and the use of calendrical proportions.

Monte Albán may have been a sacred mountain for early groups in the Valley of Oaxaca even before the city was founded. As a sacred mountain, Monte Albán may have marked spatial limits for one or more Rosario

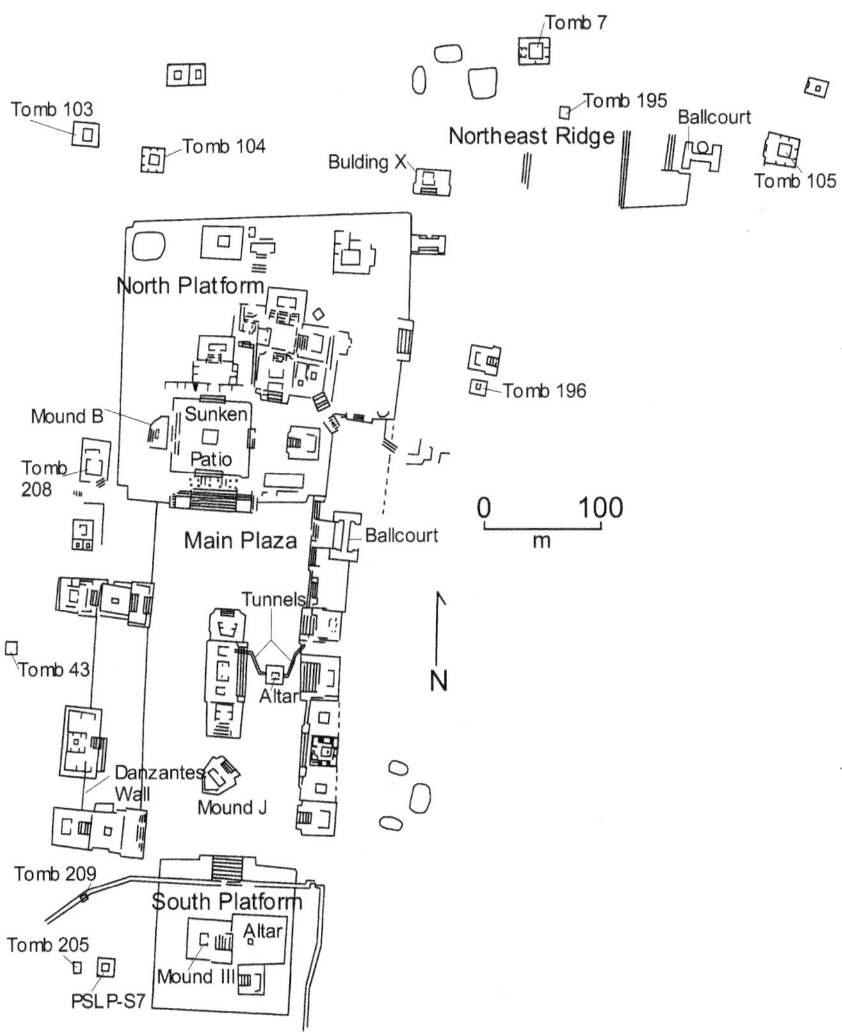

7.3. Map of the center of Monte Albán, Mexico, with locales mentioned in the chapter.

phase communities, and conflict over territorial control may have been a stimulus for initial colonization of the mountain, although Monte Albán's origins also have been attributed to the creation of a politically neutral capital (Blanton 1978; Blanton et al. 1999) or the relocation of the capital at San José Mogote (Marcus and Flannery 1996).

Monte Albán eventually became an emblematic sacred mountain recognized by many people throughout the valley and nearby mountainous regions, many of whom could see Monte Albán from their communities. As time passed, Monte Albán was probably thought of as home of the gods, the place where deities were first conceived or at least manifested on ceramic urns or carved stones. Monte Albán is depicted in Postclassic Mixtec codices as a symbol of political legitimacy (Jansen 2001; Pohl 2000). Today it remains a sacred spot, a tourist attraction and thus a source of riches, and a place where shamans take clients for performance of therapeutic and propitiatory rites.

Both domestic and communal ritual activities were performed at Monte Albán. Life-cycle rituals carried out in household or domestic contexts at Monte Albán include, most notably, mortuary practices (Winter 2002). Zapotecs at Monte Albán, continuing pre-urban traditions, generally buried their dead beneath house floors or just outside the house, along with vessels probably containing food and drink for the journey to the afterlife. In contrast to the Middle Formative in the Valley of Oaxaca prior to the founding of Monte Albán, social distinctions between commoners and elite became more accentuated at the ancient city, which is reflected in the size and elegance of houses and in the elaborateness of mortuary treatment. These characteristics differ by phase, but from earliest times (Danibaan phase) and especially in the Xoo phase, status variation was evident at Monte Albán. Commoner burials had relatively simple offerings of one or two vessels, whereas elite adults were buried in elaborate tombs, some with painted walls and abundant offerings.

Urban centers flourish and persist through time only if they are able to hold their populations together. Early Monte Albán was a pristine case in which new mechanisms were forged to overcome the centrifugal effect of individual family autonomy and to supersede kinship ties. Community ritual performances and religious concepts expressed in monumental public architecture at Monte Albán would have been major factors unifying the center's inhabitants, and it is clear that the public domain of religion was controlled by the elite or high-status families. Earliest examples of deity representations are found in association with elite households and in tombs but are not present in commoner households. Elite individuals are represented on carved stones and depicted with attributes and symbols of deities. So ideology was a type of power controlled by the elite.

Examples of religious activities in the non-household, public sphere at Monte Albán include Nisa phase (perhaps Pe phase) temples built on high platforms and used for religious celebrations. They usually had a wide door so the public could see the priest during the ritual. Portions of two columns found on the North Platform, originally set in a temple entrance, exhibit carvings of men dressed as priests. These high-status individuals may have been priest-leaders.

Temples had *tlecuiles* (built-in, sub-floor hearths) containing embers perhaps transferred to portable braziers and *sahumadores* (censers) for use in ceremonies. Some temples show burned areas on the floor (San José Mogote Structure 35 [Marcus and Flannery 1996:185, figure 213], Macuilxóchitl Mound 36), although it is not clear if these areas were burned during ritual activities or resulted from burning during abandonment or renovation of the structure (see Barba et al., Chapter 3, for a discussion of chemical residues from floors).

Excavation of Mound 55 at Macuilxóchitl revealed part of a hollow ceramic jaguar head found at the base of the stairway leading up to the temple. This fragment was probably part of a large effigy kept in the temple (Figures 7.4 and 7.5). The jaguar was a symbol of power among the Zapotecs and many other groups, including the Olmecs. Olmec sculptures of creatures part human and part jaguar perhaps reflect the concept of nahualism, or animal double, common in Mesoamerica. Xoo phase Zapotec leaders are often portrayed dressed in jaguar costumes. Some figurines from Macuilxóchitl portray a man with a monkey head in his headdress, another possible example of nahualism.

Offering boxes associated with temples at Monte Albán, San José Mogote, and other sites have been found containing artifacts such as ceramic and stone effigies used in ceremonies. At Monte Albán, east of Mound III on top of the South Platform, is a sacred axis formed by pits arranged along an east-west line and containing offerings (Gámez Goytia 2002).

The Sunken Patio built on the North Platform during the Nisa phase has a central altar perhaps used for performing sacrifices, and the temple-patio-altar (TPA) architectural complexes of the Xoo phase usually have altars in the center of the patio, probably used for the same function. In the Xoo phase some palaces are next to TPA complexes, ballcourts, and a market space, indicating elite control of religious, political, and economic activities.

What role did commoners play in all of this activity? At the household level, commoner and elite rituals contrast in terms of elaborateness of ceremony, and commoners and elites did not necessarily participate together. Community or public rituals, however, drew people from different social sectors. Commoners helped to build the site centers. Rituals performed in temples, at altars, or in ballcourts presumably had commoner spectators,

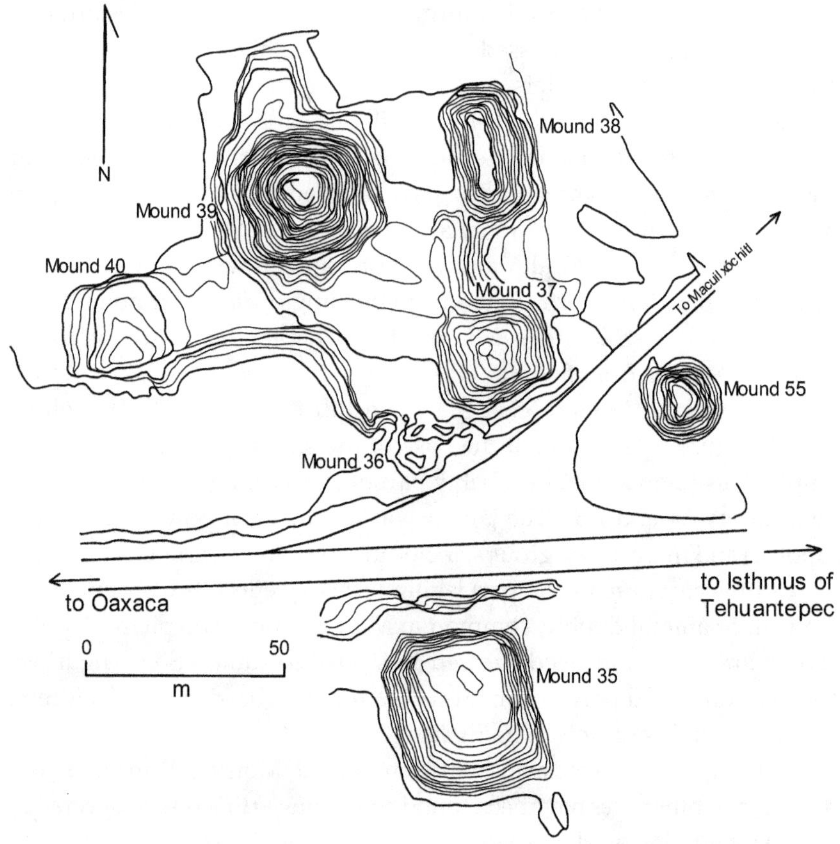

7.4. Map of Xoo phase complex excavated at Macuilxóchitl, Oaxaca, Mexico.

although elites, as intellectual authors and controllers of religion and ideology, may have orchestrated the events (see Gonlin, Chapter 4, and Joyce and Weller, Chapter 6).

ARCHAEOLOGICAL EVIDENCE FOR RITUAL AND IDEOLOGY IN THE LIOBAA PHASE

Around A.D. 800, Monte Albán, Macuilxóchitl, and other Xoo phase centers in the Valley of Oaxaca collapsed. Population may have declined and construction of temples and other monumental structures ceased. Writing, figurines, urns, and representations of deities drop out of the archaeological record. The characteristic Xoo phase carved slabs depicting elite personages and commemorating their rites of passage are no longer found.

7.5. Ceramic jaguar head found on the stairway of Mound 55, Macuilxóchitl, Oaxaca, Mexico.

Liobaa phase structures and deposits have been elusive and only a few have been documented thus far. Examples from Monte Albán include a residence (PSLP-7), two reused tombs (Tombs 208 and 209), and two

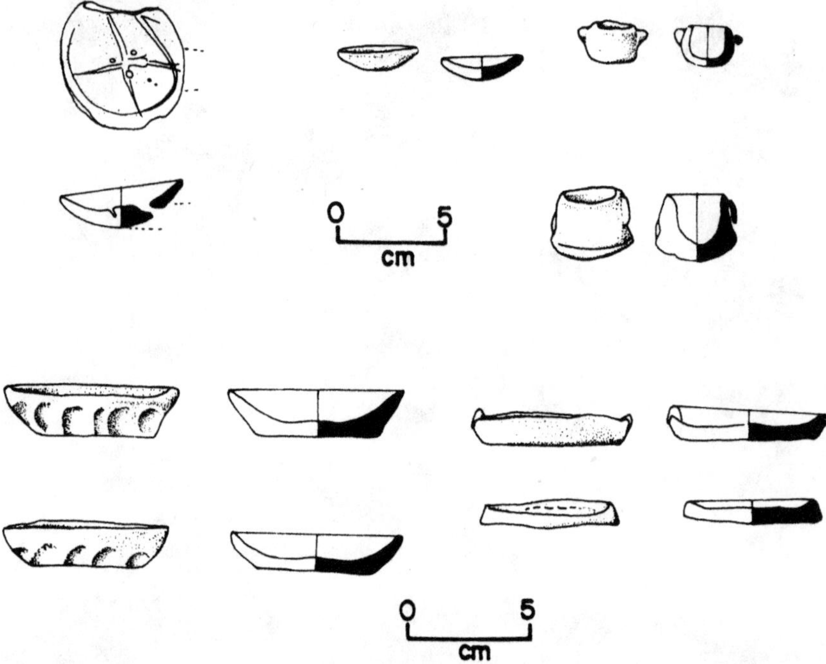

7.6. Monte Albán: miniature vessels from the South Platform altar and Mound B offerings, Oaxaca, Mexico.

concentrations of artifacts in offerings.[1] Examples at Macuilxóchitl include possible remains of a residence and two concentrations of artifacts that may have served as offerings. These four artifact concentrations are particularly important because they reflect a type of religious manifestation not documented for earlier periods in the Zapotec region. They occur in special, non-domestic contexts that evidently functioned as shrines or sacred spots visited repeatedly, perhaps during one or several generations. The evidence is as follows.

1. Monte Albán, South Platform altar offering (Figure 7.6). On and around the altar just east of Mound III was a concentration of several thousand artifacts. Of 2,347 registered objects, 1,674 are ceramic (40.68 percent are *sahumadores* and 48.62 percent are miniature vessels of Liobaa phase), 642 are lithic (beads, pendants, and greenstone *penates* [small elongated ornaments with a stylized carved human face], prismatic blades, perforators, and projectile points), 29 are shell (beads, pendants, and worked and unworked

fragments including complete shells), and 2 are metal (copper eyes, inlays from masks). The majority of the material corresponds to the Liobaa phase but some dates to the Chila phase (Herrera Muzgo Torres et al. 1999).

2. Monte Albán, Mound B offering. A concentration similar to that on the South Platform was found in excavations on the North Platform around Mound B and on the slope west of the mound. Recovered objects include an estimated 202 Xoo phase vessels, 1,265 Liobaa phase vessels, and 8 Chila phase vessels. Also found were 18 lithic objects (similar to those from the South Platform altar) and 40 shell ornaments. Vessel forms include claw vessels and handled jars known from the Xoo and Liobaa phases. Abundant in the Liobaa phase assemblage are *sahumadores* (29.96 percent) and miniature vessels (52.41 percent).

3. Macuilxóchitl, Mound 35, Feature 14. The Mound 35 residential platform was occupied during the late Xoo, Liobaa, and Chila phases, judging by groups of vessels found beneath presumed room and patio floors. Feature 14 was a concentration on the west slope of the mound. An estimated 370 Liobaa phase vessels were recorded (45.5 percent *sahumadores* and 34.12 percent hemispherical bowls ranging in size from large to miniature) and included jars, *patojos* (shoe-shaped vessels), and hemispherical bowls with high walls, all characterized by the same brown-yellow paste and brushed surfaces typical of the miniatures; fine grayware, known as G3M, vessels (hemispherical and composite silhouette bowls and *cántaros,* or "water jars"); and some fine brown paste *comales* (tortilla griddles). The feature also included three medium-size river cobbles with carved faces roughly resembling the style of the faces carved on Postclassic *penates* (Figure 7.7).

4. Macuilxóchitl, Mound 36, Feature 31. A Liobaa phase offering was also found in excavations on the preserved portion of the top of Mound 36. Only a small area was preserved since most of the platform had been destroyed years ago by construction work. It consisted of an estimated 84 Liobaa phase vessels (41.37 percent *sahumadores* and 40.22 percent hemispherical bowls from large to miniature in size).

The Monte Albán and Macuilxóchitl offerings include high percentages of small *sahumadores* and miniature vessels (Figure 7.8). These objects seem to be typical of Liobaa phase ritual deposits and also occur in the reused Monte Albán tombs mentioned previously. The offerings from the two sites, however, also exhibit differences.

7.7. Macuilxóchitl Mound 35, one of the stone sculptures representing a penate (scale = 30 cm), Oaxaca, Mexico.

First, at Monte Albán, the South and North Platform locales had been used for public rituals during the Xoo phase, whereas the Macuilxóchitl locales had been a residence (Mound 35) and a temple (Mound 36) associated with an elite family. Second, the offerings at Monte Albán are more numerous and varied than those at Macuilxóchitl. One scenario that accounts for this difference (although others are equally possible) is that more people participated in the rituals at Monte Albán and/or the Monte Albán locales were used for a relatively long time. Also, it is likely that both males and females participated in the rituals at Monte Albán. Projectile points (male-related items) were found in the South Platform altar offering, and ethnographic data from present-day Oaxaca villages document participation of both sexes in ceremonies of petition in which miniatures are left as offerings.

In contrast, the simplicity and smaller number of offerings at Macuilxóchitl Mounds 35 and 36 imply a smaller and more homogeneous group, perhaps the descendants of the elite family and their followers who lived atop Mound 35 during the Xoo phase. Also, the offerings may have been deposited during a relatively short time of perhaps one or two generations. The carved stones presumably formed part of the shrine.

During the Liobaa phase, burials and small tombs are known in the Valley of Oaxaca, indicating that household mortuary ritual continued. Yet, no elite tombs like those of Xoo or Chila have been documented, and no evidence of a powerful elite group has been found. The archaeological remains recovered from Monte Albán and Macuilxóchitl are attributable to commoners. Change in social structure is reflected in change in ritual.

Three principal factors influenced the changes noted in Liobaa ritual from those common in the previous Xoo phase. First, buildings used

Ceramic Form	Monte Albán		Macuilxóchitl	
	Mound III and Altar	Mound B	Mound 35, Feature 14	Mound 36, Feature 31
	X	X	X	X
	X	X	X	X
	X	X	X	X
	X	X		
			X	X
	X	X		
	X	X		
			X	X

7.8. Comparative table of miniature vessels from Monte Albán and Macuilxóchitl, Oaxaca, Mexico.

for public ritual during the Xoo phase were no longer maintained in the Liobaa phase; they had been abandoned and were in disrepair and perhaps no longer fit for celebration of public ritual (or they may have been deliberately avoided). Second, religious ideology was no longer under formal elite control so commoners had more choice about where and how to celebrate rituals. Third, the specialized ritual artifacts used in the Xoo phase were no longer being produced. So in Liobaa times, at both Monte Albán and Macuilxóchitl, important Xoo phase spaces became shrines used by individuals for rituals. Copal was burned in *sahumadores* and offerings were made in simple, miniature homemade vessels.[2]

The frequent occurrence of *sahumadores* and miniature vessels in the documented Liobaa phase ritual contexts implies that a specific kind of ritual was carried out. *Sahumadores*, used in Zapotec rituals as early as Danibaan times, are especially common in the Xoo phase and were used for burning copal to produce incensed smoke. Claw vessels were used to hold liquids. Miniature vessels were used for symbolic offerings, perhaps similar to those documented ethnographically in Oaxaca, by members of various ethnic and linguistic groups (Barabas 2003).

The Liobaa phase rituals documented at both Monte Albán and Macuilxóchtl are evidence of propitiatory rites celebrated by individuals. The intensity of activity, especially at Monte Albán, may have been a response to the crisis brought on by the urban collapse. The relatively few Liobaa people in the valley may have requested help from the old gods, and these offerings are the evidence.

ARCHAEOLOGICAL EVIDENCE FOR RITUAL AND IDEOLOGY DURING THE CHILA PHASE

By the Late Postclassic Chila phase, population in the Valley of Oaxaca had recovered and grown to exceed Xoo phase levels. Chila phase archaeological materials are better known than those of the Liobaa phase. Here, as a comparative case study, we include data from recent explorations at Macuilxóchitl.

Excavations in Mound 1 at Macuilxóchitl have brought to light a well-preserved residence dating to the Late Postclassic Chila phase (A.D. 1250–1521) that is striking for its similarity in layout to the palaces of Yagul (Bernal and Gamio 1974) and the Palace of the Columns at Mitla. Given the comparatively small size of the residence, its single small tomb, and household debris containing few polychrome sherds, it is likely that the Mound 1 residence housed a family of commoner status. Like the palaces at Yagul and Mitla, the Macuilxóchitl residence consists of two patios, each of which is enclosed on three or four sides by rooms and/or walls. Based on details of architectural layout, the compound was probably divided into private and (relatively more) public areas. The north patio appears to have served as the residents' private living quarters and the south patio served as a workspace and area for interaction with neighbors and other families (Figure 7.9).

The north patio is enclosed on all sides by rooms. Access to the patio was restricted to two openings at the southwest and southeast corners. The south patio, by contrast, is much more accessible to the community beyond, as its south side is defined by a single step running east-west. The compound's most important structure is located on the north side of the patio, facing the entrance. It occupies the space between the two patios and was most likely the residence of the head of the household. This

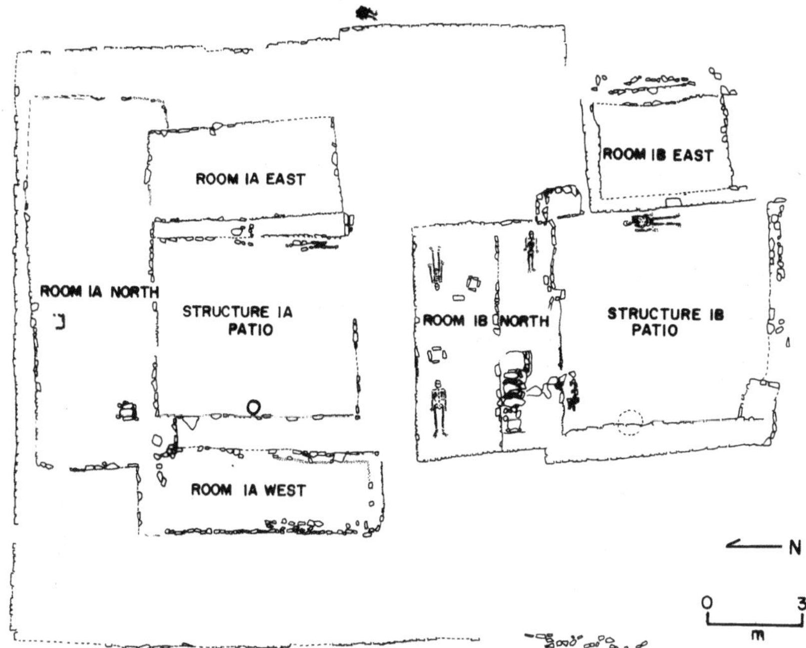

7.9. Macuilxóchitl Mound 1: plan of the excavated residential patios, Oaxaca, Mexico.

spacious building contains the compound's tomb, and all but one of the compound's adult residents were found buried beneath the floor.

Two kinds of commoner ritual were documented in the Mound 1 excavations: mortuary rituals and rituals involving burial of vessels beneath the patio floors. Four adults were interred in the structure located between the two patios. Adult burials in simple graves were found in the northwest, northeast, and southeast corners of the structure. In the southwest corner a single adult was buried in the compound's small tomb. The individuals were laid to rest on their backs with legs extended and arms at their sides or, in one case, with hands resting on the pelvis. A fifth adult burial was found beneath the floor of the south patio, adjacent to the structure on the patio's east side. A sixth burial, that of a child, was found just beyond the compound's east wall, immediately outside the residence. The child was buried seated with its head resting on its knees. The burial of family members in tombs and graves beneath household floors or within the confines of the residence during the Chila phase continues the Zapotec tradition of funeral practices that crystallized during the Middle Formative period.

Each of the grave and tomb offerings of Mound 1 consists of three to five pottery vessels typical of the Chila phase. Common are the fine grayware paste semispherical and composite silhouette bowls with or without elongated supports that also abound in domestic refuse deposits. Small *ollas* with restricted mouths and perforated vertical strap handles attached to the vessel sides made from gray or brown-cream paste are also frequent in the funerary contexts at Mound 1. These vessels appear only in mortuary contexts during the Chila phase (Markens 2004). Other offerings, such as greenstone beads, are rare. Interestingly, the adult burial pattern of extended dorsal position exhibits continuity with the Xoo phase.

A notable contrast to Xoo and Liobaa phase burials and tombs, however, is the absence of *sahumadores*. This absence is striking since *sahumadores* continued in use during the Late Postclassic period and are abundant in the domestic refuse at Mounds 1 and 35 at Macuilxóchitl. The miniatures appearing in Late Xoo phase tombs and common in Liobaa phase tombs and burials are also absent from Mound 1 funerary contexts. Polychrome pottery, although present in small quantities in the household refuse at Mound 1, was not found in any of the funerary contexts.

Commoner ritual at Mound 1 is also represented by more than fifty ceramic vessels recovered from beneath the floors of the north and south patios (Figure 7.10). The vessels were left in different sectors of the patios, often buried in pairs so that one was inverted to cover the mouth of the other. Other sub-patio offerings consist of a single vessel whose mouth was covered by a single large potsherd. Although offerings of paired vessels were found grouped together, the individual vessel pairs were probably buried at different moments since each pair is found at a slightly different depth beneath the patio floor. The kinds of vessels selected most often for the sub-patio offerings were brown paste *ollas* and *patojos* heavily discolored by soot. They were found incomplete or damaged, presumably because of prior heavy domestic use. Grayware semispherical and composite silhouette bowls or fragments of *ollas* also are common and were found inverted, covering an *olla* or *patojo*. More elegant grayware composite silhouette *ollas*, in addition to *ollas* and cups with long legs, were also found in the patios covered by an inverted semispherical bowl or an *olla* fragment. These fancier vessels showed signs of heavy use and the tripod supports were almost always missing (Figure 7.11). An identical pattern has been documented for the palaces at Yagul where similarly paired vessels were found buried beneath the floor of Patio B (Bernal and Gamio 1974:37–38, photos 41–49). Here then is an

7.10. Macuilxóchitl Mound 1: paired vessels from south patio, Oaxaca, Mexico.

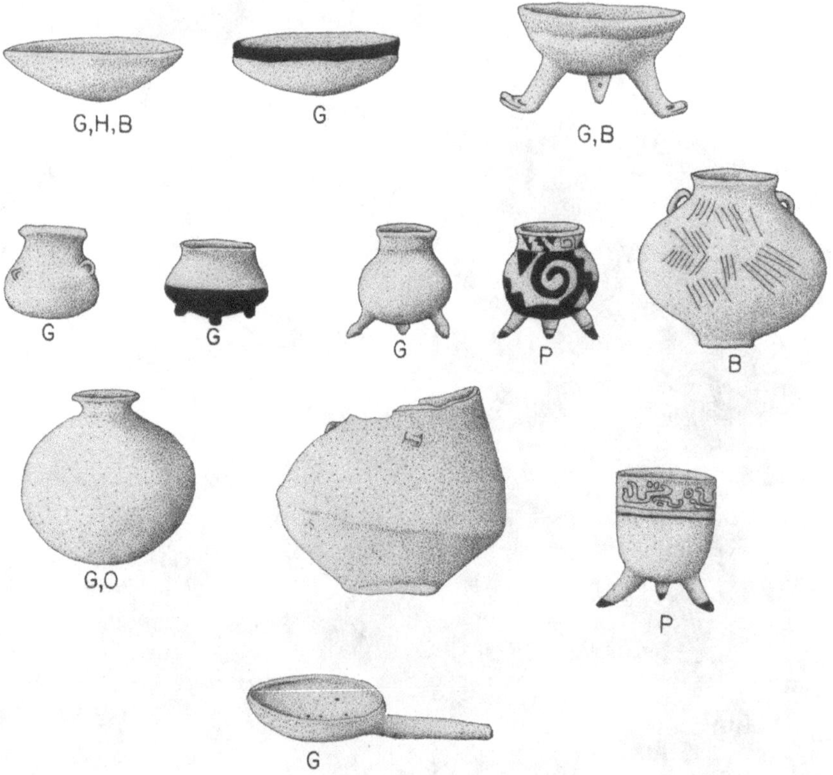

7.11. Vessels representative of the Chila phase forms found in Mound 1 at Macuilxóchitl, Oaxaca, Mexico, including gray (G), Huitzo Polished Cream (H), brown (B), polychrome (P), and orange/yellow (O).

important similarity between commoner and elite ritual during the Late Postclassic period.

Although the meaning of this ritual is enigmatic, Elsie Clews Parsons's (1936:76) account of a Mitla ritual comes to mind here. She documents for Mitla, as well as for other Zapotec valley towns, the practice of storing the umbilical cord of each newborn in two ceramic vessels, one of which is inverted to cover the other. This arrangement prevents dirt from entering the container, because it is believed that if dirt enters the vessel, the child's vision might be damaged. The vessels are buried beneath the floors of the house. The fifteen to twenty paired vessels found within the Macuilxóchitl Mound 1 residence could have been deposited during perhaps two or three generations of occupation. Most of the vessels may correspond to a life-cycle ritual, whereas others may have to do with propitiatory rituals, for example, incorporated within the domestic sphere.

The nature of Chila phase public ritual is hard to grasp, but, nevertheless, archaeological evidence and historical documents provide some clues. By the Late Postclassic period, the leaders of the individual city-states occupying the Valley of Oaxaca appear to have invested relatively fewer resources in the construction of temples, as temple platforms are rare at sites dating to this interval. Such is the case at Macuilxóchitl, where it appears that the Xoo phase temple crowning Cerro Danush was allowed to fall into a state of disrepair by the end of the Classic. The reduction in temple construction during this time appears to signal an important shift in the role elites played in public rituals and correspondingly in how they went about validating their privileged status. This shift finds expression in the surviving prehispanic and Colonial era Oaxacan codices, *lienzos,* and other historic sources (Pohl 1994).

At the time of the conquest, paramount political leadership of the *queche,* or "city-state," in the Valley of Oaxaca was vested in the office of the *coqui,* or "king," a direct descendant of the polity's putative founding ancestor (Oudijk 2002). Perhaps the single most important symbol of the *coqui*'s royal authority was the *quiña,* or "sacred bundle," which was stored in the royal palace and for which the *coqui* acted as steward on behalf of the community (Pohl 1994). The *quiña* appears to have embodied powerful spiritual forces, for it is often embellished in Mixtec pictorial codices with the likeness of a *dzahui,* or rain god, or with a *ñuhu* figure, another Mixtec primeval spirit force. During the Postclassic period, Mixtec and Zapotec religions appear to have embraced a cult of ancestor worship that focused on the polity's royal descent line. It may be that much of the public ritual shifted from the venue of temples to the spacious courtyards of the city-state's royal palace, like those known from Mitla and Yagul. There the ruling lord may have demonstrated through ritual involving the *quiña* his right to rule and his control over, or access to, the vital spirit forces essential for the well-being of the community. Commoners carried out rituals in domestic contexts associated with birth, death, and other life-cycle events. They also may have made pilgrimages individually or collectively to shrines, as the villagers of Macuilxóchitl do at Cerro Danush today.

Macuilxóchitl shows parallels to Monte Albán even though it continued to be occupied during the Postclassic. In the Xoo phase, the principal palace and most important temple were on top of Cerro Danush. Thus, following Barabas's model and the previous discussion of Monte

7.12. Celebration of the Santa Cruz atop Cerro Danush at Macuilxóchitl, Oaxaca, Mexico (photograph by R. Markens, 2003).

Albán, the elite controlled the sacred mountain, religion, and the symbols of fertility on which life depended. During the Postclassic the temple atop Danush continued to be a sacred place; dozens of broken *sahumadores* and braziers are found on the surface. Today the people of Macuilxóchitl, like those in towns throughout Oaxaca, celebrate on May 3 the fiesta of the Santa Cruz, a ritual involving petition for rains and fertility, as noted by Barabas (2003). Macuilxóchitl villagers walk up to the top of Danush, leave miniature representations of animals and other objects, and request bountiful crops and economic well-being. These beliefs are also part of an oral tradition today. Several informants claim that many believe there is gold or treasure inside Cerro Danush and tell of an enormous serpent that lives in Danush, which in Barabas's terms (2003) is the guardian of the hill's symbolic resources (Figure 7.12).

SUMMARY AND CONCLUSIONS

The Classic-Postclassic period transition is generally perceived to be a time of sweeping transformation across Mesoamerica (see Joyce and Weller, Chapter 6). In the Valley of Oaxaca, Monte Albán ceased to be an important political and urban center while other large communities—such as Jalieza, Lambityeco, and Suchilquitongo—appear to have been abandoned by the end of the Classic period. The nature of the social, political, and economic reorganizations that took place in the subsequent Early Postclassic period have remained to a large extent unclear because of the long-standing inability of archaeologists to define a ceramic phase corresponding to this interval. Because of this obstacle, communities, residences, palaces, and public buildings dating to the Early Postclassic remain for the most part unidentifiable. Recently progress has been made in defining the pottery from this phase based on excavations at Monte Albán (Herrera Muzgo Torres et al. 1999), Macuilxóchitl, and a seriation of curated tomb and burial offerings recovered from different parts of the valley (Markens 2004).

The tomb and grave lots used in this ceramic seriation and those recovered from excavations at Macuilxóchitl suggest a change in domestic burial practices related to social ranking with the onset of the Early Postclassic period. Perhaps most striking during this interval is the absence of large, ostentatious tombs containing lavish offerings, like those documented for both the Late Classic and Late Postclassic periods.

The Early Postclassic appears to mark the sudden cessation at Macuilxóchitl and throughout the Valley of Oaxaca of what one might refer to in Robert Redfield's (1956) terms as the Zapotec Great Tradition. At this time, the use of elaborate funerary urns depicting individuals impersonating gods, as well as the use of writing carved in stone or painted in murals to record the events involving individuals of exalted status, comes to an end. Seen in this light, the Early Postclassic period appears to be a time of political crisis in the valley, marked by a simplification of the social-rank hierarchy and the dispersion of the valley population into smaller communities. This trend appears to end by the threshold of the Late Postclassic period (A.D. 1200–1521), just at the time when archaeological (Bernal and Gamio 1974) and ethnohistoric (Oudijk 2002) evidence documents the emergence of the competitive territorially compact kingdoms or city-states known to the Spanish in the sixteenth century variously as *cacicazgos* or *señoríos.*

Despite these abrupt changes during the Early Postclassic period, a number of emerging lines of evidence suggest that some aspects of domestic and ritual life remained constant. During the Early and Late Postclassic periods the dead continued to be laid to rest in both tombs and simple graves, much as they had been in the centuries preceding the end of the Classic period. The skeletal remains of adult men and women are found in household tombs in approximately equal numbers and probably represent a number of generations of related male and female household heads. There is also evidence for more diversified burial practices, especially in the Late Postclassic period, such as the reuse of tombs constructed centuries earlier, as exemplified by Tomb 7 (Caso 1969; Winter 2001), or the use of tombs as ossuaries containing the bones of dozens of individuals (Robles García and Molina 1998).

The Early Postclassic data from Monte Albán and Macuilxóchitl provide evidence of ongoing innovation and religious ritual activity when compared with the offerings found in previously significant spaces. This pattern is a result of the disappearance of earlier, organized public ritual, which correlated with the political crisis or failure that resulted in the simplification of the social hierarchy throughout the Valley of Oaxaca. In the Late Postclassic, richly appointed tombs appear again in the archaeological record, as is the case with Tomb 7 of Monte Albán and Tombs 1 and 2 of Zaachila, indicating the presence of individuals of unusually high status. The emergence of a new political elite in the Valley of Oaxaca at the beginning of the Late Postclassic period appears to have been based on a new ideology emphasizing descent from founding ancestors of individual city-states and control over the symbols of community well-being. The enactment of public rituals may have shifted in large part away from temples to the city-state royal palace, as the palace became the new seat of political and religious authority.

ACKNOWLEDGMENTS

The authors thank Juan Cruz Pascual and Harry Baudouin for preparing the line drawings.

NOTES

1. Monte Albán residence PSLP-7 is a simple house and follows the Xoo phase pattern of a central patio surrounded by rooms. The rounded exterior corners are distinctive and no tomb or burials were found.

2. The use of miniature vessels as offerings goes far back in time in the Valley of Oaxaca. For example, Rosario phase Burial 68 at San José Mogote (Marcus and Flannery 1996:122) contained miniatures, and Danibaan phase Tomb 43 at Monte Albán (Caso et al. 1967) contained miniatures deposited as offerings. Both are high-status interments and the miniatures are unique examples. In the Xoo phase, at Lambityeco (Tomb 11) and at Monte Albán (Tombs 172, 188, 195, 196, and 205),

miniatures occur in tombs as offerings, along with normal-size vessels. These miniatures and the later Liobaa miniatures may have been substitutes for full-size vessels. They used much less raw material and could have been made by almost anyone, that is, non-specialists in a household context. Because of size they are more economical to leave as offerings and do not suggest that a useful cooking or serving vessel was taken out of circulation. They also take up less space, which may have been why they were used in Xoo phase tombs, which were often crowded with utilitarian vessels. Finally, the miniatures are similar if not analogous to the miniatures left today at *pedimentos* (shrines) as documented ethnographically, for example, at Mitla and Teotitlan del Valle.

REFERENCES CITED

Barabas, Alicia M.

2003 Etnoterritorialidad Sagrada en Oaxaca. In *Diálogos con el territorio: Simbolizaciones sobre el espacio en las culturas indígenas de México,* Volume 1, edited by Alicia Barabas, pp. 39–119. Instituto Nacional de Antropología e Historia, México, D.F.

Bernal, Ignacio, and Lorenzo Gamio

1974 *Yagul: El Palacio de los Seis Patios.* Instituto de Investigaciones Antropológicas, Universidad Nacional Autónoma de México, México, D.F.

Bernal, Ignacio, and Arturo Oliveros

1988 *Exploraciones arqueológicas en Dainzú, Oaxaca.* Colección Científica 67. Instituto Nacional de Antropología e Historia, México, D.F.

Blanton, Richard E.

1978 *Monte Albán: Settlement Patterns at the Ancient Zapotec Capital.* Academic Press, New York.

Blanton, Richard E., Gary M. Feinman, Stephen A. Kowalewski, and Linda M. Nicholas

1999 *Ancient Oaxaca: The Ancient Monte Albán State.* Cambridge University Press, Cambridge.

Carrasco, Davíd

1990 *Religions of Mesoamerica.* Harper & Row, San Francisco.

Caso, Alfonso

1969 *El tesoro de Monte Albán.* Memorias del Instituto Nacional de Antropología e Historia 3, México, D.F.

Caso, Alfonso, Ignacio Bernal, and Jorge R. Acosta

1967 *La cerámica de Monte Albán.* Memorias del Instituto Nacional de Antropología e Historia 13, México, D.F.

Drennan, Robert D.

1976 Religion and Social Evolution in Formative Mesoamerica. In *The Early Mesoamerican Village,* edited by Kent V. Flannery, pp. 345–368. Academic Press, New York.

Flannery, Kent V., and Joyce Marcus

1976 Formative Oaxaca and the Zapotec Cosmos. *American Scientist* 64:374–383.

Gámez Goytia, Gustavo

2002 El Eje Sagrado en Monte Albán: Elemento central de la arquitectura religiosa Zapoteca. In *La religión de los Binnigula'sa',* edited by Victor de la Cruz and Marcus Winter, pp. 199–217. IEEPO-IOC, Oaxaca.

Greenberg, James B.

2001 Chatino. *The Oxford Encyclopedia of Mesoamerican Culture,* Volume 1, edited by Davíd Carrasco, pp. 175–176. Oxford University Press, New York.

Herrera Muzgo Torres, Alicia

2002 Ritos Postclásicos en Monte Albán. In *La religión de los Binnigula'sa',* edited by Victor de la Cruz and Marcus Winter, pp. 345–370. IEEPO-IOC, Oaxaca.

Herrera Muzgo Torres, Alicia, Gustavo Gámez Goytia, Marcus Winter, and Cira Martínez López

1999 *Exploraciones en la Plataforma Sur,* Volume 8. Proyecto Especial Monte Albán 1992–1994, Informe Final, edited by Marcus Winter. Centro Instituto Nacional de Antropología e Historia Oaxaca.

Jansen, Maarten

2001 Monte Albán y el origen de las dinastías Mixtecas. In *Memoria de la Primera Mesa Redonda de Monte Albán: Procesos de cambio y conceptualización del tiempo,* edited by Nelly M. Robles García, pp. 149–164. CONACULTA and Instituto Nacional de Antropología e Historia, México, D.F.

Joyce, Arthur A.

2000 The Founding of Monte Albán: Sacred Propositions and Social Practices. In *Agency in Archaeology,* edited by Marci-Anne Dobres and John E. Robb, pp. 71–91. Routledge, London.

Koontz, Rex, Kathryn Reese-Taylor, and Annabeth Headrick (editors)

2001 *Landscape and Power in Ancient Mesoamerica.* Westview Press, Boulder.

Kowalewski, Stephen A., Gary M. Feinman, Laura Finsten, Richard E. Blanton, and Linda M. Nicholas

1989 *Monte Albán's Hinterland, Part II.* University of Michigan Museum of Anthropology, Memoirs 23, Ann Arbor.

Marcus, Joyce, and Kent V. Flannery

1996 *Zapotec Civilization*. Thames and Hudson, London.

Markens, Robert

2004 Ceramic Chronology in the Valley of Oaxaca, Mexico, During the Late Classic (A.D. 500–800) and Postclassic (A.D. 800–1521) Periods and the Organization of Ceramic Production. Ph.D. dissertation, Brandeis University. University Microfilms, Ann Arbor.

Martínez López, Cira

2002 La residencia de la Tumba 7 y su templo: Elementos arquitectónico-religiosos en Monte Albán. In *La religión de los Binnigula'sa'*, edited by Victor de la Cruz and Marcus Winter, pp. 221–272. IEEPO-IOC, Oaxaca.

Martínez López, Cira, Robert Markens, Marcus Winter, and Michael D. Lind

2000 *La cerámica de la Fase Xoo (Epoca IIIB–IV) del Valle de Oaxaca*. Contribución 8 del Proyecto Especial Monte Albán 1992–1994. Centro Instituto Nacional de Antropología e Historia Oaxaca.

Monaghan, John

1995 *The Covenants with Earth and Rain*. University of Oklahoma Press, Norman.

Oudijk, Michel R.

2002 The Zapotec City-State. In A *Comparative Study of Six City-State Cultures,* edited by Mogens Herman Hansen, pp. 73–90. Reitzels Forlag, Copenhagen.

Parsons, Elsie Clews

1936 *Mitla: Town of the Souls and Other Zapoteco-Speaking Pueblos of Oaxaca, Mexico*. University of Chicago Press, Chicago.

Peeler, Damon E., and Marcus Winter

1992–1993 Mesoamerican Site Orientations and Their Relationship to the 260-Day Ritual Period. *Notas Mesoamericanas* 14:37–62. Universidad de las Américas Puebla, Cholula.

1995 Building J at Monte Albán: A Correction and Reassessment of the Astronomical Hypothesis. *Latin American Antiquity* 6:362–369.

Pohl, John M.D.

1994 *The Politics of Symbolism in the Mixtec Codices*. Vanderbilt University Publications in Anthropology, No. 46, Nashville.

2000 The Lintel Paintings of Mitla and Other Frescoes. *Notebook for the Mixtec Pictographic Writing Workshop at Texas*, No. 7. March 9–19, Austin.

Redfield, Robert

1956 *Peasant Society and Culture*. University of Chicago Press, Chicago.

Reilly, F. Kent, III

1999 Mountains of Creation and Underworld Portals. In *Mesoamerican Architecture as a Cultural Symbol,* edited by Jeff Kowalski, pp. 15–39. Oxford University Press, New York.

Robles García, Nelly, and Guillermo Molina V.

1998 Exploración de una tumba prehispánica en el sitio Llaadzie en la comunidad de Mitla, Oaxaca. *Cuadernos del Sur* 12:21–52.

Schele, Linda

1996 The Olmec Mountain and Tree of Creation in Mesoamerican Mythology. In *The Olmec World: Ritual and Rulership,* pp. 105–117. The Art Museum, Princeton University, Princeton.

Schele, Linda, and Julia Guernsey Kappelman

2001 What the Heck's Coatépec? The Formative Roots of an Enduring Mythology. In *Landscape and Power in Ancient Mesoamerica,* edited by Rex Koontz, Kathryn Reese-Taylor, and Annabeth Headrick, pp. 29–53. Westview Press, Boulder.

Smith Stark, Thomas C.

2002 Dioses, sacerdotes y sacrificio: Una mirada a la religión Zapoteca a trevés del vocabulario en lengua Capoteca (1578) de Juan de Córdoba. In *La religión de los Binnigula'sa'*, edited by Victor de la Cruz and Marcus Winter, pp. 91–195. IEEPO-IOC, Oaxaca.

Sugiyama, Saburo

2004 Governance and Polity at Classic Teotihuacan. In *Ancient Mesoamerica,* edited by Julia Hendon and Rosemary Joyce, pp. 97–123. Blackwell, Malden.

Urcid, Javier

2001 *Zapotec Hieroglyphic Writing*. Dumbarton Oaks, Washington, D.C.

Winter, Marcus (editor)

1994 *Monte Albán: Estudios recientes*. Proyecto Especial Monte Albán 1992–1994. Contribución 2. Centro Instituto Nacional de Antropología e Historia, Oaxaca.

Winter, Marcus

2001 *Tesoros de Oaxaca*. Gobierno Constitucional de Oaxaca and Instituto Nacional de Antropología e Historia, México, D.F.

2002 Religión de los *Binnigula'sa'*: La evidencia arqueológica. In *La religión de los Binnigula'sa'*, edited by Victor de la Cruz and Marcus Winter, pp. 47–88. IEEPO-IOC, Oaxaca.

CHAPTER EIGHT

ALTAR EGOS

Domestic Ritual and Social Identity in Postclassic Cholula, Mexico

GEOFFREY G. MCCAFFERTY

INTRODUCTION

Domestic ritual is a defining practice in social reproduction. It can provide significant points of contrast for distinguishing social identities, such as ethnicity, gender, class, and religion—defining the "us" as opposed to the "them." It can take different forms, including religious and secular celebrations, as well as mundane practices such as cooking, childcare, and yard work. Behavioral associations constitute fundamental elements in definitions of self, whereas shared rituals are primordial processes for the construction of group identity. Objects of domestic ritual frame these shared moments, serving as materializations of emotional ties. Christmas decorations and wedding rings are passed down through generations, adding time depth to these links. Foodways, including preparation as well as consumption practices, provide a multisensory mosaic of flavors, smells, and activities that orient at the same time that they organize. From my own experience I think of the annual battles over Northern-style white bread stuffing as opposed to my wife's cornbread dressing, as the Civil War reignites every Thanksgiving. Does the altar-like placement of the television set—adorned with family photos (ancestor worship?), the *TV Guide* (an almanac for predicting the future?), and the remote control (a wand of power?)—constitute the ritual center of early twenty-first-century houses?

Archaeological evaluation of pre-Columbian domestic contexts can reveal similar patterns relating to ritual practices. This chapter will consider domestic remains from the site of Cholula, Puebla, Mexico, a Postclassic urban center famous for its religious and economic importance (Figures 0.1 and 0.2). Cholula is known from ethnohistorical and archaeological evidence as a city that has been continuously occupied for more than 3,000 years (G. McCafferty 1996a). It also offers potential for ethnographic studies of traditional practice and modern development (e.g., Bonfil Batalla 1973). Among other aspects of its culture history, Cholula was a multiethnic city subject to several ethnic invasions and consequent factionalism (G. McCafferty 2003). I will draw on ethnographic and ethnohistoric sources to inform interpretations of the archaeological evidence from an Early Postclassic house from the UA-1 locus on the campus of the Universidad de las Américas, Puebla.

Household archaeology offers an important contrast to traditional studies of ceremonial centers and the palaces of the rich and famous. As noted by Jon Lohse in Chapter 1, the Dominant Ideology Thesis has long been the paradigm that shaped Mesoamerican archaeology, with the implication that elites constructed society in their image and non-elites had no choice but to follow. This thesis ignores important alternatives developed in allied social sciences (Abercrombie et al. 1980; Scott 1985, 1990; Wolf 1999) and elaborated in Marxist archaeology (Miller and Tilley 1984; Paynter and McGuire 1991), in which dominant ideologies are juxtaposed against strategies of resistance. Resistance can take many guises, from outright rebellion to subtle twisting of cultural norms to archaisms that emphasize the past over a less palatable present (see Joyce and Weller, Chapter 6). In addition to resistance are concepts of cultural pluralism that can include social identities such as ethnicity, gender, status, and religion. Urban centers are defined by multiculturalism, and conceptualizations of Mesoamerican cities should incorporate this principle. The result of all of these alternatives is a postmodern cacophony of agency, as a multitude of social actors strategically manipulated their lives in dialectical relationship with their cultural surroundings. Instead of assuming static behavioral norms, this approach assumes diversity and seeks to reveal patterns from the bottom up as more and more examples generate similarities as well as specialized outliers.

The use of household archaeology to generate patterns of past social behavior is still in relative infancy (but see contributions in MacEachern et al. 1989; Santley and Hirth 1993; and Wilk and Ashmore 1988), and therefore it is most tenuous to attempt generalizations from a handful of case studies (but see Olson 2001). The problem is even more acute in Cholula, where only one Postclassic house has been investigated in detail (McCafferty 1992). Yet even if generalizations are not possible, the explication of the UA-1 Structure 1 house and its associated material culture is important because they can be compared with other Postclassic houses of Central Mexico and also with ethnohistorical and ethnographic data.

Was the UA-1 Structure 1 a "commoner" house? Because this structure is unique in Cholula's archaeological record, this determination is still subject to speculation. The site locus was more than one kilometer from the Early Postclassic site center surrounding the Great Pyramid, presumably where elite residences would have been located. The four-room structure measured only about 60 square meters in area, at the low end of dwelling sizes from Aztec Cihuatecpan (Evans and Abrams 1988). The presence of architectural elements, such as painted plaster floors and walls, an altar, *temazcal*, and evidence of decorative façades, however, all points to investment above the level of the simplest of the Cihuatecpan houses. Thus, although this household might have had some wealth, it probably was not an elite household. It should serve, therefore, as a contrast to dominant ideologies of Cholula. Until more comparative examples have been adequately excavated, analyzed, and published, however, questions of the degree of representativeness will remain.

Although little is known of the commoners of Cholula, ethnohistorical sources provide a relatively vivid account of the dominant society of the Postclassic. This ideology revolved around the cult of Quetzalcoatl, with a prominent role played by the long-distance merchants who were also associated with the ritual center (Rojas 1927 [1581]). Cholula was a center for highly skilled artisans who produced ceramics and textiles in the Mixteca-Puebla style, and the Cholula market was noted for its fine metal- and feather-work (Durán 1971 [1576–1579]). As a pilgrimage center, nobles from many parts of Central Mexico maintained "vacation homes" for their visits during festivals. Because Cholula was the focus of several ethnic migrations, its population consisted of a complex mix of Olmeca-

Xicallanca, Tolteca-Chichimeca, as well as other groups (Olivera and Reyes 1969). The conclusion of this chapter will examine how the UA-1 Structure 1 household compares with the norms of the dominant society.

HOUSEHOLD RITUAL IN ETHNOGRAPHIC AND ETHNOHISTORIC SOURCES

Pre-Columbian Cholula was noted as one of the major ceremonial centers of ancient Mesoamerica, featuring the largest and longest-used pyramid in the world (Marquina 1970; McCafferty 1996b, 2001a). During the Postclassic, Cholula was known as the center for the pan-Mesoamerican cult of Quetzalcoatl (Carrasco 1982; McCafferty 1999, 2001a; Ringle et al. 1998). People made long pilgrimages to the temples of the city, and these pilgrims included nobles who came to Cholula for confirmation of their semi-divine authority (Rojas 1927 [1581]). Abundant ethnohistorical records describe public ritual of the city. Unfortunately, but not uncharacteristically, domestic ritual received only minimal attention from Colonial period chroniclers. Since Cholula continued as a major center for religious pilgrimage and celebration, however, ethnographic and ethnohistoric sources provide useful information that may relate to prehispanic practices (e.g., Bonfil Batalla 1973; Olivera 1970).

Historical accounts of Cholula households indicate the importance of religious altars. Fredrick Starr (1908:110) recorded that one-room houses in late-nineteenth-century Cholula featured pictures of saints and the Virgin pinned to the wall with burned candles in front of them. Adolph Bandelier (1976 [1884]) found that indigenous houses in the mountains near Cholula featured a main room, or *teopantzintli,* with an altar consisting of a wooden shelf on which were a religious image, vases for flowers, and "little trinkets of clay or wood" (1976:143).

These historical accounts bear a strong resemblance to ethnohistorical descriptions of Aztec household organization based on Colonial legal documents found by Susan Kellogg (1993). Specific rooms were labelled *teopantzonca,* or "rooms with an altar." The Spanish *corregidor* of Cholula, Gabriel de Rojas, wrote in the late sixteenth century that "there is no house that does not have an altar with many images of saints" (1581:31; reprinted in Bonfil Batalla 1973:43, translation by author). Other shrines were described as being in courtyards. One of the first Catholic priests in New Spain, Fray Toribio de Benavente Motolinía, recorded this description of domestic ritual:

> Each day women awoke early with a smiling heart and placed their offering to the gods on an altar in the courtyard of their house. On the altar was a round brazier [*brasero*] with a burning coal and there the woman offered incense to the same fire kept in honor of the god, and/or in honor of the sun and the other gods. She also placed on the altar a clay vessel [*vaso*] with feet, filled it with clean water, and added flour of maize or *tlaulli* and also offered this to the gods. She then took some coals in a vessel like a frying pan but of clay, and holding this by the handle, threw incense onto the coals. And then she raised her hands with the brazier to the four directions. She also placed [on the altar] some vessels with food and later cleaned the vessels. To this offering they said, "Tlatlalchipahuacihuatl," which means "the beautiful woman, the earth." It should be noted that with this offering to the sun, to fire, to the earth, and to the other gods, they believed that they would have a good day, and that the sun would follow its course well and illuminate the earth, and by this bear fruit and maintain life. (Motolinía 1996 [1540]:433 in Smith 2002:98)

Household rituals were probably the unifying symbol of the social group and incorporated a specific gender ideology in ritual practice. In addition to the above quotation, Diego Durán (Heyden 1994:164–165) noted that the maintenance of the household altar was one of the primary responsibilities for female members of the group. Elizabeth Brumfiel (1996) demonstrates the importance of female imagery in Aztec domestic ritual through a study of Postclassic figurines, concluding that in contrast to a male-centered state ideology, female figurines predominate in household contexts, perhaps in resistance to dominant ideologies. Female figurines are also abundant in Postclassic Morelos (Smith 2002:103; Olson, Chapter 9). This evidence supports the importance of female-centered domestic ritual.

Susan Evans (1990) has identified ritual activities associated with *temazcales*, especially those relating to curing rituals accompanied by female figurines, and Durán (1971 [1576–1579]:270) reported idols and offerings placed within the sweatbath. Fray Bernardino de Sahagún's encyclopedic *Florentine Codex* provides a detailed description of midwifery practiced in the *temazcal* (1950–1982 [1547–1585], 6:149–160). The firebox was called the *xictli*, or "navel," in reference to the belief that the sweatbath was the womb of the Mother Goddess (Sullivan 1982:18), as further evidence for the important role of women in domestic ideology. The goddess of midwives and healers, known by the Aztecs as Toci, was closely associated with *temazcales* (*Codex Magliabechiano* 1983 [1903]:figure 65).

Finally, ethnohistoric sources indicate that burials were often part of domestic ritual. The Aztecs believed that different fates awaited the deceased depending on the cause of death. The most common burial practice was for individuals, along with their worldly possessions, to be cremated in preparation for the journey to Mictlan, the land of the dead located in the distant north. The bones were then placed in a pot, with a greenstone that represented the heart, and were buried in the home (Sahagún 1950–1982 [1547–1585], 3:43–45). If the deceased was a noble, then slaves were killed and cremated to accompany him or her. Diego Durán (Horcasitas and Heyden 1971:121–122) also described the variety of burial practices: "Some people were buried in the fields; others in the courtyards of their own homes; others were taken to shrines in the wood; others were cremated and their ashes were buried in temples." Gabriel de Rojas (1927 [1581]:164, translation by author) described the indigenous burial practice at Cholula: "[W]hen they died they were buried in front of an idol, in a round hole, not lying extended but rather drawn up or squatting."

The distinction between cremation among the Aztec and direct, primary interment at Cholula is one notable difference between the two Postclassic cultures. For example, numerous pots containing cremated remains and often accompanied by a single greenstone bead were found by Edward Sisson (1974:31–33) at Late Postclassic Coxcatlan Viejo, part of the Aztec empire to the south of Cholula. Otherwise, however, relatively few Aztec cremation burials have been found. Non-cremation burials have occasionally been found in Postclassic residential areas, as at Cihuatecpan in the Valley of Mexico (Evans and Abrams 1988), Tetla-11 at Chalcatzingo (Norr 1987) and Cuexcomate and Capilco (Smith 2002) in the Valley of Morelos, Tula (Healan 1988), and Coxcatlan in the Tehuacan Valley (Sisson 1973, 1974). In part because of the scarcity of Postclassic burials and the relatively high percentage of adults in burial populations, Michael Smith (2002:108–109) suggests that there may have been cemeteries, perhaps associated with public buildings or with older parts of sites. In this sense, the hundreds of Postclassic burials found at Cholula's Great Pyramid (López Alonso et al. 1976), largely abandoned during the Middle and Late Postclassic, may constitute a cemetery (discussed later).

THE UA-1 STRUCTURE 1 COMPLEX

This chapter draws on these historical and ethnohistorical insights to interpret material remains found at a Middle (A.D. 900–1050) to Late (A.D.

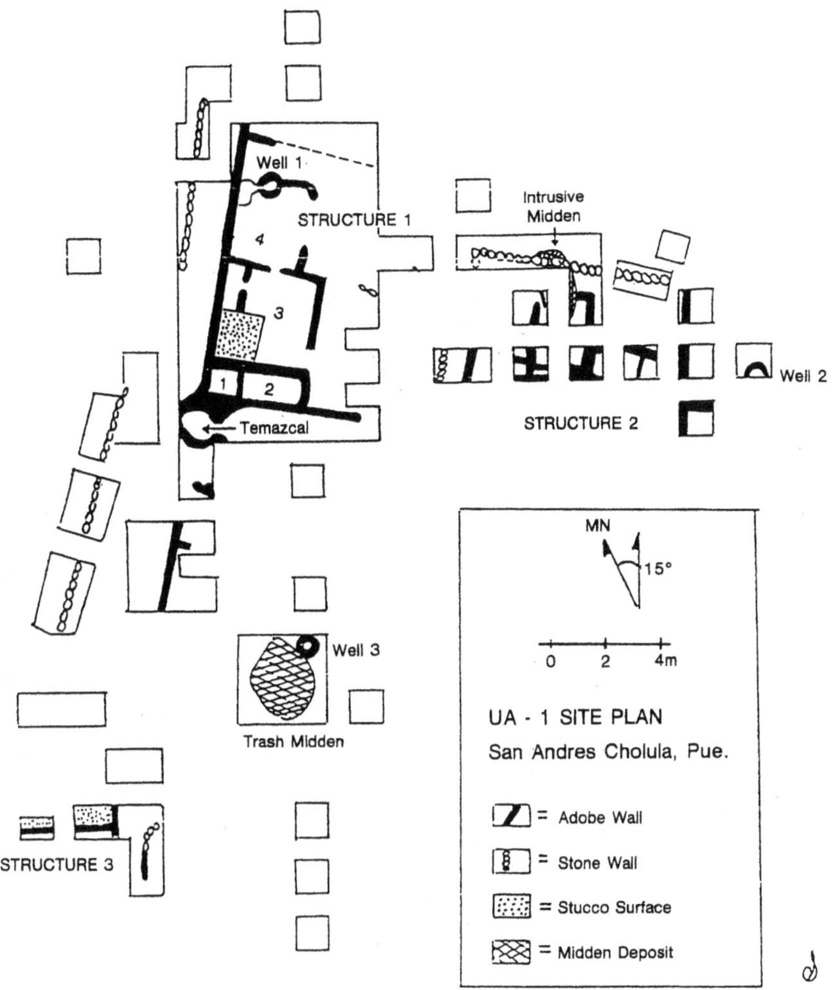

8.1. Plan of UA-1, Cholula, Mexico.

1050–1200) Tlachihualtepetl period house from the eastern edge of prehispanic Cholula. The UA-1 project was conducted as a field school in 1968 under the direction of the late Daniel Wolfman (1968; McCafferty 1992). It completely exposed Structure 1 and sampled the Early Cholollan (A.D.1200–1400) Structure 2 (Figure 8.1). Ceramics from discrete depositional contexts were seriated and linked to radiocarbon dates to redefine the Postclassic chronology (McCafferty 1996a, 2001b).

Structure 1 is notable because it seems to have been abandoned rapidly, probably as the result of fire and perhaps militarism (McCafferty 1992, 2003). A thick layer of ash covered the floor beneath the collapsed walls, the stucco floor was charred, and a high concentration of projectile points was found in the area (102 points or point fragments in just over 200 m^2 of excavated area). A nearly empty sub-floor cache box was found that contained a piece of carved bone with ash at the bottom, suggesting that it was open when the house burned, possibly evidence of looting or the hurried recovery of family heirlooms. Finally, a group burial was found in Room 4, where a mature woman and five children were placed in a hole dug through the plaster floor. Some of the skeletal remains projected above the floor level, indicating that interment occurred after the building was abandoned, but the burials were sealed beneath the collapsed adobe walls of the structure. A three-centimeter layer of ash was also found at the base of the burial pit.

Structure 1 featured four rooms, two porch areas, and a possible *temazcal* sweatbath. It backed up against a compound wall and faced onto a patio that included a trash pit; artifacts from the midden cross-mended with artifacts from the floor contact, indicating that they were part of the same systemic context at the time of abandonment (Schiffer 1972). Room 1 was very small, barely 1 x 1 m, and may have been connected to the adjacent sweatbath. Room 2 measured 1 x 2 m, with a variety of objects on the floor, including *comales, manos, metates,* and remains of a spinning and weaving kit with spindle whorls, bone awl, and a bowl with dye. Room 3 was the largest room; it featured a raised platform, a storage cubicle, a three-stone hearth, and the previously mentioned cache box. Room 4 was probably added after the original three, as indicated by a doorway connecting it to Room 3 that had apparently been made by breaking through an existing wall. It contained another hearth, as well as the multiple burial described previously and an intrusive well dating to the Late Cholollan phase (A.D. 1400–1520). The porch areas may have been partially covered by the roof, and a low curb would have diverted rainwater away from this area and the interior rooms. The entire structure was elevated above the natural ground surface by 50 cm of rubble fill, although it could not be determined if this platform had been intentionally filled or simply constructed over the remains of an earlier structure. It was not determined if this house was isolated or part of a patio group with other contemporary residential structures. Seriation of ceramics from the adjacent Structure 2 clearly indicated that it was from a separate ceramic phase, so this structure may represent a subsequent but not contemporary occupation of the area.

Based on the presence of multiple small rooms, hearths, domestic artifacts, remains relating to both male and female activities, and adult and child skeletons, it was concluded that

> (1) Structure 1 was a residential structure occupied between approximately A.D. 900 and 1200;
> (2) it was occupied for an extended period of time, resulting in modification of the structure (perhaps in relation to the domestic cycle as mature children married but continued to live in the same household);
> (3) the house was destroyed by fire and rapidly abandoned, leaving important artifacts in situ and thus providing valuable insights into the systemic context of domestic behavior; and
> (4) although the presence of some architectural elaboration (e.g., altar, sub-floor cache box, and painted stucco floors) suggests a degree of wealth, the small overall size of the house and distance from the urban center suggest that this structure was a non-elite, or commoner, household. (McCafferty 1992)

EARLY POSTCLASSIC DOMESTIC RITUAL

At Cholula, the UA-1 Structure 1 provides important information on domestic ritual and, through these data, insights into the construction of social identity in the Early Postclassic. Architectural elements and sub-floor features, as well as artifacts, relate to ritual practices that took place within the residential complex.

ARCHITECTURE

The most prominent architectural feature for inferring domestic ritual is the low platform from Room 3 (Figure 8.2). It is approximately square, measuring 1.34 x 1.38 m and 37 cm in height. The platform was made of adobe bricks covered by a thin layer of mud and then a layer of plaster. This structural form is similar to what Susan Evans and Elliot Abrams (1988) identified as a bench or sleeping platform from the Aztec site of Cihuatecpan but also corresponds to what Sisson (1973) called "altars" from Postclassic Coxcatlan in the Tehuacan Valley. The UA-1 Structure 1 platform was found with two small bowls, a spindle whorl, ceramic ball, and bone on the surface, perhaps as offerings similar to the "little trinkets

8.2. Platform altar in Room 3, UA-1, Cholula, Mexico.

of clay and wood" mentioned by Bandelier (1976 [1884]:143). Adjacent to the adobe platform was a cubicle containing ceramic urns, and in front of the platform were sub-floor pits containing whole vessels, probably representing ritual interments. These features reinforce the interpretation that the platform functioned as an altar.

The cubicle measured only about 1 m in length by 30 cm in depth and opened off Room 3 near the platform/altar. Inside the cubicle were one fragmentary and two complete urns, which measured about 30 cm in height, were biconical in form, and featured appliqué decoration on the exterior in anthropomorphic form (Figure 8.3). Similar vessels from Cholula are illustrated in Florencia Müller (1978:204–205). Sisson (1991/92) found more examples of these vessel forms, which he called *xantiles,* in the Tehuacan Valley and inferred that the iconography represented deities. Similar urns are also known from Cacaxtla, where they are brightly painted and include "Maya" blue paint. The anthropomorphic appliqués resemble deities and warriors and may fulfill a role similar to that of the urns from the Zapotec religion that have been interpreted as representing semi-divine ancestors (Marcus 1983; Sellen 2002), although the Zapotec urns are characteristically found in burial contexts. Since no comparable form is known from Classic period Cholula, it is likely that the use of *xantiles* is a ritual practice introduced during the Epiclassic period, possibly

8.3. *Anthropomorphic braziers, or* xantiles, *found in the niche next to the altar, UA-1, Cholula, Mexico.*

associated with the Olmeca-Xicallanca ethnic group (McCafferty 2000). It is uncertain how the *xantiles* may have functioned in the UA-1 Structure 1 context, but their proximity to the platform/altar suggests their placement on the altar during special ceremonies.

A three-stone hearth, dug about 12 cm into the stucco floor, was located to the northeast of the adobe platform/altar. A second hearth was found in Room 4; it was 24 cm in diameter and lined with potsherds. Much attention has been focused on the cosmic significance of the three-stone hearth in recent archaeological literature, particularly for the Maya for whom the hearthstones represented a world axis (Freidel et al. 1993; Headrick 2001; Schele and Mathews 1998). For the Aztec, the word for hearth (*xictli*) was the same as for navel, the center of the body and link to the womb (see also reference to the *temazcal* firebox). Thus, the three-stone hearth may be conceptualized as the axis mundi of the domestic sphere (e.g., Sahagún 1950–1982 [1547–1585], 6:131). That UA-1 Structure 1 had two hearths may further indicate that it was a multifamily dwelling, perhaps relating to developments in the domestic cycle.

In front of the platform/altar and beside the hearth were several small pits dug through the plaster floor, with complete vessels (bowls) placed at the bottom of the feature. In the northeast corner of the room a buried tripod bowl contained a greenstone celt. Sahagún (1950–1982 [1547–1585], 6:131) recorded the Aztec custom of burying the placentas of baby girls beside the family hearth as a means of ensuring that the girl would remain in the home until marriage and would be a "good wife." A similar practice was noted ethnographically by Elsie Clews Parsons (1936:76) from Mitla, Oaxaca, with the additional comment that the bowls were covered to prevent blindness (see Chapter 7); covered bowls were recovered from the Zapotec Tlailotlacan compound at Teotihuacan (Spence 2002:59). Although no organic materials were noted from the ceramic vessels at UA-1 Structure 1, it can be speculated that these bowls may have been part of a related practice of ritual interment specifically related to female ideology.

Adjacent to Structure 1 was an unusual structure that most closely corresponds to a *temazcal*, or sweatbath. It was circular in form, about 1 m in diameter, and with a narrow passageway opening onto the main chamber (Figure 8.4). The adobe walls were fire reddened. The overall form is similar to *temazcales* recorded ethnographically in the Cholula area by Gloria Castillo Rella (1970:206–209; Figure 8.4). These measure about 1 m in diameter and feature a firebox connected to the main chamber so that heat and herbal vapors could enter the occupied bathing area. As

8.4. Temazcal, or sweatbath, with circular seating area connected to tunnel to firebox, UA-1, Cholula, Mexico.

noted, sweatbaths were important arenas for ritual practice, as they were used in healing and also in preparation for and cleansing after childbirth (Sahagún 1950–1982 [1547–1585], 6:149–160). Notably, a figurine of a human face with closed eyes was found in the passageway from the firebox and may represent an object used in a curing ritual, as indicated by Durán (1971 [1576–1579]:270).

Mortuary Practices

Skeletal remains of nineteen individuals were found at UA-1, with eighteen associated with the Structure 1 house. Preliminary identification of the skeletons was prepared by Arturo Romano of the Museo Nacional de Antropología, Mexico, and recorded in Wolfman's preliminary report (1968; also McCafferty 1992:143–157, 207–220). Information on location, orientation, burial position, age, and sex is presented in Table 8.1. Seventeen of the burials were primary interments, and only Burials #13 and #14 were secondary. The flexed, seated posture was the predominant burial position, and where orientation could be determined, all but one of the skeletons were facing in a northerly direction, toward Mictlan, the Nahua land of the dead.

Although most of the burials were found with Structure 1, only Burial #8 can be stratigraphically linked with the occupation phase of the house. (Seriation suggests that the S6/W3 burials may also have been contemporary with the occupation; see discussion later in this chapter.) Burial #8 was placed in a pit dug into the stucco floor of the southeast corner of Room 4 prior to the construction of the overlying wall. The skeleton was of a child, age four to six years, with evidence for tabular erect skull shaping. An obsidian blade was the only object associated with the burial.

The other seventeen burials from Structure 1 were associated with post-abandonment processes; although based on the relationship of the burials to collapsing adobe walls, it is likely that the interments took place soon after the house burned. The most complex of the burial contexts was a multiple burial involving six individuals (#4, #5, #6, #7, #11, and #12) who were placed in a pit dug through the floor of Room 4, just east of the main structural wall. Burials #4, #5, #6, and #7 were enclosed within a small adobe enclosure, whereas #11 and #12 were outside of the enclosure, suggesting that they may have been interred at a later time (Figure 8.5). Burial #4 was an adult female, and the other individuals were sub-adults (#12 was identified as an infant). Grave goods included beads (including one located in the mouth of Burial #7), a ceramic ball, a blue-green stone celt, shells (including a shell whistle), two obsidian eccentrics (including a red obsidian butterfly), a Cocoyotla Black on Natural bowl, and a concentration of red seeds. The greatest concentration of objects was associated with Burial #7, a child.

A second concentration of burials was located in unit S6/W3, south of the house, against an adobe wall aligned with the main north/south wall of Structure 1. The burials rested on a hard-packed surface and were

Table 8.1. Burial data for Structure UA-1, Cholula, Mexico (after Wolfman 1968:table 4)

Burial #	*Orientation*	*Position*	*Age*	*Grave Goods*
1	—	—	fetus	none
2	—	—	fetus	none
3	north	seated flexed	infant	bowl rim, obsidian fragment, copper ring
4	north	seated flexed	adult	bowl, red seeds[1]
5	northwest	dorsal flexed	child	1
6	east	dorsal flexed	child	1
7	north	seated flexed	child	beads, a ceramic ball, greenstone celt, shell, shell whistle, obsidian eccentric "M," obsidian eccentric butterfly
8	north	seated flexed	child	obsidian blade
9	north	seated flexed	child	bowl[2]
10	north	dorsal flexed	infant	bowl
11	north	dorsal flexed	infant	1
12	northeast	ventral flexed	child	1
13	—	—	adult	none
14	north	seated flexed	infant	2 large sherds
15	—	—	fetus	none
16	north	seated flexed	infant	bowl
17	?	seated flexed	child	obsidian blade, large sherds
18	?	?	infant	obsidian blade, large sherds
19	north	seated flexed	child	carved bone, polishing stone, chert projectile point

Notes:

1. Several objects were found in proximity to Burials #4, #5, #6, #7, #11, and #12 but could not be clearly associated with individual skeletons, nor are they clearly grave goods. These items included a chert point, an obsidian scraper, a spindle whorl, and a figurine head.
2. Objects were also found with Burials #9, #10, #14, #16, #17, and #18 that could not be associated with any individual skeleton. These items included a high frequency of obsidian blades and scrapers, two projectile points, two figurines, a spindle whorl, and numerous ceramic balls.

covered by the collapsed wall. Based on the seriation of associated ceramics (McCafferty 2001b:109), this context may date to the occupation phase prior to the final abandonment of Structure 1. Burials #17 and #18 were interred together inside an *olla,* with an obsidian blade and several large potsherds. Bowls were also found with Burials #9, #10, and #16, and large sherds were found with Burial #14. Other objects included frequent obsidian blades and scrapers, two projectile points, two figurines, a spindle whorl, and numerous ceramic balls.

A single Torre Polychrome bowl contained three fetuses (Burials #1, #2, and #15). The bowl was found in the trash midden located in the house patio, but it is unclear if the burials were directly associated with the midden deposit or if the bowl was intrusive and therefore postdated the feature.

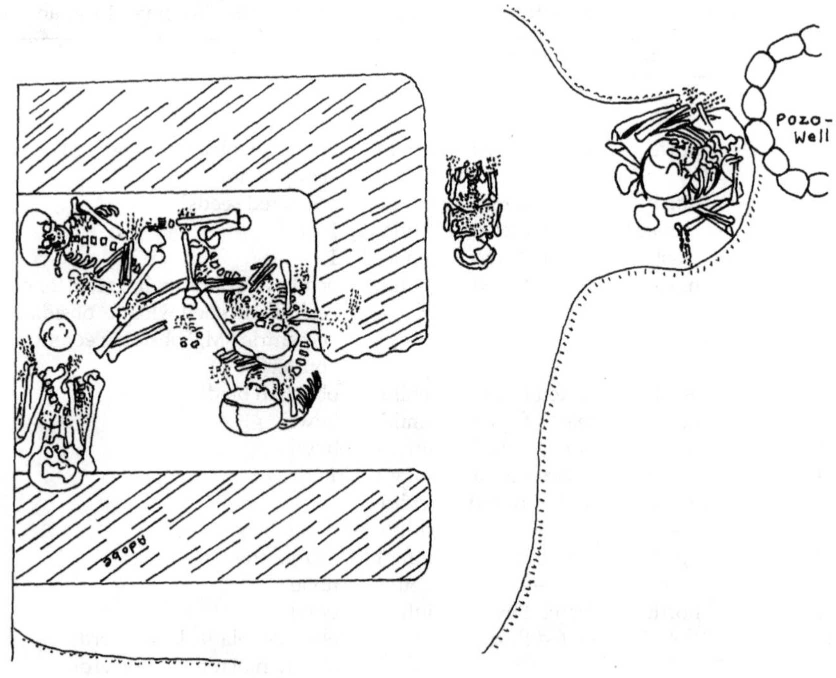

8.5. Multiple burial at Cholula, Mexico.

Torre Polychrome was a common ceramic type in the Trash Midden assemblage, totaling 8 percent of all rim sherds (McCafferty 2001b:93, table 5.2), so the bowl with the three fetus burials is not obviously anachronistic.

Two isolated burials were also found in Structure 1. Burial #3 was an infant buried in a flexed seated position, located in the porch area south of the house wall. It was badly disturbed, perhaps because of a wall collapse after interment. A large bowl rim was found beneath the burial, and a piece of obsidian and a copper ring with a filigree design of an anthropomorphic face were also associated with the burial. Burial #19 was a young child buried above the floor level near the intersection of two walls in Room 1. Objects found near the burial included a piece of carved bone, a polishing stone, and a white chert projectile point, although these could not be conclusively related to the burial as grave goods.

The mortuary remains found associated with Structure 1 represent primarily children, who were buried with modest grave goods and minimal formal preparation. They provide a contrast to the demographic profile of the burials found at the Great Pyramid of Cholula (Hayward 1986;

López Alonso et al. 1976; G. McCafferty and S. McCafferty 2002), where children made up only 42 percent of the 302 identifiable Postclassic burials. Life tables of the Postclassic burials from the ceremonial center indicate a low life expectancy, with most individuals in the 25–34-year age class (Hayward 1986:219–220). Although Hayward attempted to generalize from these data about the Postclassic Cholula population, it seems likely that the dramatically different pattern found at the UA-1 domestic context indicates a distinct burial strategy and therefore should be used to supplement and correct the Great Pyramid's burial population. The Postclassic burials at the Great Pyramid should be considered a specialized cemetery area, perhaps similar to the suggestion of Smith (2002) that adults and elites may have been buried in separate sectors of Postclassic sites, away from the residential zones. As such, the Great Pyramid "cemetery" is probably more representative of dominant ideological norms than is the UA-1 household context.

Artifacts

In addition to the architectural and mortuary features, numerous artifacts relating to domestic ritual were recovered from Structure 1, including incense burners, musical instruments, and figurines.

Incense was burned in many different ritual practices, as the smoke represented a form of communication with the supernatural. Pre-Columbian pictorial manuscripts depict incensing ceremonies occurring in shrines and before ancestral bundles (e.g., *Codex Selden* 1964:9-I). Spanish chroniclers commented that incense was a regular feature of religious rituals, including domestic ritual (Motolinía 1996 [1540]:433; Sahagún 1950–1982 [1547–1585]).

Four different *incensario* forms were found in the UA-1 excavations: long-handled *sahumadores,* tripod *incensarios* with carved lattice sides, pinched appliqué *braseros,* and lantern censers (Figure 8.6). The long-handled *sahumadores* were of the San Pedro Polished Red type and were often decorated with incised patterns filled with a gray graphite paint. No complete examples were found, but about 1 percent of the UA-1 Trash Midden ceramics were sahumador fragments (McCafferty 2001b:114, table 5.12), suggesting that their use was fairly common within the domestic context.

The carved lattice *incensarios* were rare at UA-1 but are notable because similar vessel forms have been found at Tula and in the Mixteca

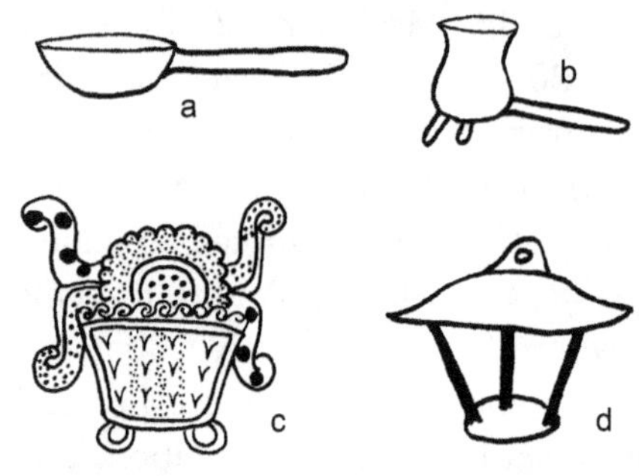

8.6. Common forms of UA-1 incense burners, Cholula, Mexico: (a) long-handled sahumadores, *(b) tripod* incensarios, *(c) pinched appliqué* braseros, *and (d) lantern censers.*

Alta, indicating a wide regional distribution of this particular form. They were also of the San Pedro Polished Red type, with a well-burnished exterior surface treatment and occasional black painted decoration.

The pinched appliqué *braseros* have thick walls that are often striated and coated in white stucco and then occasionally painted in blue or black. They typically have pinched nubs on the exterior and occasionally include appliqué "cords" of clay on the rim. Vessels resembling this form appear in the *Codex Borgia* (e.g., 1963:folio 18), a pre-Columbian pictorial manuscript that was likely painted in the Cholula area (Nicholson 1966; Nicholson and Quiñones Keber 1994:xii). *Braseros* occur in the Cerro Zapotecas Sandy Plain type and again made up about 1 percent of the Trash Midden deposit (McCafferty 2001b:114, table 5.12).

The final form of incense burner is called a "lantern" censer. This form consists of a round base and three supports holding up a "roof" (Figure 8.6d; see Müller [1978:128–129] for a complete example, although it is unclear if the placement of the lantern censer within a tripod bowl is contextually accurate). The roof has a loop handle on top, where it could be suspended, and often a coating of soot on the interior ceiling. The interior of the roof is often rough, like the bottom of a *comal,* but can be distinguished by its smaller diameter, greater pitch, remains of the three support posts, and occasional incised decoration on the upper surface to resemble a thatched roof. Smith (2002:101) identifies these as "scored censers" and reports them from domestic middens in Morelos (also Séjourné 1970:figure 39; 1983:figure 119). They constituted about 0.5 percent of the UA-1 Trash Midden assemblage (McCafferty 2001b:114, table 5.12).

Another artifact class that probably had a ritual function was the ceramic flute. No complete examples were found, but numerous fragments of thin-walled, ceramic tubes about 2 cm in diameter were found, many of which had perforations that would have served as finger holes. The use of flutes is known from ethnohistorical accounts relating to public ritual,

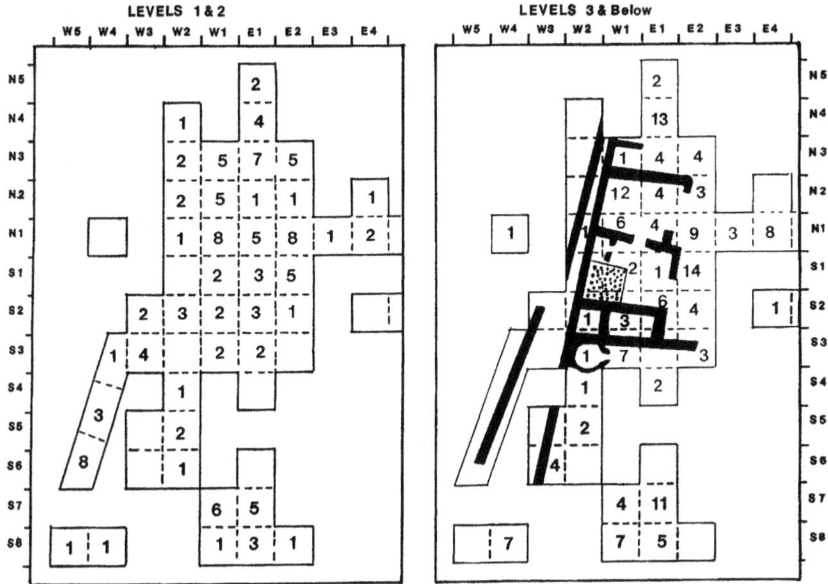

8.7. Distribution of figurines at UA-1 Structure 1, Cholula, Mexico.

especially during the Feast of Toxcatl, dedicated to the god Tezcatlipoca (Olivier 2002). Traditional flutes are still played in Cholula to welcome the sunrise during ritual occasions. Their presence in the UA-1 household context may imply use in domestic rituals or, alternatively, that members of the UA-1 household performed in public rituals but discarded their broken instruments in their private trash midden.

Small ceramic figurines had a somewhat ambiguous function, but that undoubtedly included domestic ritual (see Olson, Chapter 9, for a discussion of Postclassic figurines from Morelos, Mexico). Three hundred eighty-nine figurines were found in the UA-1 excavation, with 154 found in association with Structure 1 (Figure 8.7). Although figurine fragments were found in virtually every 2 x 2 m excavation unit, they clearly were concentrated in specific locations, usually in the porch areas just outside the house or in the Trash Midden. The only concentration within the house occurred in the northwest corner of Room 4, a possible kitchen. There was a relative absence of figurines in Room 3, which was associated with the platform/altar. Based on the spatial distribution, a more comfortable interpretation would be that most of these figurines were used in areas associated with children's play.

Of the figurine forms found associated with Structure 1, the great majority were anthropomorphic, with few bird and mammal (including monkey) figures. Only one of these objects was complete enough to include both a head and torso (Figure 8.8a), and it probably represented a woman with arms crossed against her chest as if holding something; she wore ear spools, a large lip plug, and a skirt. Interestingly, this figurine was not broken below the waist but ended in a bulb of clay as if it were intended to have a cloth wrapped around it, as seen in some historic dolls. A second figurine was headless but included a torso and one leg (Figure 8.8b). This figurine was of a male, based on lack of breasts and use of a *maxtlatl* loincloth. Notable about this figurine was a circular hole in the chest to represent heart sacrifice.

The majority of the other diagnostic figurines were heads broken from the torso. Some of these had ear spools or headdresses, but there was little diagnostic symbolism to identify these items with specific deities. Of the few figurines that included gender-related attributes, females outnumbered males. A curious feature of several of the faces was that they were concave on the back and featured perforations so that they could be tied onto other figurines, or perhaps onto fingers, as masks (Figure 8.8c).

The most common identifiable figurine form was of Tlaloc (Figure 8.8d), the Nahua storm god characterized by goggle eyes and a long *bigote,* or moustache, which covers the mouth. There was one probable female head with a headdress of draped cloth that may represent a member of an earth/fertility goddess complex, such as Tlazolteotl (Figure 8.8e). A large, flat figure with a nose bar, as well as some of the Tlaloc figures, featured a clay strap on the back, similar to "rings" used in the *Codex Borgia* as identified by Gabriela Uruñuela and colleagues (1996). The prominence of Tlaloc imagery is notable because Tlaloc is not present in the Morelos figurine corpus reported by Smith (2002; also Olson, Chapter 9) and therefore may constitute another difference in commoner ideology separating Cholula from the Aztecs.

Although not technically a figurine, another common deity image was that of the old god, Huehueteotl, who often appeared as an anthropomorphic vessel support on polychrome bowls. Huehueteotl was associated with fire, and sculptures of the old fire god with a vessel on his head were made during the Classic period at Teotihuacan (Cowgill 1997). The old god vessel supports may be conceptually related to these earlier sculptures.

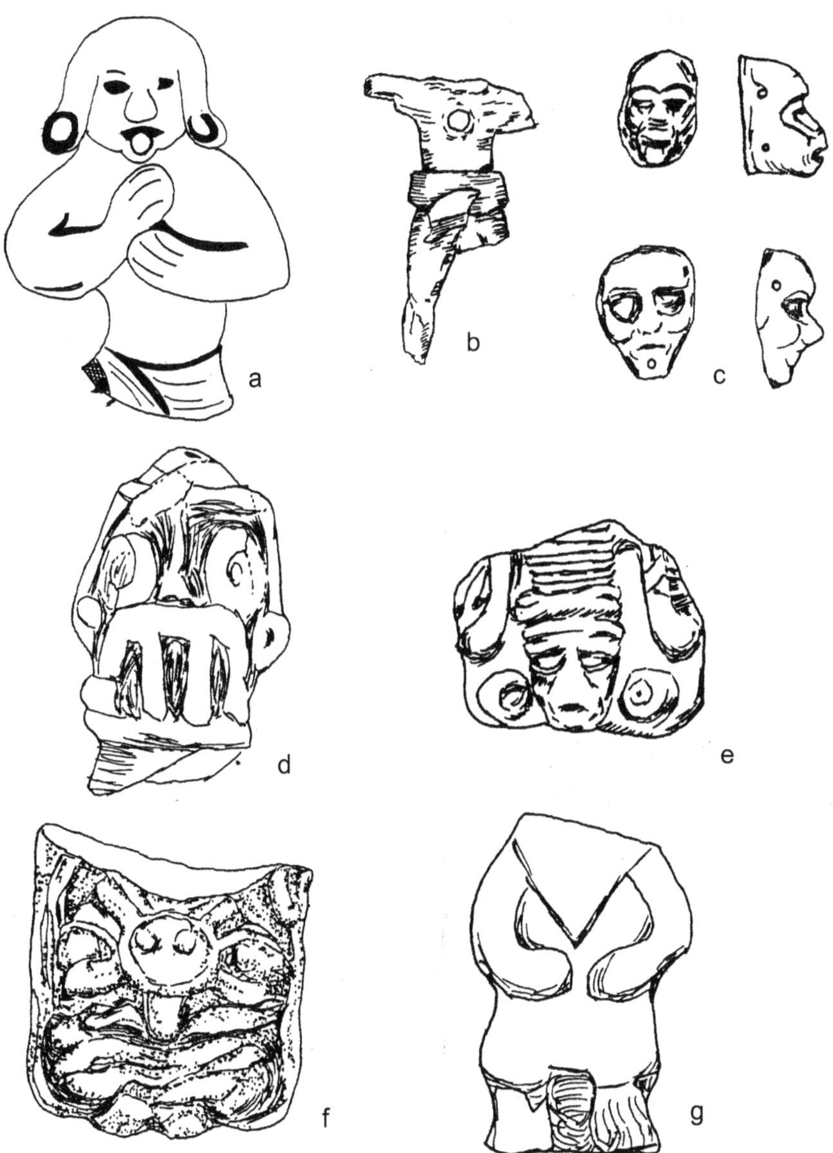

8.8. (a) Complete head and torso (UA-1); (b) male sacrificial victim (UA-1); (c) miniature figurine masks; (d) Tlaloc head (UA-1); (e) possible figurine of Tlazolteotl (UA-1); (f) figurine of seated female from Well 3; (g) figurine of standing female from Well 1.

As discussed previously, a figurine was found in the *temazcal* and therefore may represent a ritual context relating to healing. Another context where figurines were found that may have ritual content is in the bottom of wells. Three wells were excavated in the UA-1 project and in two of the three, female figurines were found at the deepest level (the third, Well 2, dated to the historical period). In Well 3, located beneath the Trash Midden, a cross-legged female is seated against a vertical slab, possibly representing a throne back (Figure 8.8f). She is identified as female based on costume elements, including a long skirt and triangular *quechquemitl.* She wears a large disk on her chest as a pendant with two circular appliqués (similar disk pendants are found on female figures on *xantiles*). Traces of blue paint are found on the figurine. Two nearly identical figurines have been found: one that is illustrated in Noguera's (1954:161, figure b) book on Cholula ceramics and another found by the archaeologist Sergio Suárez Cruz at the bottom of an Early Postclassic well (Suárez C. 1995).

The second UA-1 figurine was found in Well 1, the Late Cholollan phase feature that passed through the floor of Room 4. This example was a slab figurine of a standing female wearing a long skirt and *quechquemitl* (Figure 8.8g). All of these figurines were headless, perhaps relating to a ritual termination in which the "spirit" is released (e.g., Mock 1998). The practice of dropping a female figurine into a well may correspond to ethnohistoric accounts of fertility offerings made to the goddess Chalchihuitlicue in order to facilitate conception (Durán 1971 [1576–1579]:269).

In summary, the figurine evidence from Structure 1 does not support their exclusive use in religious ritual, as the greatest concentrations were in porch areas that would probably have been used for daily activities, such as child's play. Additionally, since identifiable deities are rare, most of the figurines are interpreted as representing mortals. Based on these data, I believe that the UA-1 figurines functioned primarily as "action figures" used by children in play and, concurrently, in the enculturation process. The presence of a figurine representing a heart sacrifice may relate to a "commoner ideology" of victimization, but this interpretation is clearly speculative. Those figurines that were found in more ritually significant contexts, such as the *temazcal* and the bottom of wells, may have been used as a means of interacting with supernatural forces to promote curing or fertility. When figurines could be identified with members of the Postclassic pantheon, Tlaloc was the most common deity representation.

Foodways as Domestic Ritual

As suggested in the opening commentary on the significance of Thanksgiving food rituals, foodways can carry important symbolic meanings relating to social identity. Learned from an early age, aromas and flavors carry multisensory meanings for self-identification. Special meals are prepared to mark rites of passage and ritual events. The early Colonial accounts provide rich descriptions of the feasts that accompanied different calendar periods (e.g., Durán 1971 [1576–1579]). Archaeological ceramics interpreted from the perspective of vessel form can provide a sensitive means for inferring changing foodways, including both the food items consumed and the rituals practiced in consumption (e.g., feasting).

A major shift in Cholula foodways occurred during the Classic to Postclassic transition with the introduction of the comal, a wide, low-profile griddle used primarily for heating tortillas. In the Late Classic domestic context excavated at the Transito site (McCafferty 1996a), no comal rims were found. An elite residence on the northeast platform of the Great Pyramid contained Early Tlachihualtepetl phase (A.D. 700–900) refuse in construction fill with about 9 percent of all rim sherds from *comales*. The UA-1 Structure 1 contexts correspond to the subsequent phases of the Early Postclassic, and comal rims are even more abundant, averaging about 20 percent and occurring in both Momoxpan Orange and San Andrés Red types (McCafferty 2001b). Similarly high frequencies occur in other Postclassic contexts from Cholula, indicating that tortilla consumption continued as an important component of domestic foodways.

The dramatic increase in tortilla use, as evidenced in the huge proportion of comal fragments in domestic refuse, implies a radical shift in food consumption as well as a significant reallocation of women's labor (Brumfiel 1991). Women were the major food producers in Mesoamerica, and grinding corn for tortillas was a cornerstone of female identity. Ethnographic studies indicate that the preparation of maize dough for tortillas is a physically demanding and labor-intensive practice that would have consumed a large part of the workday, while also keeping women planted in their domestic compound. In contrast, tortillas are a very portable food that may have been produced in part for men who worked relatively far from home (Brumfiel 1991:241). Feasts were noted for the consumption of vast quantities of tortillas, including specially made ritual tortillas with elaborate forms and exotic ingredients (e.g., Sahagún 1950–1982 [1547–1585], 1:19).

Other changes in the Early Postclassic ceramic assemblage at UA-1 further indicate significant changes in domestic foodways. Most apparent is the dramatic increase in decorated serving wares, including the beginnings of the famous Cholula polychrome tradition (McCafferty 1994). Late Classic serving wares were plain, gray/brown conical bowls (Tepontla Burnished Gray/Brown), almost completely lacking in decoration (McCafferty 1996a, 2001b). Changes began in the Epiclassic with a transition that introduced sloppily painted bichrome black-on-orange subhemispherical bowls (Cocoyotla Black on Natural). Beginning in the Middle Tlachihualtepetl phase, polychrome serving wares featured brilliant orange, red, white, and black painted decoration that often included codex-style motifs (Figure 8.9). Following Martin Wobst's (1977) perspectives on style as symbolic communication, the colorful and iconographically charged serving wares probably indicated an increased ritual significance for food consumption in which public display or the private reinforcement of group identity took on a more prominent role.

In addition to the bright colors of the polychrome pottery, many new types and vessel forms were found in the domestic assemblage. Whereas the Late Classic domestic context included only three major types (Tepontla, Acozoc, and Teotihuacan Thin Orange), the UA-1 Early Postclassic assemblage featured ten types that each made up at least 2 percent of the total rims (McCafferty 2001b:93–94). Added to this increase in types was a greatly increased variety of vessel forms (McCafferty 2001b:112). More research needs to be done, but the preliminary indication is that ritualized foodways may have contributed to the increased diversity of ceramic types and forms.

Early Postclassic foodways, as inferred from the UA-1 Structure 1 ceramic assemblage, mark a radical shift from the domestic patterns of the Late Classic and even Epiclassic. Greater diversity in forms suggests a greater diversity of foodstuffs, as tortillas became a staple of the diet. Both wet and dry foods were consumed (based on bowl as well as plate forms), and a variety of jar (olla) and pot (*cazuela*) forms suggest specialized cooking practices. The vibrant colors of the polychrome serving wares suggest that feasting may have played a role in group integration. The large Trash Midden associated with the Structure 1 Patio had a relatively high frequency of cup (*copa*) forms (McCafferty 2001b:116), which may have been used for consuming pulque (the fermented juice of the maguey) during ritual gatherings. Iconography on polychrome vessels may relate to mythical events associated with religious or ethnic affiliation. Within the

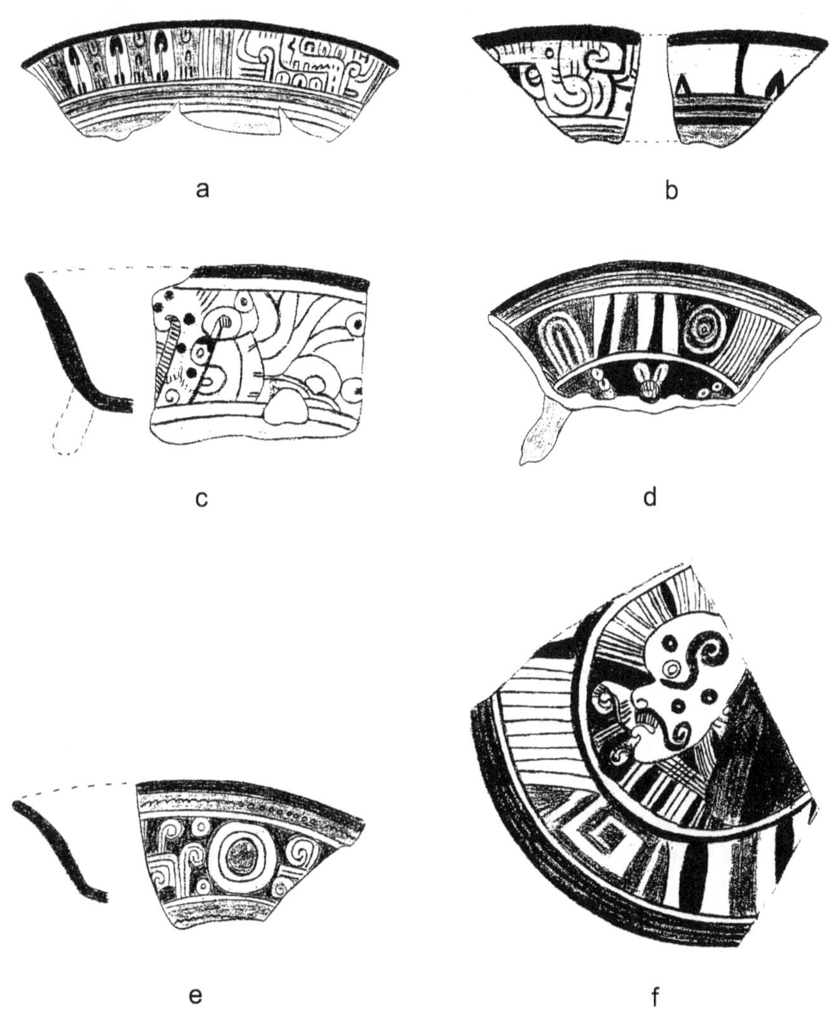

8.9. Polychrome pottery from UA-1 Structure 1, Cholula, Mexico.

multicultural city of Cholula, foodways may have been a significant factor in the ritual practice of group identity.

SUMMARY AND CONCLUSIONS

The UA-1 Structure 1 excavation produced a rich artifact assemblage in primary contexts associated with the architectural remains of a residential dwelling from the Early Postclassic period. Evidence of burning, among other clues, suggests that the site was abandoned rapidly with de facto refuse left in situ. Consequently these data are useful for a range of interpretations about Early Postclassic domestic practice, including ritual activities, of a non-elite household.

The major locus of ritual practice was Room 3, where a platform altar, three-stone hearth, sub-floor caches, and a niche containing three *xantiles* were all found. These features are consistent with ethnohistorical and ethnographic descriptions of *teopantzonca*, "rooms with altars," which were important arenas of domestic ritual. Other activities that would have been practiced in association with these areas probably included burning incense as a form of communication with the supernatural, perhaps including semi-divine ancestors represented as biconical *xantiles*, and playing music to attract the attention of supernatural forces. A variety of incense burners and flute fragments support the idea that these activities were practiced in and around Structure 1.

Figurines, an artifact class often associated with ritual practice, were rare in Room 3 but were found in most other parts of the residential area, with concentrations on the porches, areas more typically associated with child's play. This contextual argument, plus the fact that few of the figurines could be readily identified with specific deities of the Mesoamerican pantheon, suggests that figurines were more in the realm of children's toys. This interpretation does not ignore the significance of toys as an important means of enculturation but suggests a more secular than religious tone to that process.

Finally, some deity figures identifiable from the figurine assemblage include the storm god Tlaloc, a member of the female earth/fertility cult (perhaps Tlazolteotl), and the old god Huehueteotl as tripod vessel supports. Headless female figurines in Wells 1 and 3 suggest a practice analogous to that documented for the deity Chalchihuitlicue, involving offerings to influence female reproduction. Although sparse because of the small sample of identifiable deity figures at UA-1, this assemblage can be used to generate a local pantheon, at least for commoner religious practice. Notable from the UA-1 pattern is the absence of Ehecatl/Quetzalcoatl, despite the fact that Quetzalcoatl is widely noted as the patron deity of Cholula during the Postclassic (McCafferty 1999), and the prominence of Tlaloc, in contrast to the figurine assemblage from Morelos (Olson, Chapter 9).

Another important aspect of domestic ritual documented at UA-1 Structure 1 was the high number of burials. Although only one of the individuals could be clearly linked to the occupation of the house, many others seem to have been buried shortly after the house was burned and abandoned. Of the eighteen burials from Structure 1, only one was an adult. This pattern contrasts dramatically with the demographics of burials from around Cholula's Great Pyramid, which featured a majority of adult burials (Hayward 1986; López Alonso et al. 1976; G. McCafferty and S. McCafferty 2002). Most of the UA-1 burials were in a flexed, seated position facing north. This pattern corresponds well with the Postclassic burial pattern from the ceremonial center and with the description of a "squatting" position as noted by Rojas (1927 [1581]:164). The northerly orientation of the burials corresponds with the direction of Mictlan.

A final observation on commoner ritual at Postclassic Cholula relates to food rituals, as inferred from the ceramic inventory. In contrast to earlier Classic and Epiclassic assemblages, the Early Postclassic ceramics from Structure 1 featured brightly decorated polychromes using codex-style motifs. There was a significant increase in the numbers of both ceramic types and vessel forms, suggesting that ceramics may have become a much more meaningful category of symbolic communication. The most dramatic change in the kitchen "tool-kit" was in the introduction and preponderance of *comales*, linked to tortilla production. Since tortilla production in particular and foodways in general were ideologically linked to female practice, the ceramic assemblage indicates a possible redefinition of female roles within the household.

The engendering of the UA-1 Structure 1 household as female space reappears in a variety of aspects: the prominence of the three-stone hearth, ritually interred pots around the hearth, the altar (ethnohistorically linked to female practice), the *temazcal* used in healing and midwifery, the high number of female figurines, the many child burials along with an adult female burial, and the increased importance of food rituals. The UA-1 site also produced a high number of spindle whorls (S. McCafferty and G. McCafferty 2000) to go with the spinning and weaving kit found in Room 2. Spinning and weaving were another cornerstone of female ideology (Brumfiel 1991; S. McCafferty and G. McCafferty 1991). The UA-1 data strongly suggest that the Postclassic house was a nexus of female activities and ritual practice, in contrast to more public or state-level religious practices (e.g., Brumfiel 1996).

The dominant ideology of the Early Postclassic, inferred from ethnohistoric accounts and archaeological remains from the ceremonial center surrounding the Great Pyramid, indicates the major importance of the cult of Ehecatl/Quetzalcoatl, god of the wind, planet Venus, and priestly knowledge. Archaeological support for this theme has been found in the final occupation of the Great Pyramid (McCafferty 2001a), where carved stone monuments feature serpent imagery and a mural (now missing) depicted a polychrome feathered serpent (Acosta 1970:66). Numerous stamp-bottom bowls found at the Great Pyramid, dating to the Epiclassic and Early Postclassic, have representations of Ehecatl's diagnostic shell motif, while another has a representation of Venus as evening star (McCafferty and Suárez C. 2001).

As the major religious center of Central Mexico, however, Cholula was also associated with other gods and goddesses, including Xochiquetzal and Centeotl. During the Late Postclassic, after the ceremonial center was moved from the area surrounding the Great Pyramid to the area of the modern civic center of San Pedro Cholula (where a "new" Pyramid of Quetzalcoatl was erected), a rain god called Chiconauquiahuitl was worshipped on top of the partially abandoned Great Pyramid (McCafferty 2001a; Rojas 1927 [1581]). Representations of the shrine in the *Historia Tolteca-Chichimeca* (e.g., 1976 [1547–1560]:folio 7) depict a large frog, and an altar stone that may have been rolled down from the summit also represents a frog (McCafferty 2001a; see Gonlin, Chapter 4, for a discussion of frog iconology in Mesoamerica).

In contrast to these aspects of the "dominant" religious ideology, the UA-1 household lacked iconography relating to Quetzalcoatl. Tlaloc, the major rain god who was included in the domestic context, cannot be confused with the frog-like Chiconauquiahuitl of the Great Pyramid. These discrepancies further suggest a difference in religious ideology between the dominant culture and household-level practices.

Other decorative elements from the ceremonial center represent Cholula as a multicultural city, with iconographic references to Teotihuacan, the Gulf Coast, the Maya, and the Mixteca of Oaxaca (McCafferty 2000, 2001a). This multiculturalism may relate to the role of Cholula as a pilgrimage center of the Quetzalcoatl cult (Ringle et al. 1998). The *pochteca* merchants were affiliated with Yiacatecuhtli, an avatar of Quetzalcoatl, and their prominence must have added to the internationalism of the city. The Mixteca-Puebla stylistic tradition (McCafferty 1994; Nicholson 1982; Smith and Heath-Smith 1980), also known as the International Postclassic style (Robertson 1985), facilitated symbolic discourse that crosscut linguistic and cultural boundaries, much as did the Zuyuan culture described by Alfredo López Austin and Leonardo López Luján (2000).

The UA-1 Structure 1 household did have some items obtained through long-distance trade, particularly marine shells and obsidian. Ceramics decorated in the Mixteca-Puebla style were prominent in the ceramic assemblage, although a more detailed iconographic analysis would be useful in differentiating between domestic and "dominant" themes. Michael Lind (1994) found that images of sacrifice were an important theme in Late Postclassic polychromes from Cholula, in vessels of the elite Coapan Laca ("Catalina" in Lind's terminology) type. In contrast to the Coapan Laca designs involving hearts, skulls, and bloodletting tools, the UA-1 household assemblage lacked such images but rather featured symbols relating to possible mythological scenes. This difference suggests not just a distinction in iconography but also a different set of ideological themes.

Burials are another element of ritual practice that provides a contrast between "commoner" and "dominant" ideologies. From the Postclassic burial population recovered by the Proyecto Cholula around the Great Pyramid (G. McCafferty and S. McCafferty 2002; López Alonso et al. 1976), there were 176 adults (99 males and 77 females) compared with 126 sub-adults (12 infants, 103 children, 11 juveniles). In contrast, of the 18 individuals associated with UA-1, 17 were sub-adults (3 fetuses, 6 infants, 8 children) with only 1 adult (female). This pattern indicates a strong difference in burial practices, with a much greater association between sub-adults and household contexts. The predominant burial position and orientation at both the Great Pyramid and UA-1 were flexed, seated burials facing north, indicating an overarching religious structure relating to mortuary ritual. Yet, there was a greater variation in the amount of grave goods associated with burials found in the Great Pyramid cemetery, with some individuals accompanied by great wealth, whereas the majority lacked grave goods altogether. In contrast, all individuals buried at UA-1 Structure 1, other than the fetuses, had relatively modest grave goods. The comparison between these two data sets therefore indicates shared beliefs relating to position and orientation between the public burials of the Great Pyramid and the household-level mortuary rituals of UA-1 Structure 1. Distinctions occur in decisions of who was selected for public burial in the possible cemetery and the degree of wealth interred with an individual.

The study of domestic ritual provides important insights into a key element of household organization, as religion and associated practices are used as defining elements of social identity. Through the outstanding systemic context provided by the UA-1 Structure 1, a richly textured reconstruction of Early Postclassic life can be achieved, albeit for this single case. These patterned behaviors, in turn, can be compared with earlier, later, and spatially distinct patterns to begin to chart culture change and continuity and can even be contrasted with more public-level ritual to infer the degree to which state-level ideologies were adopted or resisted at the household level. Through this kind of high-resolution study, archaeology can realize its potential for studying diachronic processes as well as multi-dimensional social identities.

A final caveat, however, must be restated regarding the UA-1 assemblage. Cholula was a complex, multicultural center for at least 3,000 years. So few domestic contexts have been properly excavated, analyzed, and published that comparative interpretations are virtually impossible. To use this one context to characterize "commoner" practice in the Early Postclassic is therefore premature. It is also ingenuous, in my opinion, to assume that there will ever be one identifiable "commoner ideology" in a plural society such as urban Cholula. As such, this case study is presented as the first of what will hopefully become many examples of Postclassic identity strategies representing a diversity of commoner rituals and commoner ideologies.

ACKNOWLEDGMENTS

This analysis owes much to the outstanding data recovery and field recording of the late Daniel Wolfman and members of his UA-1 field school. Considering the early period of this project—years before Kent Flannery's *Early Mesoamerican Village* (1976) brought "household clusters" to archaeological attention—it was remarkably innovative.

My research on the UA-1 materials was supported by grants from Sigma Xi and SUNY Binghamton. This chapter was finalized during a research sabbatical provided by the Faculty of Social Sciences of the University of Calgary. Many people have provided constructive input to this research, including Liz Brumfiel, John Hoopes, Bill Isbell, Mickey Lind, Randy McGuire, Jan Olson, Dave Peterson, Ann Stahl, and Sergio Suárez. As always, Sharisse McCafferty has been integral to all phases of my research.

REFERENCES CITED

Abercrombie, Nicholas, Stephen Hill, and Bryan S. Turner
1980 *The Dominant Ideology Thesis*. Allen and Unwin, London.

Acosta, Jorge R.

1970 Patio Sureste. In *Proyecto Cholula,* edited by Ignacio Marquina, pp. 57–66. Serie Investigaciones 19. Instituto Nacional de Antropología e Historia, Mexico, D.F.

Bandelier, Adolph E.

1976 [1884] *Report of an Archaeological Tour in Mexico, in 1881.* AMS Press, New York.

Bonfil Batalla, Guillermo

1973 *Cholula: La ciudad sagrada en la era industrial.* Instituto de Investigaciones Históricas, Universidad Nacional Autónoma de México, Mexico, D.F.

Brumfiel, Elizabeth

1991 Weaving and Cooking: Women's Production in Aztec Mexico. In *Engendering Archaeology: Women and Prehistory,* edited by Joan M. Gero and Margaret W. Conkey, pp. 224–251. Basil Blackwell, Oxford.

1996 Figurines and the Aztec State: Testing the Effectiveness of Ideological Domination. In *Gender and Archaeology,* edited by Rita W. Wright, pp. 143–166. University of Pennsylvania Press, Philadelphia.

Carrasco, Davíd

1982 *Quetzalcoatl and the Irony of Empire: Myths and Prophecies of the Aztec Tradition.* University of Chicago Press, Chicago.

Castillo Rella, Gloria

1970 Sección de Estudios Urbanisticos. In *Proyecto Cholula,* edited by Ignacio Marquina, pp. 183–209. Serie Investigaciones 19, Instituto Nacional de Antropología e Historia, Mexico City, Mexico, D.F.

Codex Borgia

1963 *Codice Borgia* (facsimile). Fondo de Cultura Economica, Mexico, D.F.

Codex Magliabechiano

1983 [1903] *The Book of the Life of the Ancient Mexicans Containing an Account of Their Rites and Superstitions.* Translated with commentary by Zelia Nuttall. University of California Press, Berkeley.

Codex Selden 3135 (A.2)

1964 *Codex Selden.* Facsimile with commentary by Alfonso Caso. Sociedad Mexicana de Antropología, Mexico, D.F.

Cowgill, George L.

1997 State and Society at Teotihuacan, Mexico. *Annual Review of Anthropology* 26:129–161.

Evans, Susan T.

1990 Household Ritual in Aztec Life. Paper presented at the 55th Annual Meeting of the Society for American Archaeology, Las Vegas.

Evans, Susan T., and Elliot M. Abrams

1988 Archaeology at the Aztec Period Village of Cihuatecpan, Mexico: Methods and Results of the 1984 Field Season. In *Excavations at Cihuatecpan: An Aztec Village in the Teotihuacan Valley*, edited by Susan T. Evans, pp. 50–234. Vanderbilt University Publications in Anthropology, No. 36. Nashville.

Flannery, Kent V. (editor)

1976 *The Early Mesoamerican Village*. Academic Press, New York.

Freidel, David, Linda Schele, and Joy Parker

1993 *Maya Cosmos: Three Thousand Years on the Shaman's Path*. William Morrow and Company, New York.

Hayward, Michelle H.

1986 A Demographic Study of Cholula, Mexico, from the Late Postclassic and the Colonial Period of 1642–1738. Ph.D. dissertation, Pennsylvania State University. University Microfilms, Ann Arbor.

Headrick, Annabeth

2001 Merging Myth and Politics: The Three Temple Complex at Teotihuacan. In *Landscape and Power in Ancient Mesoamerica*, edited by Rex Koontz, Kathryn Reese-Taylor, and Annabeth Headrick, pp. 169–195. Westview Press, Boulder.

Healan, Dan (editor)

1988 *Tula of the Toltecs: Excavations and Survey*. University of Iowa Press, Iowa City.

Heyden Doris (translator)

1994 *The History of the Indies of New Spain, by Diego Durán*. University of Oklahoma Press, Norman.

Historia Tolteca-Chichimeca

1976 [1547–1560] *Historia Tolteca-Chichimeca*. Edited and translated by Paul Kirchoff, Lina Odena G., and Luis Reyes G. Instituto Nacional de Antropología e Historia, Mexico, D.F.

Horcasitas, Fernando, and Doris Heyden (translators and editors)

1971 *Book of the Gods and Rites of the Ancient Calendar, by Fray Diego Durán*. University of Oklahoma Press, Norman.

Kellogg, Susan

1993 The Social Organization of Households Among the Tenochca Mexica Before and After the Conquest. In *Prehispanic Domestic Units in Western Mesoamerica: Studies of the Household, Compound, and Residence*, edited by Robert S. Santley and Kenneth G. Hirth, pp. 207–224. CRC Press, Boca Raton.

Lind, Michael D.

1994 Cholula and Mixteca Polychromes: Two Mixteca-Puebla Regional Sub-Styles. In *Mixteca-Puebla: Discoveries and Research in Mesoamerican Art and Archaeology,* edited by Henry B. Nicholson and Eloise Quiñones Keber, pp. 79–100. Labyrinthos Press, Culver City.

López Alonso, Sergio, Zaid Lagunas R., and Carlos Serrano

1976 *Enterramientos humanos de la Zona Arqueológica de Cholula, Puebla.* Colección Científica 44, Departamento de Antropología Física, SEPINAH, Mexico, D.F.

López Austin, Alfredo, and Leonardo López Luján

2000 The Myth and Reality of Zuyua: The Feathered Serpent and Mesoamerican Transformations from the Classic to the Postclassic. In *Mesoamerica's Classic Heritage: From Teotihuacan to the Aztecs,* edited by Davíd Carrasco, Lindsay Jones, and Scott Sessions, pp. 21–87. University Press of Colorado, Boulder.

MacEachern, Scott, David J.W. Archer, and Richard D. Garvin (editors)

1989 *Household and Communities: Proceedings of the Twenty-First Annual Conference of the Archaeological Association of the University of Calgary.* The University of Calgary Archaeological Association, Calgary.

Marcus, Joyce

1983 Rethinking the Zapotec Urn. In *The Cloud People: Divergent Evolution of the Zapotec and Mixtec Civilizations,* edited by Kent V. Flannery and Joyce Marcus, pp. 144–148. Academic Press, New York.

Marquina, Ignacio

1970 Pirámide de Cholula. In *Proyecto Cholula,* edited by Ignacio Marquina, pp. 31–46. Serie Investigaciones 19. Instituto Nacional de Antropología e Historia, Mexico, D.F.

McCafferty, Geoffrey G.

1992 The Material Culture of Postclassic Cholula, Mexico: Contextual Analysis of the UA-1 Domestic Compounds. Ph.D. dissertation, State University of New York at Binghamton. University Microfilms, Ann Arbor.

1994 The Mixteca-Puebla Stylistic Tradition at Early Postclassic Cholula. In *Mixteca-Puebla: Discoveries and Research in Mesoamerican Art and Archaeology,* edited by Henry B. Nicholson and Eloise Quiñones Keber, pp. 53–78. Labyrinthos Press, Culver City.

1996a The Ceramics and Chronology of Cholula, Mexico. *Ancient Mesoamerica* 7:299–323.

1996b Reinterpreting the Great Pyramid of Cholula, Mexico. *Ancient Mesoamerica* 7:1–17.

1999 Reading the Fine Print About Quetzalcoatl at Cholula. Paper presented at the 64th Annual Meeting of the Society for American Archaeology, Chicago.

2000 Tollan Cholollan and the Legacy of Legitimacy During the Classic/Postclassic Transition. In *Mesoamerica's Classic Heritage: From Teotihuacan to the Aztecs*, edited by Davíd Carrasco, Lindsay Jones, and Scott Sessions, pp. 341–367. University Press of Colorado, Boulder.

2001a Mountain of Heaven, Mountain of Earth: The Great Pyramid of Cholula as Sacred Landscape. In *Landscape and Power in Ancient Mesoamerica*, edited by Rex Koontz, Kathryn Reese-Taylor, and Annabeth Headrick, pp. 279–316. Westview Press, Boulder.

2001b *Ceramics of Postclassic Cholula, Mexico: Typology and Seriation of Pottery from the UA-1 Domestic Compound*. Monograph 43, Cotsen Institute of Archaeology. University of California, Los Angeles.

2003 Ethnic Conflict in Postclassic Cholula, Mexico. In *Ancient Mesoamerican Warfare*, edited by M. Kathryn Brown and Travis W. Stanton, pp. 219–244. Altamira Press, Walnut Creek.

McCafferty, Geoffrey G., and Sharisse D. McCafferty

2002 Boys and Girls Interrupted: Mortuary Evidence on the Children of Postclassic Cholula, Mexico. Paper presented at the Annual Meeting of the American Anthropological Association, New Orleans.

McCafferty, Geoffrey G., and Sergio Suárez C.

2001 Stamp-Bottom Bowls of Cholula Mexico (with Sergio Suárez Cruz). *La Tinaja: A Newsletter of Archaeological Ceramics* 13:4–10.

McCafferty, Sharisse D., and Geoffrey G. McCafferty

1991 Spinning and Weaving as Female Gender Identity in Post-classic Central Mexico. In *Textile Traditions of Mesoamerica and the Andes: An Anthology*, edited by Margot Schevill, Janet Catherine Berlo, and Edward Dwyer, pp. 19–44. Garland Publishing, New York.

2000 Textile Production in Postclassic Cholula, Mexico. *Ancient Mesoamerica* 11:39–54.

Miller, Daniel, and Christopher Tilley (editors)

1984 *Ideology, Power, and Prehistory*. Cambridge University Press, Cambridge.

Mock, Shirley Boteler

1998 Prelude. In *The Sowing and the Dawning: Termination, Dedication, and Transformation in the Archaeological and Ethnographic Record of Mesoamerica*, edited by Shirley Boteler Mock, pp. 3–18. University of New Mexico Press, Albuquerque.

Motolinía, Fray Toribio de Benavente

1996 [1540] *Memoriales (Libro de oro, MS JGI 31)*. Biblioteca Novohispana 3. El Colegio de México, Mexico, D.F.

Müller, Florencia

1978 *La Alfarería de Cholula*. Serie Arqueología, Instituto Nacional de Antropología e Historia, Mexico, D.F.

Nicholson, Henry B.

1966 The Problem of the Provenience of the Members of the "Codex Borgia Group": A Summary. In *Summa Antropológica en homenaje a Roberto J. Weitlaner,* edited by A. Pompa y Pompa, pp. 145–158. Instituto Nacional de Antropología e Historia, Mexico, D.F.

1982 The Mixteca-Puebla Concept Re-visited. In *The Art and Iconography of Late Post-Classic Central Mexico,* edited by Elizabeth H. Boone, pp. 227–254. Dumbarton Oaks, Washington, D.C.

Nicholson, Henry B., and Eloise Quiñones Keber

1994 Introduction. In *Mixteca-Puebla: Discoveries and Research in Mesoamerican Art and Archaeology,* edited by Henry B. Nicholson and Eloise Quiñones Keber, pp. vii–xv. Labyrinthos Press, Culver City.

Noguera, Eduardo

1954 *La cerámica arqueológica de Cholula*. Editorial Guaranía, Mexico, D.F.

Norr, Lynette

1987 The Excavation of a Postclassic House at Tetla. In *Ancient Chalcatzingo,* edited by David Grove, pp. 400–408. University of Texas Press, Austin.

Olivera de V., Mercedes

1970 La importancia religiosa de Cholula. In *Proyecto Cholula,* edited by Ignacio Marquina, pp. 211–242. Serie Investigaciones 19. Instituto Nacional de Antropología e Historia, Mexico, D.F.

Olivera de V., Mercedes, and Cayetano Reyes

1969 Los Choloques y los Cholultecas: Apuntes sobre las relaciones etnicas en Cholula hasta el siglo XVI. *Anales del INAH* 7:247–274.

Olivier, Guilhem

2002 The Hidden King and the Broken Flutes: Mythical and Royal Dimensions of the Feast of Tezcatlipoca in Toxcatl. In *Representing Aztec Ritual: Performance, Text, and Image in the Work of Sahagún,* edited by Eloise Quiñones Keber, pp. 107–142. University Press of Colorado, Boulder.

Olson, Jan Marie

2001 Unequal Consumption: A Study of Domestic Wealth Differentials in Three Late Postclassic Mexican Communities. Ph.D. dissertation, State University of New York at Albany. University Microfilms, Ann Arbor.

Parsons, Elsie Clews

1936 *Mitla: Town of the Souls and Other Zapotec-Speaking Pueblos of Oaxaca, Mexico.* University of Chicago Press, Chicago.

Paynter, Robert, and Randall H. McGuire

1991 The Archaeology of Inequality: Material Culture, Domination, and Resistance. In *The Archaeology of Inequality,* edited by Randall H. McGuire and Robert Paynter, pp. 1–27. Basil Blackwell, Cambridge.

Ringle, William M., Tomás Gallareta Negrón, and George Bey III

1998 The Return of Quetzalcoatl: Evidence for the Spread of a World Religion During the Epiclassic Period. *Ancient Mesoamerica* 9:183–232.

Robertson, Donald B.

1985 The Cacaxtla Murals. In *Fourth Palenque Round Table, 1980,* edited by Merle Green Robertson and Elizabeth P. Benson, pp. 291–302. Pre-Columbian Art Research Institute, San Francisco.

Rojas, Gabriel de

1581 Descripción de Cholula hecha en 1581 por Gabriel de Rojas. Manuscript on file, Rare Books Library, University of Texas, Austin.

1927 [1581] Descripción de Cholula. *Revista Mexicana de Estudios Historicos,* Tomo I (6):158–170.

Sahagún, Bernardino de

1950–1982 [1547–1585] *Florentine Codex: General History of the Things of New Spain.* Edited and translated by Arthur J.D. Anderson and Charles E. Dibble, 13 volumes. University of Utah Press, Salt Lake City, and School of American Research, Santa Fe.

Santley, Robert S., and Kenneth G. Hirth (editors)

1993 *Prehispanic Domestic Units in Western Mesoamerica: Studies of the Household, Compound, and Residence.* CRC Press, Boca Raton.

Schele, Linda, and Peter Mathews

1998 *The Code of Kings: The Language of Seven Sacred Maya Temples and Tombs.* Scribner, New York.

Schiffer, Michael B.

1972 Archaeological Context and Systemic Context. *American Antiquity* 37: 156–165.

Scott, James C.

1985 *Weapons of the Weak: Everyday Forms of Peasant Resistance.* Yale University Press, New Haven.

1990 *Domination and the Arts of Resistance.* Yale University Press, New Haven.

Séjourné, Laurette

1970 *Arqueología del Valle de Mexico: 1. Culhuacan*. Instituto Nacional de Antropología e Historia, Mexico, D.F.

1983 *Arqueología e historia de Valle de Mexico: De Xochimilco a Amecameca*. Siglo Veintiuno Editores, Mexico, D.F.

Sellen, Adam T.

2002 Storm-God Impersonators from Ancient Oaxaca. *Ancient Mesoamerica* 13:3–19.

Sisson, Edward B.

1973 *First Annual Report of the Coxcatlán Project*. Robert S. Peabody Foundation for Archaeology, Andover.

1974 *Second Annual Report of the Coxcatlán Project*. Robert S. Peabody Foundation for Archaeology, Andover.

1991/92 Los dioses de Coxcatlán, Puebla. *Notas Mesoamericanas* 13:5–23.

Smith, Michael E.

2002 Domestic Ritual at Aztec Provincial Sites in Morelos. In *Domestic Ritual in Ancient Mesoamerica*, edited by Patricia Plunket, pp. 93–114. Monograph 46, Cotsen Institute of Archaeology. University of California, Los Angeles.

Smith, Michael E., and Cynthia M. Heath-Smith

1980 Waves of Influence in Postclassic Mesoamerica? A Critique of the Mixteca-Puebla Concept. *Anthropology* 4:15–50.

Spence, Michael W.

2002 Domestic Ritual in Tlailotlacan, Teotihuacan. In *Domestic Ritual in Ancient Mesoamerica*, edited by Patricia Plunket, pp. 53–66. Monograph 46, Cotsen Institute of Archaeology. University of California, Los Angeles.

Starr, Frederick

1908 *In Indian Mexico: A Narrative of Travel and Labor*. Forbes and Company, Chicago.

Suárez C., Sergio

1995 La cerámica Lisa Choluteca. *Arqueología* 13–14:109–120.

Sullivan, Thelma

1982 Tlazolteotl-Ixcuina: The Great Spinner and Weaver. In *The Art and Iconography of Late Post-Classic Central Mexico*, edited by Elizabeth H. Boone, pp. 7–36. Dumbarton Oaks, Washington, D.C.

Uruñuela, Gabriela, Patricia Plunkett, Gilda Hernández, and Juan Albaitero

1996 Biconical God Figurines from Cholula and the *Codex Borgia*. *Latin American Antiquity* 8:63–70.

Wilk, Richard R., and Wendy Ashmore (editors)

1988 *Household and Community in the Mesoamerican Past*. University of New Mexico Press, Albuquerque.

Wobst, Martin

1977 Stylistic Behavior and Information Exchange. In *Papers for the Director: Research Essays in Honor of James B. Griffin*, edited by Charles E. Cleland, pp. 317–342. Anthropological Papers, No. 61. Museum of Anthropology, University of Michigan, Ann Arbor.

Wolf, Eric R.

1999 *Envisioning Power: Ideologies of Domination and Crises*. University of California Press, Berkeley.

Wolfman, Daniel

1968 Preliminary Report on Excavations at UA-1, July 1968. Report submitted to the Departamento de Monumentos Prehispanicos. Manuscript on file at the Department of Anthropology, Universidad de las Américas, Santa Catarina Martir, Puebla.

CHAPTER NINE

A SOCIOECONOMIC INTERPRETATION OF FIGURINE ASSEMBLAGES FROM LATE POSTCLASSIC MORELOS, MEXICO

JAN OLSON

INTRODUCTION

The tradition of producing, trading, and consuming ceramic figurines was of great significance in the religion of Central Mexican Postclassic cultures. Figurines with images depicting women, men, plants, animals, temples, and deities have been found in public arenas (e.g., temples) but more notably in domestic contexts (e.g., middens). Unfortunately, although early Spanish chroniclers described the public religion as including processions, offerings, and sacrifices, they neglected to mention domestic activities and rituals (cf. Durán 1971:272; Ruiz de Alarcón 1984:49–63). Thus, they left almost no ethnohistoric information on the use or significance of small ceramic figurines commonly found in the domestic contexts of commoners and elites.

All segments of society, however, did not participate equally (qualitatively or quantitatively) in these domestic rituals (see Lohse, Chapter 1).

Richard Netting (1993) found in his cross-cultural study of agricultural households that diversity in domestic activities was not unusual—rather it was the norm. To assume that all commoners or households operated in a similar manner would be to ignore essential differences based on where people resided, what position in society they held, and under what economic and political conditions they lived. Therefore, it is important to investigate ritual behavior at many societal levels.

In this chapter I analyze figurine assemblages from elite and non-elite households residing in three various-sized communities in Morelos, Mexico. Archaeological excavations of Aztec period houses at the sites of Yautepec, Cuexcomate, and Capilco in Morelos (see Figures 0.1 and 9.1) have provided a great quantity of ceramic figurines to demonstrate that household rituals and ideology varied depending on socioeconomic group and time.

These sites were occupied from the Middle Postclassic to Colonial times (Figure 0.2). The Middle Postclassic period, ca. A.D. 1100–1300/1350, covers the Temazcalli phase in western Morelos and the Pochtla phase at Yautepec. Late Postclassic–A period, A.D. 1300/1350–1440, corresponds to the Early Cuauhnahuac and Atlan phases; Late Postclassic–B period, A.D. 1440–1540, to the Late Cuauhnahuac and Molotla phases; and the Colonial period, A.D. 1540–1650, to the Santiago phase at Yautepec (Hare and Smith 1996).

Two rural sites, the village of Cuexcomate and the hamlet of Capilco, were first excavated in 1985 under the aegis of the Postclassic Morelos Archaeological Project (Smith et al. 1992). During the Middle Postclassic phase, Capilco was a small hamlet of approximately 6 houses and Cuexcomate had not yet been established. In the Late Postclassic–A phase, Capilco grew to approximately 14 houses, while some 43 houses were established at Cuexcomate, three kilometers to the east of Capilco. In the Late Postclassic–B, Capilco continued its steady growth until there were 21 occupied houses. Cuexcomate underwent a tripling of population to approximately 146 houses covering more than 14.2 hectares (Smith 1992).

Because Yautepec's Postclassic residential area is located underneath a modern town, it is not possible to know the entire number of Postclassic domestic structures. Nonetheless, an intensive survey determined that by A.D. 1519, central Yautepec covered an area of 209 hectares and had an estimated population of 15,000 people. In 1993, fourteen domestic middens were excavated under the Urban Yautepec Project, seven of which were associated with house structures (Smith 1994a; Smith and Heath-

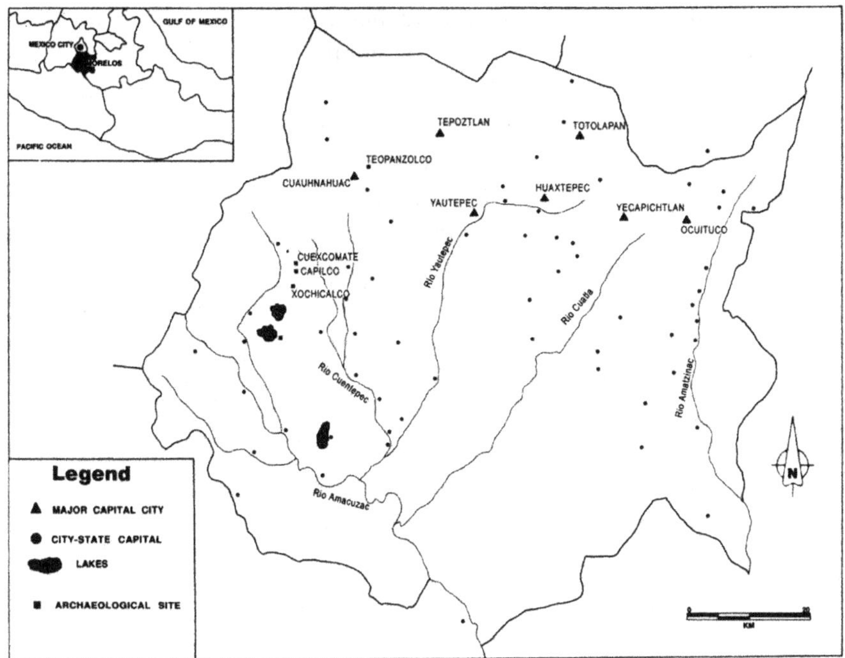

9.1. Map of Postclassic sites Yautepec, Cuexcomate, and Capilco in Morelos, Mexico (map by M. Smith, 1992).

Smith n.d.; Smith et al. 1994). From these excavations, more than a million artifacts, including ceramic sherds, figurines, burials, ground stones, metal, jade, and obsidian, were recovered that date from the Middle to Late Postclassic periods.

This analysis relies on figurines from middens reflecting patterns of discard in residential contexts. The middens were arranged by time period, classified into rural and urban contexts, and categorized into elite and commoner classes (Olson 2001). Although much argument revolves around the identification of class in the archaeological context (see Chase and Chase 1992), for this project we relied on domestic architecture as the primary indicator of class. In his cross-cultural study of houses and their symbolic meanings, Richard Blanton (1994) points out that the domestic structure is the foremost resource of most family or household groups. Not only is the house a physical structure that shelters its occupants from the natural environment, it also reflects the household's organization, goals, and strategies for acquiring wealth and status. This assessment is shared in Elliot M. Abrams's (1989, 1994) energetics model for examining architecture. This model evaluates construction volume, quality of materials, and complexity of architectural features and decoration as sensitive indicators of social inequality (Deetz 1982; Price 1982; Sanders and Santley 1983).

Some Morelos middens were not associated with a house and thus artifacts found in these middens were used as secondary indicators of class. Therefore, distance statistical measurements, such as t-test, discriminant function, and ANOVA, were used to identify whether midden remains resembled known (based on architecture) elite or commoner assemblages. Because the variable distribution is expressed at the local level, I identified class at each site based on local-per-site archaeological variables. These techniques returned values for which I ordered the remaining unclassed middens from the largest to smallest number. I hypothesized that the middens with a value farthest away from a known elite midden were poor commoner households and those that were closer were relatively wealthier (Olson 2001:167–202).

METHOD OF ANALYSIS

The figurines from Cuexcomate and Capilco were initially studied by Cynthia Otis Charlton in the 1980s. In 1988, Michael E. Smith and I reanalyzed 1,499 figurines from the Yautepec excavations and 691 from Capilco and Cuexcomate, using a classification method that differed from the conventional methods used by earlier researchers. A monothetic classification was developed in which types are formed by discrete combinations of attributes and can be formally defined. Because monothetic types can be determined by the presence or absence of attributes, it was felt that the use of such a classification allowed us to better describe the collection to others and also to more effectively analyze the data. We, however, were not without comparative sources in 1998 and thus we consulted many previous studies in preparing our analyses (Boas and Gamio 1921; González Rul 1988; Guilliem Arroyo 1997; Heyden 1996; Séjourné 1970, 1983).

We employed two basic crosscutting typologies, one for groups and one for types, each of which comprised a series of mutually exclusive classes (Olson et al. 1999). Each artifact was classified as a member of a group as well as a type. A "group" designation primarily refers to a figurine's place of origin and is defined by paste and overall form, as shown in Table 9.1. Examples of the figurine group classification are found in Figure 9.2. The "type" classification refers to the design of the figurine

Table 9.1. Figurine group categories for Postclassic Central Mexico

Figurine Group	*Description and Comment*
Aztec Orange paste	Hard, fine orange Aztec paste characteristic of wares from the Basin of Mexico. For the purposes of this project, it was assumed that these were imports to Morelos, an interpretation that has been confirmed for sherds of this paste (Smith et al. 1999). No figurines have yet been tested with neutron activation analysis.
Classic and Formative	Assumed to be heirlooms deliberately saved by Postclassic occupants, as they were found in securely dated Postclassic levels or items picked up by children and carried home.
Coarse paste/Orange slip	Distinctive orange/buff paste with numerous inclusions and a thick orange slip. Many or most examples appear to be the well-described female hollow rattle figurines characteristic of the Basin of Mexico (Parsons 1972).
Colonial	Identified from clothing, hairstyles, horses, and other traits that are obviously Spanish in style or origin.
Cookie Cutter	A highly distinctive category of flat figurines found only at Yautepec. Since there are no identified examples yet reported from outside the Yautepec Valley, we believe they are a local product.
Cuexcomate Orange	A distinctive red-orange hard paste first identified in the Cuexcomate and Capilco collections by Cynthia Otis Charlton (personal communication). This group, present in 1 to 5 percent of the figurines at those sites, is also found in small amounts at Yautepec, where they are classified as imports.
Fine Buff paste	Very fine buff paste with little or few inclusions. Since there are no other ceramics in Morelos with this kind of paste, it is likely that these were also imports, probably from the western Basin of Mexico (Michael E. Smith, personal communication).
Local paste	Because the pastes resemble the local Yautepec Valley plain ware paste, we believe that most of these were produced locally.
Mazapan	A rare group of brown paste human figurines from the west.
Miniature	A catchall category of figurines smaller than 6 cm in length.
Unknown	Fragments that cannot be assigned to any of the above categories.

image, with categories such as male, female, animal, rattle, and deity, as shown in Table 9.2. Figure 9.3 contains examples of the figurines' type classification.

9.2. Figurines from the Mexican Postclassic sites Yautepec, Cuexcomate, and Capilco that illustrate the figurine group classification: (a) Local Female, (b) Cookie Cutter, (c) Fine Buff, (d) Miniatures, (e) Colonial, (f) Mazapan, (g) Cuexcomate Orange.

Figurine attributes were also taken to identify special features of figurines. These characteristics include Body Part, Position, Headdress, Skirts, Perforations, Necklace Designs, and Deity Image. Although I have discussed many of these attributes elsewhere (Olson 2001), for the purposes of this analysis I will discuss only the figurine position (standing, kneeling, seated, lying down, and other). Elizabeth Brumfiel (1996), citing Esther Pasztory (1983:210), argues that the kneeling position represents a lower status, one of submission and of traditional female activities, such as grinding and weaving. She argues that higher status is noted in a standing or

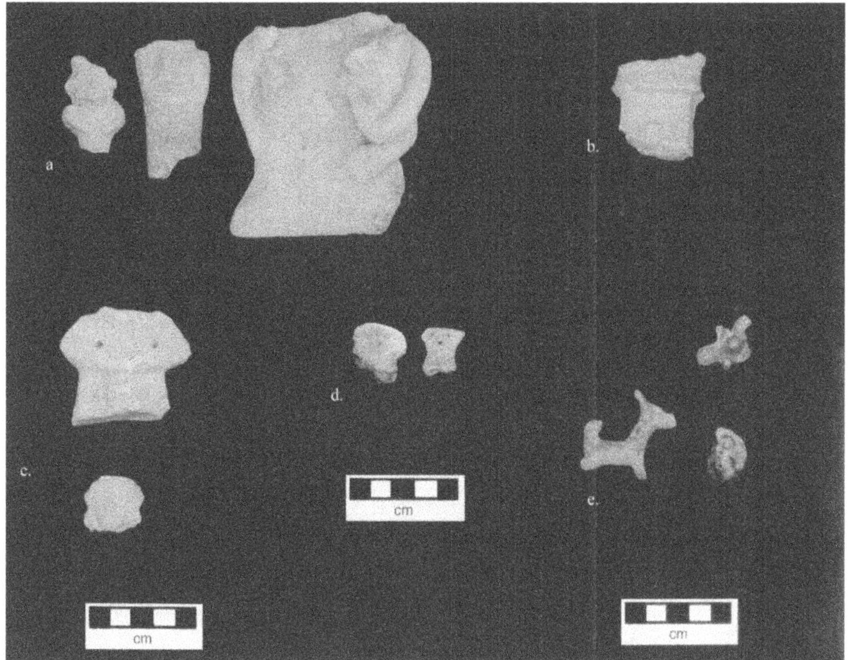

9.3. Figurines from the Mexican Postclassic sites Yautepec, Cuexcomate, and Capilco that illustrate the figurine type classification: (a) Female, (b) Temple, (c) Male, (d) Ghost, (e) Animals: Dog, Turtle, Monkey.

seated position. Although Brumfiel identifies interesting symbolic differences in the position of figurines in relation to work and social status in the community, her hypothesis needs to be tested with a larger data set to ascertain if positions are associated with elite or non-elite contexts (Marcus 1998:20–21).

To assess change in the groups and types of figurines in domestic ritual, I ordered the data presented in Table 9.3 by time period and socioeconomic class for each site. The basic unit of analysis is the domestic unit, which for this project has been defined as a well-phased midden deposit (Smith, personal communication). The mean percentages of figurine positions are arranged in Table 9.4, whereas Table 9.5 contains mean percentages of animal species for known animal figurines. The numbers of domestic units and total figurines in each column are given at the bottom of the table (the first and last columns do not contain means because each of these categories has only a single domestic unit). When comparing classes and sites over time, only house middens with more than six figurines were

Table 9.2. Figurine type categories for Postclassic Central Mexico.

Figurine Type	*Description*
Animals	Most common were dogs, birds, and opossums.
Females	Clothing, hairstyles, headdresses, facial expressions, and the presence of breasts.
Ghost	Crude solid cylindrical figurine with simple punctate facial features. Brumfiel and Hodge (1996) call figurines of this type from Xaltocan "mud men" and suggest that a local identity is evident in their production.
Human	Anthropomorphic figurines whose gender was indeterminable. Because we were conservative in assigning gender to fragments and to broken figurines, there are a large number of figurines that are typed as human without gender.
Infant	Rare figurines of children in cradles.
Males	Breechcloths, hairstyles, drums, and lack of breasts.
Puppet	Based on examples published elsewhere (González Rul 1988; Uruñuela et al. 1996), thin curving cylindrical pieces were identified as appendages for figurines.
Rattle	Fragments of hollow spherical rattles, most of which had twisted handles. Rattles were an important part of special ritual activity (Monjarás-Ruiz 1970).
Temple	Common in the Basin of Mexico but quite rare in Morelos.
Unknown	Includes fragments that are figurines but cannot be classified into another type category.

used for statistical analysis. Not all middens contained the required quantity of figurines for statistical validity and thus not all status groups are included for each period.

RESULTS OF ANALYSIS: COMPARISONS OF FIGURINE ASSEMBLAGES

Figurines from the Middle Postclassic Period (a.d. 100–1300/1350)

City-states founded during the Middle Postclassic period competed for control of tribute and land, promoted trade, and sought intercity alliances. Agricultural and craft production intensified to meet the demands of a growing population, and markets thrived. Both Yautepec and Capilco were founded during this period. The urban site of Yautepec had a larger population than that of the rural hamlet, and its community members

Table 9.3. Percent data for figurines ordered by chronology and socioeconomic class for Cuexcomate, Capilco, and Yautepec in Morelos, Mexico.

Phase	*Middle Postclassic*		*Late Postclassic–A*				*Late Postclassic–B*				*Colonial*
Site	*Cap*[1]	*Yau*	*Cap*	*Cuex*	*Yau*	*Yau*	*Cap*	*Cuex*	*Yau*	*Yau*	*Yau*
Class	*com*	*com*	*com*	*elite*	*com*	*elite*	*com*	*com*	*com*	*elite*	*com*
GROUPS[2]											
Aztec Orange paste	0.0	0.6	0.0	0.0	1.8	0.0	1.3	1.1	2.8	1.7	0.0
Classic	0.0	1.3	0.0	0.0	0.5	3.6	2.4	0.4	0.7	1.7	0.0
Coarse paste or slip	0.0	1.8	3.8	1.7	4.7	0.0	10.9	3.3	2.8	8.5	0.0
Colonial	0.0	0.0	0.0	0.0	0.5	0.0	1.3	0.0	3.0	1.7	7.7
Cookie Cutter	0.0	3.0	0.0	0.0	5.3	7.1	0.0	0.0	4.2	6.8	3.8
Cuexcomate Orange	33.3	0.0	6.5	8.4	0.7	0.0	8.5	10.1	0.1	0.0	0.0
Fine Buff paste	0.0	11.1	5.6	6.7	9.3	17.9	5.6	12.5	16.7	12.7	19.2
Formative	0.0	0.0	0.0	0.0	0.6	0.0	0.0	0.0	1.1	0.8	0.0
Local paste	50.0	66.6	83.2	81.7	70.3	50.0	69.9	65.2	63.5	62.7	65.4
Mazapan	0.0	0.0	0.0	0.0	0.0	0.0	0.0	0.0	0.0	0.8	0.0
Miniatures	16.7	15.6	1.0	1.7	6.4	21.4	0.0	7.3	4.2	2.5	3.8
Modern	0.0	0.0	0.0	0.0	0.0	0.0	0.0	0.0	0.2	0.0	0.0
Unknown	0.0[3]	0.0	0.0	0.0	0.0	0.0	0.0	0.2	0.5	0.1	0.1
TYPES											
Animal	0.0	8.2	13.0	13.4	10.6	3.6	12.6	9.0	13.5	10.2	15.4
Female	16.7	22.3	17.8	11.7	29.3	28.6	19.8	12.7	19.3	38.1	11.5
Ghost	16.7	4.7	1.0	0.0	0.6	3.6	1.3	1.2	0.8	0.0	0.0
Human	16.7	33.7	27.0	20.0	25.5	35.6	24.7	18.6	27.8	23.7	15.5
Infant	0.0	2.3	0.0	0.0	0.2	0.0	0.0	0.0	0.0	0.8	0.0
Male	16.7	2.9	27.0	8.4	8.8	14.3	12.0	19.3	11.5	15.3	26.9
Puppet	33.3	2.4	3.8	10.0	0.2	0.0	6.8	8.4	2.1	1.7	3.8
Rattle	0.0	11.0	1.9	5.0	9.8	3.6	12.6	9.9	12.0	3.4	7.7

continued on next page

Table 9.3—*continued*

Phase	*Middle Postclassic*		*Late Postclassic–A*				*Late Postclassic–B*				*Colonial*
Site	*Cap*[1]	*Yau*	*Cap*	*Cuex*	*Yau*	*Yau*	*Cap*	*Cuex*	*Yau*	*Yau*	*Yau*
Class	*com*	*com*	*com*	*elite*	*com*	*elite*	*com*	*com*	*com*	*elite*	*com*
Temple	0.0	0.0	0.0	0.0	0.0	0.0	0.0	0.0	0.6	1.7	0.0
Unknown	0.0	10.5	8.6	31.7	14.4	10.7	10.2	21.0	12.4	5.1	19.2
Special/Other	0.0	1.9	0.0	0.0	0.7	0.0	0.0	0.0	0.0	0.0	0.0
Imports	0.0	13.5	9.4	8.3	16.5	17.9	17.8	16.9	22.4	22.9	19.2
Local	100.0	86.5	90.6	91.7	83.5	82.1	82.2	83.1	77.6	77.1	80.8
Total no. of figurines	6	88	47	36	258	28	49	117	980	118	26
No. figurines/1,000 sherds	1.2	1.69	1.33	1.30	1.91	2.44	1.37	1.64	1.31	1.66	3.00

Notes:

1. Cap = Capilco; Cuex = Cuexcomate; Yau = Yautepec; com = commoner.
2. Frequencies are calculated separately for groups and types. Figurines are from well-phased middens with n>6.
3. Figures are mean percentages for the domestic units in each column. The last two rows contain simple quantities.

Table 9.4. Mean percentages for figurine positions by chronology and socioeconomic class at Yautepec in Morelos, Mexico

Phase	*Middle Postclassic*	*Late Postclassic–A*		*Late Postclassic–B*		*Colonial*
Class	com[1]	com	elite	com	elite	com
Total	18	34	6	150	31	5
Kneeling (%)	0.00	2.22	16.60	12.88	12.90	0.00
Seated (%)	0.00	17.22	16.67	9.32	19.35	20.00
Standing (%)	92.31	80.56	66.00	77.33	67.74	80.00
Other (%)	7.69	0.00	0.00	0.16	0.32	0.00

Note:
1. com = commoner.

Table 9.5. Mean percentages of animal species for known animal figurines by chronology and socioeconomic class at Yautepec in Morelos, Mexico

Phase	*Middle Postclassic*	*Late Postclassic–A*		*Late Postclassic–B*		*Colonial*
Class	com[1]	com	elite	com	elite	com
Total	9	18	0	79	13	3
Bird (%)	0.0	33.3	0.00	12.0	15.4	0.0
Dog (%)	40.0	16.7	0.00	26.9	61.5	100.0
Feline (%)	0.0	0.0	0.00	2.5	7.7	0.0
Monkey (%)	20.0	19.4	0.00	15.5	7.7	0.0
Lizard (%)	40.0	4.2	0.00	2.5	0.0	0.0
Opossum (%)	0.0	11.1	0.00	26.6	7.7	0.0
Rabbit (%)	0.0	4.2	0.00	6.9	0.0	0.0
Other (%)	0.0	11.1	0.00	7.2	0.0	0.0

Note:
1. com = commoner.

were also wealthier (Olson 2001). All middens of this time period are associated with the commoner class (Figure 9.4).

Although a widespread ideology that deified natural elements existed throughout Morelos, most figurines used in rituals employed local pattern and imagery (Smith 2002; Smith and Heath-Smith n.d.). For example, the Cuexcomate Orange figurine group was found only in Capilco, whereas the Cookie Cutter group was exclusive to the urban center of Yautepec. Other community patterns show that rattles are present in all Yautepec units but they are absent from the Capilco excavations. Conversely, puppet and hand-molded ghost figurines are found in small frequencies in Yautepec and in large frequencies in Capilco. This shift to molded figurines may have reached the smaller hamlet site after reaching the urban center.

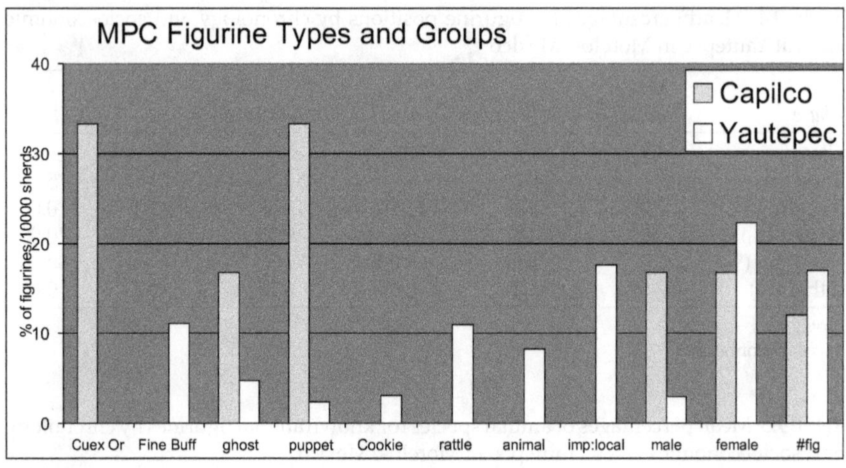

9.4. Middle Postclassic period figurine type and group for Capilco and Yautepec, Mexico.

Although local imagery is clearly important during this time period, excavations from the urban center have revealed a few indications of trade with the Valley of Mexico. Not surprisingly, evidence shows that the burgeoning urban center was more involved in interregional trade than was the rural hamlet. Trade differences are also noted in frequencies of imported ceramic vessels in the communities (Olson 2001). This discrepancy suggests that an ideology was transferred first to larger centers and then to the smaller communities, which were likely more isolated from the emerging market system.

Figurines from the Late Postclassic–A Period (A.D. 300/1350–1440)

City-states such as Cuauhnahuac in central Morelos and Huaxtepec in eastern Morelos expanded their powers across the landscape to incorporate other city-states into conquest-states. The conquest-states of Morelos eventually formed alliance networks through interstate elite marriages and the exchange of invitations to elite ceremonies and festivities (Smith 1994b).

Trade, rather than tribute, was the major form of economic relationship between the states of Cuauhnahuac and Huaxtepec (Smith 1994b). Yet, the evolution of these conquest-states resulted in more levels of hierarchy and one more level of tribute responsibilities for rural residents to fulfill. This extra burden, combined with a rising population, negatively affected the standard of living (Olson 2001). The drop in the standard of living was likely influenced not only by an increase in economic responsibilities involving tribute payments to higher levels of social organization but also by a significant increase in population (Smith and Doershuk 1991). Between the Middle Postclassic and the Late Postclassic–A, Yautepec increased in size and population, as did the smaller rural site of Capilco, at an estimated annual rate of 1.6 percent (Smith and Heath-Smith 1994:363). Cuexcomate was founded during this time period, which coincided with a notable intensification of local agriculture through the introduction of cross-check dams and terraces.

In this time period, we have evidence for both commoner and elite classes. I thus will discuss differences between the elite and commoner classes within a site and then make comparisons between the sites (see Figures 9.5 and 9.6).

Yautepec. The percentage of figurines made from local paste is even higher than in the Middle Postclassic middens. Although the commoner middens contained a significantly higher percentage of locally made figurines than the elite middens, they also contained a few imported ones, such as Aztec Orange paste figurines. In fact, these Valley of Mexico imports are restricted to commoner middens. Other Valley of Mexico imports, such as the Fine Buff paste figurines, were found in both commoner and elite middens but in significantly higher concentrations in the elite midden, as were unique Miniature figurines. It is likely that the political economic models that identify acquisition based on price and importation do not apply in this case.

A difference between socioeconomic groups is also noted in the percentage of human and animal images. The commoner middens have a considerably higher percentage of animal figurines, whereas the elite unit has a higher percentage of human images. Similarly to the Middle Postclassic commoner middens, the animal images identified are primarily birds, with both eagles and ducks represented. Dogs, monkeys, and opossums, along with a few rabbits and lizards, are also found in the middens. There is considerable variation among the units in terms of the animal images identified, except that the percentage of birds was constant in almost every unit. It is unclear at this point why commoners would have more animal imagery in their figurine assemblage than the elite household did.

In terms of the sexed figurines, females are by far the most common, yet variation exists in terms of the male figurines. These male figurines

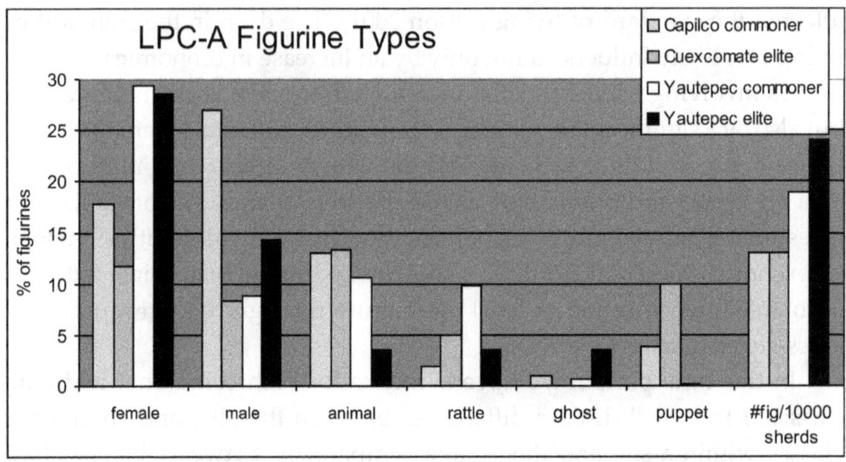

9.5. Late Postclassic–A period figurine types for Capilco commoner, Cuexcomate elite, Yautepec commoner, and Yautepec elite, Mexico.

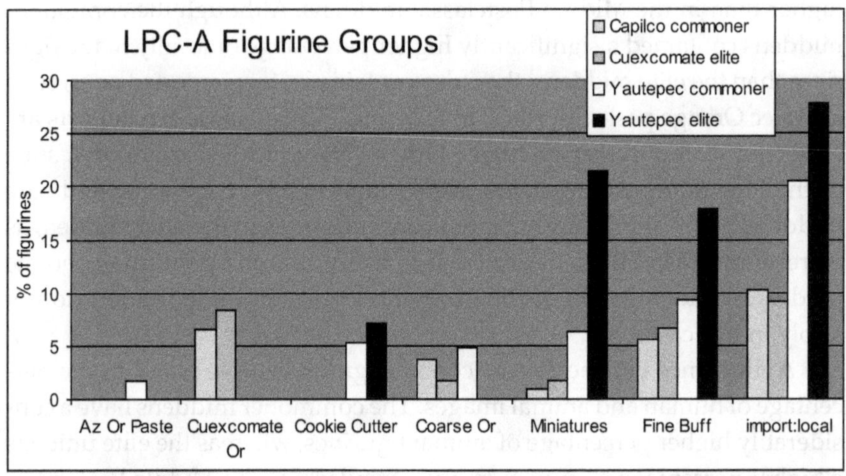

9.6. Late Postclassic–A period figurine groups for Capilco commoner, Cuexcomate elite, Yautepec commoner, and Yautepec elite, Mexico.

appear to play a more important role in the ritual of this period than in the previous one and more so in the elite household. Yet, it should be stated that these percentages are still considerably small and that the domestic rituals are focused around the female activities, probably specific curing rites and those denoting changes in important life stages (Brumfiel 1996; Cyphers 1993; Olson et al. 1999; Otis Charlton 1994; Smith 2002).

Puppet and ghost figurines are found in a few commoner middens but in significantly smaller percentages than in the Middle Postclassic period. It appears that the role these early figurines played during the early trading relations of this area lessened in significance and possibly changed. Puppet figurine fragments are completely absent in elite middens, but the hand-molded ghost figurines are surprisingly more prominent. I would have expected that elite households would not have used hand-molded images. It is possible that these figurines were given special import as heirloom or family pieces relating to local cults.

The positions of figurines are primarily standing, particularly in the commoner households. It is in the elite household that variation in positions is noted. Of the non-standing figurines, kneeling and seated positions are equally common. Kneeling females are typically found in the codices, such as the *Primeros Memoriales* (Sahagún 1997), where they are depicted performing artisanal activities such as grinding. The expectations of elite women are more fully elaborated than those for the commoners (Sahagún 1950–1982), which may be revealed in the figurine assemblage.

The commoner households overall have more figurines than the elite households do. Michael E. Smith (1987) has suggested that the ethnographic data identify poorer households as having a greater affinity to religious items in the house.

Capilco. Except for the consumption of figurines from local paste, considerable group variation is noted among commoner households. Within the commoner grouping there is no distinction between the figurine assemblage of wealthier commoners and poorer commoners. Although all contexts have locally made figurines, a mixture of households used imported items, such as Fine Buff figurines, which previously had only been found in the larger center. These imported items are evidence of the community's growing economic and ritual connections with other areas, even with the larger communities of the Basin of Mexico.

As in the larger center of Yautepec, a significant decrease in the percentage of puppet figurines and ghost figurines from the Middle Postclassic period is observed. Again, it is possible that the local ritual practices that involved these forms of figurines became obsolete or altered because of foreign influences.

Of the sexed figurines, the percentage of females is slightly lower than in the previous period, which highlights a difference between this very small hamlet and the larger center. It appears that in the smaller community, rites involving males were important enough to leave evidence in the archaeological record. As to what these rituals may have entailed is yet to be determined.

Not all of the figurines, however, are classified as human; animal figurines are finally introduced into the Capilco assemblages. The animals represented are primarily birds, resembling the urban centers' earlier introduction of animals (birds) into their household rituals. It is difficult to determine if this evidence demonstrates that Capilco was entering into a regional system of trade or adopting new ideological beliefs or that other structuring forces were at play.

Cuexcomate. Although figurines were present in many units, only the elite middens had more than six, the minimum number for analysis. The import-to-local ratio is low, indicating a high percentage of locally made figurines, yet imported Fine Buff figurines are present in small numbers. Of these figurines the majority are anthropomorphic, with only a few more female than male images. There are equal percentages of figurines in the standing and kneeling positions. A high percentage of animal figurines are also found. Thus, the assemblage represents many elements from the smaller hamlet and a few from the larger urban center.

Inter-site comparison. Some important similarities were observed between rural and urban assemblages. No significant differences were found between Capilco and Cuexcomate in relation to figurine types and groups, suggesting that the rural sites used very similar assemblages in their ritual activities. In contrast to rural households, urban units had imported Aztec Orange paste and Fine Buff paste figurines. The presence of these kinds of figurines in the urban middens contributed to Yautepec's higher ratio of imported to locally produced artifacts. Local paste figurines, however, remained the most frequently occurring of all figurine groups.

Although some categories of figurines were found at all sites, site variation did exist. As in the Middle Postclassic period, the urban residents used Cookie Cutter figurines in their rituals, whereas the rural inhabitants used their local Cuexcomate Orange figurines. Unfortunately, no evidence for production has been found.

Although all sites had a high percentage of anthropomorphic figurines, only the rural sites had a high percentage of male images, with a statistically significant difference found between Capilco and Yautepec. Rural areas used more puppet figurines than urban centers did, but this distinction may have been a preference based on geographical location rather than on community size. Figurine images of animals were found in all but the urban elite middens, with birds the most common animal species. This pattern suggests that lower-status households used more animal images in their rituals. Another difference between community contexts is the high frequency of kneeling figurines in the poorer rural middens in comparison with urban ones.

Figurines from the Late Postclassic–B Period (A.D. 1440–1540)

Early in the Late Postclassic–B period the Triple Alliance formed between the states of Mexico-Tenochtitlan, Texcoco, and Tlacopan in A.D. 1427. Soon after, in A.D. 1438, the empire incorporated the Tlahuica peoples of Morelos. In western Morelos, Cuexcomate and Capilco, which had been part of the conquest-state of Cuauhnahuac, started paying tribute to Texcoco, while Yautepec began paying tribute to the king of Mexico-Tenochtitlan. In this period, a definite decrease in standard of living was observed at all households investigated, but the two rural sites were even lower than the urban center (Olson 2001). The decrease in the standard of living may have resulted from the higher tribute demands imposed by conquest-states and the imperial capital or from a population increase that created a shortage of available land. The population continued to be high in this period, but the annual rate of growth decreased between periods from 1.6 percent to 1.0 percent (Smith and Heath-Smith 1994).

As remains of both commoner and elite households were excavated, I will discuss intra-site differences between classes followed by inter-site comparisons (see Figures 9.7 and 9.8).

Yautepec. An interesting change in this period is the general decrease in artifact and wealth variation between the two socioeconomic groups. This decrease is also noted in the figurine assemblage, as the commoners have an increased frequency of imported items and the elite have a reduced frequency. This pattern represents an overall change in the relations between elites and commoners that even extended into the ritual area. Although the exact rituals being performed are unknown, we can at least determine that the two groups used similar items with similar symbolism. This change may have resulted from increasing markets or the Aztec empire conquest.

In commoner middens, human figurines in the standing position were the dominant type, with an increase in the kneeling position from those

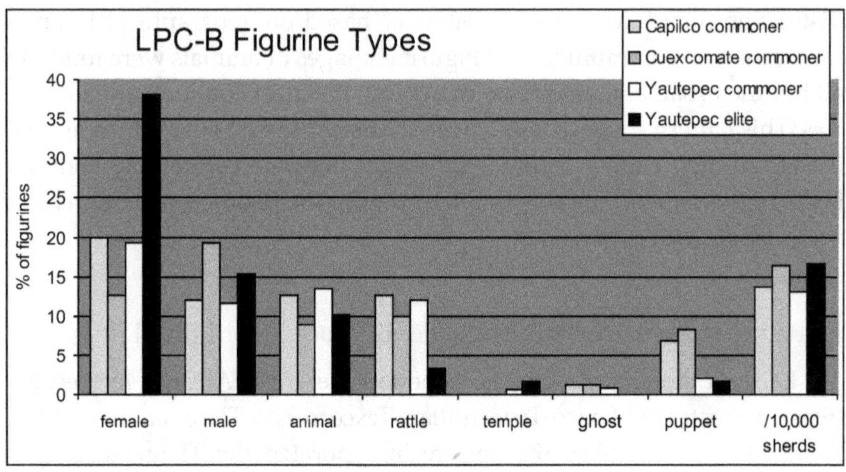

9.7. Late Postclassic–B period figurine types for Capilco commoner, Cuexcomate commoner, Yautepec commoner, and Yautepec elite, Mexico.

found in the Late Postclassic–A. In comparison with the commoner middens, the elite unit has double the percentage of seated figurines as seen previously. A wealthy commoner unit also had high percentages of seated figurines, almost triple the commoner average. Unlike in other periods where I do not feel that we can determine if position is related to status, I argue that in this case Brumfiel's model (1996) holds merit. It is possible that these particular figurines are representative of political and economic status; however, because the two groups are becoming more similar in the rest of the assemblages, I believe that the seated position has less import to the actual rituals.

Temple figurines are also associated with high-status middens, which include the elite midden and a very wealthy commoner midden. Although the variations in figurine origins decreased, the distinctions in figurine imagery between classes increased. Thus, although all households have access to imported goods and local styles, it is the imagery that is proving to be the most notable difference.

Animal figurines also showed some peculiar differences between elite and commoner middens in the urban setting of Yautepec. Dogs represented a great source of protein for the Aztecs and were often shown as a food resource (Coe 1994). Overall there is a dramatic increase in the frequency of dog figurines between earlier time periods and the Late Postclassic–B. As the wealthier elites and mid-commoner groups would have been more

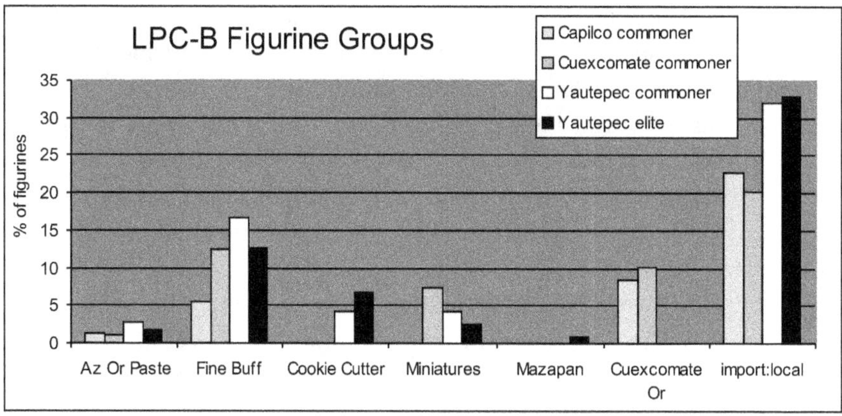

9.8. Late Postclassic–B period figurine groups for Capilco commoner, Cuexcomate commoner, Yautepec commoner, and Yautepec elite, Mexico.

able to afford protein meals, it is not surprising that they would have a much higher frequency of dog figurines compared with the commoners. Poor commoner households, however, have a high frequency of opossums, which may be connected to curing and birthing rituals, and a lesser frequency of monkeys and birds.

Capilco. The figurine assemblage of Late Postclassic–B Capilco is more varied than in the Late Postclassic–A, as is the variability between houses. Orange paste figurines are particularly prevalent. Aztec Orange paste figurines, along with a great increase in general Orange slipped and Cuexcomate Orange figurines, were found in the assemblage. The ratio of female to male is substantially higher than previously, as male figurines decrease in importance in domestic ritual. Even more so than in the Late Postclassic–A, these households were involved in trade with other areas and likely adopted ideologies from elsewhere. Although these ideologies may be part of a larger belief system, it is likely that the community ignored much of the imperial ideology and continued to practice its own unique forms.

Cuexcomate. Only commoner units had more than the minimum six figurines for analysis; therefore, elite middens are excluded in the Cuexcomate analysis. Local paste figurines are the least variable group and most common of all the figurines. Yet, the variety of figurines increased over the Late Postclassic–A as imports began to come into the community. Imported Fine Buff paste figurines and Miniature figurines from the Valley of Mexico were found in almost all middens. As with the Yautepec figurines, male figurines are positively correlated with imports that are mostly seated or kneeling.

Inter-site comparison. Consumption of figurines in the latter half of the Late Postclassic period decreased considerably in the urban context, increased in the town setting of Cuexcomate, and remained the same in the hamlet of Capilco. This pattern perhaps mimics Smith's (1987) model of religious image acquisition found in ethnographic contexts.

Some regional distinctions between the rural and urban areas concerning figurine images continue to be noted. Yautepec middens exclusively contained Cookie Cutter and temple figurines, whereas the more crudely made Cuexcomate Orange figurines are found at rural sites. The puppet figurines are one of the few types that are significantly more prevalent in the rural sites of Capilco and Cuexcomate, suggesting that they may have continued to play some role in a local cult.

The imagery of the figurines has changed considerably from earlier periods. With the expansion of the Aztec empire into the Tlahuica area, a greater variety of animals are found on the figurines and the variety corresponds to an increase in the number of imports at all sites. Although there is an increase in imports in this period, the urban population used figurines with more animal variety than did their rural counterparts.

The rural communities caught up to the urban center in the frequency of non-standing figurines. During this period the kneeling figurines were found in commoner contexts, suggesting relations to status or occupations that previously may have been the domain of the elite.

Figurines from the Colonial Period (a.d. 1540–1650)

The disruption caused by the Spanish Conquest had a great effect on the residential patterns of Central Mexican peoples as they left their destroyed house compounds (Kellogg 1993). Yet, James Lockhart writes that the early stages of post-Conquest evolution of the Nahua peoples, "despite great revolutions, reorientation, and catastrophes, [showed] little changes in Nahua concepts, techniques, or modes of organization." He further notes that later during the Colonial period, "Spanish elements came to pervade every aspect of Nahua life, but with limitations, often as

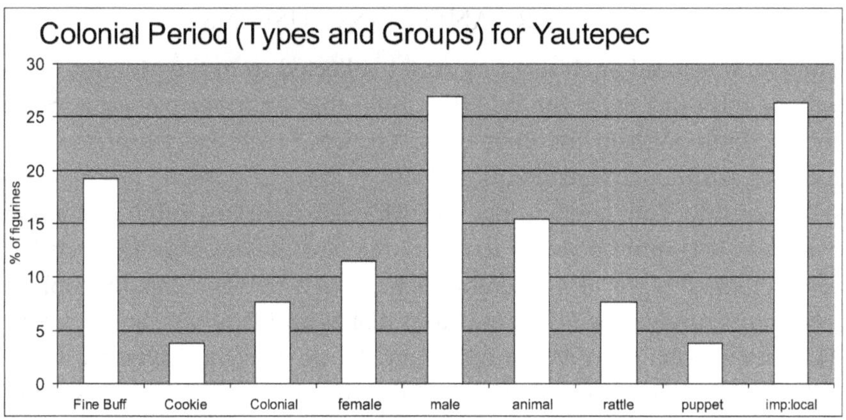

9.9. Colonial figurine types and groups from Yautepec, Mexico.

discrete additions within a relatively unchanged indigenous framework" (Lockhart 1992:429).

Yautepec. Only one midden was excavated that corresponded to the Colonial period and this midden is of the commoner class (Figure 9.9). The most plentiful figurines are made from the local paste, and the second most common style is the imported Fine Buff. Also represented were Colonial figurines, which were identified by Spanish clothing styles. All the other figurine groups were of very low percentages—such as Cookie Cutter and Miniature figurines—or had disappeared completely—such as ghost and temple types. Changes in imagery were especially prevalent. Whereas in the Postclassic period bird imagery was dominant, dog figurines were the only type found in the Colonial period. These changes likely reflect some of the ideological changes occurring as the Postclassic world was crumbling. Even though domestic households did not change much in terms of ceramic and lithic artifacts, the ritual items showed some modification. I do not believe that these transformations occurred because the Spanish were in the households of the Tlahuica but instead because of the ideological changes occurring as a people experienced alterations in the natural and human world around them.

Also in this period, the frequency of female figurines plummets, so that males make up a large percentage of Colonial assemblages. Along with this dramatic shift in the ritual gender imagery of the Colonial period, 20 percent of the figurines are seated.

SUMMARY AND CONCLUSIONS

This multifactored analysis of figurines collected from the Morelos excavations indicates there can be little doubt that figurines played a major role in households at the three sites. Yet, what their exact function was requires additional consideration. With respect to possible associations with reproduction and curing, the Morelos figurines offer intriguing evidence. It is quite possible that ceramic figurines were used in curing ceremonies. Images of Chalchihuitlicue, the water goddess (Nicholson 1988), are found in the *Florentine Codex* (Sahagún 1950–1982) and *Primeros Memoriales* (Sahagún 1997) in which one figure wears a circle-and-wave-patterned *quexquemitl huipil* set resembling the Cookie Cutter images found at Yautepec. If these figurines represent the water goddess, this symbolism may suggest a local cult appealing for assistance from Chalchihuitlicue during curing ceremonies.

Animal species also exhibit associations with reproduction. Like the monkey, the opossum was important in childbirth. Included in the Morelos figurine collection are numerous opossum images, first identified by Salvador Guilliem Arroyo (1997). Fray Bernardino de Sahagún (1950–1982, 3:156) states that an opossum's tail was an ingredient in a drink made to induce labor in women. This statement suggests the association of opossums with pregnancy, perhaps best represented by one of the Yautepec figurines, which depicts an opossum holding its abdomen and apparently in the process of giving birth.

The Morelos figurine assemblage also indicates some intriguing changes over time and differences between class and size of community. It is expected that an increase in long-distance market trade over time would likely lead to an increase in foreign symbols. This pattern, in fact, is borne out in the Morelos data, yet whether this factor is the only one affecting the belief systems is unknown at this point. The urban center of Yautepec, which has more overall ceramic imports than the rural communities (Olson 2001), also has more foreign images in its figurine assemblages. For example, in the Middle Postclassic period, only the urban middens contained imported figurines, but by the Late Postclassic–A every site had imported figurines, with the urban center still holding a higher frequency of imported images. But by the Late Postclassic–B, trade increased in the empire and the distinction between urban and rural in terms of ratio of imported to locally made figurines decreased.

All communities participated in a religious tradition relating to the natural world, but unique local styles were observed for each geographical location. The rural residents appear to have had a local belief system more dependent on male images than were the beliefs of the urban dwellers (except for Capilco in the Late Postclassic–B). In general, a greater percentage of puppet figurines are found in the rural sites than the urban center, which further suggests differences in ritual activity. These differences, however, may likely be material manifestations of different aspects of a similar belief system.

In the Late Postclassic–A, data are consistent with models in which elite groups consume a greater frequency of foreign symbols, perhaps to distinguish themselves from other social classes (Douglas and Isherwood 1996; Orlove and Rutz 1989). But, like the decrease in distinction between urban and rural areas between the Late Postclassic–A and the Late Postclassic–B, class distinctions are also reduced. Some distinctions, however, remain, such as the exclusive association of state images of power (represented by seated images on thrones and temple figurines) with the wealthy. Animal figurines also showed some peculiar differences between elite and commoner middens in the urban setting of Yautepec. Overall, there is a dramatic increase in the frequency of dog figurines in elite middens between earlier time periods and the Late Postclassic–B. Poor commoner households, however, have a higher frequency of opossum figurines (Coe 1994).

The Morelos data suggest that figurines were an important part of the belief system of the Tlahuican peoples of Central Mexico. Both commoners and elites used the artifacts in domestic contexts, but the types of symbols they chose were different. This data set identifies particular variability within the commoner group. As time progressed, markets opened, communities increased trade of knowledge, empires evolved more variability, and choice in how to enact rituals appeared in this provincial area.

This data set also reveals that rural inhabitants used symbols and images that were distinct from urban dwellers and probably for different rites and ceremonies. As Jon Lohse rightly states in his introduction to this volume, not all ideology and symbols used by the majority of people were constructed by the elite few. Although it appears from this data set that the elite may have opened up avenues to express rituals, the commoners truly developed their own practices of rite participation. These practices varied, from continuing with local cults and ideas to incorporating ideas from the larger urban centers and elite and even influencing the elite and larger centers with their ritual practices. The precise function of figurines is yet to be determined, but figurines are important archaeological clues to understanding the complex socioeconomic and ideological world of Central Mexican peoples.

ACKNOWLEDGMENTS

Support for this project has been provided through the fellowship program at the Social Sciences and Humanities Research Council of Canada, the International Federation of Women, and various grants based out of SUNY-Albany, including the DeCormier Scholarship through the Institute for Mesoamerican Studies, the Benevolent Society, the Department of Anthropology, and the graduate studies office. This chapter was derived from my doctoral dissertation at SUNY-Albany. I thank my committee members—Robert Carmack, Louise Burkhart, and Marilyn Masson—and particularly my advisor, Michael E. Smith, who allowed access to the artifacts from Yautepec, Cuexcomate, and Capilco. Special thanks go to Vicenta Ortiz, Alma Sanchez, and Betty Sanchez for many fruitful hours spent working on the artifacts in the lab. I also thank Jon Lohse and Nancy Gonlin for their comments on this chapter and their work in putting this collection together.

REFERENCES CITED

Abrams, Elliot M.

1989 Architecture and Energy: An Evolutionary Perspective. In *Archaeological Method and Theory,* Volume 1, edited by Michael B. Schiffer, pp. 47–86. University of Arizona Press, Tucson.

1994 *How the Maya Built Their World*. University of Texas Press, Austin.

Blanton, Richard E.

1994 *Houses and Households: A Comparative Study*. Plenum, New York.

Boas, Franz, and Manuel Gamio

1921 *Album de colecciones arqueológicas*. Imprenta del Museo Nacional de Arqueología, Historia, y Etnografía, Mexico, D.F.

Brumfiel, Elizabeth M.

1996 Figurines and the Aztec State: Testing the Effectiveness of Ideological Domination. In *Gender and Archaeology,* edited by Rita P. Wright, pp. 143–166. University of Pennsylvania Press, Philadelphia.

Brumfiel, Elizabeth M., and Mary G. Hodge

1996 Interaction in the Basin of Mexico: The Case of Postclassic Xaltocan. In *Arqueología Mesoamericana: Homenaje a William T. Sanders,* Volume 1, edited by Alba Guadalupe Mastache, Jeffrey R. Parsons, Robert S. Santley, and Mari Carmen Serra Puche, pp. 417–437. Instituto Nacional de Antropología e Historia, Mexico, D.F.

Chase, Arlen F., and Diane Z. Chase

1992 Mesoamerican Elites: Assumptions, Definitions, and Models. In *Mesoamerican Elites: An Archaeological Assessment,* edited by Diane Z. Chase and Arlen F. Chase, pp. 3–17. University of Oklahoma Press, Norman.

Coe, Michael D.

1994 *Mexico: From the Olmecs to the Aztecs.* Fourth edition. Thames and Hudson, New York.

Cyphers, Ann

1993 Women, Rituals, and Social Dynamics at Ancient Chalcatzingo. *Latin American Antiquity* 4:209–224.

Deetz, James J.F.

1982 Households: A Structural Key to Archaeological Explanation. *American Behavioral Scientist* 25:717–724.

Douglas, Mary, and Baron Isherwood

1996 *The World of Goods: Toward an Anthropology of Consumption.* Second edition. Basic Books, New York.

Durán, Fray Diego

1971 *Book of the Gods and Rites and the Ancient Calendar.* Translated by Fernando Horcasitas and Doris Heyden. University of Oklahoma Press, Norman.

González Rul, Francisco

1988 *La cerámica en Tlatelolco.* Colección Científica 172. Instituto Nacional de Antropología e Historia, Mexico, D.F.

Guilliem Arroyo, Salvador

1997 Figurillas de Tlatelolco. *Arqueología* 17:111–138.

Hare, Timothy S., and Michael E. Smith

1996 A New Postclassic Chronology for Yautepec, Morelos. *Ancient Mesoamerica* 7:281–297.

Heyden, Doris

1996 La posible interpretación de figurillas arqueológicas en barro y piedra según las fuentes históricas. In *Los arqueólogos frente a las fuentes,* edited by Rosa Brambila Paz and Jesús Monjarás-Ruiz, 322:129–146. Colección Científica 322. Instituto Nacional de Antropología e Historia, Mexico, D.F.

Kellogg, Susan M.

1993 The Social Organization of Households Among the Tenochca Mexica Before and After the Conquest. In *Prehispanic Domestic Units in Western Mesoamerica: Studies of the Household, Compound, and Residence,* edited by Robert S. Santley and Kenneth G. Hirth, pp. 207–224. CRC Press, Boca Raton.

Lockhart, James

1992 *The Nahuas After the Conquest: A Social and Cultural History of the Indians of Central Mexico, Sixteenth Through Eighteenth Centuries.* Stanford University Press, Stanford.

Marcus, Joyce

1998 *Women's Ritual in Formative Oaxaca: Figurine-Making, Divination, Death and the Ancestors.* Prehistory and Human Ecology of the Valley of Oaxaca 11. Museum of Anthropology Press, Ann Arbor.

Monjarás-Ruiz, Jesús

1970 Figurillas-sonaja Aztecas del Valle de México. In *Los Mexicas y la Triple Alianza,* Volume 3, edited by Elena Limón and María de la Cruz Paillés H., pp. 257–283. Obras de Robert H. Barlow. Instituto Nacional de Antropología e Historia, Mexico, D.F.

Netting, Robert McC.

1993 *Smallholders, Householders: Farm Families and the Ecology of Intensive, Sustainable Agriculture.* Stanford University Press, Stanford.

Nicholson, Henry B.

1988 The Iconography of Deity Representations in Fray Bernardino de Sahagún's *Primeros Memoriales:* Huitzilopochtli and Chalchihuitlicue. In *The Work of Bernardino de Sahagún: Pioneer Ethnographer of Sixteenth-Century Aztec Mexico,* edited by Jorge Klor de Alva, Henry B. Nicholson, and Eloise Quiñones Keber, pp. 229–254. Institute for Mesoamerican Studies, Albany.

Olson, Jan Marie

2001 Unequal Consumption: A Study of Domestic Wealth Differentials in Three Late Postclassic Mexican Communities. Ph.D. dissertation, State University of New York at Albany. University Microfilms, Ann Arbor.

Olson, Jan Marie, Michael E. Smith, and Elizabeth DiPippo

1999 Ceramic Figurines and Domestic Ritual at Late Postclassic Sites in Morelos, Mexico. Paper presented at the 64th Annual Meeting of the Society for American Archaeology, Chicago.

Orlove, Benjamin S., and Henry J. Rutz

1989 Thinking About Consumption: A Social Economy Approach. In *The Social Economy of Consumption*, edited by Henry J. Rutz and Benjamin S. Orlove, pp. 1–57. University Press of America, Lanham.

Otis Charlton, Cynthia

1994 Plebians and Patricians: Contrasting Patterns of Production and Distribution in the Aztec Figurine and Lapidary Industries. In *Economies and Polities in the Aztec Realm*, edited by Mary G. Hodge and Michael E. Smith, pp. 195–219. Institute for Mesoamerican Studies, Albany.

Parsons, Mary H.

1972 Aztec Figurines from the Teotihuacán Valley, Mexico. In *Miscellaneous Studies in Mexican Prehistory*, Volume 49, edited by Michael W. Spence, Jeffrey R. Parsons, and Mary H. Parsons, pp. 81–164. Anthropological Papers. Museum of Anthropology, University of Michigan, Ann Arbor.

Pasztory, Esther

1983 *Aztec Art*. Harry N. Abrams, New York.

Price, Barbara J.

1982 Cultural Materialism: A Theoretical Review. *American Antiquity* 47: 709–741.

Ruiz de Alarcón, Hernando

1984 *Treatise on the Heathen Superstitions That Today Live Among the Indians Native to New Spain, 1629*. Translated and edited by J. Richard Andrews and Ross Hassig. University of Oklahoma Press, Norman.

Sahagún, Fray Bernardino de

1950–1982 *Florentine Codex: General History of the Things of New Spain. 12 books.* Translated and edited by Arthur J.O. Anderson and Charles E. Dibble. School of American Research, Santa Fe, and University of Utah Press, Salt Lake City.

1997 *Primeros Memoriales: Paleography of Nahuatl Text and English Translation*. Translated by Thelma D. Sullivan. University of Oklahoma Press, Norman.

Sanders, William T., and Robert S. Santley

1983 A Tale of Three Cities: Energetics and Urbanization in Pre-Hispanic Central Mexico. In *Prehistoric Settlement Patterns: Essays in Honor of Gordon R. Willey*, edited by Evon Z. Vogt and Richard M. Leventhal, pp. 243–291. University of New Mexico Press, Albuquerque.

Séjourné, Laurette

1970 *Arqueología del Valle de México, I: Culhuacan*. Instituto Nacional de Antropología e Historia, Mexico, D.F.

1983 *Arqueología e historia del Valle de México: De Xochmilco a Amecameca*. Siglo Veintiuno, Mexico, D.F.

Smith, Michael E.

1987 Household Possessions and Wealth in Agrarian States: Implications for Archaeology. *Journal of Anthropological Archaeology* 6:297–335.

1992 *Archaeological Research at Aztec-Period Rural Sites in Morelos, Mexico,* Volume 1, *Excavations and Architecture/Investigaciones arqueológicas en sitios rurales de la Epoca Azteca en Morelos,* Tomo 1, *Excavaciones y arquitectura*. University of Pittsburgh Memoirs in Latin American Archaeology 4.

1994a Excavaciones de casas Postclassicas del centro urbano de Yautepec, Morelos: Informe tecnico partial. Unpublished report submitted to the Instituto Nacional de Antropología e Historia, Mexico, D.F.

1994b Economies and Polities in Aztec-Period Morelos: Ethnohistoric Introduction. In *Economies and Polities in the Aztec Realm,* edited by Mary G. Hodge and Michael E. Smith, pp. 313–348. Institute for Mesoamerican Studies, Albany.

2002 Domestic Ritual at Aztec Provincial Sites in Morelos. In *Domestic Ritual in Ancient Mesoamerica,* edited by Patricia Plunket, pp. 93–114. Monograph 36, Cotsen Institute of Archaeology. University of California, Los Angeles.

Smith, Michael E., and John F. Doershuk

1991 Late Postclassic Chronology in Western Morelos, Mexico. *Latin American Antiquity* 2:291–310.

Smith, Michael E., and Cynthia Heath-Smith

1994 Rural Economy in Late Postclassic Morelos: An Archaeological Study. In *Economies and Polities in the Aztec Realm,* edited by Mary G. Hodge and Michael E. Smith, pp. 349–376. Institute for Mesoamerican Studies, Albany.

n.d. *Archaeological Research at Aztec-Period Rural Sites in Morelos, Mexico,* Volume 2, *Artifacts and Dating*. Volume in preparation.

Smith, Michael E., Cynthia Heath-Smith, Ronald Kohler, Joan Odess, Sharon Spanogle, and Timothy Sullivan

1994 The Size of the Aztec City of Yautepec: Urban Survey in Central Mexico. *Ancient Mesoamerica* 5:1–11.

Smith, Michael E., Hector Neff, and Ruth Fauman-Fichman

1999 Ceramic Imports at Yautepec and Their Implications for Aztec Exchange Systems. Paper presented at the 64th Annual Meeting of the Society for American Archaeology, Chicago.

Smith, Michael E., Osvaldo Sterpone, and Cynthia Heath-Smith

1992 Modern Adobe Houses in Tetlama, Morelos. In *Archaeological Research at Aztec-Period Rural Sites in Morelos, Mexico,* Part I, *Excavations and Architecture,* edited by Michael E. Smith, 4:405–418. University of Pittsburgh Monographs in Latin American Archaeology.

Uruñuela, Gabriela, Patricia Plunket, Gilda Hernández, and Juan Albaitero

1996 Biconical God Figurines from Cholula and the *Codex Borgia. Latin American Antiquity* 8:63–70.

CHAPTER TEN

STEPS TO A HOLISTIC HOUSEHOLD ARCHAEOLOGY

MARK W. MEHRER

INTRODUCTION

Mesoamerica offers the archaeologist interested in commoner ritual and ideology a rich prehistory, a written record of ancient practices, an ethnohistorical record of contact times, and some modern groups who have maintained strong continuities with their past. This book's treatment of these topics encourages a new theoretical approach that balances the ancient lives. Commoner and elite are incorporated into our modern understanding of the past, a treatment that promises continuing invigoration of Americanist archaeology. The volume's issues have roots in household archaeology as it has developed during the last thirty years or so (e.g., Flannery 1976; Flannery and Winter 1976). By expanding the scope of household archaeology far beyond its more functional processualist beginnings, the contributors to this volume address theory, architecture, artifacts, and broad social contexts.

THEORY

Among the theoretical perspectives considered, the idea of social power (Lohse, Chapter 1; Joyce and Weller, Chapter 6) figures prominently, which seems to underlie the whole question of who determines the agenda of ritual and ideology in an ancient culture or society. Power itself is devilishly intractable to define and it is difficult to explain how individuals attained and retained it. Here, ideology is not considered to be a monolithic given for most of ancient society but rather a way of life that pervades all levels of society, elite and common, with variations appropriate to each level. This understanding challenges the notions of Great Tradition versus Little Tradition (Uruñuela and Plunket, Chapter 2; Winter et al., Chapter 7) and the Dominant Ideology Thesis (Lohse, Chapter 1), which emphasize distinctions between commoner and elite in matters of ideology and ritual but give prominence (or dominance) to elites and downplay the social power expressed by commoners in their rituals and ideologies. These differences in theoretical perspectives can be glossed as the distinction between a "top-down" approach and a "bottom-up" approach. The strengths of the bottom-up approach are made clear where such an approach is appropriate, as is the value in a balanced perspective that favors neither the top nor the bottom.

Dominance and resistance (Joyce and Weller, Chapter 6; Lohse, Chapter 1) are aspects of social power that are pertinent to a consideration of commoner ritual and ideology, especially when seen from a bottom-up perspective. From a top-down perspective, resistance can be viewed as an aberration of the social norm—a transient social phenomenon, expressed overtly or covertly—that can be resolved, successfully or otherwise, by elites. When considered from the bottom up, resistance can be seen in a much broader form that includes not only active but passive phenomena, transient or persistent, but especially subtle ways of life that need not be directed specifically or self-consciously at resisting elite domination. In this way, commoner ritual and ideology may be considered as a way of resistance—or as a way of persistence—in the face of elite domination. Of course, the counterpoint is elite ritual and ideology, which are understood to promote elite domination. By invoking resistance and defining the distinction between elite and commoner ritual and ideology, the authors legitimize the idea that commoner ritual and ideology are not merely subordinate copies of elite versions (see Douglass, Chapter 5; Lohse, Chapter 1; Uruñuela and Plunket, Chapter 2; and Winter et al., Chapter 7). John Douglass goes so far as to state that commoners can enjoy some level of autonomy—via their rituals, paraphernalia, and sacred landscapes—in their access to the supernatural. The notion of any degree of relative autonomy for commoners can be controversial for some. In Mississippian studies in North America, for example, the controversy seems to be whether it is appropriate to consider commoners' roles from a bottom-up perspective (Emerson 1997; Mehrer 1995; Milner 1998, 2003; Pauketat 1994).

Jon Lohse's theoretical and methodological insights resonate with my own in some ways. I especially appreciate his view that some current theories overemphasize the ideological dominance of elites over commoners and thereby "impeach" themselves when they disregard commoners as "inert" in religious affairs. He and Nancy Gonlin (Chapter 4) correctly perceive the imbalance in some archaeological analyses with respect to the relative importance of elite versus commoner social domains. Like them, I feel that archaeologists should seek to create a narrative of the past that includes the participation of commoners. Equally appealing is the unbiased notion that studies of ritual and ideology should recognize the roles of both commoners and non-commoners. Ritual, ideology, and social power should no longer be topics of inquiry that remain focused on only one segment of society.

Lohse appropriately adds power to the book's topics of ritual and ideology. Ritual and ideology are often considered as ways that imbalances in social power are established and maintained by elite manipulation. Dominance and resistance (Joyce and Weller, Chapter 6) are general social postures in the unequal power struggle that permeates social hierarchy. If dominance is the posture of powerful elites in a society, resistance is the counter-posture of commoners. As Arthur Joyce and Errin Weller also point out, resistance can be manifested as hidden transcripts that are not obvious even in life, much less long after death. The realms of ritual and ideology, however, are good places for archaeologists to look for evidence of domestic resistance to domination.

Geoffrey McCafferty (Chapter 8) also uses ethnographic and ethnohistoric records to understand domestic ritual in the architectural space of courtyards, shrines, and altars. His study deals with figurines but in the well-defined context of a thoroughly excavated room complex at Cholula. The accounts tell of household altars and courtyard shrines, which lend strength to his interpretations of ritual room functions for parts of his archaeological example. The contexts described ethnohistorically give credence to his rich interpretations of a commoner household based firmly on the excavated architectural and artifactual evidence.

Ancient social leaders, in addition to a corps of elite artists, architects, and logistical management experts, are usually assumed to have been in command of all interesting aspects of religion, ritual, and ideology. Commoners themselves usually figure into these narratives only as abundant labor to build monuments, to provide surplus commodities for elites to manage, and to be the audience at ritual performances. Lohse stipulates that one way for archaeologists to begin incorporating commoners in their narratives of the past is to realize that the messages of "materialized ideology"—such as monuments—were often fluidly contextualized by the audience and situation. I agree and add that such media are multivocal and therefore especially difficult to evaluate archaeologically. In like manner, archaeologists who interpret such media do not constitute a single objective audience. There are many archaeological perspectives, each one an archaeological "audience" with its own perceived message. We might do well to be more self-conscious or reflective when we assume that monuments require large bodies of drudge labor that are strictly overseen by strongly centralized, hierarchically ordered, and specialized groups of elites and their minions.

This point raises the question of domestic and other non-elite architecture and what messages it embodies. Methodologically, the study of commoner architecture is closely related to the archaeology of households and inevitably to the rites and artifacts associated with their built space.

ARCHITECTURAL FEATURES OF RITUAL AND IDEOLOGICAL SIGNIFICANCE

Rituals take place in built space, or the built environment—the anthropogenic context that transforms a natural environment into a culturally constructed space. This space includes rooms, courtyards, and patios that are marked by features such as floors, sweatbaths, altars, hearths, shrines, and burials. Aspects of the built environment, such as their special composition and arrangement, are often what signify the special presence of ancient ritual activity. But the built environment should also include features of the landscape, such as caves and sacred mountains (i.e., the ritual landscape), and even ideological features, such as the *axis mundi,* as indicated in Douglass's and Gonlin's chapters. In this manner, the ritual landscape can be considered built space because it was socially constructed although not physically constructed. Many of the authors emphasize elements of built space, which is in reality a conceived or conceptualized space.

Two of the chapters, one by Gabriela Uruñuela and Patricia Plunket (Chapter 2) and another by Luis Barba, Agustín Ortiz, and Linda Manzanilla (Chapter 3), examine Teotihuacan, emphasizing the analysis of architectural features but in widely different ways. Uruñuela and Plunket consider that rural domestic traditions of architecture and ritual constructions were transformed into state-level canons of high-style architecture and city planning during the process whereby the new urban center grew out of the influx of immigrants from various regions near and far. They find patterns of rural life and belief embedded in urban contexts. These patterns are visible in *talud-tablero* architecture, mortuary patterns, and patio shrines at both the rural site of Tetimpa and the urban site of Teotihuacan. Their thesis is a refreshing reversal of the more popular take on comparing elite and commoner ritual and ideology. Rural families, or corporate residence groups, re-created their domestic spheres using urban-style apartment compounds that in some ways resonated with their ancient traditions and in other ways required innovations. Uruñuela and Plunket correctly point out that the rural, lineage-based social units would have persisted in the new urban context even though the state-level organization superseded them. The persistence of ancient, lineage-based lifeways, modified for urban life, is probably a phenomenon that was replicated around the world whenever state-level organizations coalesced out of less socially complex antecedents. The result is the familiar hierarchy—not of social classes but of organizational or governing units—that persists even today in the form of nations comprising a set of states or provinces that in turn govern their counties and cities (cf. Adams 1975:204).

One of the most intriguing ideas in Chapter 2, for me, was the idea that the Pyramid of the Sun, which lacks *talud-tablero* architecture, may be a multivocal monumental reference to both household shrines and volcanism that helped integrate the numerous diverse lineages, with diverse heritages, into the city. It would seem productive to examine early monuments in other regions throughout the globe to identify the architectural elements that potentially resonated with diverse commoners and elites alike.

Uruñuela and Plunket, however, do not completely refute Robert Redfield's (1956) outmoded dichotomy between the Great and Little traditions. A devil's advocate might say that the Tetimpa/Teotihuacan linkage and transformations actually illustrate how the reflective few appropriated the unreflective commoners' rituals and ideologies and used them to create or exaggerate a social hierarchy to their own benefit. The counterargument favored here, of course, is that ancient commoner traditions were the keys to formulating a successful urban domain that incorporated many folks from many different yet compatible backgrounds. The authors' emphasis is on the persistence and validity of rural lifeways even in times of change. The important distinction is between a top-down and a bottom-up theoretical perspective, as discussed above, a distinction mentioned specifically by several of the volume's authors. Household archaeology, by the very nature of its subject matter, must necessarily favor the bottom-up perspective, unless one were to focus primarily on the ancient households of the rich and famous (e.g., Christie 2003). Uruñuela and Plunket offer a new insight in that, on a grand scale, Teotihuacan embodies the Tetimpa household layout in its Three Temple Complexes of the city. This idea is worthy of more in-depth exploration in a separate offering.

In a different way, Barba and his colleagues (Chapter 3) examine the architecture of Teotihuacán's apartments and courtyards to identify ritual spaces in courtyards and their related storerooms. They use the spatial distribution of chemical residues and artifacts to map ritual spaces and activity areas within domestic complexes. One must ask, however, if we can ascertain that the chemical residues are signatures of ritual activities rather than other processes, such as food preparation. This method has great potential for identifying ritual behavior that might be identifiable to specific individual ethnic groups.

This potential is reminiscent of Stanley South's (1977) work in North American historical archaeology where he identified and distinguished among several British debris discard patterns. South showed that patterns among the relative proportions of artifact types, such as nails, wine bottles, and ceramics, were good distinguishing characteristics that differentiated between military and domestic sites in the relatively settled parts of the colonies. In a similar way, more distant frontier forts and trading posts had distinct patterns as well. He also recognized distinct spatial patterns of debris discard characteristic of the different areas within settlements. Refuse, for example, routinely accumulated immediately outside the doorways of houses, shops, and forts (South 1977:48). South's method emphasized quantified data and ethnohistorical information from many sites. His rhetoric, characteristic of the time, was cast in strongly processualist terms, but his point is still valid: abundant quantified data can be used to reveal patterns of debris distribution relative to architectural features to display regular patterns of ancient behavior. It seems clear that as more chemical residue samples are analyzed from additional contexts at Teotihuacan and elsewhere, patterns likely will emerge that might reveal a better picture not only of commoner rituals but of many other aspects of life as well.

McCafferty examines a Postclassic commoner domicile at Cholula with an abundant artifactual assemblage that seems to represent catastrophic abandonment as the result of a fire. A small room complex yielded figurines, deity figures, flute fragments, *comales,* censers, and features such as altars, sweatbaths, hearths, and burials. This rich assemblage in good architectural context depicts some aspects of commoner ritual life that contrast with the ritual complex of the state-level ideology. Burial composition and configuration and the various deities represented at the commoner abode do not match those represented at Cholula's ceremonial centers. This important distinction validates the notion that commoner ritual and ideology were not merely derived from the/a dominant ideology. As noted elsewhere in the volume, dominance implies resistance, so we should expect to see evidence of active or passive resistance to domination. But we can also interpret such evidence in less rhetorically charged terms as the persistence of folkways even in the heart of a large center, which at higher social levels is guided by politically centralized elite rituals and ideologies. In a related vein, McCafferty correctly points out that one depiction of commoner ritual life in the context of Cholula's much larger multicultural population does not represent all commoner ritual and ideology there. So much the better; we can expect future work to illuminate a diversity of commoner groups within Cholula. Meanwhile we remain confident that their various ideological lives were not merely small versions of those of their elite neighbors.

Gonlin also references ideological pluralism among commoners at Copán, as do Uruñuela and Plunket and also Barba and his colleagues at Teotihuacan, where ancient ethnic neighborhoods with distant roots have long been recognized. Gonlin, however, points out two different ways that ritual practice at Copán helped knit the social fabric: "shared practices that transcended social boundaries" and "idiosyncratic practices observed on the domestic level." These ideas seem to call for a heterarchical interpretation of social order. *Heterarchy* in this sense would mean simply that society could be simultaneously ordered according to more than one scheme—that a single social hierarchy would not be adequate to explain all relations of social order. A hierarchical order would be reflected in the distinctions among social classes who were integrated via the dominant ideology. One or more other orders in the same society would have integrated some individuals or groups in ways that crosscut, or were otherwise irrelevant to, the dominating hierarchy. When commoner ritual and ideology are more fully explicated, it seems likely that they will be seen to reflect such supplemental orders in ancient society, ones that crosscut or were somewhat independent of the dominant, hierarchical ideology.

ARTIFACTS OF RITUAL AND IDEOLOGICAL SIGNIFICANCE

The use of artifactual evidence is emphasized by most of the authors. Several types of artifacts are especially relevant to commoner ritual and ideology in Mesoamerica: figurines, incense burners, *candeleros,* bark beaters, mirrors, paper, small sculptures, and flutes, *ocarinas,* and whistles—many in a variety of forms. Douglass considers that there may even have been a commoner "ritual kit" composed of a variety of several such items that were readily available and readily replaceable by their owners. Such items, or kits, are to be considered vernacular in the sense that their creation and use were under the direct control of the producers themselves, always with the proviso that some items may have been attained locally through exchange. This vernacular aspect of ritual items emphasizes commoner ritual and ideology as a domain in its own right rather than being derivative or dependent on elite ritual and ideology. I use the term *vernacular* to distinguish from *high-style,* which would be controlled by a centralized, elite school of thought, as characterized by the practice of ritual by elites at ceremonial centers. Importantly, Douglass points out that by controlling their own ritual kits, commoners likely gained some autonomy in their access to the supernatural—that is, they were not totally dependent on elites for their supernatural well-being. Douglass's idea of a vernacular ritual kit fits nicely with Barba and colleagues' mapping of the domestic ritual areas and the idea that architectural patterns or ritual space and the composition of ritual kits might be two useful kinds of cultural or ethnic identifiers. Also, Douglass's consideration that commoners may have enjoyed some level of relative autonomy from elite control is helpful when trying to understand many crosscutting aspects of ancient commoner life. A degree of autonomy or independent agency is a key element in any bottom-up perspective or a heterarchical interpretation of social order.

Figurines are prominent among the analyses, and they are doubly enigmatic because of the uncertainty of how they functioned. McCafferty points out that it is not clear in most instances whether specific figurines (or figurines in general) were created to serve some ritual purpose, to be portraits, or children's toys. Moreover, although the individual item may have gone through one or more changes of function before finally being discarded, the archaeological context of figurines, as with other items, can give only an indication of their final roles.

At Cholula, McCafferty seems to have discovered a virtually intact altar room in a structural complex. These kinds of findings greatly aid our comprehension of the role of ritual in ancient commoner lives. Interestingly, in the figurine assemblage, he found some items that seem to have been ancient "action figures," reminding us that the past was not totally devoted to sober practices. Once again, McCafferty calls attention to the fact that commoners had a rich ritual life that was not simply constructed around elite domination. The variety of figurines, their morphologies, their various contexts, and the multitude of ways they were probably used strongly reinforce this interpretation.

Jan Olson (Chapter 9) examines figurines from many residential middens in Morelos, analyzing their contexts and attributes to suggest variation among social class and community size as well as change through time. Olson demonstrates that figurines did play a major role in ritual life but also that rural and urban folk used different symbols probably for different rituals. Through time, access to imported items tended to spread from urban to rural contexts as a result of the increasing effectiveness of long-distance trade routes that indirectly penetrated rural commoner settings away from the urban centers. This finding highlights the idea that domestic ritual was a viable part of folk lifeways, not a static tool of oppression imposed ideologically from above by local or regional elites. Olson demonstrates that figurines show stylistic variation on several scales, such as rural-urban and commoner-elite. From this evidence we could infer that variation in domestic ritual life, as demonstrated by figurine variability, might reflect some of the complex social ordering that was no doubt part of ancient family and community life.

THE WIDER CONTEXT OF COMMONER RITUAL AND IDEOLOGY

Two of the chapters (Chapters 4 and 7) are somewhat wider in scope than most of the others, while still treating the architectural and artifactual lines of evidence in considerable detail. These authors (Gonlin and Winter et al.) consider the broader social context of domestic ritual with the understanding that individuals were involved at various levels in their social hierarchy and that as the power of regional elite social strata rose or fell, the meaning and purpose of domestic rituals changed as well.

Marcus Winter, Robert Markens, Cira Martínez López, and Alicia Herrera Muzgo T. describe several examples of Postclassic commoner ritual in the Valley of Oaxaca at a time for which it is clear that society had lost much or all of its public ritual and religion and was no longer based on community-wide ceremonialism. Yet, even though the regional Great Tradition seems to have ended with simplification of social hierarchy and population dispersal, domestic life and rituals continued. Here, again, is an example where commoner folk demonstrate a level of relative autonomy that allows them to persist in altered conditions after the elite social classes have dissolved or lost social control. This Oaxaca example recalls the case of Copán, where it is clear that rural commoner lifeways persisted long after the royal lineages had lost their power (Webster and Gonlin 1988; inter alias).

Gonlin focuses on commoner domestic ritual and ideology in the Copán Valley but regards it in a regional scope that includes lineage-scale and polity-scale ritual and ideology as well. This focus resonates with Olson's assertion that ritual behavior should be investigated at many levels of society. Considering the architectural context and the artifactual evidence, Gonlin offers an unusually thorough consideration of the individuals themselves. She considers gender roles, noting that royal men and women are depicted in art as ritual performers while reflecting that among commoners, too, there were probably roles for both women and men. She likewise considers age-based roles in rituals, noting that children and the aged were likely to have been involved in ritual performances. Children, for example, would have acted in some rituals, even if only as part of their socialization into adult society or as the objects of rites of passage.

Both Winter and colleagues and Gonlin remind us that ancient life was rich and varied in many of the same ways that all ethnographically known lifeways are. Rarely are aspects of social life simple or narrowly scoped. Even rarer are cases where social power is so completely centralized via a dominant ideology that a simple hierarchy replaces all other ways of ordering a society (see Adams 1975, 1988; Lohse, Chapter 1). Resistance persists in the face of dominance (Joyce and Weller, Chapter 6) and it is in this resistance (or persistence) that one can sometimes see the degree of relative autonomy enjoyed by commoners in some social matters (Douglass, Chapter 5; Mehrer 1995; Milner 1998, 2003).

SUMMARY AND CONCLUSIONS

The chapters in this volume focus neatly on the later prehistoric periods during which we could expect ritual and ideology to have been dynamic institutions in the lives of most ancient Mesoamericans, commoner and non-commoner, rural and urban, male and female, child and adult. Perhaps one of the reasons that archaeologists have often considered ritual and ideology to be the provinces of elites is that much of the archaeology that has been done in the last 100 years or so has been done in and around ancient monuments, temples, palaces, and other such elite contexts.

It seems likely that there may be more variability demonstrated among commoners at the household level than among elites at the collective level. McCafferty has pointed out the diversity we may expect for commoners in multicultural urban settings. We likewise can expect diversity among rural commoner households as demonstrated by Gonlin (1994) for Copán.

Gonlin reminds us that there were several hierarchically ordered ritual spaces that corresponded with the polity, the lineage, and the domestic family. Focusing on the domestic setting of rural folk, she demonstrates that commoners had rich ritual lives and were active participants in their own spiritual well-being. Her chapter reminded me that if we interpret commoners only in terms of their role as subjugated persons, we unselfconsciously adopt a dominant viewpoint, a view from the top down, which is a bias that most anthropologists traditionally have been loathe to take.

Applied theoretical aspects of age and gender in prehistory will continue to inform the ways that artifacts are analyzed and interpreted. Although childhood comes to mind in the study of figurines, surely those of advanced age might also be visible in the archaeological record if we only look the right way. This topic is beyond the scope of discussion here, but the more general issue of the changing roles of ancient individuals throughout their lives suggests itself for further archaeological inquiry.

Ritual and ideology can now be added to the more economic topics, such as subsistence and craft specialization, which have long been studied as part of household archaeology. The authors in this volume have defined new ways of doing fieldwork, analysis, and theorizing about ancient family life. Household archaeology has developed much since its beginnings in the mid-1970s with the New Archaeology. It is not now so much "generalist or law and order" as it is holistic (see de Montmollin [1989:248–249] for a critique of processualist household archaeology). Refreshingly, the chapters here do not rely on a postmodern critique as a way to examine ritual and ideology. Fidelity to data and analysis is a hallmark of each contribution.

REFERENCES CITED

Adams, Richard Newbold

1975 *Energy and Structure: A Theory of Social Power*. University of Texas Press, Austin.

1988 *The Eighth Day: Social Evolution as the Self-Organization of Energy*. University of Texas Press, Austin.

Christie, Jessica Joyce (editor)

2003 *Maya Palaces and Elite Residences: An Interdisciplinary Approach*. University of Texas Press, Austin.

de Montmollin, Olivier

1989 *The Archaeology of Political Structure: Settlement Analysis in a Classic Maya Polity*. Cambridge University Press, Cambridge.

Emerson, Thomas E.

1997 *Cahokia and the Archaeology of Power*. University of Alabama Press, Tuscaloosa.

Flannery, Kent V. (editor)

1976 *The Early Mesoamerican Village*. Academic Press, New York.

Flannery, Kent V., and Marcus C. Winter

1976 Analyzing Household Activities. In *The Early Mesoamerican Village*, edited by Kent V. Flannery, pp. 34–47. Academic Press, New York.

Gonlin, Nancy

1994 Rural Household Diversity in Late Classic Copan, Honduras. In *Archaeological Views from the Countryside: Village Communities in Early Complex Societies*, edited by Glenn M. Schwartz and Steven E. Falconer, pp. 177–197. Smithsonian Institution Press, Washington, D.C.

Mehrer, Mark W.

1995 *Cahokia's Countryside: Household Archaeology, Settlement Patterns, and Social Power*. Northern Illinois University Press, DeKalb.

Milner, George R.

1998 *The Cahokia Chiefdom: The Archaeology of a Mississippian Society*. Smithsonian Institution Press, Washington, D.C.

2003 Archaeological Indicators of Rank in the Cahokia Chiefdom. In *Theory, Method, and Practice in Modern Archaeology*, edited by Robert J. Jeske and Douglas K. Charles, pp. 133–148. Praeger Publishers, Westport.

Pauketat, Timothy R.

1994 *The Ascent of Chiefs: Cahokia and Mississippian Politics in Native North America*. University of Alabama Press, Tuscaloosa.

Redfield, Robert

1956 *Peasant Society and Culture*. University of Chicago Press, Chicago.

South, Stanley

1977 *Method and Theory in Historical Archeology*. Academic Press, New York.

Webster, David, and Nancy Gonlin

1988 Household Remains of the Humblest Maya. *Journal of Field Archaeology* 15:169–190.

CONTRIBUTORS

LUIS BARBA—Instituto de Investigaciones Antropológicas, Universidad Nacional Autónoma de México, México, D.F.

JOHN G. DOUGLASS—Statistical Research, Inc., and University of California, Riverside, USA

NANCY GONLIN—Bellevue Community College, Bellevue, Washington, USA

ALICIA HERRERA MUZGO T.—Centro Instituto Nacional de Antropología e Historia, Oaxaca, México

ARTHUR A. JOYCE—University of Colorado at Boulder, USA

JON C. LOHSE—University of New Mexico, Albuquerque, USA

CIRA MARTÍNEZ LÓPEZ—Centro Instituto Nacional de Antropología e Historia, Oaxaca, México

LINDA MANZANILLA—Instituto de Investigaciones Antropológicas, Universidad Nacional Autónoma de México, México, D.F.

ROBERT MARKENS—Centro Instituto Nacional de Antropología e Historia, Oaxaca, México

GEOFFREY G. McCAFFERTY—University of Calgary, Alberta, Canada

MARK W. MEHRER—Northern Illinois University, DeKalb, USA

JAN OLSON—Grant MacEwan College, Edmonton, Alberta, Canada

AGUSTÍN ORTIZ—Instituto de Investigaciones Antropológicas, Universidad Nacional Autónoma de México, México, D.F.

PATRICIA PLUNKET—Universidad de las Américas, Puebla, México

GABRIELA URUÑUELA—Universidad de las Américas, Puebla, México

ERRIN T. WELLER—University of Colorado at Boulder, USA

MARCUS WINTER—Centro Instituto Nacional de Antropología e Historia, Oaxaca, México

INDEX

Page numbers in italics indicate illustrations

Abandonment, 63; of Cholula UA–1 structures, 220, 237–38; of Xunantunich, 168–69

Activity areas, chemical analysis of, 67–78, 286–87

Agriculture, xxiv, xxxi; water symbolism and, 102, 103

Aguateca (Copán), 104

Altars, *45*, 58, 61, 65, 91, 95, 169, 283; Cholula household, 216–17, 221–22, 238; stone sculptures of, 103–4; at Tetimpa, 42–43, *44*

Altun Ha, 158–59, 169

Ancestor veneration/worship, xxvii, xxxi, 45, 161, 205; at Tetimpa, 36, 42–43

Apartment compounds: floor analyses in, 67–78; Oztoyahualco, xxvii–xxviii, 61–63; ritual areas in, 59–60; Teotihuacan, 43, *45*, 47–48, 56

Architecture, 145, 283, 285; Cholula, xxix–xxx, 221–25; in Copán Valley, xxviii, *86;* domestic Maya, 90–93; exclusionary, 152–60; at Monte Albán, 190–91; monumental, 8–9, 15–18, 56, 162; Río Viejo, 165–66. *See also by type*

Artifacts, 85; Cholulan ritual, 229–37; ideotechnic, 5–6; Liobaa phase, 195–200; locally available, 161–62; Maya ritual, 95–107; Naco Valley ritual, 130–35

Atemoztli, 47

Atetelco apartment compound, 61

Atlan phase, 252

Axis mundi, 284; landscape of, 125–26; at Monte Albán, 152, 154, 193

Aztecs, 12, 218, 224, 252

Baking Pot, exclusionary architecture at, 159–60

Ballcourts, ballgame, xxxi–xxxii, 13–14, 128

Bark beaters, 105, 135, 288

Barrio centers, 60

Bat Palace (Dos Pilas), 168
Belize, 18–19, 23
Beverages, fermented, 105, 106
Blood/bloodletting, 102, 135
Blue Creek, 159
Book of Chilam Balam of Chumayel, 143
Braseros, 229, 230
Bufo marinus, 102
Building compounds, at Tetimpa, 35, 42. *See also* Apartment compounds
Burials, xxvii, 19, 57, 161, 162, 169, 192, 198, 285; in apartment courtyards, 61–62; Cholula, xxix, 218, 220, 226–29, 238–39, 241, 287; Late Classic Maya, 93–95; Oaxaca Valley, xxix, 201; at Teotihuacan, 41, 66; at Tetimpa, 35, 37, 39–41, 42–43; Zapotec, 207–8
Butterfly God, *62*

Caana (Caracol), 155–56
Cacaxtla, 101, 222
Caches, Maya, 95–99, 162
Campeche, *17*
Candeleros, 64, 288; from Copán, 99, 100; from Naco Valley, 130–31, *131*, 134
Capilco, xxx, 218, 263; figurines from, 252, 254, 258, 261, 265–66, 267, 269, 270, 273
Caracol, 162, 170; ceremonial precinct at, 155–56, 159
Cardinal directions/cardinality, in site plans, 18–21, 190
Castillo (Xunantunich), 156
Catalina, Inquisition testimony of, 143–44
Caves, 106, 111(n2), 188, 189
Censers, 39, 288; from Cholula, 229–30; from Copán, 91, 99; from Naco Valley, 130, 132–33, 134; from Teotihuacan, 14, 64, 66, 73
Centeotl, 240
Ceramics, xxiv, xxix, 208–9(n2); in Chila phase ritual, 202–5; Cholula ritual, 219, 222, 229–37, 239; Cholula trade in, 215, 241; in Liobaa phase ritual, 197, 199–20. *See also* Censers; *Comales;* Figurines; Whistles
Ceremonial precincts: at Altun Ha, 158–59; at Caracol, 155–56; as exclusionary, 159–60; at Monte Albán, 152–55; at Xunantunich, 156–58
Ceren, 91
Cerro Danush, 186, 205, *206*
Cerro de la Campana, 186
Cerro Gordo, 45
Chac, 102
Chalcatzingo, 218
Chalchihuitlicue, 238, 272
Chan Kom, 98, 102
Chan Nòohol, 18, 22, 168
Chemical analyses: of apartment complex floors, 67–78; of ritual activities, 56–57, 58, 286–87
Chicanná, *17*
Chichén Itzá, 185
Chiconauquiahuitl, 240
Chila phase, 186; ritual and ideology during, 200–206
Childbirth, symbolism of, 272
Children, 94, 108; Cholulan burials of, 227, 228–29; figurines and, xxx, 231, 234; Tetimpa burials of, 39, 40
Cholula, 15, 101, 214, 289; abandonment patterns at, 237–38; burials in, 238–39, 241; commoner households in, xxix–xxx, 287; Ehecatl/Quetzalcoatl cult at, 14, 240; foodways in, 235–37; household ritual in, 216–18; immigration to, 38–39; mortuary practices in, 226–29; multicultural population of, 215–16, 240; ritual-associated artifacts from, 229–34; UA–1 Structure 1 complex at, 218–26
Chorti, 102
Cihuatecpan, 215, 218, 221
Cists, Maya, 95–99
Ciudadela (Teotihuacan), 14
Class. *See* Commoners; Elites; Social status
Classic period, xxvii, xxix, 15, 64; collapse, xxviii–xxix, 144–45, 150, 171–72, 185–86; domestic architecture, 92–93; household ritual, 89–90; Maya, xxviii, 83–84; resistance during, 161–69; Zapotec religion during, 189–94
Cobá, 91
Codex Borgia, 230
Collective memory, 168; knowledge as, 12–13
Colonial period, figurines from, 252, 270–71
Colors, symbolism of, 18
Comales, at Cholula, 235, 239

Commoners, xxvi–xix, xxvii, xxviii–xxx, xxxiii, 1–2, 22–23; definition of, xxi–xxiii, 85, 87; exclusion from state ritual of, 152, 155–56; material evidence of, xxiv–xxv; Maya, 83, 84; and public ritual, 193–94; resistance by, 147–48; social power of, 282–83; social status of, 8–9
Communication, ritual and symbolic, 4–5, 7
Copal, 58
Copán, xxi, xxv, 64, 84, 111(nn1, 2), 126, 128, 160, 169, 290; caches at, 95–99; food in ritual context, 105–7; hierarchy of sites at, 85–87; household ritual at, 107–10; ideological pluralism in, 287–88; Late Classic burials from, 93–95; ritual artifacts in, 99–105; scales and loci of ritual at, 88–90
Copán Pocket, 85, 98, 111(n1); Late Classic Burials in, 93–95
Copán Valley, xxiv, xxviii, 91, *97*, 101, 150, 290
Corporate groups, 89; commoner participation in, 108–9
Corporate states, 14, 15
Cosmology, 17; in house lot structures, 18–22; Tetimpa's place in, 41–42
Courtyards, xxxi, 63; apartment, 59–60; altars in, 61, 283; chemical analyses of, 70–78
Coxcatlan, 218, 221
Coxcatlan Viejo, 218
Coyol nut, 106
Crypts, Dos Hombres household, 19
Cuauhnahuac, 262–63, 267
Cuauhnahuac phase, 252
Cuexcomate, xxx, 218, 263; figurines from, 252, 254, 266, 267, 269–70

Dainzú, 186
Danibaan phase, 190, 192
Danzantes Wall (Monte Albán), 190
Dedication rituals, 161
Deities: Cholula, 239–40; patron family, 61, *62*; representations of, xxix, 232, 238, 272. *See also by name*
Depopulation, during Classic period collapse, 150
DIT. *See* Dominant Ideology Thesis
Divination, 105
Dogs, as figurine and food items, 268–69
Domestic sphere: ritual in, xxxi–xxxii; at Teotihuacan, 63–66
Dominant Ideology Thesis (DIT), xix, 3 , 7–8
Dos Hombres, house lot organization, 18–21
Dos Pilas, 168
Dueños, 189
Durán, Diego, 217, 218

Early Postclassic period, xxiii, xxix, xxxii, 145, 173(n1), 185, 186; at Cholula, 221–37, 239–40, 242; at Río Viejo, 165–68; Zapotec ritual during, 207–8
Effigies, 91, 190; jaguar, 193, *195;* volcano, 41, *42*, *47*, 47–48
Ehecatl/Quetzalcoatl cult, 14, 238, 240
Elites, xxi, xxxii, 12, 85, 126, 173(n1), 205, 281, 291; dominant ideologies of, 146–47; exclusionary control of ritual, 152–56; figurine use, 264, 268–69; ideology and, 6–7; Late Classic period, 170–71, 194; Monte Albán, 162–63; Naco Valley, xxviii, 128, 129, 134–36; public ritual, xxxi–xxxii, 148–49; ritual maintenance of, 8–9; social power, 282–83, 290; societal control, 16–17; at Xunantunich, 168–69
El Jaral (Copán Valley), 91–92, 101
El Raizal (Copán), 90
Ethnohistory, 283; in Cholula, 215, 216; flute use in, 230–31
Etlatongo (Oaxaca), 143–44

Families, 59, 91, 96; patron deities of, 61, *62*
Feasting, 161; at Cholula, 236–37
Fertility, 189
Fetuses, Cholulan burials of, 227–28
Figurines, xix, 64, 193, 217, 251, 259–60(table), 261, 288–89; analysis methods, 254–58; from Cholula, xxix–xxx, 231–32, *233*, 234, 238; Colonial period, 270–71; from household middens, 253–54; Late Postclassic, 262–70; in Maya ritual, 99–100; Naco Valley, 131–32, 134
Fire God, 66
Floors, chemical analyses of, 56–57, 67–78
Florentine Codex, 272
Flutes, 288; ceramic, 230–31

Food, 286; in Cholulan ritual, 235–37, 239; in Copán ritual, 105–7; dogs as, 268, 269
Formative period, 15, 34–35, 46
Frogs, 240; Maya iconography and use of, 101–3
Funerary cults, 63. *See also* Ancestor veneration/worship

Gender, 198, 291; Copán household ritual, 108, 290; of figurines, 263–64, 265–66, 273; of household burials, 39–40
Genealogy, 46
Giddens, Anthony, Structuration Theory, 10–12
Gods, lineage, 66. *See also* Deities; *various deities by name*
Great Plaza (Copán), *86,* 88–89, 108
Great Plaza (Tikal), 160
Great Pyramid (Cholula), 240; Postclassic burials at, 218, 228–29, 239, 241
Great Temple of Tenochtitlan, 58
Guardians, 189
Guelaguetza celebration, 13
Guiengola, 186

Hall of the Eagles (Tenochtitlan), 58
Hallucinogens, 105
Heavens, 125. *See also* Cosmology
Hidden Transcripts, 3, 11–12; archaeological evidence of, 160–69; of resistance, 148–49, 151
Hieroglyphic Stairway (Copán), 95
Historia Tolteca-Chichimeca, 240
Households, xvii, xviii, 35, 59, 163, 252, 291; archaeology of, 84–85, 215, 281, 291–92; Cholula, xxix–xxx, 214, 216–37, 241–42, 287; Classic Maya, 89–90, 95; at Copán, 107–9, 109–10; figurines associated with, 253–54; hierarchical organization of, 76, 78; Naco Valley, 129, 133–36; Oztoyahualco, 62–63, *63;* Río Viejo, 166–67; ritual practices in, xxxi–xxxii, 18–19, 161–62; Teotihuacan, 63–66
House lots, cardinal organization of, 18–21, 23n1
Houses: burials in, 39–41; at Tetimpa, 35, *36,* 39–41
Huaxtepec, trade, 262–63
Huehueteotl, images of, *62,* 64, 66, 232, 238

Iconography, toad or frog, 101–3, 240
Ideology, 1–2, 8, 84, 146, 148, 217, 261, 282; Chila phase, 200–206; defining, 3, 5–6; elite maintenance of, 6–7; Liobaa phase, 195–200; pluralism, 287–88; state, 39, 44–45
Immigrants, at Teotihuacan, 38–39, 45
Incense, 229
Incensarios. See Censers
Independence, 147
Infants, burials of, 39, 40, 66
Inquisition, 143–44
Intoxication, 105–6
Itzamná, 102
Izapa, 101

Jaguar, 193, *195*
Jalieza, 186, 207

Knowledge, xxxii, 6, 11, 18; as collective memory, 12–13

Labná, *17*
Labor, 16, 17
Lambityeco, 186, 207
Landa, Bishop de, 135
Landscapes, xvii, 124; sacred and ritual, xxxii, 125–26, 188
La Sierra (Honduras), 128–29, 132, 134
Las Sepulturas, 96, 100, 101, 104
Late Classic period, 123, 186; at Teotihuacan, 55–56; exclusionary architecture, 154–60; in Naco Valley, 126–36; resistance during, 145, 162–69; rural burial patterns, 93–95; state-sponsored ceremonies, 150–51; state power during, 149–50, 170–71
Late Formative period, at Tetimpa, xxvii, 15, 33–34
Late Postclassic period, 96, 185, 205, 218, 252; figurines, xxx, 262–71, 272; Zapotec culture, 186, 207–8
La Ventilla compound, 60, 61, 66
Lineages, 40, 66, 89; maintenance of, 46–47; and Tetimpa shrines, 41, 42
Liobaa phase, 186; ritual and ideology, 195–200
Living space, structuring, 18–22
Los Achiotes (Copán), 90

Macuilxóchitl, xxxii, 186, *194*, 208; Chila phase, 200–205; Liobaa phase, 196–200; ritual at, 193, 205–6
Main Group (Copán), *87*, 88, 101, 108, 111(n1)
Main Plaza (Monte Albán), *153*, 163; as ritual space, 152, 190; exclusionary structure of, 154–55
Maize (*Zea mays*): fermenting, 106
Males, burials of, 39–40
Maquixco, 65
Margarita tomb (Copán), 101, 104
Marx, Karl, class definition, xxii
Maya, xxvi, xxviii, 9, 64, 143, 240; Classic period, 83–84; commoner ritual artifacts, 99–107; domestic caches, 95–99; domestic ritual architecture, 90–93; exclusionary ritual architecture, 155–60; frog and toad iconography, 101–3; rural burial patterns, 93–95
Maya Lowlands, Late Classic period collapse, 164, 168–69
Mayapan, 96
Memory: collective, 12–13; historical and autobiographical, 13–14
Mexico, Basin of, depopulation of, 45
Mexico-Tenochtitlan, 267
Mictlan, burials oriented toward, 226, 239
Middens, figurines from, xxx, 253–54, 261, 267–68
Middle Postclassic period, figurine assemblages, 252, 258, 261–62, 265, 272
Migration: to Cholula, 215–16; to Teotihuacan and Cholula, 38–39, 45
Mirrors, 288; from Copán, 104–5
Mitla, 186, 200, 204, 224
Mixe, 189
Mixteca, 192, 205, 240
Mixteca Alta, 229–30
Molotla phase, 252
Momoztli, *58*
Monte Albán, 101, 170, 186, 208; ceremonial precinct at, 152–55; Classic period collapse of, 185, 206–7; commoner resistance at, 162–63; Liobaa phase, 195–200; religious structure of, 190–94
Monuments, construction of Olmec, 8–9
Morelos, 218, 230, 289; figurine assemblages from, 252, 254–74; Late Postclassic in, xxx, 262–63
Mortuary practices, xxxi; Cholula, 226–29; Tetimpa, 35, 285
Motagua Valley, 134
Motolinía, Toribio de Benavente, 216–17
Mountain monsters (*witz*), 126
Mountains: and axis mundi, 125–26; Monte Albán as, 190–92; pyramids as sacred, 44–45; as sacred, 188–89
Moyotlan (Tenochtitlan), 58
Multiculturalism, of Cholula, 215–16, 240
Mundo Perdido, 169
Murals, on monumental buildings, 15–16, 56

Naco Valley, xxviii, 123, 126; candeleros and figurines, 64, 100; household ritual in, 133–36; occupation of, 127–29; ritual artifacts from, 130–33
Nahualism, 193
Nahua speakers, xxiv; Spanish Conquest, 270–71
Newborn ritual, 204, 224
New-house ceremony, 98
Nisa phase, 190, 192–93
Nobility. *See* Elites
North Platform (Monte Albán), 193

Oaxaca Valley, xxix, 13, 18, *187*, 208–9(n2), 290; Chila phase, 200–206; exclusionary architecture in, 152–55; Late Classic period collapse, 164–65, 185–86, 206–7; Liobaa phase, 194–200
Ocarinas, 288; from Naco Valley, 131–32, 134
Offerings, xxxii, 217; Liobaa phase, 196–98; Maya cached, 96–99; Monte Albán, 193, 196
Olmec, 8–9, 14
Olmeca-xicallanca, 215–16, 224
Operation 19 house group, 19, *20*
Operation 25 house group, 19–*21*
Opossums, as figurines and food, 269, 272
Oral histories/tradition, 173(n2), 206
Oratorios, domestic Maya, 90–93
Otherworld, 125
Oxkintok, 57
Oztoyahualco apartment compound, xxvii–xviii, 60; domestic ritual artifacts in, 64, *65*, *66*; evidence for ritual in, 56–57, 61–63; floor analyses, 67–78

Palenque, 99, 185
Paper, 105, 135, 288
Parsons, Elsie Clews, 204, 224
Patios: Macuilxóchitl residential, 200–201; shrines, 35, 44
Pe phase, 190
Petén, 150, 169
Petroglyphs, frog or toad, 101
Piedras Negras, xix, 102, 104
Pilgrimages, to Cholula, 14, 215, 216
Plants, hallucinogenic and intoxicating, 105, 106
Platforms, 188; Cholula domestic, 221–22; talud-tablero, 35, 36–38, 39, 40–41, 285
Pluralism, 214; ideological, 287–88
Pochteca, at Cholula, 240
Popocatépetl: eruption of, 15, 35, 38, 45; symbolic representation of, 41, 46, 47–48
Postclassic period, xxii, xxix–xxx, 186, 192, 205, 206, 290; at Cholula, 215–37
Pottery. *See* Ceramics
Power, 9, 12, 46, 152; elite ritual and, 134–35; imbalances in, xxxiii–xxxiv; Late Classic period, 163–64, 170–71; monumental architecture and, 15–16; public performances of, 148–49; social, 282–84, 290; social relations and, 145–46; of state polities, 149–50
Primeros Memoriales, 272
Principal Group (Copán), 169
Private sphere, at Tetimpa, 35, 43. *See also* Domestic sphere; Households
Public spaces, 55; Late Classic period ritual and, 150–51
Public sphere, 216; elite power and, 148–49; Monte Albán, 192–93; at Teotihuacan, 35–36; Xoo phase ritual, 198–99
Pyramid of the Moon complex (Teotihuacan), xxvii, 39; as sacred mountain, 44–45; talud-tablero system at, 37, *38*
Pyramid of the Sun (Teotihuacan), 37, 39, 126, 285; symbology of, 45, 46
Pyramids, 156, 216; as sacred mountains, 44–45

Quetzalcoatl, 238; cult of, 215, 216, 240
Quiña, 205

Rabbit deity, *62*
Rebellion, 143, 149
Reciprocity, human-supernatural, 189
Red Courtyard (Teotihuacan), 76
Re-inscription, 168
Religion, 6, 33, 56, 150, 285; Classic to Early Postclassic, xxix, 240; commoners and, 1–2; defining, 3–4; prehispanic Zapotec, 187–94, 196–97
Residences, Río Viejo, 166–68
Resistance, 3, 10, 12, 143, 147, 214, 290; archaeological evidence of, 15, 160–69; Classic period collapse and, 144–45, 171–72; hidden forms of, 148–49, 151; social power and, 282–83
Río Amarillo, 96, 97, 101
Río Viejo, 164; Late Classic period collapse at, 165–68
Ritual, xvii–xix, xxxi, 1–2, 6, 17, 22–23, 46, 170, 283; in apartment compounds, 59–60; chemical evidence of, 56–57, 58, 67–78, 286–87; Chila phase, 200–206; Copán, 88–90; defining, 3, 4–5; defining domestic, 213–14; in household organization, 19–21; Liobaa phase, 195–200; Monte Albán, 192–93; Naco Valley, 133–35; private vs. public, 35–36, 43; and social status, 8–9, 14; Teotihuacan, 63–66; village, 34–35
Ritual kits, xxviii, 288
Rosario phase, at Monte Albán, 190–91
Rulership, symbolism of, 14, 105

Sacred spaces, 126, 136
Sacrifices, 58; human, 42, 102, 144
Sahagún, Bernardino de, 217, 272
Sahumadores, 197, 199, 202, 229
San José Mogote, 18, 21, 193
San Lorenzo, 8–9, 15, 168, 169
San Marquitos, 165
San Pedro Cholula, 240
Santa Cruz fiesta, *206*
Santiago phase, 252
Satunsat building (Oxkintok), 57
Sculptures, 126, 288; toad and frog, 101–3
Sepulturas. *See* Las Sepulturas
Shamans, 102, 108
Shells: jute, 106–7; *Spondylus,* 133, 135
Shrines, xxvii, 35, 283; domestic Maya, 90–93; Liobaa phase, 196–97, 199; Tetimpa and Teotihuacan, 41–44

Siyah K'ak', 101
Site plans, monumental, 17–18
Slaves, resistance by, 144
Social order, 34, 173(n1), 205; Copán, 287–88; Late Classic period collapse and, 163–64
Social power, 17, 282–84, 290
Social status, xxiii–xxiv, 6, 10, 90, 108, 109, 159; defining, xxi–xxii; ritual maintenance of, 8–9, 14
Space, ritual organization of, 17–18
Spanish colonial era: figurines, 270–71; resistance and rebellion during, 143–44
Spirits, 188, 189. *See also* Deities
Springs, 188, 190
State polities: collapse of, 163–64, 169; Late Classic period, 149–50
Stone monuments: denigration and reuse of, 166–67, 168; at Río Viejo, 164, *165*
Stone tables, from Las Sepulturas, 104
Street of the Dead (Teotihuacan), 47
Structuration Theory, 3, 10–11; knowledge in, 12–13
Suchilquitongo, 207
Sula Plain, 131
Sunken Patio (Monte Albán), 190, 193
Sweatbaths, 217, 224–25, *225*
Symbolism, 7, 12, 18, 41, 164; frog and toad, 101–3; Monte Albán, 190–93; of natural features, 188–89; of pyramids, 44–45; rebellion and resistance and, 167–68; ritual, 4–5, 14; talud-tablero, 37–38
Symbols, 16; destruction of royal, 167–68, 169

Talud-tablero systems, 35, 36, 44, 285; at Teotihuacan, 37–38, *38*, 64
Tecuhtli ceremony, 14
Tehuantepec, 186
Temazcales, 217, 224–25, 234, 239
Temple models, in apartment compounds, 64, 65–66
Temple-patio-altar (TPA) complexes, at Monte Albán, 154–55, 193
Temples, 56, 64, 156, 188, 205, 216; and axis mundi, 125–26; domestic Maya, 90–93; at Monte Albán, 192–93
Templo Mayor, 101
Tenochtitlan, 58
Teopancazo apartment compound, 60, 66
Teopantzintli, 216
Teopantzonca, 216, 238
Teotihuacan, 14, 15, 33, 43, 44, 101, 126, 160, 224, 240, 285, 286, 287; apartment compounds at, 59–61; burials at, xxvii, 40, 41; domestic cult at, 63–66; immigrants in, 38–39, 45; Late Classic Period collapse, 164, 169, 185; lineage maintenance at, 46–47; Oztoyahualco apartment compound at, xxvii–xxviii, 56–57, 61–63, 67–78; public ritual at, 35–36; talud-tablero symbolism at, 37–38; as urban development, 55–56
Tepantitla apartment compound, 64
Tepeilhuitl, 47
Terminal Classic period, xxiii; Xunantunich, 156–57, 169
Terminal Formative period, 45, 154; at Tetimpa, xxvii, 33–34
Termination rituals, household, 161
Terrestrial world, 125
Tetimpa, xxvii, 15, 35, *44*, 285, 286; ancestor veneration at, 42–43; burials at, 39–41; kin groupings at, 46–47; occupation of, 33–34; shrines at, 41–42; talud-tablero system at, 36–37
Tetitla apartment compound, *45*, 59, 60, 61; ritual artifacts in, 65, 66
Texcoco, 267
Textiles, Cholula trade in, 215
Tezcatlipoca, 231
Thatched huts, as symbolic architecture, 16, *17*
Three Temple Complexes (Teotihuacan), 47
Tikal, xxxii, 90, 91, 101, 160, 169, 185
Tlachihualtepetl period, Cholula houses of, 219–21
Tlacolula, 186
Tlacopan, 267
Tlahuica, 267, 270, 273
Tlailotlacan compound (Teotihuacan), 224
Tlaloc, images of, *62*, 64, 66, 232, *233*, 235, 238, 240
Tlamimilolpa apartment compound, 60, 66
Toads, Maya iconography of, 101–3
Toci, 217
Tolteca-Chichimeca, 216
Tombs, 169, 198; Zapotec, 207–8. *See also* Burials
Tortillas, production of, 135, 239

Toxcatl, Feast of, 231
TPAs. *See* temple-patio-altar complexes
Trade, xxiv, 241; Late Postclassic, 262–63, 272
Triple Alliance, 267
Tripods, Teotihuacan, 66
Tula, 185; *incensarios*, 229–30
Type 1 sites (Copán), 87, *88*, 111(n1); Late Classic burial patterns at, 93–95; sculptures at, 103–4
Type 2 sites (Copán), 87, 104, 111(n1)
Type 3 sites (Copán), 104, 111(n1)
Type 4 sites (Copán), xxi, xxv, 111(n1)
Tzotzil, 98

UA-1 Structure 1 complex (Cholula), 218–20, 241–42; abandonment of, 237–38; architecture and domestic ritual, 221–25; artifacts and domestic ritual, 229–37; burials in, 238–39; mortuary practices, 226–29
Underworld, 38, 41, 46, 125, 189, 190
Upper classes. *See* Elites
Urban centers, 15, 39, 85; deity imagery in, 261–62; Monte Albán as, 190–94; religion of, 33, 285
Urban Core (Copán), 85, 87, 103, 108, 110; caches in and cists, 96, 98

Value systems, 10, 11
Verde, Río, Late Classic period collapse, 164–65
Vessels, 208–9(n2), 222; Chila phase ritual, 202–5; in Liobaa phase ritual, 197, 199–20. *See also* Ceramics
Villages, 33, 34–35
Volcanoes: effigies of, *47*, 47–48; eruption of, 15, 35, 38; shrine models of, 41, *42*

Water, xxiv; symbolism of, 102–3, 189, 190
Water lily, as symbolic motif, 103
Weber, Max, on social status, xxi–xxii
Whistles, 131–32, 288. *See also* Ocarinas
Wind God, 14
Wine, from Copán, 106
Witz monsters, 126
Women: roles of, 55, 108, 217, 235
World Tree, 18, 125
Worldview. *See* Ideology

Xantiles, 222–24, 238
Xochiquetzal, 240
Xolalpan apartment compound, 60, 66; chemical analysis of, 70, *71*
Xoo phase, 186, 192, *194*, 208–9(nn1, 2); Macuilxóchitl, 205–6; ritual spaces, 198–99
Xunantunich, 18, 170, 172; abandonment of, 168–69; exclusionary architecture at, 156–58, 159

Yagul, 186, 200, 202, 204
Yanhuitlán, Inquisition trial, 143–44
Yautepec, xxx, 253; figurines, 252, 254, 258, 261, 263–65, 267–69, 271, 272, 273
Yayahuala apartment compound, 59–60, 61, 64, 65
Yiacatecuhtli, 240
Yucatán, symbolic architecture in, 16–17
Yucatec Maya, 98

Zaachila, 186, 208
Zacuala apartment compound, 59, 60, 61, 64, 65
Zacuala patios, 66
Zapotec culture, xxix, 18, 185–86, 224; Chila phase, 200–206; Liobaa phase, 195–200; religion, 189–94
Zapotec Great Tradition, 207
Zempoaltépetl, 189
Zuyuan culture, 240

www.ingramcontent.com/pod-product-compliance
Lightning Source LLC
Chambersburg PA
CBHW060024030426
42334CB00019B/2174

* 9 7 8 1 6 0 7 3 2 5 8 8 8 *